A HISTORY OF MODERN PSYCHOLOGY

A HISTORY OF MODERN PSYCHOLOGY

Duane P. Schultz
The University of North Carolina at Charlotte

ACADEMIC PRESS NEW YORK AND LONDON

ACADEMIC PRESS, INC.
111 Fifth Avenue, New York, New York 10003

United Kingdom Edition published by
ACADEMIC PRESS, INC. (LONDON) LTD.
Berkeley Square House, London W.1

LIBRARY OF CONGRESS CATALOG CARD NUMBER: 68-8433

PRINTED IN THE UNITED STATES OF AMERICA

To My Parents

PREFACE

A BASIC PREMISE of this text is that psychology has reached the stage where it has a significant and respectable history in its own right. This work, therefore, focuses on the history of psychology as a separate and independent discipline, concentrating on the last 100 years or so of its development. It does not attempt to cover earlier philosophical thought except where such thought relates directly to the establishment of psychology as a separate discipline. In short, it is a history of modern psychology—not of psychology and philosophy.

There is no denying that Plato, Aristotle, and other early scholars speculated on problems concerning the nature of man. Certainly they did, but in my opinion their influence on the later development of psychology as an independent and primarily experimental science is quite limited.

The master historian of psychology, Edwin G. Boring, said in 1929: "There is too much psychology now for psychologists to master their own material and philosophy too. Psychology ought to fare better when it can completely surrender its philosophical heritage, in fact as well as in voiced principle, and proceed, unimpeded by a divided soul, about its business." The working psychology of today has surrendered its philosophical heritage in fact. It is time to surrender it in voiced principle also.

Psychology is truly a product of the nineteenth and twentieth centuries, for only in the last 100 years have psychologists defined their subject matter and established its foundation, thus asserting psychology's independence from philosophy. While the early philosophers concerned themselves with problems that are generally of interest to psychology today, they approached these problems in a vastly different manner.

While not covering the early philosophical precursors, our discussion of the history of psychology does include the more immediate philosophical context. Psychology became a distinct and experimental science at a time when European thought was imbued with the spirit of positivism, empiricism, and materialism. The idea that the methods of science could be applied to mental phenomena is inherited from philosophical notions of the nineteenth century, the exciting era that is the starting point for our discussion.

One of the most striking characteristics of the century-old history of psychology is the continuous development, and subsequent decline, of different systematic positions or schools of thought. Consequently, our approach considers each distinct school and presents its historical development up to its influence on contemporary psychology. There is a definite continuity in the development of the various schools of thought in psychology's history. As Heidbreder noted in 1933: "The rise and fall of schools and systems form not a chaos, but a pattern." In my opinion, this pattern appears to be the most meaningful framework within which to understand the history of psychology.

The development and decline of each school are discussed in terms of the general intellectual and social climate of the era or region in which it occurred. Thus, the influence of the *Zeitgeist* is noted as it continuously affected the changing systematic positions in psychology. This approach enables the student to see that shifts in psychological thinking were very often influenced and augmented by broader changes in man's attitudes toward himself and the world around him. The important figures in the development of psychology are discussed, not as great men who alone altered the course of psychology, but as men of genius and insight who were, nevertheless, agents of the inevitable, whose ideas were accepted only because the times were ready for them. Each systematic position is thus presented as a reflection of contemporary intellectual trends in science or the general culture.

Modern trends emerging from the various systems are considered, including present-day developments. The more recent the development, however, the less comprehensive the coverage, as the student will already be familiar with it from other courses. The point demonstrated is the continuity of development from the old to the new.

Discussion of each school includes commentary on criticisms as well as contributions of the positions, so that students can see the weaknesses of the various systems and understand why they have been replaced by something better.

Several original source materials representing important contributions to psychological development are included throughout the book. For example, Chapter X contains the behaviorist manifesto of John B. Watson, an original paper from the *Psychological Review* that shattered many existing beliefs and helped set psychology on a new course. There are not many of these, but it is believed that students benefit from reading an original work in the context of the discussion of the man and his position.

The first chapter, "The Study of the History of Psychology," discusses several points of value to the student beginning this course of study. It includes a general overview of the development of psychology as a separate discipline, general comments on the development of the various schools of thought, an attempt to explain the value of an understanding of the history of the field, and a discussion of the recent upsurge in interest in this area among psychologists. Also considered are two approaches to the study of scientific history: the "great man" or personalistic approach, and the naturalistic or inevitability approach.

Chapters II and III present the immediate philosophical and physiological antecedents to modern psychology. In Chapters IV through XIV, the development of the various schools of thought is presented. It is shown how each system began as a revolt against the existing order and how each, in turn, inspired a revolution that opposed its own way of thinking. Specific individuals and their contributions are discussed, and each person is considered in the total context of the systematic position he helped to either formulate, advance, or destroy. Thus, for the most part, the focus of the book is on the historical progress of schools of thought, as each was developed, reacted against, and destroyed by various individuals. Each school is discussed in terms of three stages or levels of development: (a) the historical antecedents or anticipations; (b) the formal founding and development; (c) the contemporary influence of the school.

The concluding chapter discusses the role of the schools in the development of psychology and the eventual dissolution of most of them as distinct systematic positions. The growth, influence, and nature of contemporary American psychology are described and the four major research areas in psychology today (learning, perception, motivation, and personality) are commented on. Contemporary psychology in other countries is also noted. The chapter concludes with a brief discussion of a new challenge to contemporary psychology: the humanistic movement.

At the end of each chapter are suggestions for additional reading for the student who wishes to investigate further a particular issue or individual. This book is written for undergraduate courses in the history of psychology; however, since it discusses the major theoretical systems in terms of their formal development and impact on contemporary psychology, it may also be suitable for a course in systems.

Several people have been of great help in the preparation of this work. For reading and commenting on the entire manuscript, I am extremely grateful to my colleague Dr. George Windholz, and to Dr. Antos C. Rancurello of the University of Dayton, Ohio. Mr. Alva Stewart (now Head Librarian, North Carolina Wesleyan College) and Miss Jenny Gibson Brown (of the J. Murrey Atkins Library of the University of North Carolina at Charlotte) have been most helpful in locating source materials. My greatest debt is to my wife, Sydney Ellen, for her cogent criticisms, expert editing, tireless typing, and, above all, her understanding and patience during this project.

DUANE P. SCHULTZ

CONTENTS

THE APPLICATION of the experimental method to the problem of mind is the great outstanding event in the history of the study of the mind, an event to which no other is comparable.

E. G. Boring

I

THE STUDY OF THE HISTORY
OF PSYCHOLOGY

Introduction

THE ANCESTRY OF modern psychology can be traced to the earliest of inquiring minds. Man always seems to have been fascinated by his own behavior, and ruminations on human nature and conduct fill many philosophical and theological volumes. Generally speaking, the same kinds of questions now asked about the nature of man were asked centuries ago. The important difference between modern psychology and its intellectual precursors is not so much the kinds of questions as the methods used to seek the answers.

Until the last quarter of the nineteenth century, man attempted to study himself by nonscientific means, by speculation, intuition, and generalization from his own experiences. The major change or breakthrough occurred when man tried to answer his questions about human nature by using the tools and methods of science, which had already been demonstrated successful in answering questions in the natural sciences. When men tried to use carefully controlled experimentation and data collection to study human nature, then and only then did psychology begin to attain some independence from its philosophical antecedents.

In order to break away from philosophy, psychology had to develop a more precise and objective way of dealing with its problems than its forebears had used. Much of the history of psychology after its break with philosophy involves, as we shall see, the continuing refinement of its tools, techniques, and methods of study in order to achieve increased precision and objectivity in both its answers and questions.

The first sign of a distinct field of inquiry known as psychology, then was the adoption, in the last quarter of the nineteenth century, of the scientific method as the means for attempting to solve its problems. During that period there were several formal indications that psychology

1

was beginning to flourish. In 1879[1] in Leipzig, Germany, Wilhelm Wundt established what is generally considered the first psychological laboratory in the world. Wundt also established, in 1881, a journal, *Philosophische Studien*, considered to be the first journal of psychology containing experimental reports. In 1888, the University of Pennsylvania appointed James McKeen Cattell as professor of psychology, the first professorship in psychology in the world. Prior to that time, psychologists received appointments in departments of philosophy. With Cattell's appointment, however, psychology received formal recognition in academic circles of its independence from philosophy. In 1887, G. Stanley Hall established the *American Journal of Psychology*, the first American psychology journal.

Between 1880 and 1895, dramatic and sweeping changes took place in psychology in the United States. During that time, 24 psychological laboratories and 3 psychology journals were established. In 1892, the first scientific organization of psychologists, the American Psychological Association, was founded (its membership now exceeds 26,000).

In 1908, psychology was defined by William McDougall as the "science of behavior," apparently for the first time. Thus, by the early part of the twentieth century, psychology had succeeded in gaining its independence from philosophy, developing laboratories in which to use the methods of science, establishing its own scientific organization, and giving itself a formal definition as a science—the science of behavior.

The Physiological Influence

Much of psychology's heritage comes from philosophy. However, while early philosophers were preparing the way for an experimental attack on the functioning of the mind, another group of scholars was independently approaching some of the same problems from an entirely different direction. Early physiologists were making great strides toward understanding the neural mechanisms underlying the mental processes. Obviously, the methods of study of the physiologists differed markedly from those of the philosophers. The eventual union of these disparate

---

[1] There is some dispute as to whether 1875 or 1879 was the founding year for the first experimental laboratory. Boring (1963) noted that Wundt was given space for experimental demonstrations in 1875, but it was not until 1879 that the space was used for independent research. Watson (1963, 1966) accorded the honor to 1875, while other sources (Chaplin & Krawiec, 1960; Flugel & West, 1964; Miller, 1962; Murphy, 1949; Peters, 1953) agreed on 1879. Boring and Watson noted (as did other sources) that 1875 also saw William James equipping a small laboratory at Harvard. The significance of the event, however, is far more important than the precise date on which it occurred.

disciplines produced a field of study in which, at least in the more formative years, an attempt was made to preserve the conflicting traditions and beliefs of both. Fortunately, psychology eventually succeeded in attaining an identity and stature of its own.

It should be pointed out that there is some disagreement among psychologists on the facilitating influence of physiology on psychology. Marx and Hillix (1963) noted that physiology played a very small direct role. The man generally considered the father of experimental psychology, Wilhelm Wundt, called his psychology an experimental physiological psychology, although there was really no physiological experimentation in his research program. Marx and Hillix suggested that psychology sought association with the name "physiology" only because of the latter's prestige, prestige that the young science of psychology rather desperately wanted and needed. "Accordingly, physiology was, and even today is, often invoked to illustrate the scientific respectability of psychology in general and of specific theories in particular" (Marx & Hillix, 1963, p. 30).

Whatever the eventual role in the new psychology, in the period just prior to the emergence of psychology as an experimental science (from 1800 through the 1870s), physiologists were working on problems of great relevance to psychology. In Chapter III we will examine the work of some of these physiological precursors to psychology.

The Development of Schools of Thought in Psychology

As noted earlier, and discussed in more detail in the next two chapters, psychology evolved as a separate scientific discipline in the last quarter of the nineteenth century. In these early years, the direction of the new psychology was primarily the work of one man, Wilhelm Wundt, who had very definite ideas as to what form this new science should take. He alone determined the subject matter, proper method of research, topics on which research should be performed, and goals of the new science. He was guided, or at least strongly influenced, of course, by the spirit of the times in which he lived and the then current thinking in philosophy and physiology. Nevertheless, it was Wundt in his role as agent of the times who drew together various lines of thought and, through the force of his personality and his intensive and exacting writing and research, fashioned the new psychology. He was a compelling and forceful "agent of the inevitable." And so, for a number of years, psychology was molded in his image.

In a comparatively short period of time, however, the situation in psychology changed radically, for by 1900, a great deal of controversy and cleavage had developed among the growing number of psychologists. The spirit of the times was changing and new ideas were forming in other sciences as well as in the general culture. Reflecting these new currents of thought, some psychologists took issue with Wundt's view of psychology and proposed their own views. Thus, by the turn of the century, several different systematic positions or schools of thought were in existence.

The term "school" refers to a group of psychologists who became associated ideologically, and sometimes geographically, with the leader of a movement. For the most part, the members of a school worked on common problems and shared a common theoretical or systematic orientation.

The emergence of different schools of thought and their subsequent decline is one of the most striking characteristics of the history of psychology. The phenomenon is not unique to psychology, however, for all the sciences experienced a similar period early in their respective histories when competing schools of thought divided the field of study (Kuhn, 1962).

Each of these schools was a movement of protest, indeed a rebellion, against the prevailing systematic position. Each pointed out what it saw as the shortcomings and failures of the older point of view and each presented new definitions, concepts, and research strategies designed to correct the perceived weaknesses. When a new school of thought captured the scientific community's attention, it resulted in the rejection of the once honored position. These intellectual combats between incompatible positions (the old and the new) were fought with feverish tenacity on both sides.

Very often, the leaders of the older school were never wholly convinced about the wisdom of the "new path to truth." Usually older in years, these leaders were too deeply committed to their position, intellectually as well as emotionally, to change. Many of their adherents, particularly the younger, hence less committed, became converts to the new position, while others continued to cling to the old traditions, working in increasing isolation and loneliness. As Boring (1950) commented:

> There are certain limitations in the progress of thought which an individual cannot readily overcome. He may modify and revise with the utmost honesty, but, the farther he goes on, the less able is he to change direction radically or to check the weightier lines of his development. It is a psychological law of inertia, as against both change of direction and change of speed. What would happen to science if its great men did not eventually die, no one can guess. What does happen is that a new man takes up the work of an older man without the constraint of inertia from his past, that he thinks, works and writes more simply and directly, and that thus from the old he creates something new that gradually itself accumulates inertia (p. 399).

Thus, several different schools of thought developed in the early years of psychology, each one an effective protest against what had gone before. Each new school used its older opponent as a base from which to push to gain momentum. Each position proclaimed proudly and loudly what it was not, *i.e.*, how it differed from the older theoretical system. As the new system developed and grew in numbers and influence, it served to inspire opposition and the whole combative process began anew. What was once a pioneering, aggressive movement then became the older, less flexible, tradition and then succumbed to the vigorous force of a new youthful movement.

Even though the dominance of at least some of these schools was only temporary in nature, each played a vital role in the development of psychology. Their influence can be seen in contemporary psychology even though the psychology of today bears little similarity to the earlier systems (for new doctrines again have replaced the old). Heidbreder (1933) compared the role of the schools of psychological thought to that of the scaffolding used in erecting a tall structure. Without the scaffolding from which to work, the building could not be erected. And yet, the scaffolding does not remain—it is torn down when it is no longer needed. In analogous fashion, the structure of today's psychology has been built within the general framework and guidelines established by the schools.

We cannot look on any of the schools as complete accounts of scientific fact; they are not finished products in any sense. Rather, they provided the tools, methods, and conceptual schemes that psychology has used to accumulate and organize a body of scientific fact. This is not meant to imply that the psychology of today is in a finished form. New guidelines have replaced the schools but nothing guarantees their permanence in the evolutionary process of science-building. The schools of psychology, therefore, were temporary but very necessary stages in the development of psychology.

It is in terms of the historical development of these systems—these revolutions—that the exciting advance of psychology can best be understood. Individuals stand out as making pioneering pronouncements and contributions, but their full significance is most notable when considered in the context of the ideas that preceded theirs (on which they often built) and the work that followed them.

After a detailed look at the beginnings of experimental psychology (Chapters II and III), we will consider each of the major psychological schools at three different levels: (a) the prescientific development of the position, including the work of earlier scholars who developed their insights without the use of the experimental method; (b) the early

TABLE 1

HISTORICAL DEVELOPMENT OF THE PSYCHOLOGICAL SCHOOLS

	1650	1700	1750	1800	1850	1900	1930
Structuralism						Wundt, Titchener, Brentano, Stumpf, Külpe	
Functionalism					Darwin, Galton, Spencer; James	Hall, Cattell; Dewey, Angell	Carr, Woodworth
Associationism	Locke	Berkeley, Hume, Hartley		J. Mill, J. S. Mill		Ebbinghaus, Müller; Pavlov, Bekhterev	Thorndike
Behaviorism					Comte, Romanes	Morgan, Loeb	Watson, Weiss, Holt, Lashley, Tolman, Guthrie, Hull, Skinner
Gestalt				Kant	Mach	von Ehrenfels	Wertheimer, Koffka, Köhler, Lewin
Psychoanalysis		Leibnitz		Herbart	Charcot, Janet	Freud, Adler, Jung	Horney, Fromm

attempts to attack particular problems using the tools of science; and (c) the formal establishment of each school and its influence on the contemporary psychological scene.

A schematic representation of the historical development of the various psychological systems in terms of representative great men, is given in Table 1. The table serves to indicate the key figures in each school and the relative periods of their contributions. The order of the schools in the table does not represent any sort of ranking in terms of importance.

The Relevance of the Past for the Present

This section might aptly be entitled, "Why study the history of psychology?" The methods of present-day psychology certainly bear little formal resemblance to those used in the early psychological laboratories and even less resemblance to the prescientific philosophical approach. Indeed, the development of psychology has been so dynamic that psychology of only 25 years ago seems remote. Will knowledge of the history of the field produce a better understanding of today's psychology? Considering the vast amount of material to be studied in psychology, is it worth the effort to know what happened 50 or 100 years ago?

We consider, first, evidence of psychologists' own interest in the history of their field, on the assumption that this reflects their feelings about the importance of the study of the history of psychology. One such point of evidence is that your psychology department offers the course you are now taking. Most psychology departments give such a course and some think it important enough to require it for undergraduate and graduate degrees (Nance, 1962). Most other science departments do not offer courses in the history of their field. A general course in the history of science is sometimes offered by the humanities division of a university, but it is seldom taught by a scientist. Psychologists feel that the history of psychology is a useful addition to their curriculum.

In 1958, a committee of the American Psychological Association reported on a survey of graduate departments in psychology in American universities. The survey sought to determine which courses composed an ideal undergraduate curriculum for prospective graduate students. The results revealed that History of Psychology, and Schools and Systems, were rated among the top ten ideal courses for preparing prospective graduate students in psychology (American Psychological Association, 1958).

At the professional level there are definite signs of growing interest among psychologists in the history of psychology. In 1965, the Division of the History of Psychology of the American Psychological Association was formed and the *Journal of the History of the Behavioral Sciences,* under the editorship of a psychologist, was begun. Also in 1965, the Archives of the History of American Psychology was established, at the University of Akron (Ohio), to serve the needs of scholars by collecting and preserving source materials of the history of psychology. Textbooks such as this one, and professional monographs dealing with aspects of psychology's history, appear frequently, reflecting the importance that psychologists attribute to the study of the history of psychology.

Why is psychology unique among the sciences in its expression of interest in its own background? It has been suggested that of all the sciences, psychology is unique in that it has attracted man's attention and interest for centuries. From the beginnings of recorded time, man has attempted to study and understand his own behavior and has reached many respectable insights and conclusions. Of course, a number of inaccuracies and myths about human nature have also survived from man's early attempts to understand himself. Because of man's extreme complexity, many questions asked about human nature centuries ago are still asked, in one form or another. There is, then, a continuity of problems and questions (if not of methods) in psychology that is not found in the other sciences. Thus, there exists a more immediately visible and tangible link with the past in psychology, a connection that many psychologists find interesting to explore.

Does the knowledge of psychology's past contribute to an understanding of psychology's present? Boring has said that without a degree of historical sophistication in his field, the psychologist "sees the present in distorted perspective, . . . mistakes old facts and old views for new, and . . . remains unable to evaluate the significance of new movements and methods. In this matter I can hardly state my faith too strongly. A psychological sophistication that contains no component of historical orientation seems to me to be no sophistication at all" (1950, p. ix). Since scientific facts or data are most meaningful when considered in the light of earlier related facts or data, modern psychology is most meaningful when related to its past developments.

The scientist must also be concerned with the history of his field in order to avoid repeating the past. As we shall see, the history of science contains several instances of supposedly new discoveries and insights that, as it turned out, had been anticipated years earlier—the new discovery being made in ignorance of the earlier work.

Knowledge of the past might help predict the future. Boring took issue with this idea noting that, "The past is not a crystal ball" (1963, p. 5) in which one may foresee the future. Esper (1964), however, argued strongly for the position that the past is the only basis on which one may intelligently plan for the future. Since one purpose of the study of the history of a science is to better understand the present, Esper asked what the functional significance of this understanding would be if not to provide some preparation for the future.

Wertheimer (1966) suggested two additional reasons for the study of the history of psychology. First, the complexity and vastness of contemporary psychology may tend to confuse students in their attempts to relate the various concepts, areas, and approaches to one another. An understanding of the history of psychology can help to integrate the many areas and subareas that compose modern psychology and to recognize the existence of interrelationships between the various facts and theories.

Wertheimer's second reason, probably the best of all those cited, is sheer intellectual curiosity. The study of history, he suggested, really needs no defense or attempt at justification. The fascination of the story is reward enough. The chapters that follow contain much in the way of human drama, revolutionary ideas and movements, and despair-filled defeats of individuals and their ideas.

Upon completing this course, you will have hopefully gained some appreciation of the great progress that has been made in knowledge and methodology in the comparatively short time since psychology became an independent discipline. There were false starts and mistakes, but overall there is a thread of continuity moving toward increasing precision and objectivity in subject matter and techniques, a goal toward which psychology as a science has always striven, strengthened by its past mistakes and victories alike.

Conceptions of Scientific History: Personalistic and Naturalistic

There are two approaches that can be taken to a study of scientific history. One is from the standpoint of the massive achievements and contributions of certain individuals: the so-called great man or personalistic theory. The other approach, the naturalistic theory, sees the great men and their contributions as reflections of the climate of the times.

As we read the history of any science, it appears obvious that science is the work of extremely creative and intelligent men. Suppose, for example, that Copernicus had not had the insight to see that a heliocentric view of the solar system was much more plausible than a geocentric view? Would someone else have demonstrated this burst of brilliance in the same era? The naturalistic theory of history says yes, because men's attitudes toward themselves were shifting at that time and the heliocentric theory was inevitable.

The personalistic theory of history says, "The man makes the times," but suppose the times are not yet ready for what the man has to say?

The history of science is replete with instances of lack of acceptance of new discoveries or insights at given points in time. Even the greatest of minds (perhaps especially the greatest of minds) have often been constrained by what has been called the *Zeitgeist*—the spirit or intellectual climate of the times. The acceptance and use of a discovery, therefore, may be limited by the dominant patterns of thought in a given culture, region, or era. Thus, an idea that is too novel or too preposterous to gain acceptance in one period of civilization may be accepted readily and easily a generation or perhaps a century later. Slow change seems to be the rule for scientific progress.

Perhaps, then, the notion that the man makes the times is not entirely correct. Perhaps, as the naturalistic theory of history would have it, "The times make the man," or at least make possible the acceptance of his theories. Unless the *Zeitgeist* is ready for what the great man has to say, he may not be heard (or he may be laughed at, or burned at the stake—this too may depend on the *Zeitgeist*).

The inhibiting or delaying capacity of the *Zeitgeist* is operative not only at the level of the general culture but within science itself, and its effects are perhaps even more pronounced at this "local" level. There are, in the history of psychology, many instances of early discoveries that remained dormant for long periods before being recognized and accepted. The concept of conditioning of responses, for example, was first suggested by Robert Whytt in 1763. It was over 100 years later that Ivan Pavlov expanded these early observations into the basis for a new system of psychology. Mendel's work on genetics was ignored for about 35 years (possibly because of its publication in an obscure journal), before making its impact.

Instances of simultaneous discovery also support the naturalistic theory of history. For example, there have been highly similar discoveries by individuals working far apart geographically and often in complete ignorance of one another's work. Postman (1962) noted that in 1900 three different investigators, working independently (indeed unknown to one another), rediscovered Mendel's work. "If one scientist won't do it, then another will; or if one scientist does it at the wrong time, three others will do it at the right time!" (Postman, 1962, p. 26).

Existing theoretical positions in a field of science can often exert a negative influence by standing in the way of further progress. An existing theory may so thoroughly dominate a discipline that investigation (or even consideration) of a new field of inquiry is inhibited. Existing theories can also influence, indeed determine, the way in which the phenomena or data pertaining to a problem are categorized. This, of course, may prevent the scientist from looking at the data in a new way.

This inhibiting effect of the *Zeitgeist* within science can operate with methods and techniques of investigation as well as with theoretical formulations. And it can also operate with regard to what is considered to be the proper subject matter for investigation. We shall see in later chapters the tendency to focus on consciousness and mental aspects of man in the early years of scientific psychology. Even as the methods of study began to be more objective and precise, the focus of study continued for a long time to be subjective in nature. Psychology had to wait until the second decade of this century before it finally lost its mind!

The truth probably lies somewhere between the two extremes of the personalistic and naturalistic theories of history. The intellectual climate of the times certainly has played a vital role in facilitating or inhibiting new points of view. Herrnstein and Boring (1965) suggested that modern historical analysis has served to reduce the role of the great man in scientific progress. Virtually every major step forward in science turns out, on historical investigation, to have been anticipated by past discoveries. The new discovery is assigned to the great man whose name it bears because the *Zeitgeist* had prepared the way for its acceptance in his time (rather than earlier), and/or because the great man's demonstrations were more thoroughly convincing than those of his predecessors.

The great men, as Boring (1963) has suggested, have become eponyms; *i.e.,* their names have been given to systematic positions or laws, and this process has fostered the belief that the discovery was the result of a sudden insight by these great men. In point of historical fact, the development of the discovery has usually been much more gradual. Eponymy may thus serve to distort history by not taking proper account of the *Zeitgeist* and earlier neglected contributions.

A history of a science such as this one must, it seems, be eponymous, for it chooses representative great men to exemplify the development of the science. What would the history of psychology be like if the names of all the great men were left out? It would still exist, but would be less meaningful, for the historian would be forced to find other labels with which to designate eras, schools of thought, and the like. Also, an eponymous account of the growth of psychology need not distort historical development as long as we remember that the thinking of the great man and the acceptance of what he had to say were strongly influenced by the spirit of the times in which he lived.

The naturalistic view of history is broader in scope and includes the personalistic view, for it shows genius not only as the antecedent of new thought but also as the consequence of its antecedent conditions. Thus we may think of the "Great Men as the consequences of the Great Events" (Boring, 1963, p. 16).

It should be clear by now that a history of psychology, to be discussed adequately, must be considered in terms of both theories of history. The *Zeitgeist*, however, appears to play the major role, for no matter how great is the man, if he is too far out of phase with the climate of the times, he and his insights will die in obscurity.

SUGGESTED FURTHER READINGS

The suggested further readings listed at the end of each chapter are not meant to include all source materials available on the various people and positions discussed. Only those the author feels are particularly noteworthy, interesting, and informative are listed. General reference works on the history of psychology are noted in the Bibliography.

Boring, E. G. *Psychologist at large: An autobiography and selected essays.* New York: Basic Books, 1961.

Boring, E. G. *History, psychology, and science.* New York: Wiley, 1963.

Crutchfield, R. S., & Krech, D. Some guides to the understanding of the history of psychology. In L. Postman (Ed.), *Psychology in the making: Histories of selected research problems.* New York: Knopf, 1962. Pp. 3–27.

Kuhn, T. S. *The structure of scientific revolutions.* Chicago: University of Chicago Press, 1962.

II

DIRECT PHILOSOPHICAL INFLUENCES ON PSYCHOLOGY

The Beginnings of Modern Science: Descartes

THE HISTORY OF modern psychology may be conveniently divided into three periods: (a) the philosophical, from Descartes (1650) to Fechner (1860); (b) the institutional or systematic, from Wundt (1874) to the 1920s; and (c) the factual, from about 1930 to the present. Chapters II and III are concerned with the so-called philosophical period.

At the beginning of the modern scientific era in the seventeenth century, some philosophers, notably Descartes, began to rebel against the kind of "psychology" that had come down from the early Greek philosophers. Although this rebellion did not attempt to divorce psychology from philosophy, it did attempt to bring psychological thinking into line with the rapid new developments in the physical sciences. Revolutionary developments had taken place in physics and astronomy through attempts on the part of Galileo and others to describe physical processes in terms of motion and inertia. In physiology, the discovery of the circulation of the blood by Harvey in 1628 led to attempts to explain physiological processes in physical terms. The stage was thus set for the attempt to apply the new physics to an understanding of human and animal behavior.

The overall trend in science in the seventeenth century was empiricism; that is, science appealed primarily to observation rather than to dogma and authority. There was a growing distrust of the past and a desire for the new. It was a time of great revolt against the old, a groping toward freedom from philosophical presuppositions, and remarkable advances in the physical and physiological sciences. It was a truly golden era, illuminated by the discoveries and insights of many great men, who successfully created (or reflected) a changing atmosphere in which scientific inquiry could and did flourish. They are, therefore, of great importance in the history of science in general. For the

13

most part, though, they were not *directly* related to the evolution of psychology.

One scholar, however, did contribute directly to the history of modern psychology; more than anyone else, he freed inquiry from the rigid theological and traditional dogmas that had dominated it for centuries. "Not since Aristotle had a philosopher constructed a new and influential system of thought that took into account the sum of knowledge, which in two thousand years had grown so significantly" (Herrnstein & Boring, 1965, p. 581). This great man, who symbolizes a transition from the Renaissance to the modern period of science, and who, many feel, represents the beginnings of modern psychology, was René Descartes.

THE LIFE OF DESCARTES (1596–1650)

Descartes was born in March, 1596, at La Haye in Touraine, France. His father was a councilor at the parliament of Brittany and from him Descartes inherited enough money to support his life of study and travel. That Descartes, unlike others in similar circumstances, did not lead a life of dilettantism was apparently attributable to his sheer genius, curiosity and hunger for knowledge, indifference to dogmatic authority, and constant desire for evidence and proof.

From 1604 to 1612 he was a student at the Jesuit College at La Flèche, where he received good training in the humanities and mathematics and displayed considerable talent, particularly in the latter discipline. Because Descartes' health was frail, the rector, Father Charlet, excused him from the morning religious duties and allowed him to lie in bed instead, a habit he retained all his life. It was during these mornings abed that he studied his lessons and did his most creative thinking.

After his formal education, he sampled the pleasures of Paris for awhile and then, finding this existence tiresome, went into seclusion to study mathematics. In 1617 he became a gentleman volunteer in the army of Prince Maurice of Nassau, a seemingly strange thing for one of such contemplative existence to do.

Returning to Paris in 1623, Descartes once again pursued his favorite study of mathematics but found Parisian life too distracting and moved to Holland in 1628. So great was his need for solitude and seclusion that, during the next 20 years in Holland, he lived in 13 different towns and 24 different houses, always keeping his address unknown to all but his most intimate friends, with whom he corresponded voluminously. His only other apparent requirements, in addition to seclusion, were proximity to a Catholic Church and a university.

Most of his important works were written during the years in Holland, where freedom of thought was characteristic during the seventeenth century. His freedom was slightly marred by some degree of attempted religious persecution, from which he was protected by the French Ambassador and the Prince of Orange. At one time, booksellers were forbidden to sell his works and he was brought before the magistrates to answer charges brought by the theologians of Utrecht and Leyden that he was an atheist and a profligate—serious charges for a devout Catholic. White (1965) noted that Descartes "was condemned by Catholics and Protestants alike. Since Roger Bacon, perhaps, no great thinker had been so completely abased and thwarted by theological oppression" (p. 80).

Descartes' growing fame led to an invitation from Queen Christina of Sweden to instruct her in philosophy. Reluctant though he was to give up his freedom and seclusion, he nonetheless had a great respect for royal prerogative and went to Sweden on the warship sent for him. Apparently the Queen was not a very good student and, to make matters worse, insisted on having her lessons three times a week at 5 A.M. in her cold library during an unusually bitter winter. One can imagine Descartes' chagrin at having to be up so early in the morning, much less to have to instruct a not very bright pupil. He withstood the early rising and extreme cold for four months before dying of pneumonia on February 11, 1650.

THE CONTRIBUTIONS OF DESCARTES

In addition to his importance in the later development of psychology, Descartes was also a pioneer in modern mathematics, having laid the foundations of analytic geometry, which apparently came to him in a series of dreams! He has often been called the father of modern philosophy as well as the father of physiological psychology and reflexology.

His most important work, from the standpoint of the future development of psychology, is probably his attempted resolution of the mind-body problem, which had been a controversial issue for centuries. Scholars throughout the ages had argued about how the mind, or purely mental qualities, could be distinguished from the body and all other physical qualities.

Before discussing Descartes' treatment of this problem, let us very briefly consider earlier conceptions of the mind or soul. Primitive man endowed all things in the world with a spirit or soul not unlike his own. He tended to anthropomorphize the things he found in nature, to regard nature as a conscious living force. This naïve conception of causality has been called *animism*. Thus, primitive thought maintained that in every material being there exists a second being, a kind of demon or spirit that is of a different substance from that of the body, if not completely without substance. It was believed that this demon or soul is capable of temporarily leaving the body in sleep and dreams, and permanently leaving it in death. In other words, the soul was seen as capable of an existence independent of (and beyond) the body. There was thus recognized a disparity or distinction between psychic or mental phenomena (the soul) and the material body. There were later attempts to associate the soul with specific organs of the body—the nerves, blood, heart, sex organs—but hardly ever the brain. These attempts frequently led to the notion of separate organ souls, each with a different function.

The Greek notions of the human soul were to influence rather strongly the later development of Western psychology. There were some attempts to trace the soul back to material substances. Some philosophers, for instance, considered the soul equivalent to water, some to air, some to fire. For Plato, the soul was not only a principle of earthly life but also arose from a divine preexistence and was immortal after death. The views of Aristotle were more advanced for, although he viewed the soul as metaphysical in origin, he considered it primarily as the life principle. There were several separate souls for Aristotle: the vegetative soul, which even plants possess; the perceptive or sensitive soul, which animals have; and the thinking soul, which only man possesses and which rules over the lower souls.

During the Christian Middle Ages the dominant concern was the eternal salvation of the soul. The Christian theory of the immortal human soul conceived of it as divorced from the body and composed of an immaterial substance always striving to unite with God.

Descartes was the first to offer an approach to this problem that focused attention on a strictly physical–*psychological* dualism. In so doing, he turned attention away from the study of the soul, in its abstract sense, to the study of the mind and the mental operations it performs. Methods of inquiry changed as a result from metaphysical analysis and deduction to induction and objective observation. Where the soul could only be speculated upon, the mind and its operations of cognition, volition, and sensation could be *observed*.

Mind and body, according to Descartes, are two distinct entities. There is no qualitative similarity between the body, or the world of the physical, and the mind. Matter and the body are extended substances that operate by, and can be explained in terms of, mechanical principles. The soul or mind is unextended, free, and insubstantial, or lacking in substance. Descartes then went a step further and stated that mind and body, though totally separate and distinct, are capable of interacting in the human organism. The mind can influence the body and the body can influence the mind—the so-called mind–body theory of interactionism.

Let us take a more detailed look at Descartes' conception of the body.

Since the body is made up of physical matter, it must share those characteristics common to all matter: extension in space and capability of movement. If the body is matter, then the laws of physics and mechanics that account for movement and action in the physical world must also be applicable to the body.

The body, when it is considered apart from the mind (and it can be so considered since the two are separate entities), is like a machine, the operation of which can be adequately explained by the mechanical laws of the movement of objects in space. With this line of reasoning, Descartes developed his "physics of physiology" (Boring, 1950, p. 162).

The *Zeitgeist* was ready for the acceptance of such a mechanical interpretation of the workings of the human body. One reason is that exciting new advances in physiology supported the notion. In 1628, Harvey had discovered the gross facts about the circulation of the blood and much was being discovered about the process of digestion. It was also known that the muscles of the body work in opposing pairs and that sensation and movement are somehow dependent upon the nerves. Physiological research had taken great strides in understanding the human body, though far from completely. The nerves, for instance, were considered to be hollow tubes through which animal spirits flow. The point of importance, however, is not the accuracy or completeness of the knowledge of human physiology, but rather that it was consonant with a mechanical, physical interpretation of the body.

In addition to these physiological contributions to the explanation of the body is the fact that mechanical models were among the wonders of the age. The gardens of the times were adorned with fountains so constructed that water running in tubes would move manikins, play instruments, and so on. Descartes saw a similarity between these water pipes and the nerve tubes in the human body. The statues and figures were caused to move in the absence of voluntary action on their part and this was reflected in Descartes' observation that movements of the body could frequently occur without conscious intention on the part of the individual. From this line of analogizing, he arrived at the idea of the *undulatio reflexa*, a movement not supervised or determined by a will to move. For having formulated this notion, he is often called the author of the theory of reflex action.

The body was therefore considered to operate like a machine. Since animals did not possess souls, they were considered to be automata, or machines that move themselves. Thus, the difference between man and animals so important to Christian religion was preserved. These views were part of an overall trend toward the notion that the behavior of man is predictable. The mechanical body will move and behave in predictable ways so long as the inputs are known. Animals, being completely machinelike, belong entirely in the area of physical phenomena. Hence, animals have no immortality, are not capable of thought, and have no freedom of will (since they have no will). Descartes made some minor adjustments in his thinking on animals in later years, but he never changed his basic conviction that animal behavior can be explained mechanistically.

The nonmaterial mind, according to Descartes, has the capacities of thought and of consciousness, and consequently provides us with knowledge of the external world. It has none of the properties of matter. The most important characteristic of the mind is its capacity to think; this sets it apart from the physical world of matter. This "thinking thing" is free, immaterial, and unextended.

Since the mind perceives and wills, it must somehow influence, and be influenced by, the body. Descartes recognized that when the mind "decides" to move from one point to another, for example, this decision is carried out somehow by the nerves and muscles of the body. Similarly, when the body is stimulated in some fashion, as by light or heat, the mind recognizes and interprets these sensory data and makes a decision as to the appropriate response.

Thus, Descartes was led to formulate what is perhaps the most important part of his theory: the interaction of these two totally different entities. He had to find a point of interaction where the mind and the body could engage in their mutual influence. Several considerations were involved in the search for this place of interaction. First, Descartes conceived of the soul as being unitary, which meant that it must interact with only one part of the body. Descartes was also convinced that the point of interaction must be somewhere within the brain, for research was demonstrating ever more clearly that sensations travel to the brain and that movement originates within the brain. Clearly, then, the brain had to be the focal point for the mind's functions. Since the only structure of the brain that is single and unitary (*i.e.*, not divided and duplicated in both hemispheres) is the pineal gland or conarium, Descartes considered it the only logical choice for a point of interaction.

The manner in which this interaction between mind and body takes place is treated in mechanistic terms by Descartes. Movement of the animal spirits in the nerve tubes produces an impression on the conarium and from this impression the mind produces a sensation. What occurs is that a quantity of motion (the flow of animal spirits) produces a purely mental quality (a sensation). The reverse also occurs, in that the mind can somehow make an impression on the conarium (in a manner never made clear), which in turn, by inclining to one direction or another, influences the direction of flow of the animal spirits to the muscles, which results in a movement. Thus, a purely mental quality can influence motion, a property of the body.

It is important to remember that Descartes did not maintain that the soul is confined or contained in the conarium. The conarium is simply the point of interaction and nothing more. Descartes believed that the soul is united with all parts of the body and thus the entire body becomes the "seat of the soul."

Because of its profound influence on the subsequent development of psychology, another of Descartes' formulations—his doctrine of ideas—deserves mention. Descartes believed that the mind gives rise to two different kinds of ideas: derived and innate. Derived ideas are those produced by the direct application of an external stimulus, such as the sound of a bell or the sight of a tree. These derived ideas, then, are a product of the experiences of the senses.

Of far more importance is the notion of innate ideas, which are not derived from sensory experience. These ideas are not produced by objects in the external world impinging on the senses. The label "innate" describes their source: They develop out of the mind or consciousness alone. Their innate tendency or potential existence is independent of sense experience, though they may be realized or actualized in the presence of appropriate sense experience. Some of these innate ideas, according to Descartes, are the ideas of self, God, the geometric axioms, perfection, and infinity.

This notion of innate ideas is discussed again in later chapters, for it eventually culminates in the nativistic theory of perception and the Gestalt school. We also will see its influence in terms of the spirited opposition it inspired among the early English empiricists and associationists and among the more modern empiricists, such as Helmholtz and Wundt.

The work of Descartes served as a most important catalyst for many trends later prominent in psychology. His most important systematic conceptions are his mechanistic conception of the body, his mind–body theory of interactionism, the localization of the mind's functions in the brain, and the doctrine of innate ideas.

Nineteenth-Century Influences

After Descartes, the development of modern science in general and of psychology in particular was most rapid and prolific. By the middle of the nineteenth century, the long period of what has been called pre-scientific psychology came to an end. During this time European philosophical thought became dominated by a new spirit: positivism. The term and the concept are the work of Auguste Comte, who was working on a systematic survey of all knowledge—an ambitious project indeed! To make the project more manageable, Comte wanted to limit his work strictly to facts the truth of which was beyond question, *i.e.*, those facts determined through the methods of science.

Positivism, then, refers to a system based exclusively on facts that are immediately observable and undebatable. All else of a speculative or inferential nature is rejected as illusory. A positivistic philosophy deals with only those things that can be known through the senses.

Other ideas quite supportive of antimetaphysical positivism were also extant in philosophy. The materialists strongly believed that all things could be described in physical terms and understood in the light of the physical properties of matter and energy. They further believed that consciousness could be explained in the terms of physics and chemistry. In discussions of mental phenomena, they tended to focus on their physical aspect, the anatomical and physiological structure of the brain.

A third group of philosophers, the empiricists, were also quite active by the nineteenth century, particularly in England. They were concerned with how the mind acquires knowledge and argued that the only valid source of knowledge is sensory experience.

Nineteenth-century man's conception of himself and the world around him was rapidly changing. Positivism, empiricism, and materialism were to become the philosophical foundations of the new psychology. Discussions of psychological phenomena were beginning to be conducted within a framework made up of a reliance on factual, observational evidence based on sensory experience. More focus was being placed on the physiological processes involved in mental functioning (see Chapter III). Of the three new traditions or orientations, empiricism played the major role in shaping the early development of the new science of psychology.

English Empiricism

Empiricism provided the new psychology with both a methodological and a theoretical framework. The method of the empiricists is observation and to some extent experimentation. In contrast to the older, rational and speculative methods of inquiry, the empirical method relies completely on objective observation and is more "scientific" in nature.

The theoretical aspect of empiricism relates to the growth of the mind—how it acquires knowledge. The empiricistic view is that the mind grows through the progressive accumulation of sensory experiences. This attitude is in distinct opposition to the nativistic viewpoint, as exemplified by Descartes, which says that some ideas are present at birth (*i.e.*, are innate). We now consider some of the major English empiricists.

JOHN LOCKE (1632–1704)

The son of an attorney, Locke studied at Westminster and Oxford, receiving his bachelor's degree in 1656 and his master's degree soon after that. He remained at Oxford for several years, tutoring in Greek, rhetoric, and philosophy, and then took up the practice of medicine. He had also developed an interest in political matters while at Oxford and in 1667 went to London, where he became secretary to the Earl of Shaftesbury and, in time, the confidant and friend of this controversial figure.

Shaftesbury's political stature and influence declined and in 1681, after his participation in a plot against Charles II, he fled to Holland. Though Locke was not involved in the plot, his close relationship with Shaftesbury brought him under suspicion and he, too, fled to Holland. In 1689, he was able to return to England, where he took the post of Commissioner of Appeals and began writing a series of works on education, religion, and economics. He was particularly concerned with religious freedom and the right of men to govern themselves. The influence of Locke's political writings was noted by Thomas Jefferson, who acknowledged his debt to Locke when he was preparing the Declaration of Independence (Watson, 1963, p. 170). Locke's writings brought him much fame and influence and he was heralded throughout Europe and England as a champion of liberalism in government.

Locke's major work of importance to psychology is *An Essay Concerning Human Understanding*, which appeared in 1690 and was the culmination of some 20 years of study and thought. This classic, which went through four editions by 1700 and was translated into French and Latin, marked the formal beginning of English empiricism.

Locke was concerned primarily with the question of how the mind acquires knowledge. In attacking this question he first denied the existence of innate ideas, arguing that man is not equipped at birth with any knowledge whatever. He admitted that certain ideas may appear to be innate to an adult because he has been constantly taught the idea (such as the idea of God) from childhood and cannot remember any time when he was not aware of it. Therefore, the adult comes to believe that he must have had the idea since birth. Thus, apparent innateness of ideas is explained by Locke in terms of learning and habit.

How, then, does the mind acquire knowledge? To Locke, the answer was, emphatically, through experience: all knowledge is empirically derived.

In an often quoted passage from his *Essay,* Locke noted:

> Let us then suppose the mind to be, as we say, white paper void of all characters, without any ideas:—How comes it to be furnished? Whence comes it by that vast store which the busy and boundless fancy of man has painted on it with an almost endless variety? Whence has it all the *materials* of reason and knowledge? To this I answer, in one word, from EXPERIENCE. In that all our knowledge is founded; and from that it ultimately derives itself (Book II, Chapter 1).

Locke recognized two different kinds of experience, one deriving directly from sensation and the other from reflection. Some ideas arise from direct sensory input from physical objects in the environment. They are simply sense impressions. In addition to the operation of sensations upon the mind, however, the operation of the mind itself—reflection—can give rise to ideas. It is important to remember that the mental function of reflection as a source of ideas is also dependent on sensory experience. The ideas produced by reflection are based on those already experienced sensorially.

In the development of the individual, sensation comes first. It is a necessary precursor to reflection, for there must exist a reservoir of sense impressions in order for the mind to be able to reflect. In reflection, the individual remembers past sensory impressions and combines them in various new ways to form abstractions and other higher-level ideas. All ideas, then, no matter how abstract and complex, arise from these two sources, but the overall origin remains sense impressions or experience.

Locke also made the distinction between simple and complex ideas. Simple ideas can arise from both sources, are received passively by the mind, and are elemental or unanalyzable; *i.e.,* they cannot be further reduced to simpler ideas. As we have seen, the mind, through the process of reflection, can actively create new ideas through combinations of other ideas. These derived ideas are what Locke called the complex ideas and they arise from simple ideas of both sensation and reflection. Thus, complex ideas are compounded or "built up" out of simple ideas and hence are capable of being analyzed or resolved into simple ideas.

This notion of a mental combination or compounding of ideas (and their analysis) marks the beginning of the so-called mental chemistry that characterizes the notion of association. This decomposition of mental life into elements (simple ideas), and the compounding of these elements to form complex ideas, subsequently formed the core of the new scientific psychology.

One other Lockian doctrine of considerable interest to psychology in his notion of primary and secondary qualities as they apply to simple ideas of sense. Primary qualities exist in the object whether we perceive them or not. For instance, the size and shape of a building are primary qualities, whereas the color of the building is not inherent in the object but is dependent on the experiencing person.

The secondary qualities, such as colors, odors, sounds, and tastes, are not in the object; rather, they exist in one's perception of the object. The tickle of a feather is not in the feather itself but in one's reaction to the feather. These secondary qualities exist, then, only in the act of perception. If you did not bite into a peach, the taste would not exist. The primary qualities, such as the shape of the peach, exist in the object whether we perceive them or not.

Thus, Locke fully recognized the subjective nature of perception—the fact that different people may perceive a given stimulus situation in different ways. The secondary qualities were introduced in an attempt to explain the fact that there is not always an exact one-to-one correspondence between the physical world and an individual's perception of it.

GEORGE BERKELEY (1685–1753)

Locke's immediate successor in British empirical philosophy, Berkeley was a deeply religious man born and educated in Ireland. At the age of 24, he was ordained a deacon in the Anglican Church and shortly thereafter published two important philosophical works that were to exert an influence on psychology: *An Essay Towards a New Theory of Vision* (1709) and *A Treatise Concerning the Principles of Human Knowledge* (1710).

With these two books, his contribution to psychology ended. Thereafter he traveled extensively in Europe and returned to Ireland to hold a number of posts, including teaching at Trinity College. He became financially independent through the gift of a large amount of money from a woman whom he had apparently met only once at a dinner. He traveled in the United States, spent three years at Newport, Rhode Island, and gave his house and library to Yale University when he left. The last years of his life were spent as Bishop of Cloyne in Ireland.

Berkeley agreed with Locke that all knowledge of the external world comes from experience but disagreed with Locke's doctrine of primary and secondary qualities by arguing that there are no primary qualities at all. There are only what Locke called secondary qualities for, to Berkeley, all knowledge is a function of the experiencing or perceiving person. The name given to this position some years later was "mentalism," to denote Berkeley's emphasis on purely mental phenomena.

Berkeley argued that perception is the *only* reality of which we can be sure. We cannot know with absolute certainty the nature of physical objects in the experiential world. All we can know for sure is how we perceive these objects and, since our perception is within ourselves and thus individually subjective, we do not mirror the external world in our perception. Thus, to Berkeley, a physical object is nothing more than an accumulation of sensations that we have experienced together, so that force of habit renders them associated in our minds. The experiential world is the summation of our sensations.

There is, then, no material substance, at least none of which we can be certain, for if we take away the perception, the quality disappears. There can be no color, for instance, without the perception of color. Things exist only in being perceived. This extremist point of view never really gained much support, for it inevitably leads to solipsism, which, of course, precludes any possibility of a collective philosophy or science.

Of greater value to psychology is Berkeley's work on depth perception. In his *An Essay Towards a New Theory of Vision,* he attacked the problem of how we perceive the third dimension of depth with a retina of only two dimensions. His answer was that we perceive the third dimension of depth as a result of experience—as a result of the recurring association of visual impressions with sensations of touch and movement that occur in ocular adjustments in looking at objects at different distances, or in bodily movements in moving toward or away from seen objects.

In other words, the continuing sensory experiences of walking toward or reaching for objects, and the sensations from the eye muscles, become associated to produce the perception of depth. For example, when an object is brought closer to the eyes, the pupils will move inward toward one another or converge. This convergence diminishes when the object moves away at a greater distance. Thus, depth perception is not a simple sensory experience, but rather an association of ideas that must be learned.

Perhaps for the first time, a purely psychological process was explained in terms of association of sensations. Berkeley thus continued the growing associationistic tradition in empiricism. His explanation rather accurately anticipated the modern view of depth perception in that he discussed the important influences of the physiological cues of accommodation and convergence.

DAVID HUME (1711–1776)

A philosopher and historian, Hume studied law at the University of Edinburgh but did not graduate. He tried the world of business but found this not to his liking, so he lived on his small income during three years of self-study in philosophy in France. After returning to England, he published *A Treatise of Human Nature,* his most important work for psychology, in 1739.

Other books followed, and he gained much fame as a writer while also working as a tutor, companion, secretary, librarian, and judge-advocate in a military expedition. He was very well received in Europe and England and held several posts in government.

Hume reemphasized Locke's notion of the compounding of simple ideas into complex ideas, developing and making more explicit the notion of association. He agreed with Berkeley on the nonexistence of the material world except when it is perceived, but took yet another step. He abolished mind as a substance and said that the mind is a secondary quality like matter! It, too, is observable only through perception. Hume believed that mind is nothing more than the flow of ideas, sensations, memories, and so on.

Of greater importance to psychology, however, is the clear distinction he drew between the two kinds of mental contents: impressions and ideas. Impressions are the basic elements of mental life and are akin to "sensation" and "perception" in today's terminology. An idea is the mental experience we have in the absence of any stimulating object; the modern equivalent is "image."

Hume did not define these two mental contents either in physiological terms or in reference to any external stimulating object. He was quite careful not to assign any ultimate causes to impressions. These two mental contents differ not in terms of their source or point of origin, but in terms of their relative strength or vivacity: Impressions are strong and vivid, whereas ideas are weaker by comparison.

Furthering his notion of difference between ideas and impressions, Hume said that ideas are weak copies of impressions. Both of these mental contents may be simple or complex, with a simple idea resembling its simple impression. Complex ideas, however, do not necessarily resemble any simple idea, since the complex idea evolves from a combination of several simple ideas in some new and novel pattern.

Complex ideas are compounded from simple ideas by association and Hume's two ultimate laws of association are resemblance or similarity, and contiguity in time or place. The more similar and contiguous are two ideas, the more readily they will be associated. Hume's work fit into the continuing development of empiricism and associationism.

DAVID HARTLEY (1705–1757)

Hartley, the son of a minister, was preparing for a career in the church himself, but because of doctrinal difficulties, turned to medicine instead. He led a quiet and uneventful life, practicing medicine and studying philosophy. In 1749 he published *Observations on Man, His Frame, His Duty, and His Expectations,* his single most important work, often considered the first systematic discourse on associationism.

Hartley is considered important, not for the originality of his work

on associationism, but for the great clarity and precision of his organization and systematization of previous work on associationism. The basic
premises of this doctrine are certainly not new with Hartley, but he
served the very important function of bringing together the earlier
threads of thought, and is acknowledged as the founder of associationism
as a formal doctrine.

Boring (1950) discussed Hartley and the nature of formal foundings
of doctrines and schools as follows:

> He took Locke's little-used title for a chapter, "the association of ideas,"
> made it the name of a fundamental law, reiterated it, wrote a psychology
> around it, and thus created a formal doctrine with a definite name, so that
> a school could repeat the phrase after him for a century and thus implicitly
> constitute him its founder. It is apt to be thus with "founding." When the
> central ideas are all born, some promoter takes them in hand, organizes them,
> adding whatever else seems to him essential, publishes and advertises them,
> insists upon them, and in short "founds" a school. . . . origination and found-
> ing may be very different matters (pp. 193–194).

This passage makes a most important point and should be remembered
as the various "foundings" in the history of psychology are discussed.

Hartley's fundamental law of association is contiguity, by which he
attempts to explain memory, reasoning, emotion, and both voluntary
and involuntary action. Those ideas or sensations that recur together, either
simultaneously or successively, become associated, so that future occurrences of one result in a repetition of the other. Thus, repetition, in
addition to contiguity, is necessary for the formation of associations.

Hartley agreed fully with Locke that all ideas and knowledge are
derived from sensory experience; there are no associations present at
birth. As the child grows and accumulates a variety of sensory experiences, connections and trains of association of greater and greater complexity are established. In this fashion, higher systems of thought are
developed by the time adulthood is reached. Thus, higher-order mental
life is capable of analysis or reduction to the elements or atoms from
which it was formed through the mental compounding of associations.
Hartley became the first to use the doctrine of association to explain
all types of mental activity.

THE MILLS: FATHER AND SON

Educated at Edinburgh, James Mill (1773–1836) was for a short time
a clergyman, but left the Church of Scotland to gain his livelihood
as a writer. His writings were many and varied, and his most famous
literary work is his *History of British India,* a book that took 11 years
to write. His most important contribution to psychology is *Analysis of
the Phenomena of the Human Mind,* which appeared in 1829.

James Mill held that sensations and ideas are the only two kinds of mental elements. In the by now familiar empiricist-associationist tradition, he said that all knowledge begins with sensations, from which are derived the higher-level complexes of ideas through the process of association. Association is a matter of contiguity or concurrence alone and may be either synchronous or successive.

James Mill believed that the mind has no creative function because he felt that association was a purely passive process. In other words, sensations that have occurred together in a certain order are mechanically reproduced as ideas, and these resulting ideas occur in the same order as their corresponding sensations. Association was thus treated in very mechanistic terms, with the resulting ideas being merely the accumulation or sum of the individual elements.

James Mill's son, John Stuart Mill (1806–1873) was a brilliant child whose entire education was conducted by his father, whom he both admired and feared. He wrote influentially in a number of areas, including philosophy, economics, political science, and psychology.

Of greatest importance to psychology is his reaction against the extreme mechanical and atomistic (or elementistic) position of his father. John Stuart Mill argued that in the associative process of the acquisition of knowledge, the mind has a very active role. Complex ideas do not merely summate through the association of simple ideas, as his father had said. The son argued instead that the complex ideas generated from simple ideas are not merely the sum of the individual parts (simple ideas) but rather involve a new quality that is not present in the original elements. Adding blue, red, and green lights in proper proportions yields white—an entirely new quality. In this so-called "creative synthesis" point of view, the combination of mental elements always produces something new.

Contributions of Empiricism to Psychology

With the development of empiricism, philosophy was turning somewhat away from its older tradition of rationalism and dogmatism. It was still concerned with many of the same problems, but its method of attacking these problems was becoming more empirical, atomistic, and mechanistic.

Consider again the emphases of empiricism: the primary role of the processes of sensation; analysis of conscious experience into elements; synthesis of elements to form more complex mental experiences through the mechanism of association; and emphasis on conscious processes. The major role empiricism played in influencing the new scientific psychology will be evident, for we will see that these areas stressed by empiricism form the basis of the subject matter of psychology.

By the mid-nineteenth century, when psychology was on the verge of becoming a science, its philosophical anticipators had become empirical in both subject matter and method. Philosophy had done all it could. What was needed now was an experimental attack on the subject matter.

SUGGESTED FURTHER READINGS

Mind–Body Problem

Feigl, H. Mind–body, *not* a pseudo problem. In S. Hook (Ed.), *Dimensions of mind*. New York: New York University Press, 1960. Pp. 24–36.

McDougall, W. *Body and mind*. New York: Macmillan, 1911 (paperback edition, Boston: Beacon Press, 1961).

Reeves, W. *Body and mind in Western thought*. Glasgow: Penguin, 1958.

Scher, J. M. (Ed.) *Theories of the mind*. New York: Free Press, 1962.

Descartes

Balz, A. G. A. *Descartes and the modern mind*. New Haven: Yale University Press, 1952.

Pirenne, M. H. Descartes and the body–mind problem in physiology. *British Journal of the Philosophy of Science*, 1950, **1**, 43–59.

General

Feigl, H. Philosophical embarrassments of psychology. *American Psychologist*, 1959, **14**, 115–128.

Gustafson, D. (Ed.) *Essays in philosophical psychology*. Garden City, New York: Doubleday, 1964.

Hall, A. R. *The scientific revolution: 1500–1800*. Boston: Beacon Press, 1956.

Sarton, G. *Six wings: Men of science in the Renaissance*. Bloomington: Indiana University Press, 1957.

III

PSYCHOLOGY COMES OF AGE

As WE HAVE SEEN, the anticipators of a separate discipline of psychology had become empirical in nature; the next step was to become experimental. That great step was facilitated by the influence of experimental physiology, which provided the kinds of experimentation that laid the foundation for the new psychology.

Developments in Early Physiology: An Overview

Physiology became an experimentally oriented discipline during the 1830s, primarily under the influence of Johannes Müller (1801–1858), who strongly advocated the application of the experimental method to physiology. Müller wrote a *Handbook of Physiology* (appearing in several revisions between 1833 and 1840), which summarized the physiological research of the period and contained a large body of knowledge. The almost immediate publication of revisions, citing much new work, indicates how prolific research in experimental physiology had become. The need for such a book was reflected in the rapid translation into English of the first volume in 1838 and the second in 1842.

Müller is also of great importance in both physiology and psychology for his doctrine of the specific energies of nerves. The doctrine states that the arousal or stimulation of a given nerve always gives rise to a characteristic sensation because each sensory nerve has its own specific energy. This idea stimulated a great deal of research that sought to localize functions within the nervous system and to delimit sensory receiving mechanisms on the periphery of the organism.

Several early physiologists made substantial contributions to the study of brain functions. Their work is of importance to psychology because of their discoveries of specialized areas of the brain and their development of research methods that became widely used in later physiological psychology.

A pioneer in the investigation of reflex behavior was Marshall Hall

29

(1790–1857), who observed that decapitated animals continued to move for some time if subjected to appropriate forms of stimulation. Hall concluded that various levels of behavior depend on different parts of the brain and nervous system. Specifically, he postulated that voluntary movement depends on the cerebrum, reflex movement depends on the spinal cord, involuntary movement depends on direct stimulation of the musculature, and respiratory movement depends on the medulla.

Pierre Flourens (1794–1867), in extending Hall's research, systematically destroyed various parts of the brain and spinal cord and observed the resulting changes in animal behavior. He concluded that the cerebrum controls the higher mental processes, parts of the midbrain control visual and auditory reflexes, the cerebellum controls coordination, while the medulla governs heartbeat, respiration, and certain other vital functions.

The findings of Hall and Flourens, though still generally valid, are second in importance, for our purposes, to their introduction of the method of extirpation. This technique essentially consists of investigating the function of a given part of the brain by removing or destroying it and observing the resulting changes in the animal's behavior.

In the middle of the nineteenth century, two experimental approaches to the study of the brain were introduced. The clinical method was developed in 1861 by Paul Broca in performing an autopsy on a man who had been unable to speak intelligibly for many years. The autopsy revealed a lesion in the third frontal convolution of the cerebral cortex; Broca labeled this section of the brain the speech center (since called, appropriately enough, Broca's area).

The clinical method has since become a very useful supplement to study by extirpation, since it is somewhat difficult to secure human subjects who will agree to removal of part of the brain. As a sort of posthumous extirpation, the clinical method provides the opportunity of finding the damaged brain area assumed to be responsible for a behavioral condition that existed before the patient died.

The other new experimental approach to brain study was that of electrical stimulation, introduced by Fritsch and Hitzig in 1870. As its name suggests, the method involves the exploration of the cerebral cortex with weak electric currents. Fritsch and Hitzig found that stimulating certain cortical areas resulted in motor responses. With the development of more sophisticated and precise electronic equipment, the method of electrical stimulation has become probably the single most productive technique for studying the functions of the brain.

These few developments in early physiology indicate the kinds of research techniques and discoveries that were supportive of a scientific approach to the psychological investigation of the mind. Students interested in the history of physiology should consult appropriate sources, particularly Boring (1942, 1950) and Lachman (1963). We have simply pointed out how the direction of research in physiology influenced the newly emerging psychology. The major point is that, while philosophy was paving the way for an experimental attack on the mind, physiology was experimentally investigating the physiological mechanisms underlying mental phenomena. The next step, which was not long in coming, was to apply the experimental method to the mind itself.

The Beginnings of Experimental Psychology

Four men are considered directly responsible for the initial applications of the experimental method to the subject matter of psychology: Ernst Weber, Gustav Fechner, Hermann von Helmholtz, Wilhelm Wundt. All four were German, well trained in physiology, and considerably aware of the impressive developments taking place in physiology in the middle of the nineteenth century.

WHY GERMANY?

Although generalizations may be suspect and exceptions to the rule frequently found, it is nonetheless possible to suggest that the times favored Germany as the place of origin for the new psychology. For a century, German intellectual history had paved the way for an experimental science of psychology. Experimental physiology was firmly established in Germany and received a degree of recognition not yet achieved in France and England. There were very good reasons for this. The so-called German temperament was better suited to taxonomic description than that of France or England. While France and England favored the deductive and mathematical approach to science, Germany, with its emphasis on conscientious, thorough, and careful collecting of observational fact, favored the classificatory or inductive approach.

Since biological and physiological science does not lend itself well to grand generalizations from which facts can be deduced, France and England were slow to accept biology into the scientific community. Germany, however, with its interest and faith in morphological description, welcomed biology to its family of sciences. It can be suggested that biology and physiology throve in Germany as a result.

ERNST WEBER (1795–1878)

Weber was born in Wittenberg, Germany, the son of a theology professor. He received his doctorate at Leipzig in 1815 and taught anatomy and physiology there from 1817 until his retirement in 1871. His primary research interests dealt with the physiology of the sense organs, an area in which he made outstanding and lasting contributions.

Previous research on the sense organs had been confined almost exclusively to the higher senses of vision and audition. Weber's work consisted largely of exploring new fields, notably cutaneous and muscular sensations. He is particularly noteworthy for his brilliant application of the experimental methods of physiology to problems of a psychological nature. In particular, his experiments on the sense of touch mark a fundamental shift in the status of the subject matter of psychology. The ties with philosophy were, if not severed, at least severely weakened. Weber allied psychology with the natural sciences and helped to pave the way for the use of experimental investigation in the study of the mind.

Two-Point Threshold. Specifically, Weber made two major contributions to the new psychology. One involves his experimental determination of the accuracy of the two-point discrimination of the skin—the distance necessary between two points before the subject reports two distinct sensations. Without the use of vision, a subject is asked to report whether he feels one or two points touching the skin. When the two points of stimulation are close, the subject reports a clear sensation of being touched at only one point. As the distance between the two sources of stimulation is increased, using an apparatus resembling a drawing compass, the subject reports uncertainty as to whether he feels one or two sensations. Finally, a distance is reached where the subject reports clearly two points of stimulation. Thus, a threshold is demonstrated at which the two points can be discriminated as such—the two-point threshold.

In further research, Weber demonstrated that this two-point threshold varies both in different parts of the body of the same subject, and from one subject to another for a given region of the body. His attempt to account for these findings by hypothesizing "sensory circles" (areas in which doubleness is not perceived) has diminished in importance, but his experimental method remains of permanent significance.

The Just Noticeable Difference. Weber's second and more significant contribution eventually led to the statement of the first truly quantitative law in psychology. He wanted to determine the smallest difference between weights—the just noticeable difference—that could be discriminated. To do so, he had a subject lift two weights, a standard and a comparison weight, and report whether one felt heavier than the other. Small differences between the weights resulted in judgments of sameness, while large differences resulted in judgments of disparity between the weights. As his research progressed, Weber found that the just noticeable difference between two weights is a constant ratio, 1:40, of the standard weight. For example, a weight of 41 gm. is reported as just noticeably

different from a standard weight of 40 gm., an 82-gm. weight just noticeably different from a standard weight of 80 gm.

Weber then undertook to investigate the contributions of muscular
sensations in the discrimination of weights of differing magnitudes. He
found that a subject could discriminate much more accurately if the
weights to be judged were lifted by the subject rather than simply
placed in the subject's hand. In lifting the weights, both tactual and
muscular sensations are operative, whereas when the weight is placed
in the hand, only tactual sensations are experienced.

Since smaller differences in weight could be discriminated when the
weights were lifted (a ratio of 1:40, as already noted) as compared
to when the weights were simply placed in the hand (a ratio of 1:30
being necessary), Weber concluded that this demonstrates the influence
of the internal muscle sense on discrimination.

From these experiments, Weber found that discrimination seems to
depend not on the absolute magnitude of the difference between two
weights, but rather on the relative difference or the ratio of one to
another. The just noticeable difference between two stimuli can then
be stated as a fraction that is constant for a given sense modality. Weber
conducted experiments involving visual discrimination and found that
the fraction was smaller than it was with the muscle sense experiments.
From this he suggested that there exists a constant fraction for just
noticeable differences for each of the senses. This provided an experimental demonstration that there is not a direct one-to-one correspondence between the physical stimulus and the perception of it.

Weber's research was experimental in the strictest sense of the term.
Under well-controlled conditions, he systematically varied the stimuli
and recorded the differential effects on the reported experience of the
subject. His experiments stimulated a great deal of research and served
to focus the attention of subsequent physiologists on the validity and
importance of experimentally approaching strictly psychological problems. "His conception of 'just noticeable differences' and his broad assumption that our responses to the world are subject to measurement
have leavened the study of everything in psychology from the simplest
feelings to the most complex social attitudes" (Murphy, 1949, p. 83).
For the first time, purely psychological phenomena were subjected to
experimental manipulation and control, and given precise quantitative
definition.

GUSTAV THEODOR FECHNER (1801–1887)

Fechner was a remarkably diverse scholar whose intellectual pursuits
ranged over an active career of more than 70 years. Consider the scope
of this man, who was a physiologist for 7 years, a physicist for 15,

an invalid for 12, a psychophysicist for 14, an experimental estheticist for 11, and a philosopher for about 40 years throughout this period (Boring, 1950, p. 283). Of all these endeavors, it is the work on psychophysics that brought him his greatest fame, even though he did not wish his name to go down in posterity as a psychophysicist. "The world, however, chose for him; it seized upon the psychophysical experiments, which Fechner meant merely as contributory to his philosophy, and made them into an experimental psychology" (Boring, 1950, p. 276).

The Life of Fechner

Fechner was born in a small village in southeastern Germany where his father was the pastor. He began medical studies at the University of Leipzig in 1817 at the age of 16, and remained at Leipzig for the rest of his life.

Even before graduating from medical school, a humanistic side of Fechner showed signs of rebellion against the prevailing materialism of his scientific training. Under the pen name "Dr. Mises" he wrote satirical essays lampooning medicine and science, a practice that he continued over the next 25 years, suggesting the continuing conflict between these two sides of his personality: a love of science and of the metaphysical. His first such essay, *Proof that Man is Made of Iodine*, attacked the then current medical fad of the use of iodine as a panacea. He was troubled by materialism and strove to establish his "day view," that the universe can be regarded from the point of view of consciousness, in opposition to what he called the "night view," which held the universe to be inert matter.

Upon completion of his medical studies, Fechner began a second career in physics and mathematics at Leipzig, at first without any official appointment. During this period, economic necessity led him to translate French handbooks of physics and chemistry into German. By 1830 he had translated more than a dozen volumes, which served to gain him prominence as a physicist. In 1824 he had begun lecturing in physics at Leipzig and undertaking research of his own. By the late 1830s he developed an interest in sensation and seriously injured his eyes by looking at the sun through colored glasses while studying afterimages.

The combination of overwork and the eye disorder was too much for him and he became, in the language of that era, a nervous invalid with neurotic depression, hypochondriacal tendencies, and thoughts of suicide. Having resigned his chair of physics in 1840, he was cut off from everyone except his wife for three years. In 1844 he was given a small pension from the university and thus officially established as an invalid. Yet, not one of the next 44 years of his life went by without a serious contribution from him.

The Contributions of Fechner

I. Quantitative Relation between Mind and Body.

The many hours spent in speculation during these years deepened Fechner's religious awareness and his concern over the problem of the soul. He turned to philosophy and began to direct the full force of his genius toward the question of the relationship between the mind and the body. He decided that the two are identical; both are aspects of the same fundamental unity. They are related to one another as the inside of a circle is related to the outside. The apparent difference between the two, Fechner said, is merely the result of the way in which they are viewed. Fechner's fame, however, comes from his psychophysics, not his philosophy; his attempt to verify his philosophical views empirically is a milestone in the history of psychology.

On the morning of October 22, 1850—an important date in the history of psychology—Fechner had an insight that the law of the connection between the mind and body can be found in a statement of quantitative relation between mental sensation and material stimulus. An increase in the intensity of a stimulus, he said, does not produce a one-to-one increase in the intensity of the sensation. Rather, a geometric series characterizes the stimulus, while an arithmetic series characterizes the sensation. For instance, adding the sound of one bell to that of an already ringing bell produces a greater increase in sensation than adding one bell to ten others already ringing. Thus, the effects of stimulus intensities are not absolute, but are relative to the amount of sensation already existing at the time.

To measure the magnitude of the sensation, Fechner proposed the use of the difference threshold (the just noticeable difference) as the unit of measure. Miller (1962) presented a clear formulation of Fechner's line of argument, which we shall follow.

To measure how bright a particular light appears to a subject—how bright it "looks"—we cannot use the physical measurement of the intensity of the light. We can, however, use the physical measurement as a basis for measuring the psychological intensity of the sensation, by first measuring how much the light must be decreased in intensity before the subject is barely able to discriminate the difference. Then the intensity of the light is changed to this new lower value and the size of the difference threshold is again measured. Since both intensity changes are just barely noticeable, Fechner assumed that they must be subjectively equal. This process is repeated until the light is no longer visible to the subject. Since every decrement in intensity is subjectively equal to every other decrement, the number of times the intensity has to be decreased, i.e., the number of just noticeable differences, can then be used as an objective measure of the subjective magnitude of the sensation. In this way, we are measuring the stimulus values necessary to give rise to a difference between two sensations.

Fechner suggested that for each sense modality there is a certain relative increase in the stimulus that always produces an observable change in the intensity of the sensation. Thus, the sensation (the mind quality) as well as the exciting stimulus (the body or material quality) can be measured and the relation between the two can be stated in the form of an equation: $S = K \log R$, in which S is the magnitude of the sensation, K is a constant, and R is the magnitude of the stimulus. The relationship is logarithmic, since one series increases arithmetically and the other geometrically.

Fechner said that this notion was not suggested by a knowledge of Weber's work, even though Weber was also at Leipzig, indeed was a near neighbor of Fechner (Flugel & West, 1964, p. 79), and had written about this matter only four years earlier. It must be remembered, however, that Weber had not pointed out the general significance of his findings, nor had he formulated a specific law. Fechner realized that his principle was essentially what Weber's results demonstrated, and Fechner gave mathematical form to the relationship.

II. Psychophysics. The immediate result of Fechner's insight was the development of a program of research on what he later called psychophysics. In the course of this research, with its classic experiments on lifted weights, visual brightness, and tactual and visual distances, Fechner developed one, and systematized two, of the three fundamental methods of psychophysics that are still basic today: the method of average error, the method of constant stimuli, and the method of limits.

Fechner developed the method of average error in cooperation with A. W. Volkmann. It consists in having a subject adjust a variable stimulus until he perceives it to be equal to a constant standard stimulus. Over a number of trials, the mean value of the differences between the standard stimulus and the subject's setting of the variable stimulus represents his error of observation. The method assumes that our sense organs are subject to variability so as to prevent the obtaining of a "true" measure. Accordingly, we obtain a large number of approximate measures, the mean of which represents the best single approximation that can be made of the true value. The technique is useful in measuring reaction time, visual and auditory discriminations, and the extent of illusions. In an extended form it is basic to much current psychological research. Every time we calculate a mean we are, in essence, using the method of average error.

The method of constant stimuli, first called the method of right and wrong cases, was originated by Vierordt in 1852 but developed as a tool by Fechner. It was used for his very elaborate work with lifted weights, which involved over 67,000 comparisons. The technique involves two constant stimuli, the aim being to measure the difference between the stimuli that is required to produce a given proportion of "right" judgments. For example, a subject first lifts the standard weight of 100 gm. and then lifts a comparison weight of, say, 88, 92, 96, 104, or 108 gm. He judges whether the second weight is heavier, lighter, or equal to the first. The procedure is continued until a certain number of judgments have been made for each comparison. For the heavier weights, subjects almost always report a judgment of "heavier," while the lightest weights almost always are reported as "lighter." From these data, the stimulus difference (standard vs. comparison weights) is determined for that point at which the subject correctly reports "heavier" 75% of the time. A number of variations of the basic procedure render the technique useful in a wide range of measurement problems in the determination of sensory thresholds and in aptitude measurement.

The third of Fechner's psychophysical methods was originally known as the method of just noticeable differences and later came to be called the method of limits. The technique has been traced back to 1700 and was formalized by Delezenne in 1827. Weber also used the method of just noticeable differences, as we have seen, but the method was given more formal development by Fechner in connection with his work on vision and temperature sensations. The method consists in presenting two stimuli and increasing or diminishing one of them until the subject reports that he detects a difference. Fechner recommended starting the variable stimulus at an intensity clearly higher than the standard stimulus at one time, and clearly lower than the standard the next time. Data from a number of such trials are obtained and the just noticeable differences are averaged to determine the differential threshold. A variation using a single stimulus presented in the ascending and descending approaches is used to determine the absolute threshold.

Comment

Fechner carried on his research for seven years, publishing part of it for the first time in two short papers in 1858 and 1859. In 1860, the formal and complete exposition of his work appeared in the *Elemente der Psychophysik,* a text of the "exact science of the functional relations or relations of dependency between body and mind."

Fechner failed in his attempt to found a philosophy on exact science, and his research findings have not withstood later criticism. At the time, however, Fechner's statement of the quantitative relationship between stimulus intensity and sensation was considered comparable to Galileo's discovery of the laws of the lever and of falling bodies (Müller-Freienfels, 1935). Fechner's efforts made it possible for the first time to measure the impalpable mind—a truly remarkable breakthrough. It was in large measure due to Fechner's psychophysical research that Wundt later conceived of the plan of an experimental psychology. More important, Fechner's methods have withstood the test of time, proving applicable to a wider range of psychological problems than Fechner ever dreamed of, and, with only minor modifications, still being used in psychological research. Boring commented that without Fechner there would have been "little of the breath of science in the experimental body, for we hardly recognize a subject as scientific if measurement is not one of its tools. Fechner, because of what he did and the time at which he did it, set experimental quantitative psychology off upon the course which it has followed" (1950, pp. 294–295).

Although Weber's work preceded Fechner's, accolades have been heaped upon the latter. Fechner seems to have used Weber's work and built on it, but he did much more than just extend Weber's research. Weber's aims were rather limited; he was a physiologist working on just noticeable differences and the larger significance of this work escaped him. As Watson (1963) noted, Weber was an "eventful" man, whereas Fechner was an "event-making" man. Fechner sought a mathematical statement of the relation of the physical to the spiritual world. His brilliant and independent insights about measuring sensations and relating them to their stimulus measures were necessary before the implications and consequences of Weber's earlier work could be recognized.

HERMANN VON HELMHOLTZ (1821–1894)

One of the greatest scientists of the nineteenth century, Helmholtz was a prolific researcher in physics and physiology. Psychology was actually in third place among his areas of scientific contributions, yet, together with Fechner and Wundt, he became a "founder" of the new psychology.

The Life of Helmholtz

Born in Potsdam, Germany, where his father taught in the gymnasium, Helmholtz was tutored at home initially because of his delicate health. At the age of 17, he entered a Berlin medical institute where no tuition was charged to those who agreed to serve as surgeons in the army after graduation. Helmholtz served for seven years, during which time he continued his studies in mathematics and physics, published several articles, and presented a paper on the indestructibility of energy in which he gave mathematical formulation to the law of conservation of energy. After leaving the army, Helmholtz accepted a position as Associate

Professor of Physiology at Königsberg. Over the next 30 years he held academic appointments in physiology at Bonn and Heidelberg, and in physics at Berlin.

Possessed of tremendous energy, Helmholtz published in several different areas. In the course of his work in physiological optics he invented the ophthalmoscope. His three-volume work *Physiological Optics* (1856–1866) was so influential that it was translated into English 60 years later. His research on acoustical problems resulted in the publication of *On the Sensations of Tone* in 1863, summarizing his own research as well as the entire available literature. He also published in such diverse areas as afterimages, color blindness, the Arabian-Persian musical scale, the form of the horopter, human eye movements, the regulation of ice, geometrical axioms, and hay fever! In later years he contributed indirectly to the founding of wireless telegraphy and radio.

The Contributions of Helmholtz

Of interest in the history of psychology are Helmholtz's investigations of the speed of the neural impulse, audition, and vision.

Previous estimates of the speed of the neural impulse had indicated that it occurred instantaneously or at least was too fast to be measured. Helmholtz provided the first empirical measurement of the rate of conduction by stimulating a motor nerve and the attached muscle from the leg of a frog (the nerve-muscle preparation), which was so arranged that the precise amount of stimulation, as well as the resulting movement, could be recorded. Working with different lengths of nerve, he recorded the delay between stimulation of the nerve near the muscle and the muscle's reaction, and then did the same for stimulation farther from the muscle. These measurements gave him the time taken for conductance. His results yielded the modest rate of 90 ft. per second.

He also experimented with the reaction time for sensory nerves with human subjects, studying the complete circuit from stimulation of a sense organ to the resulting motor response. His findings showed such enormous differences between individuals and from one trial to the next with the same subject that he abandoned the research altogether.

Helmholtz's demonstrations that the speed of conduction was not instantaneous suggested that thought and movement follow one another at a measurable interval and do not occur simultaneously, as had previously been thought. At the time, however, Helmholtz was interested only in the sheer speed of the nerve impulse and not in its psychological significance.

Helmholtz's work on vision has had a profound influence. Besides working on the external eye muscles and the mechanism by which the lenses are focused by the internal eye muscles, Helmholtz extended a theory of color vision originally published in 1802 by Thomas Young, which has since become known as the Young-Helmholtz theory of color vision. No less important was his work on audition, including perception of combination tones and individual tones, the nature of harmony and discord, and his resonance theory of hearing. The lasting influence of his theories of vision and hearing is attested to by their continued inclusion in modern textbooks of psychology.

Comment

Helmholtz was not a psychologist, nor were psychological problems his main interest, but he contributed a large and important body of knowledge to sensory psychology and helped to greatly strengthen the newly developing experimental approach to the study of psychological problems. He considered psychology a separate discipline, but thought it allied to metaphysics. The psychology of the senses was an exception, as far as Helmholtz was concerned, because of its close association with physiology. He was not really involved (or concerned) with the establishment of psychology as an independent science, yet his influence was of such magnitude that he is included among the "founders" of the new science.

The Formal Founding of the New Science

By the mid-nineteenth century the methods of natural science were being applied to purely mental phenomena. Techniques and methods of investigation had been developed, apparatus had been devised, important books had been written, and a widespread interest had been aroused. British empiricism had emphasized the importance of the senses and the Germans had described how the senses worked. The positivistic spirit of the times encouraged the convergence of these two lines of thought. Still lacking, however, was someone to organize, integrate, promote, publicize—in a word, to "found." This final touch was provided by Wilhelm Wundt.

WILHELM WUNDT

Wundt can be called the "founder" of psychology as a formal academic discipline, and is the first man in the history of psychology to be designated properly and unreservedly as a psychologist. Moreover, the Wundtian approach to psychology is important as embodying the first school of thought—structuralism. (Wundt's life and work are discussed in Chapter IV.)

As the first modern psychologist, Wundt founded the first laboratory, edited the first journal, and began experimental psychology as a science. In addition, he was a:

> great synthesizer of research findings, both of the work that preceded him and of that carried on by his students. Wundt's *forte* was not luminous ideas lighting upon the dark corners or giving us a new dazzling perspective on the old picture. Rather, he worked over a thousand details, cleaning here, repairing there, filling a crack here, so that psychology leaving his hands was an improved, more coherent picture, but still a familiar one (Watson, 1963, p. 257).

The areas Wundt investigated, including sensation and perception, attention, feeling, reaction, and association, became basic chapters in textbooks that were yet to be written. That so much of the history of psychology following Wundt consisted of opposition to his view of psychology does not detract from his achievements and contributions.

A NOTE ON "FOUNDING"

Who actually "founded" the new psychology? Fechner? He was not trying to do so. His quest was to understand the nature of the relation between the material and spiritual worlds. He sought to demonstrate his unified concept of mind and body that, although based on mystical speculation, had a scientific foundation. In this he failed. If he founded experimental psychology, he did so incidentally and involuntarily, although it is difficult to imagine the growth of experimental psychology without an *Elemente der Psychophysik* in 1860.

Helmholtz? He was not trying to "found" the new science either. While his work supported it, his main concern was with measurement of visual and acoustical phenomena.

Wundt? Boring (1963) said succinctly, "Wundt meant to found experimental psychology, and it was founded" (p. 63). In contrast to Fechner and Helmholtz, Wundt was greatly interested in promoting the idea of psychology as an independent science. Nevertheless, it is important to remember that, although Wundt is considered to have founded psychology, he did not *create* it. It had been developing from the work of Fechner and Helmholtz, among others.

On close analysis, the matter of the founding of the new science appears open to some argument. (Perhaps it is also relatively unimportant.) The founders, as Boring suggested:

> . . . are created by the student of history as distance-markers to show how far history has come and as other signs of the road to show where there is a fairly sudden, yet never very sudden, change of direction. Great men and their unexpected quick insights are for the most part created ex post facto as mnemonic aids for the student of history. . . . Great men and crucial dates are useful as they effect an analysis of history, for history, being descriptive, is necessarily analytical (1966, p. x).

It must be remembered that during the last half of the nineteenth century the *Zeitgeist* was ready for the development and application of the experimental approach to problems of mind. Wundt, a particularly vigorous agent and promoter of the inevitable, could be considered a prophet—"but prophets expound the truth, they do not make it" (Boring, 1963, p. 37).

SUGGESTED FURTHER READINGS

Early Experimental Physiology
Brazier, M. A. B. The historical development of neurophysiology. In J. Field (Ed.), *Handbook of physiology,* Vol. I. Baltimore: Williams & Wilkins, 1959. Pp. 1–58.
Fearing, F. *Reflex action: A study in the history of physiological psychology.* Baltimore: Williams & Wilkins, 1930.
Lachman, S. J. *History and methods of physiological psychology: A brief overview.* Detroit: Hamilton, 1963.

Fechner
Boring, E. G. Fechner: Inadvertent founder of psychophysics. *Psychometrika,* 1961, **26,** 3–8.
Fechner, G. *Elements of psychophysics,* Vol. I. Trans. H. E. Adler. New York: Holt, Rinehart, & Winston, 1966.
Stevens, S. S. To honor Fechner and repeal his law. *Science,* 1961, **133,** 80–86.

Helmholtz
Koenigsberger, L. *Hermann von Helmholtz.* New York: Dover, 1965.

IV

STRUCTURALISM: EARLY STAGES

An Overview on Structuralism

WUNDT'S FOUNDING OF THE new experimental science of psychology also marked the beginning of the first systematic position or school of thought in psychology, structuralism. In America, it has become customary to consider Wundt the forerunner of structural psychology and to accord the honors for more formally developing the school to the English psychologist, E. B. Titchener, who worked in this country. Wundt, however, is certainly more than a mere antecedent of the structuralist position for, as we shall see, Titchener's position is very similar to that of Wundt. Wundt mapped out the entire field of structural psychology, which for him was simply "psychology"; it remained for Titchener to coin the term "structural psychology" in 1898.

What is structuralism and why did it develop as the first systematic position in psychology? The subject matter of the new psychology, conscious experience, as well as the task, the experimental investigation of the structure of consciousness, were determined by the *Zeitgeist*. The influence of English empiricism was evident. The new psychology absorbed the experimental methods and basic approach of the older natural sciences. It adapted the scientific methods of investigation for its own use and proceeded to study its subject matter in the same way the natural sciences were studying theirs (the physical universe). The analogy to chemistry was very persuasive. All material of the universe had been reduced to a variety of combinations of less than 100 elements. If the material world could be understood by analyzing it into its most basic elementary components, why could not the world of conscious experience be explained in the same way? Thus, the spirit of the times helped to shape both the subject matter and the methods of investigation of the new psychology.

The task of the early structuralists was to discover the nature of elementary conscious experiences, *i.e.*, to analyze consciousness into separate parts. Thus, the stage was set for Wundt, and others, to discover the structure of consciousness. We shall see how they succeeded in their task and, more important, how this initial systematic position influenced the later development of psychology.

Wilhelm Wundt

THE LIFE OF WUNDT (1832–1920)

Wundt's early education was undertaken by a Lutheran vicar, presumably the assistant of Wundt's pastor-father. Apparently there was a much closer emotional attachment to this mentor than to Wundt's own parents. When the vicar was transferred to a neighboring village, Wundt became so dejected that he was allowed to live with the vicar to continue his private education. He entered the gymnasium at age 13, and was ready for the university at 19. Boring (1950) commented:

> Certainly this was a sober childhood and a serious youth, unrelieved by fun and jollity, which prepared the young Wundt for the endless writing of the ponderous tomes which eventually did so much to give him his place in history. He never learned to play. He had no friends in childhood and only intellectual companions in adolescence. He failed to find parental love and affection, substituting for the more happy relationship this deep attachment for his vicar-mentor. One can see the future man being formed—the humorless, indefatigable, aggressive Wundt (p. 317).

In order to earn a living and study science at the same time, Wundt decided to become a physician. His medical studies took him for one year to the University of Tübingen and for the next three and one-half years to Heidelberg, where he studied anatomy, physiology, physics, chemistry, and medicine. He slowly came to realize that the practice of medicine was not for him, so he shifted to physiology in order to satisfy a lifelong quest for scholarship.

After a semester of study in Berlin with the great physiologist Johannes Müller, Wundt returned to Heidelberg to take his doctorate in 1856. He held an appointment as *Dozent* in physiology at Heidelberg from 1857 to 1864. In 1858 he was appointed assistant to Helmholtz, but found his work of drilling new students in their laboratory fundamentals a dreary task and resigned after a few years of this routine. In 1864 he was made associate professor and continued at Heidelberg until 1874.

While publishing research in physiology at Heidelberg, Wundt's conception of psychology as an independent and experimental science was beginning to emerge. His initial proposal for a new science of psychology appeared in the book entitled *Beiträge zur Theorie der Sinneswahrnehmung* (*Contributions to the Theory of Sensory Perception*), various sections of which were published between 1858 and 1862. In addition to reporting his own original experiments, he expressed his views on the methods of the new psychology. In this book Wundt spoke of "experimental psychology" for the very first time. Along with Fechner's *Elemente* (1860), this work is often considered to mark the literary birth of the new science.

The *Beiträge* was followed in 1863 by another and perhaps even more important book, *Vorlesungen über die Menschen- und Thierseele*. An indication of its importance was its revision almost 30 years later with an English translation and repeated reprintings until after Wundt's death in 1920. It contains many problems that were to occupy the attention of experimental psychologists for a number of years.

Beginning in 1867, Wundt gave a course on physiological psychology at Heidelberg; this was the very first formal offering of such a course. Out of this work came what is often considered the most important book in the history of psychology, *Grundzüge der physiologischen Psychologie* (*Principles of Physiological Psychology*), which was published in two parts in 1873 and 1874, and went through six editions in 37 years, the last appearing in 1911. Undoubtedly Wundt's masterpiece, this book firmly established psychology as a laboratory science with its own problems and methods of experimentation. For many years the *Grundzüge* served experimental psychologists as a storehouse of information and a record of the progress of the new psychology. In the book's preface Wundt noted his goal: "The work which I here present to the public is an attempt to mark out a new domain of science."

Wundt began the longest and most important phase of his career in 1875 when he became professor of philosophy at Leipzig, where he worked as prodigiously as ever for 45 years. He established his laboratory at Leipzig shortly after his arrival there, and in 1881 began the journal *Philosophische Studien* (*Philosophical Studies*), the official organ of the new laboratory and the new science. With Wundt's handbook, laboratory, and scholarly journal, the new psychology was well under way.

His spreading fame and the laboratory drew a large number of students to Leipzig to work with Wundt. Among these students were many subsequent contributors to psychology, including several Americans, most of whom returned to the United States to begin laboratories of their own. Through these students, the Leipzig Laboratory exercised an immense influence on the development of psychology. It served as the model for the many new laboratories that were developed in the latter part of the nineteenth century. The many students who flocked to Leipzig, united as they were in point of view and common purpose, constituted a school of thought in psychology.

Wundt's lectures at Leipzig were very popular and extremely well attended. His classroom manner has been described by Titchener as follows:

> Wundt would appear at exactly the correct minute—punctuality was essential—dressed all in black and carrying a small sheaf of lecture notes. He clattered up the side aisle to the platform with an awkward shuffle and a sound as if his soles were made of wood. On the platform was a long desk where demonstrations were performed. He made a few gestures—a forefinger across his forehead, a rearrangement of his chalk—then faced the audience and placed his elbows on the bookrest. His voice was weak at first, then gained in strength and emphasis. As he talked his arms and hands moved up and down, pointing and waving, in some mysterious way illustrative. His head and body were rigid, and only the hands played back and forth. He seldom referred to the few jotted notes. As the clock struck the end of the hour he stopped and, stooping a little, clattered out as he had clattered in (Miller, 1962, pp. 19–20).

At the first conference with each new group of graduate students, Wundt appeared with a list of research topics, which he proceeded to assign to the students in the order in which they stood. (There was, apparently, no question of their sitting down in his presence.) Research on those assigned topics was most thoroughly supervised and Wundt held absolute power of acceptance or rejection on completion of the thesis. The spirit of German scientific dogmatism flourished openly at the Leipzig Laboratory.

In his personal life, Wundt was quiet and unassuming, his days following a carefully and totally regulated pattern. In the morning he worked on a current book or article, read student theses, and edited his journal. In the afternoon he attended examinations or visited the laboratory. After this, he walked while thinking about his lecture for the afternoon, always given at 4 o'clock. In view of his rigorous and regulated life of scholarship, it is perhaps surprising to find that many of his evenings were occupied by his interests in music and current affairs.

A laboratory and a journal established, an immense amount of research under direction, Wundt turned his tremendous energy to philosophy in the years 1880–1891, writing on ethics, logic, and systematic philosophy. In addition to these efforts, he published the second edition of *Physiological Psychology* in 1880 and the third edition in 1887, all the while contributing articles to the *Studien*.

Yet another field on which Wundt focused his considerable talent was a task he had outlined in the *Beiträge* in 1862: the creation of a social psychology. Toward the end of the nineteenth century, he returned to this project, which culminated in the nine volumes of his *Völkerpsychologie* (*Folk Psychology*), published between 1900 and 1920. Folk psychology was concerned with the investigation of the various stages of mental development in mankind as manifested in language, art, myths, social customs, law, and morals. The implications of this work for psychology are of far greater significance than its content, for it served to divide the new science of psychology into two parts, the experimental and the social. The simpler mental functions, such as sensation, perception, and memory, can and must be studied by laboratory investigation, Wundt believed. But he believed that scientific experimentation is impossible when it comes to the study of the higher mental processes, since they are so thoroughly conditioned by linguistic habits and other aspects of one's cultural training. Thus, according to Wundt, the higher thought processes could be studied effectively only by the nonexperimental approaches of sociology, anthropology, and social psychology. This contention that social forces play a major role in the development of the complicated higher mental processes is both true and important. However, Wundt's conclusion—that the higher mental processes cannot be studied experimentally—was negated by later research efforts.

Wundt's enormous productivity continued, without a break, for 63 years until his death in 1920. Consistent with his lifelong systematic habits, he died shortly after completing his psychological reminiscences. Boring (1950) noted that Wundt wrote 53,735 pages in all, an output of 2.2 pages a day from 1853 to 1920! To read his works would take nearly two and one-half years at the rate of 60 pages a day. Few men have accomplished so much, at such a high level of competence, in such a short period of time.

THE WUNDTIAN SYSTEM

Wundt's fame rests more on the impetus he provided to experimental psychology than on his systematic position in psychology. His system is essentially a body of classifications rather than a set of functional relations between variables. As such, it cannot be experimentally verified or refuted. Also, his system was constantly undergoing revision through successive editions of his books. Thus, although the original system was never completely discarded, Wundt made some rather profound theoretical modifications during his lifetime.

The Subject Matter of Psychology. Wundt stated that the subject matter of psychology is experience, or more properly, immediate experience as opposed to mediate experience. Mediate experience is used as a means of knowledge about something other than the experience itself. This is the usual form in which we use experience to acquire knowledge about our experiential world. If we look at a flower and say, "The flower is red," the statement implies that our primary interest is in the flower and not in the fact that we are experiencing red. According to Wundt, the immediate experience in looking at this flower is not in the object itself (the flower), but rather in the experience of red. Thus, immediate experience, for Wundt, is experience per se, free and unbiased by any higher-level interpretations (as in describing this experience of red as a flower). To Wundt, it is the basic experiences such as red (the experience of red) that form the basic states of consciousness or elements of the mind. Drawn by the chemical analogy mentioned earlier, Wundt wanted to analyze or break down the mind or consciousness into its most elemental components, just as the natural scientists were breaking down their subject matter, the material universe. If we carefully describe the various experiences we "feel" when we have a toothache, our concern is with immediate experience. If, however, we say "I have a toothache," we are concerned with mediate experience. Wundt wanted to describe conscious experiences in terms of the various elemental component parts of the experience.

The Method of Study. Since, according to Wundt, psychology is the science of experience, the method of psychology must therefore be the experimental method. Specifically, Wundt chose to study experience by means of self-observation or introspection. The use of introspection was not new with Wundt, for even a cursory review can trace its use back to Socrates. What was an important innovation was Wundt's application of precise experimental control over the conditions of introspection.

The use of introspection in psychology was derived, not from philosophy, but from physics, where introspection had been used to study light and sound, and physiology, where it had been used to study the sense organs. To obtain information on the operations of the sense organs, for example, the investigator would apply a stimulus to a sense organ and ask the subject to report on the sensation produced.

Wundt set forth quite explicit rules for the proper use of introspection in his laboratory: (a) the observer must be able to determine when the process is to be introduced; (b) he must be in a state of readiness or "strained attention"; (c) it must be possible to repeat the observation several times; and (d) the experimental conditions must be capable of variation in terms of controlled manipulation of stimuli. The last condition invokes the essence of the experimental method, *i.e.*, varying the conditions of the stimulus situation and observing the resulting changes in the experiences of the subject. Introspection, as practiced at Leipzig, was a skill acquired by Wundt's students only after a very long period of rigorous apprenticeship. To be able to report on the basic elements of an experience required arduous training. Introspection thus became a primary tool for the new psychology.

The Goals of Psychology. Having defined psychology's subject matter and method, Wundt then considered its threefold goal or problem: (*a*) to analyze the conscious processes into their basic elements; (*b*) to discover how these elements are connected; and (*c*) to determine their laws of connection.

The Elements of Experience. Wundt considered sensations, aroused whenever a sense organ is stimulated and the resulting impulse reaches the brain, as one of the elementary forms of experience. He classified sensations according to either their modality (vision, hearing, and so on), intensity or duration. Wundt saw no fundamental difference between sensations and images, for images are also associated with cortical excitation. In keeping with his physiological orientation, Wundt assumed the existence of a one-to-one correspondence between the excitation of the cerebral cortex and the corresponding sensory experience. He regarded the mind and body as parallel, but not interacting, systems. Thus, the mind did not depend on the body and could be studied effectively by itself.

Feelings were the other elementary form of experience, according to Wundt; he thought that both sensations and feelings are simultaneous aspects of immediate experience. Feelings are the subjective complements of sensations but they do not come directly from any sense organ. Sensations are accompanied by certain feeling qualities, and when sensations combine to form a more complex state, a feeling quality will result from this combination of sensations.

Wundt developed his famous, and highly controversial, tridimensional theory of feeling from his own introspective observations. Working with a metronome (which produces audible clicks at regular intervals), Wundt reported that at the end of a rhythmic row of clicks, some rhythmic patterns appeared to be more pleasant or more agreeable than others. He concluded that part of the experience of any such pattern is a subjective feeling of pleasure or displeasure. (Note that this subjective feeling is a simultaneous aspect of the sensation of the clicks.) He then suggested that this feeling state can be placed at a point along a continuum ranging from agreeable to disagreeable. A second kind of feeling was also detected while listening to the clicks. Wundt reported the feeling of a slight tension while waiting for each successive click, followed by a feeling of relief after the occurrence of the anticipated click. From this he concluded that, in addition to a pleasure–displeasure continuum, his feelings seemed to have a tension–relief dimension. Moreover, he reported a mildly excited feeling when the click rate was increased, and a more quiet feeling when the rate was reduced.

Through this laborious procedure of patiently varying the speed of the metronome and meticulously noting his experiences (his sensations and feelings), Wundt arrived at three independent and distinct dimensions of feeling: (*a*) pleasure-displeasure; (*b*) strain-relaxation; and (*c*) excitement–calm. Every feeling, he stated, can be located somewhere in this three-dimensional space, presented in Figure 1.

Wundt felt that emotions are complex compounds of these elementary feelings and that each of the elementary feelings could be effectively described by defining its position on each of the three dimensions. Emotions are thus reduced to conscious contents of the mind. His theory

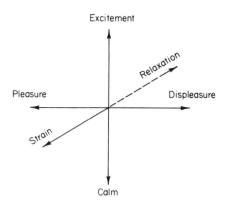

Figure 1. Wundt's tridimensional theory of feeling. From p. 21, *Psychology*, by G. A. Miller, with slight modifications. Copyright 1962 by G. A. Miller. Reprinted by permission of Harper & Row.

of feelings stimulated a great deal of research in his own and rival laboratories, but did not withstand the test of time.

The Doctrine of Apperception. How is the totality of conscious experience compounded or built up from elementary component parts? When we look at the real world we see a unity of perceptions—we see a tree as a unity; we do not "see" the many and varied sensations of brightnesses, hues, shapes, and so on, that Wundt's students reported in the laboratory. Our visual experience "comprehends" the tree as a unity and not as each of the numerous elementary sensations and feelings that might constitute the tree.

Wundt postulated his doctrine of apperception to explain how the various elements of experience are combined, or compounded, to form unified conscious experiences. He designated the actual process of relating or combining the various elements into a unity as his principle of *creative synthesis* or law of psychic resultants, which did not differ significantly from John Stuart Mill's notion of creative synthesis discussed earlier. The many elementary experiences are organized into a whole by this process of creative synthesis, which says, in essence, that the combination of elements creates new properties. As Wundt stated it, "Every psychic compound has characteristics which are by no means the mere sum of the characteristics of the elements" (1896, p. 375). Thus, something new is created out of the synthesis of the elemental parts of experience. Perhaps we might say, as the Gestalt psychologists said repeatedly, beginning in 1912, that the whole is more than the sum of its parts.

This notion of a creative synthesis was apparently drawn from the chemical analogy: the combination of the elements in chemistry produces resultants containing new properties that are not properties of the original elements. Apperception, therefore, is an active process—it is not merely acted upon by the experienced elements; rather it acts upon them in the creative synthesis of the parts to make up the whole.

Wundt emphasized the analysis of mind, the reduction of conscious experience to its elementary component parts. The notion of a creative synthesis of these parts was relatively neglected by him. Yet the fact that he did make synthesis a feature of his formal system is historically significant because this notion had important repercussions.

THE RESEARCH TOPICS OF THE LEIPZIG LABORATORY

Wundt himself stated the problems for experimental psychology during the early years of the Leipzig Laboratory. The great man assigned to his students research topics that coincided with his own aims. For a number of years the problems with which the new experimental psychology concerned itself were defined by the work done at the Leipzig Laboratory. Even more important, the extensive research performed there demonstrated, to those who doubted, that an experimentally based science of psychology was possible.

Since the methods and subject matter of the Leipzig Laboratory formed the foundation for the new science, it is important to understand the nature of the work during the early years. Wundt believed that his new science should initially be concerned with research problems that had already been investigated and reduced to some kind of quantitative form. For the most part, he did not occupy himself with new kinds of research, concerning himself chiefly with the extension and more formal development of existing research problems.

Almost all the work proceeding from the Laboratory was published in the *Studien*. Very little research was published in this journal that had not been done either at Leipzig or by Wundt's students so soon after leaving Leipzig that it still bore the imprint of the master. Over

100 studies were performed in the first 20 years of the Laboratory's existence (Boring, 1950, pp. 339–344).

The first series of studies involved the psychological and physiological aspects of vision and hearing and, to some extent, the so-called lower senses. Typical problems investigated in the area of visual sensation and perception included the psychophysics of color, color contrast, peripheral vision, negative afterimages, visual contrast, color blindness, visual size, and optical illusions. Psychophysical methods were used to investigate auditory sensations. Tactual sensations were studied as well as the time-sense, *i.e.*, the perception or estimation of intervals of varying lengths of time.

A topic that also claimed a great amount of attention in the Laboratory was reaction time. The speed of a reaction had been a research problem since the end of the eighteenth century and had been investigated by Helmholtz and by Donders, a Dutch physiologist. Wundt believed that he could demonstrate experimentally the three stages that he thought were present in a person's response to a stimulus—perception, apperception, and will. On presentation of a stimulus, the subject first perceives it, then apperceives it, and finally wills to react (from which muscular movement results). Wundt hoped to develop a "chronometry of the mind" by being able to measure the times for the various mental processes such as cognition, discrimination, will, and so on. The promise of the method was not to be realized, for in practiced subjects the three stages were not clearly apparent, and the times for the separate processes were neither constant from person to person nor from study to study.

Studies on reaction time were replaced by research on attention and feeling. Wundt considered attention to be the most vivid perception of only a small portion of the entire content of consciousness at any one time. The reference is to what is commonly called the focus of attention. Those stimuli in this focus are the most clearly perceived and are quite distinct and separate from the rest of the visual field. A simple example is the words you are now reading relative to the rest of this page and other objects in the surrounding environment that are perceived less clearly. In addition to studying the range and the fluctuation of attention in the Leipzig Laboratory, one of Wundt's students, James McKeen Cattell, performed a classic study of attention span, finding that four, five, or six units could be perceived in one short exposure.

Studies of feeling were undertaken in the 1890s to attempt to support the tridimensional theory. Fechner's method of impression was developed as the method of paired comparisons, which requires the comparison of stimuli in terms of the subjective feeling aroused. Other studies attempted to relate bodily changes, such as pulse rate, breathing, and so on, to corresponding feeling states.

Another area of investigation was the analysis of verbal associations, in which subjects are asked to respond with a single word upon the presentation of the stimulus word. Wundt proceeded to classify the types of word association discovered when single-word stimuli were presented, in order to determine the nature of all verbal association.

The experimental areas of the psychophysiology of the senses, reaction time, psychophysics, and association constituted more than half of all the work published in the first few years of the *Studien*. Wundt manifested some slight concern with child psychology and animal psychology, but apparently undertook no experimentation in these areas, believing that the conditions of study could not be adequately controlled.

IN RETROSPECT

Wolman (1960) suggested that the act of establishing the first psychological laboratory at Leipzig required a great deal of courage. To do so at that time required a man well versed not only in contemporary psychology, but also in physiology and philosophy, and capable of combining these three disciplines effectively. In order to accomplish his goal of establishing a new science, Wundt had to get rid of the nonscientific past and cut the ties between the new scientific psychology and the old mental philosophy.

By postulating that the subject matter of psychology was experience and that psychology was a science based on experience, Wundt was able to avoid discussions of the nature of the immortal soul and its relationship to the mortal body. He said simply, though emphatically, that psychology does not deal with this issue. At that time, this assertion was a great and significant step forward.

One cannot help but marvel at Wundt's outstanding creative energy and endurance for a period of more than 60 years. His creation of a scientific experimental psychology commands respect and is the source of his greatest influence. He began (as he had earlier announced his intention of doing) a new domain of science, and conducted purely psychological research in a laboratory he designed for that purpose. He published the results in his own journal and tried to develop a systematic theory of the human mind. His thoroughly trained students founded additional laboratories and continued experimenting on the problems and with the techniques set forth by the great man. Thus, Wundt provided psychology with all the accouterments of a modern science.

Murphy (1949) noted that "Before Wundt published his *Physiological*

Psychology and established his laboratory, psychology was little more than a waif knocking now at the door of physiology, now at the door of ethics, now at the door of epistemology. In 1879, it set itself up as an experimental science with a local habitation and a name" (p. 159). The times were, of course, ready for the Wundtian movement, which was the natural outcome of the development of the physiological sciences, particularly in the German universities. That Wundt was the culmination of the movement and not its originator in the strictest sense of the word does not diminish his stature. It did, after all, require the stroke of a kind of genius, a firm sense of dedication, courage, and vigor, to bring such a movement to its fulfillment. The results of his efforts represent an achievement of such overwhelming importance that Wundt is accorded a unique position among psychologists of the more modern period.

Like any great man, Wundt is subject to criticism with regard to many points of his systematic position and his experimental technique of introspection. With respect to the method he chose for the new science, it is very hard to verify his research findings. If a different person's introspection gives different results, how can we decide who is right? Experiments using introspection, unlike more objective experimentation, do not insure agreement among experimenters, since introspective observation is a strictly private affair. As such, disagreements cannot be settled by repeated observations. However, as Miller (1962) noted, "scientific psychology had to start somewhere. It was not obvious in advance that a direct attack on the mind would not be the best approach. And there was always the hope that introspective reports would parallel the physiological indicators" (p. 22).

During Wundt's lifetime, it was difficult to criticize his system, primarily because he wrote so much and so fast: By the time a critic had prepared an attack on a particular point, Wundt had changed his argument in a new edition or was writing on an entirely new and different topic. A critic, in a word, would be outwritten and buried under volumes of highly detailed and complex writings. Further, since his theories were more like classificatory schemes, they tended to be somewhat loosely knit and almost impossible to verify. There was no vital center to his program where a critic might damage him with a single stroke. As William James noted: "Cut him up like a worm, and each fragment crawls; there is no *nœud vital* in his mental medulla oblongata, so that you can't kill him all at once" (Perry, 1935, p. 68).

The Wundtian position, as boldly and forcefully advanced by his student Titchener (Chapter V), has not withstood the test of time. Structuralism is a dead issue in contemporary psychology and has been for many years. Consequently, contemporary psychologists have voiced complaints about what they now see as the narrowness of Wundt's position. As we shall see in the following chapters:

> Almost all the new schools have been founded as a protest against some one or other characteristic of Wundt's psychology, but we may welcome the schools without condoning the complaint. At any one time a science is simply what its researches yield, and the researches are nothing more than those problems for which effective methods have been found and for which the times are ready (Boring, 1950, p. 343).

Wundt's achievements, however, are not diminished by the fact that much of the history of psychology after him consisted of rebellion against some of the limitations he had placed on the field. Forward movement must have something to push against and Wilhelm Wundt provided a compelling and magnificent beginning to modern experimental psychology.

Other Early European Psychologists

Wundt had no monopoly on the new psychology, for at other laboratories in Germany the science was also beginning to flourish. Although he was obviously the most important organizer and systematizer in the early days of psychology, there were others who influenced the new science. Some of these early psychologists disagreed with Wundt on a number of points but all shared his belief that introspection was the only proper method to be used in psychology. Some of them, rather paradoxically, came to influence structural psychology by their opposition to it rather than by any direct positive contributions to the position. Even though these early non-Wundtian psychologists had different points of view, all were engaged in the common enterprise of developing the new psychology. Their endeavors made Germany the undisputed center of the new movement.

FRANZ BRENTANO (1838–1917)

At about age 16, Brentano began his training for the priesthood, studying at Berlin, Munich, and Tübingen, where he received his degree in philosophy in 1864. He was ordained the same year, and two years later began teaching philosophy at Würzburg, writing and lecturing on Aristotle.

In 1870, the Vatican Council accepted the doctrine of papal infallibility, with which Brentano could not agree. He resigned his professorship (to which he had been appointed as a priest) and left the Church. His most famous work, *Psychologie vom empirischen Standpunkte* (*Psychology From an Empirical Standpoint*), was published in 1874, the year in which the second part of the first edition of Wundt's *Principles of Physiological Psychology* was published. Brentano's book was in direct opposition to the Wundtian view, attesting to the dissent apparent in the new psychology from the outset.

Also in 1874, Brentano was appointed professor of philosophy at the University of Vienna, where he remained for 20 years, during which time his influence grew considerably. He was a popular lecturer and among his students were several men who gained their own places of prominence in the history of psychology: Carl Stumpf, Christian von Ehrenfels, and Sigmund Freud. In 1894, Brentano retired and spent his remaining years in Italy and Switzerland, engaged in study and writing.

Brentano was one of the more important non-Wundtians because of his diverse influences within psychology. (We will see, in Chapter XII, that he is one of the intellectual precursors of the school of Gestalt psychology.)

Despite their vastly different approaches, Brentano shared with Wundt the goal of making psychology a science. Whereas Wundt's psychology was plainly experimental, Brentano's was empirical. The primary method of psychology for Brentano was observation, not experimentation, though he did not reject the utility of the experimental method. An empirical approach generally is broader in scope in that it obtains its data from observation and individual experience as well as experimentation.

Brentano opposed one of Wundt's fundamental points—that psychology should study the content of conscious experience. Instead, Brentano argued that the proper subject matter of psychology was mental acts or processes; the mental act of seeing, for example, as opposed to the study of mental content (that which is seen).

Brentano's so-called act psychology thus countered the Wundtian view that the psychic processes are contents. He argued that the distinction must be drawn between "the experience as a structure and the experience as a way of acting" (Murphy, 1949, p. 225). The sensory content of red is quite different from the experience of sensing red. Brentano urged that this act of experiencing is the true subject matter for psychology.

He argued that the color red is not mental but strictly a physical quality. The act of seeing red, however, is mental. Of course, the act always involves an object, i.e., a content is always present because the act of seeing is meaningless unless something is seen. This different subject matter also necessitated a different method of study, for acts (unlike sensory contents) are not accessible through the analytical introspection of the Leipzig Laboratory.

To study mental acts requires observation on a larger scale than that practiced by orthodox introspectionists. As a result, act psychology, as we have seen, is more empirical than experimental in its methodology. This is not to imply that Brentano's psychology was a return to speculative philosophy; though not experimental in nature, it did rely on careful observation.

Brentano's position had its loyal adherents, but the Wundtian psychology of content still maintained the place of prominence in the new psychology. Since Wundt wrote much more than Brentano, his position was better known. Also, it was easier to study sensations or contents with the methods of psychophysics than to study the more elusive acts.

CARL STUMPF (1848–1936)

The son of a medical family, Stumpf came into contact with science at an early age but developed a greater interest in music. At the age of seven he began studying the violin and by age ten was composing music. As a student at Würzburg, he was captivated by Brentano and began to study philosophy and science. At Brentano's suggestion, he went to Göttingen where he received his doctorate in 1868. He held a number of academic appointments over the following years, during which time he turned seriously toward psychology.

In 1894, he received the most prized professorship in German psychology—at the University of Berlin. (Wundt, who at that time was the dean of German psychologists, would have seemed the logical choice for the position. It has been suggested that the influential Helmholtz opposed the appointment of Wundt.) With the position Stumpf acquired, as Boring put it, "a small laboratory and a large future" (1950, p. 366). The years at Berlin were extremely productive and the original laboratory of three small rooms grew into a large and important institute. Though his laboratory never rivaled Wundt's in scope or intensity of research, Stumpf is often considered Wundt's major direct competitor.

Stumpf's first psychological writings are concerned with space perception, but his most influential work is *Tonpsychologie* (*Psychology of Tone*), which appeared in two volumes in 1883 and 1890. This work and his other studies of music earned him a place second only to Helmholtz in the field of acoustics and marked the beginning of the psychological study of music.

The strong influence of Brentano was probably a reason for Stumpf's acceptance of a less rigorous form of introspection than that considered necessary at Leipzig. A bitter controversy raged between Wundt and Stumpf in a series of publications on introspection of tones, which was started by Stumpf on a theoretical level but was made more personal by Wundt. In essence, the issue involved the question of which introspectionist's reports were the more credible. When dealing with tones, should one accept the results of highly trained introspectionists (Wundt) or of expert musicians (Stumpf)? Stumpf would not accept the results obtained at Wundt's laboratory on this problem.

Continuing to write on music and acoustics, Stumpf also began a center for the collection of recordings of primitive music from all over the world, founded the Berlin Association for Child Psychology, and published a theory of feeling in which he attempted to reduce feeling to sensation. Stumpf became one of a number of Germans who maintained their independence from Wundt and so strove to enlarge the boundaries of psychology.

OSWALD KÜLPE (1862–1915)

Initially a student, disciple, and follower of Wundt, Külpe, in the course of his career, led a group of students in a movement to break away from what he considered the limitations of the master's work. Though Külpe's movement was not a revolution, it can be regarded as a sort of declaration of freedom inspired by dissatisfaction with the perceived narrowness of some of Wundt's views. Külpe worked on a number of problems that Wundt's brand of structuralism had disregarded.

After an apparently uneventful childhood, Külpe began his university training at the age of 19 at Leipzig. His original intention was to study history, but under the influence of Wundt he changed, for a while at least, to philosophy and experimental psychology, which at that time (1881) was still very much in its infancy. History still held a strong attraction for Külpe, however, because after one year with Wundt he went to Berlin to study it again for a semester. Two further academic forays into psychology and history followed before he finally (1886) returned to Wundt and Leipzig for eight years. After receiving his degree at Leipzig, he stayed on as *Dozent* and assistant to Wundt, carried on research in the Laboratory, and wrote a psychology textbook, *Grundriss der Psychologie* (*Outline of Psychology*). This text, published in 1893 and dedicated to Wundt, defined psychology as the science of the facts of experience as dependent on the experiencing individual.

In 1894, Külpe became professor at Würzburg, where two years later he established a laboratory that before long became almost as important as the Leipzig Laboratory. Among the students attracted to Würzburg were several Americans, one of whom, James Rowland Angell, was an important figure in the development of functionalism (Chapter VIII). Strangely enough, Külpe was apparently more concerned with philosophy and esthetics than with psychology during his laboratory's early years. While his writings are philosophical in nature, a great deal of research from his laboratory was published. Külpe served not only as the inspiration for his students' research, but also as observer in most of the laborious and routine introspective experiments.

In the *Grundriss*, Külpe did not discuss thought at all. In this respect his position was congruent with that of Wundt, in whose shadow he still operated. By the turn of the century, however, Külpe was convinced that the thought processes could be studied experimentally. The "higher mental process" of memory had already been studied experimentally by Hermann Ebbinghaus in 1885 (Chapter IX). If memory could be studied in the laboratory, why not thought? For the first time, experimentation was consistently applied to the higher mental processes.

Another point of difference between the Würzburg school (as it came to be called) and Wundt's system related to the method of introspection. For Wundt, introspection involved little more than having an experience and then describing it. Külpe developed a new method, called "systematic experimental introspection," involving the performance of a complex task, such as the establishment of logical connections between concepts, after which the subject was required to render a retrospective report of his experiences during the task. In other words, the subject had to perform some mental process, such as thinking or judging, and then to examine how he thought or judged. The method is systematic in that the whole experience is described quite precisely by fractionating it into time periods. Similar tasks were repeated many times so that the introspective accounts could be corrected, corroborated, and amplified. Also, introspective reports were often supplemented by questioning to direct the subject's attention to particular points.

The two forms of introspection also differed in that Külpe's subjects did not know in advance what they were to observe, whereas Wundt's subjects did.

Külpe rejected neither Wundt's subject matter of conscious experience nor his research tool of introspection, nor even his fundamental task of analyzing consciousness into its basic structure. The Würzburg school did not so much revolt against the master as attempt to expand his concept of psychology's subject matter to include the higher mental processes, and to refine the method of introspection.

What were the results of this attempted expansion and refinement? Wundt's point of view, as we have seen, stressed that conscious experience can be reduced to its component sensory or imaginal elements: all experience is composed of sensations or images. Külpe's program of direct introspection of thought processes found evidence supporting just the opposite point of view: that thinking can occur without any sensory or imaginal content! This finding came to be identified as "imageless thought," to represent the notion of meanings in thought that do not seem to involve any specific images. A nonsensory form or aspect of consciousness was thus identified.

The first important contribution from this school was a study by Karl Marbe on the comparative judgment of weights. Marbe found that although sensations and images are indeed present during the task, they seem to play no part in the process of judgment itself. The subject really does not know how the judgments (of lighter or heavier) come into his mind. This finding contradicted the belief about thought that had been held for centuries. It had been supposed that in making a judgment of this kind, the subject retained an image of the first object and compared it with the sensory impression of the second object. Marbe's experiment demonstrated that there is no such comparison of image and impression, and that the process of judgment is much more elusive than had been supposed.

These and related experiments conducted at Würzburg demonstrated that, though the conscious elements usually considered necessary for thought are not essential for thought, there are apparently other conscious states present that had not been previously suspected. These "new" states, such as hesitation, doubt, confidence, searching, or waiting for an answer, were considered to be neither sensations, images, nor feelings, and were initially called "conscious attitudes." In subsequent work, J. Orth suggested that Wundt's feelings of strain–relaxation and excitement–calm can be reduced to these same intangible and obscure conscious attitudes.

The Würzburg group also dealt with association and will. A classic study by Henry Watt demonstrated that in an associative task (e.g., asking a subject to find a subordinate or superordinate of a particular word), the subject has little relevant information to report as regards his conscious process of judgment. This finding provided a further demonstration of conscious experience that could not be reduced to Wundt's sensations and images. Watt found that his subjects were able to respond correctly without being consciously aware of intending to do so during the time of response. He concluded that the conscious work was done prior to the performance of the task, at the time when the instructions were given and understood. Upon receipt of the instructions, the subject, according to Watt, determined to react in the manner required. Upon presentation of the stimulus word, the subject carried out the instructions without any further conscious effort. Through the instructions the subject's determination had apparently established an unconscious set or "determining tendency" to respond in the way the instructions directed. Once the task had been understood and this determining tendency adopted, the actual task was performed with little, if any, conscious effort. What the Würzburgers suggested is that predispositions outside of consciousness are somehow able to control conscious activities.

A new period in the Würzburg school began in 1907 with the work of Karl Bühler, whose method involves presenting to the subject a question that requires some thought before it can be answered. The subject then gives as complete an account as possible of the steps involved in reaching the answer, with the experimenter interjecting questions about the process. Bühler's importance lies in his careful demonstration of the existence of nonsensory thought processes. This notion had already been uncovered, but it had been only an aspect, and not a major focus, of the previous Würzburg work. Bühler, more than any of the other Würzburgers, stressed the notion of elements of experience that are not sensory in nature. He asserted quite explicitly that these new types of structural elements, these thought elements, are vitally important in the process of thought and must be given serious consideration.

Not unexpectedly, Külpe's refinement of Wundt's method of introspection and the attempt to add to the list of elements evoked strong criticism from the more orthodox Wundtian structuralists. It came in the form of vigorous and scathing attacks from Wundt and his pupil, Titchener. Wundt called the Würzburgers' form of introspection "mock" experiments and said that their method did not really involve experimentation or introspection. Through it all, Külpe maintained the highest regard for both of his critics.

In a way it is strange that the Wundtians so strongly opposed the Würzburgers' notion of nonsensory mental life, for Külpe, after all, proceeded along paths that Wundt had opened. And had not Wundt himself thought along not too dissimilar lines? Was not his notion of feelings a recognition of nonsensory elements of conscious experience? It was certainly no accident that Külpe, a product of Wundtian training, had instigated this movement.

Are there really fundamental points of difference between the Würzburgers and the Wundtians? In terms of basic emphasis, goals, and methods, probably not. Külpe and his followers were still, after all, trying to find the elements of conscious experience through introspective report. They were, like Wundt, analytical in their approach and structuralists in their basic orientation.

The 15 years that Külpe remained at Würzburg were his most influential in the history of psychology. In 1909 he went to Bonn, where he founded a laboratory, and in 1913 he moved to Munich. His interest in philosophical problems, particularly esthetics, came to the fore in his post-Würzburg years. Külpe wrote very little concerning his students' work at Würzburg, and his planned description of the nature of the thought processes was never written. Boring commented that Külpe "did not in his life-time convince his critics. At the dramatic moment in this work he died, too early, at the age of fifty-three, without having yet convincingly demonstrated to the world that Wundt was wrong, or that Wundt was right, when he said that one can not experiment upon thought" (1950, p.

409). Whether the world was so convinced or not, the notions developed by the Würzburgers were, to some degree, influential for the later Gestalt psychologists.

A major contribution to modern psychology is the Würzburgers' emphasis on the area known as motivation. Their key concept of determining tendency or set certainly has a bearing on motivation as treated in today's psychology. Also, their demonstration that experience depended not only on conscious elements, but also on the unconscious determining tendencies, suggests the role of unconscious determinants of behavior, which forms a major part of Freud's systematic position (Chapter XIII).

One should not conclude, from this discussion of Külpe, that the more traditional and orthodox Wundtian structuralism was dead by the 1900s. This was decidedly not the case, as we shall see from our discussion of Wundt's stalwart standard-bearer, E. B. Titchener.

SUGGESTED FURTHER READINGS

Wundt

Boring, E. G. On the subjectivity of important historical dates: Leipzig 1879. *Journal of the History of the Behavioral Sciences,* 1965, **1,** 5–9.

Cattell, J. McK. The psychological laboratory at Leipzig. *Mind,* 1888, **13,** 37–51.

Titchener, E. B. Wilhelm Wundt. *American Journal of Psychology,* 1921, **32,** 161–178.

Brentano

Puglisi, M. Brentano: a biographical sketch. *American Journal of Psychology,* 1924, **35,** 414–419.

Rancurello, A. C. *A study of Franz Brentano.* New York: Academic Press, 1968.

Titchener, E. B. Brentano and Wundt: empirical and experimental psychology. *American Journal of Psychology,* 1921, **32,** 108–120.

Stumpf

Langfeld, H. S. Carl Stumpf: 1848–1936. *American Journal of Psychology,* 1937, **49,** 316–320.

Külpe and the Würzburg School

Ogden, R. M. Oswald Külpe and the Würzburg School. *American Journal of Psychology,* 1951, **64,** 4–19.

V

STRUCTURALISM:
FINISHED FORM

THE ORTHODOX WUNDTIAN BRAND of the new psychology was transplanted to the United States by Wundt's most outstanding pupil, E. B. Titchener, and underwent its fullest development at his hands. A knowledge of Wundt's psychology provides a reasonably accurate picture of Titchener's system, though the two positions are not identical. The pupil differed on some points with the teacher but the Titchenerian system is Wundtian in methods, content, and spirit.

Edward Bradford Titchener

THE LIFE OF TITCHENER (1867–1927)

Titchener, a fascinating man, was English by birth, German in his professional and personal temperament, and spent his most productive years at Cornell University in the United States. For Titchener, who is often pictured clad in the academic gown he invariably wore to class, every lecture was a dramatic production. The staging was carefully prepared by assistants (under Titchener's watchful eye); his staff and assistants (who attended all his lectures) entered through one door to take front-row seats, and the Professor came through another that led directly to the lecture platform. Afterwards, the lecture was solemnly discussed by the faculty and graduate students.

As Titchener put it, the wearing of his Oxford gown gave him the right to be dogmatic. Although he spent only two years with Wundt, Titchener resembled his mentor in many respects, including his autocratic nature, his very formal lectures, and even his bearded appearance.

Born in Chichester, England, of an old family that had little money, Titchener relied on his considerable intellectual abilities to win scholarships to further his education. He initially attended Malvern College and then Oxford, where he studied philosophy and the classics for four years and became a research assistant in physiology for the fifth year.

While there, Titchener became interested in Wundt's new psychology, an interest that was neither shared nor encouraged by anyone at Oxford. Quite naturally, then, he journeyed to Leipzig, the mecca for scientific pilgrims, to study under Wundt for two years, receiving his degree in 1892. There seems no doubt that Wundt made a lifelong impression on the young student, though Titchener apparently saw little of him (Wundt was 35 years older and somewhat aloof). The two years at Leipzig determined Titchener's future in psychology, that of his many future students, and to a certain extent, the destiny of American psychology for a number of years.

After receiving his degree, Titchener wanted to become the pioneer of the new experimental psychology in England. The British, however, were skeptical of a scientific approach to one of their favorite philosophical subjects. Therefore, after a few months as an extension lecturer in biology at Oxford, Titchener went to the United States to teach psychology and direct the laboratory at the new Cornell University. He was then 25 years old, and he remained at Cornell for the rest of his life.

The years 1893–1900 were spent in developing his laboratory, acquiring equipment, conducting research, and writing some 62 articles. As more and more students were attracted to Cornell, Titchener relinquished the time-consuming task of participating personally in every study and, in later years, his research was conducted almost entirely by his students.

It was through direction of his students' research that his systematic position reached fruition. Titchener gave over 50 doctorates in psychology in 35 years and most of these dissertations bear the stamp of his personal thought. He exercised great authority in the selection of his students' research problems, assigning topics that were relevant to the issue with which he was concerned at the time. In this way, Titchener built a unified systematic position, with all graduate students at a given time expected to work collectively on the problem that then occupied Titchener's attention. As Roback (1952) noted, "Titchener thus erected an ivory tower in which he was to sit aloft and direct the course of what he considered to be the only scientific psychology worthy of the name" (p. 184).

This is not to imply that Titchener's own publications were few. His bibliography lists 216 articles and notes and a number of books. Quite naturally, Titchener translated the master; when he had completed the third edition of Wundt's *Principles of Physiological Psychology*, he found that Wundt had finished a new edition. Titchener then translated this fourth edition, only to learn that the tireless Wundt had published a fifth edition!

Titchener wrote *An Outline of Psychology* in 1896, *Primer of Psychology* in 1898, and the four-volume *Experimental Psychology* in 1901–1905.

Külpe is said to have described the latter work as "the most erudite psychological work in the English language" (Boring, 1950, p. 413). These textbooks enjoyed wide popularity in this and other countries and some were translated into Russian, Italian, German, Spanish, and French.

Titchener engaged in several hobbies or avocations that tended to divert time and energy from psychology. He became so proficient in music that he conducted a small ensemble at his home every Sunday evening, and at one time substituted for a music professor at Cornell. His avid interest in coin collecting led him, with typical thoroughness, to learn such remote and difficult languages as Chinese and Arabic, in order to master the characters on the coins. In addition to his knowledge of classical languages, he was conversant with a half-dozen modern languages, including Russian. Throughout his career, he maintained a voluminous correspondence with a number of colleagues. The majority of these letters were typewritten by Titchener with added hand-written material.

As he grew older, he withdrew from social and university life. He had become a living legend at Cornell, though a number of faculty members had never met him. He did a great deal of his work at home and spent relatively little time at the university. His relations with psychologists outside his own group never were very close. Elected to the American Psychological Association by the charter members in 1892, he resigned shortly thereafter because the Association would not expel a member he accused of plagiarism. It is said that a friend paid Titchener's dues for a number of years so that his name might be listed.

In 1904, a group of psychologists called the "Titchener experimentalists" was formed and met regularly to compare research notes. As might be suspected, Titchener selected both the topics and the guests, and generally dominated these meetings.

Around 1910, Titchener began work on what was intended to be a thorough exposition of his systematic point of view. Unfortunately, it was never completed, though a few sections were published in a journal and reprinted posthumously in a book in 1929. His productivity seemed to diminish in the last 10–15 years of his life and he died of a brain tumor at age 60.

TITCHENER'S SYSTEMATIC POSITION

Titchener formally launched structural psychology in the United States in a paper entitled *The Postulates of a Structural Psychology*, reprinted on pages 69–80.

Subject Matter. The subject matter for psychology, according to Titchener, is experience. He said, however, that all sciences share the same subject matter—some aspect of the world of human experience—though each deals with a different aspect. The subject matter of psychology, as distinct from the subject matter of the other sciences, is experience as it is dependent on the experiencing person. This kind of experience is vastly different from that studied by a physicist, for example. Although light and sound may be studied by both a physicist and a psychologist, the physicist looks at the phenomena from the viewpoint of the physical processes involved, while the psychologist views them in terms of how they are experienced by a human observer.

The other sciences, Titchener said, are independent of experiencing persons. The temperature in a room may be 85 degrees whether anyone experiences the level of heat or not. If an observer stands in a room and reports that he feels uncomfortable, however, this feeling is experienced by, and is dependent on, the experiencing individual.

Titchener cautioned that in the study of experiencing one must not commit what he called the "stimulus error," *i.e.*, confusing the mental process with the object being observed. For instance, an observer seeing an apple and reporting it as an apple, instead of describing the hues, brightnesses, and spatial characteristics he is experiencing, is committing the stimulus error. The object of observation is not to be described in terms of everyday language but rather in terms of the conscious content of the experience.

When an observer focuses on the stimulus object instead of the conscious process, he fails to distinguish what he knows about the object (*e.g.*, that it is called "apple") from his own immediate experience. The only things an observer really knows about an object are its color, brightness, and spatial pattern (*e.g.*, that the object is red, shiny, and round). If he describes anything other than these characteristics, he is interpreting the object, not observing it.

Titchener defined consciousness as the sum total of a person's experiences as they exist at a given point in time. Mind is defined as the sum of a person's experiences accumulating during his lifetime. Mind and consciousness are thus generally the same, except that consciousness involves mental processes occurring at the moment rather than the total accumulation of processes.

Methods of Psychology. Psychology, like all sciences, depends on observation, but it depends on observation of conscious experience, or introspection. Titchener's form of introspection was even more highly developed and formalized that Wundt's. Titchener felt that introspection could be performed only by very well-trained observers and was strongly opposed to the use of untrained observers. He realized that everyone learns to describe experience in terms of the stimulus, and that in everyday life this is beneficial and necessary. In the laboratory, however, this habit had to be unlearned through intensive training; his trained introspectors had to relearn how to perceive so as to describe the conscious state, not the stimulus. (The difficulties in specifying precisely what observers learned to do are discussed in a later section, "Criticisms of Introspection.")

Titchener also believed that observation in psychology must be not only introspective in nature, but also experimental. Thus, he diligently observed the rigid rules of scientific experimentation, noting that:

> An experiment is an observation that can be repeated, isolated and varied. The more frequently you can repeat an observation, the more likely are you to see clearly what is there and to describe accurately what you have seen. The more strictly you can isolate an observation, the easier does your task of observation become, and the less danger is there of your being led astray by irrelevant circumstances, or of placing emphasis on the wrong point. The more widely you can vary an observation, the more clearly will the uniformity of experience stand out, and the better is your chance of discovering laws. All experimental appliances, all laboratories and instruments, are provided and devised with this one end in view: that the student shall be able to repeat, isolate and vary his observation (1909–1910, p. 20).

Aim of Psychology. Titchener's three problems or aims of psychology are very similar to those of Wundt. The psychologist seeks (*a*) to reduce conscious processes to their simplest, most basic components, (*b*) to determine how these elements are combined and their laws of combination, and (*c*) to bring the elements into connection with their physiological conditions. Thus, the aims of psychology coincide with those of the natural sciences. After a scientist decides what part of the natural world to study, he proceeds to discover its elements, to demonstrate how they are compounded into more complex phenomena, and to formulate the laws governing the phenomena.

Views on Particular Problems. We have seen that one of psychology's goals, to Titchener, is that of reducing consciousness to its component elements. How do we know if a given conscious process is elemental, *i.e.*, cannot be broken down into anything simpler? Titchener's answer is that if the process remains unchanged in the face of rigorous and persistent introspection, it is a true element. In essence, his test of the irreducibility of elements is analogous to the chemist's criterion for establishing chemical elements.

Titchener believed that there are three elementary states of consciousness: sensations, images, and affective states. Sensations, he said, are the basic elements of perception and occur in the sounds, sights, smells, and other experiences occasioned by physical objects actually present in the environment. Images are the elements of ideas and are found in the process that pictures or reflects experiences not actually present at the moment, such as a memory of a past experience. Affections are the elements of emotion and are found in experiences such as love, hate, or sadness.

In *An Outline of Psychology* (1896), Titchener presented a list of his discovered elements of sensation; it comprised more than 44,000 sensation qualities, the majority of which were visual (32,820) and auditory (11,600). Each single element was believed to be conscious and distinct from all others, and each could be blended or combined with others to form perceptions and ideas.

Although basic and irreducible, these elements could still be classified, just as chemical elements are grouped into various classes. Despite their simplicity, elements have characteristics that enable us to distinguish among them. To the Wundtian attributes of quality and intensity, Titchener added duration and clearness. He considered these four attributes basic characteristics of all sensations that are thus present to some degree in all experience.

Quality is the characteristic that clearly distinguishes each element from every other, such as cold, or red. Intensity refers to the strength or weakness, loudness or brightness, of a sensation. Duration refers to the course of a sensation over time, and clearness refers to the role of attention in conscious experience. That which is in the focus of attention is more dominant than that toward which attention is not directed.

It is noted that sensations and images possess all four of these attributes, but that affection has only three—it lacks clearness. Titchener felt that it was not possible to focus attention directly on the quality of pleasantness, for example. When we try to do so, the affective quality disappears. Some sensory processes, particularly vision and touch, also possess the attribute of extensity, in that they spread out in space.

Thus, all conscious processes are reducible to one of these elements. The findings of the Würzburg school did not cause Titchener to modify his position. He recognized that obscure and ill-defined qualities may occur during thought but he held that they were still sensory or imaginal elements. The subjects in the Würzburg laboratory had, Titchener said, succumbed to the stimulus error because they paid more attention to the object than to their conscious processes.

A good deal of research on affection or feeling was carried out in the Cornell laboratory and resulted in rejection of Wundt's tridimensional theory. As noted earlier, affection has only three attributes, quality, intensity, and duration. Thus, sensations and affections are processes of the same general type sharing these three attributes in common. They differ in that affection lacks the attribute of clearness. Titchener felt that affection had only one dimension, pleasantness–unpleasantness, denying Wundt's other two dimensions of tension–relaxation and excitement–depression.

Wundt's rigid experimentalism was exaggerated by Titchener, who held that psychology must be not only experimental, but also pure. Thus, Titchener was strongly opposed to the practical application of psychology. (In 1921, however, he became one of the directors of the Psychological Corporation, which is avowedly committed to the promotion of applied psychology.) He believed that the scientist has to remain completely free of any concern for the practical worth of his work. He was opposed to child psychology, animal psychology, indeed any area of the science that did not fit in with his introspective experimental psychology of the content of consciousness. As new movements and fields began to broaden the science, younger psychologists who had not trained under Titchener regarded him as outdated.

Boring (1950) commented that a person often stands out in history because he opposed some old thought or position. The situation seems reversed with Titchener, who "stood out in bold relief because everyone near him moved away from him. If all movement is relative, then Titchener moved—backwards with respect to his advancing frame of reference" (p. 419). The climate of American and European psychology was changing, but Titchener was not, and some came to look on his efforts as a futile attempt to cling to antiquated principles.

Titchener thought he was establishing the basic pattern for psychology but his work has proved to be but one phase in its history. The era of structuralism collapsed when Titchener died. That it was sustained as long as it was in America is an effective tribute to the commanding personality of the man himself. The following article by Titchener is often considered the foundation of the American school of structural psychology. This paper also discusses "functional" psychology and introduces us to the functionalist movement discussed in Chapter VI.

• • •

THE POSTULATES OF A STRUCTURAL PSYCHOLOGY[1]

Biology, defined in its widest sense as the science of life and of living things, falls into three parts, or may be approached from any one of three points of view. We may enquire into the structure of an organism, without regard to function—by analysis determining its component parts, and by synthesis exhibiting the mode of its formation from the parts. Or we may enquire into the function of the various structures which our analysis has revealed, and into the manner of their interrelation

[1] By Edward Bradford Titchener. Reprinted from the *Philosophical Review*, 1898, **7**, 449–465, by permission of Cornell University.

as functional organs. Or, again, we may enquire into the changes of form and function that accompany the persistence of the organism in time, the phenomena of growth and of decay. Biology, the science of living things, comprises the three mutually interdependent sciences of morphology, physiology, and ontogeny.

This account is, however, incomplete. The life which forms the subject matter of science is not merely the life of an individual; it is species life, collective life, as well. Corresponding to morphology, we have taxonomy or systematic zoölogy, the science of classification. The whole world of living things is here the organism, and species and sub-species and races are its parts. Corresponding to physiology, we have that department of biology—it has been termed "œcology"—which deals with questions of geographical distribution, of the function of species in the general economy of nature. Corresponding to ontogeny we have the science of phylogeny (in Cope's sense): the biology of evolution, with its problems of descent and of transmission.

We may accept this scheme as a "working" classification of the biological sciences. It is indifferent, for my present purpose, whether or not the classification is exhaustive, as it is indifferent whether the reader regards psychology as a subdivision of biology or as a separate province of knowledge. The point which I wish now to make is this: that, employing the same principle of division, we can represent modern psychology as the exact counterpart of modern biology. There are three ways of approaching the one, as there are the three ways of approaching the other; and the subject matter in every case may be individual or general. A little consideration will make this clear.

1. We find a parallel to morphology in a very large portion of "experimental" psychology. The primary aim of the experimental psychologist has been to analyze the structure of mind; to ravel out the elemental processes from the tangle of consciousness, or (if we may change the metaphor) to isolate the constituents in the given conscious formation. His task is a vivisection, but a vivisection which shall yield structural, not functional results. He tries to discover, first of all, what is there and in what quantity, not what it is there for. Indeed, this work of analysis bulks so largely in the literature of experimental psychology that a recent writer has questioned the right of the science to its adjective, declaring that an experiment is something more than a measurement made by the help of delicate instruments. And there can be no doubt that much of the criticism passed upon the new psychology depends on the critic's failure to recognize its morphological character. We are often told that our treatment of feeling and emotion, of reasoning, of the self is inadequate; that the experimental method is valuable for the investigation of sensation and idea, but can carry us no farther.

The answer is that the results gained by dissection of the "higher" processes will always be disappointing to those who have not themselves adopted the dissector's standpoint. Protoplasm consists, we are told, of carbon, oxygen, nitrogen, and hydrogen; but this statement would prove exceedingly disappointing to one who had thought to be informed of the phenomena of contractility and metabolism, respiration and reproduction. Taken in its appropriate context, the jejuneness of certain chapters in mental anatomy, implying, as it does, the fewness of the mental elements, is a fact of extreme importance.

2. There is, however, a functional psychology, over and above this psychology of structure. We may regard mind, on the one hand, as a complex of processes, shaped and moulded under the conditions of the physical organism. We may regard it, on the other hand, as the collective name for a system of functions of the psychophysical organism. The two points of view are not seldom confused. The phrase "association of ideas," *e.g.*, may denote either the structural complex, the associated sensation group, or the functional process of recognition and recall, the associating of formation to formation. In the former sense it is morphological material, in the latter it belongs to what I must name (the phrase will not be misunderstood) a physiological psychology.

Just as experimental psychology is to a large extent concerned with problems of structure, so is "descriptive" psychology, ancient and modern, chiefly occupied with problems of function. Memory, recognition, imagination, conception, judgment, attention, apperception, volition, and a host of verbal nouns, wider or narrower in denotation, connote, in the discussions of descriptive psychology, functions of the total organism. That their underlying processes are psychical in character is, so to speak, an accident; for all practical purposes they stand upon the same level as digestion and locomotion, secretion and excretion. The organism remembers, wills, judges, recognizes, etc., and is assisted in its life-struggle by remembering and willing. Such functions are, however, rightly included in mental science, inasmuch as they constitute, in sum, the actual, working mind of the individual man. They are not functions of the body, but functions of the organism, and they may—nay, they must—be examined by the methods and under the regulative principles of a mental "physiology." The adoption of these methods does not at all prejudice the ultimate and extra-psychological problem of the function of mentality at large in the universe of things. . . .

It cannot be said that this functional psychology, despite what we may call its greater obviousness to investigation, has been worked out either with as much patient enthusiasm or with as much scientific accuracy as has the psychology of mind structure. It is true, and it is a truth which the experimentalist should be quick to recognize and emphasize, that there is very much of value in "descriptive" psychology. But it is also true that the methods of descriptive psychology cannot, in the nature of the case, lead to results of scientific finality. The same criticism holds, as things stand, of individual psychology, which is doing excellent pioneer work in the sphere of function. Experimental psychology has added much to our knowledge, functional as well as structural, of memory, attention, imagination, etc., and will, in the future, absorb and quantify the results of these other, new coördinate branches. Still, I do not think that anyone who has followed the course of the experimental method, in its application to the higher processes and states of mind, can doubt that the main interest throughout has lain in morphological analysis, rather than in ascertainment of function. Nor are the reasons far to seek. We must remember that experimental psychology arose by way of reaction against the faculty psychology of the last century. This was a metaphysical, not a scientific, psychology. There is, in reality, a great difference between, say, memory regarded as a function of the psychophysical organism, and memory regarded as a faculty of the substantial mind. At the same time, these two memories are nearer together than are the faculty memory and the memories or memory complexes of psychological anatomy. There is, further, the danger that, if function is studied before structure has been fully elucidated, the student may fall into that acceptance of teleological explanation which is fatal to scientific advance: witness, if witness be necessary, the recrudescence of vitalism in physiology. Psychology might thus put herself for the second time, and no less surely though by different means, under the dominion of philosophy. In a word, the historical conditions of psychology rendered it inevitable that, when the time came for the transformation from philosophy to science, problems should be formulated, explicitly or implicitly, as static rather than dynamic, structural rather than functional. We may notice also the fact that elementary morphology is intrinsically an easier study than elementary physiology, and that scientific men are so far subject to the law of inertia, whose effects we see in the conservatism of mankind at large, that they prefer the continued application of a fruitful method to the adoption of a new standpoint for the standpoint's sake.

I may, perhaps, digress here for a moment, to raise and attempt to answer two questions which naturally suggest themselves: the questions whether this conservatism is wise, and whether it is likely to persist. I believe that both should be answered in the affirmative. As has been indicated above, the morphological study of mind serves, as no other method of study can, to enforce and sustain the thesis that psychology is a science, and not a province of metaphysics; and recent writing shows clearly enough that this truth has need of constant reiteration.

Moreover, there is still so much to be done in the field of analysis (not simply analysis of the higher processes, though these will of course benefit in the long run, but also analysis of perception and feeling and idea) that a general swing of the laboratories towards functional work would be most regrettable. It seems probable, if one may presume to read the signs of the times, that experimental psychology has before it a long period of analytical research, whose results, direct and indirect, shall ultimately serve as basis for the psychology of function; unless, indeed—and this is beyond predicting—the demands laid upon psychology by the educationalist become so insistent as partially to divert the natural channels of investigation.

The remaining four psychologies may be dismissed with a briefer mention. 3. Ontogenetic psychology, the psychology of individual childhood and adolescence, is now a subject of wide interest, and has a large literature of its own. 4. Taxonomic psychology is not yet, and in all likelihood will not be, for some time to come, anything more than an ingredient in "descriptive," and a portion of individual, psychology. It deals with such topics as the classification of emotions, instincts and impulses, temperaments, etc., the hierarchy of psychological "selves," the typical mind of social classes (artists, soldiers, literary men), and so forth. 5. The functional psychology of the collective mind is, as might be expected, in a very rudimentary condition. We can delimit its sphere and indicate its problems; minor contributions to it may be found here and there in the pages of works upon psychology, logic, ethics, æsthetics, sociology, and anthropology; and a few salient points— the question, e.g., of the part played by the æsthetic sentiment in the make-up of a national mind—have been touched upon in essays. But we must have an experimental physiology of the individual mind, before there can be any great progress. 6. Lastly, the labors of the evolutionary school have set phylogenetic psychology upon a fairly secure foundation, and the number of workers is a guarantee of rapid advance in our understanding of mental development.

The object of the present paper is to set forth the state of current opinion upon the question of the structural elements of mind, their number and nature. It may be doubted, at first sight, whether anything like a consensus of opinion can be made out. "Every psychologist of standing," wrote Külpe in 1893, "has his own laws of association." Every psychologist of standing in the year of grace 1898, so the reader may think, has his own favorite "unique" process. Does not Brentano advocate an ultimate "judgment," and James a "fiat of the will," and Stout an ultimate "thought"? Is there not the perennial controversy about the "third conscious element," the process of conation, the "activity experience"? Are not even the clear waters of the psychology of sensation troubled by the possibility of an "efferent" conscious process, a sensation of innervation? The questions are importunate, and cannot be lightly brushed aside. We will begin, therefore, by examining a test case: Brentano's irreducible "judgment." I select this, because Professor Ebbinghaus, in his recent Psychology, seems to put a structural interpretation upon it. He himself classifies the elements of mind (we shall return to this classification later) as sensations, ideas, and feelings; Brentano, he says, ranks alongside of ideas the element of judgment. If this account is correct, we must admit that the morphology of mind is still a battle-field for individual opinions; we shall hardly escape the difficulty by the mere statement that Ebbinghaus is an experimentalist, and Brentano not.

When, however, we turn to Brentano himself, the matter assumes a different complexion. Brentano's principal criterion of psychical, as contradistinguished from physical phenomena, is that of "intentional in-existence" or "immanent objectivity," which we may paraphrase as reference to contents, direction upon something as object. "Every psychical phenomenon contains in it something as object, though not every one in the same way. In ideation something is ideated, in judgment something admitted or rejected, in love and hate something loved and hated, in desire something desired, etc." This is evidently the language of function, not of structure. Indeed, Brentano uses the phrases *psychisches Phänomen* and *Seelenthätigkeit* interchangeably; his "fundamental" or "principal classes of psychical phenomena" are the "mental activities" of ideation (not "idea!"), judgment and interest (love and hate, the emotive processes). The spirit of his whole psychology is physiological; and when, on occasion, he discusses a point in anatomy, he leaves his reader in no doubt as to the shift of *venue*. Now the mental elements of the experimentalists, the bare sensation and the bare feeling, are abstractions, innocent of any sort of objective reference. We cannot fairly compare Brentano's "judgment" with them. Nay, more, we cannot fairly say that he would have posited an ultimate judgment process *if* he had adopted the anatomical point of view; since he has not adopted it, the speculation is absurd. The "psychology from the empirical standpoint" is a systematization of mental "activities," *i.e.*, of the mental functions of the human organism.

This wave, then, has not overwhelmed us. Escaping it, we may turn now to the positive side of our enquiry. Our appeal will lie, in the first instance, to the experimentalists; but the omission of references to works on descriptive psychology is largely due to considerations of space, and does not by any means necessarily imply that the authors of these works differ from the writers quoted. Some of the "unique" processes still left outstanding will be taken up at the end of this discussion.

We set out from a point of universal agreement. Everyone admits that *sensations* are elementary mental processes. There is, it is true, diversity of opinion as to the range of contents that the term shall cover. Wundt identifies the peripherally excited and the centrally excited processes. "For the psychological attributes of a sensation the circumstance [of external or internal initiation] is entirely irrelevant. . . . It is only the central stimulus that always accompanies sensation." Külpe retains the name "sensation" for both classes, but declares that they "must be treated separately, as they normally present characteristic differences." Ziehen and Ebbinghaus, on the other hand, draw a sharp line of distinction between the "sensation," which is externally aroused, and the "idea" (in Lotze's sense), which is its centrally aroused substitute, and so recognize two elements where Wundt and Külpe see only one. The divergence, however, is not serious. It seems to depend, primarily, upon the admission or exclusion of genetic considerations. If we rule that these are foreign to a strictly morphological examination of mind, the question of one sense element or two becomes a problem set by analysis to analysis, capable of resolution by analytic methods; it is a subject for dispute "inside the ring," and is thus upon a quite different level from the question, *e.g.*, of an elementary will process. We may note, in passing, that the innervation sensation, while it remains as a theoretical possibility, has been generally given up by the experimental school.

Simple *affective* processes, again, are regarded by a large majority as elemental. Both Wundt and Külpe are at some pains to make clear the essential difference between sensation and affection. Lehmann and Ebbinghaus are equally explicit. Ziehen does not give a place to feeling beside sensation and idea; his chapters are entitled "The Affective Tone of Sensation" and "The Affective Tone of Ideas," and his treatment makes affective tone an attribute, coördinate with the intensity and quality of sensation and the clearness and contents (meaning) of idea. Nevertheless, he speaks in one passage of the cortical substrate of this tone as "an entirely new psychophysiological process." Münsterberg, on the other hand, denies the ultimateness of feeling altogether, and seeks to reduce it to the sensations accompanying movements of flexion and extension, reflexly released. There is, further, an "inside" controversy as to the number of affective qualities. But analysis will some day settle the question whether there are two of these (Külpe), or two in the sphere of sensation and many more in that of idea (Ziehen), or an inexhaustible variety under the six heads of pleasantness and unpleasantness, tension and relaxation, excitement and tranquilization (Wundt).

It is natural, in view of the intrinsic difficulty of the subject, that the psychology of feeling should be in a less settled state than the psychology of sensation. All the more striking, when we consider the close relation that obtains between "feeling" and "will," is the unanimity with which experimentalists reject the doctrine of a specific will process. "There is no reason," writes Ebbinghaus, "for looking upon acts of will or appetitions as elementary forms of the mental life." And Wundt, Külpe, Ziehen, and Münsterberg are of the same manner of thinking.

No fourth candidate for elemental rank has appeared. No trace has been found, in all the minute analysis of the last twenty years, of a mental krypton or argon. It seems safe, then, to conclude that the ultimate processes are two, and two only, sensations and affections, though we must not forget that the first class, that of sensations, includes the two well-defined sub-species, "sensation" and "idea."

How, now, are these different processes to be distinguished? What is our justification for looking upon them as last things of mind? Disregarding function, and trying to answer the question upon the anatomical plane, we can point at least to three valid criteria. We may refer to experience itself, and note that sensation and affection are irreducible for introspection. The one cannot be derived from, identified with, the other; they "look" different or "feel" different, however far analysis be pushed. Or we may have recourse to physiology. Since the structure of mind is conditioned upon the physical organization, we may differentiate sensation and affection by reference to their physical substrates. Or, again, we may seek a descriptive formula, which shall sum up the essential characteristics of the two processes. It is in this sense that Wundt is speaking, when he says that sensation qualities range between maxima of *difference,* and affective qualities between maxima of *opposition* or antithesis. Any one of these statements is adequate to the psychological requirements. The last of them, however, as Wundt's exposition shows, implies that we are already familiar with the *attributes* of which sensation and affection are constituted. We must devote a brief space to their consideration.

Once more, we set out from a point of universal agreement. "There are two indispensable determinants of every psychical element, quality and intensity." But discussion is not slow to begin. For these two attributes or determinants are, evidently, of different kinds. Quality is specific and individual; it is quality that makes the elemental process a blue or a sweet, a pleasant or a *c* of the third octave. Intensity, on the contrary, is a general attribute, common to all modalities of sensation and qualities of affection. Hence, while some psychologists rank the two determinations together, as coördinate, others set aside quality for itself, and count intensity along with extent and duration as equipollent characteristics, whether of all the mental elements or of certain great groups of qualities. There is also much difference of opinion as to the precise place to be ascribed to the attributes of extent and duration. For Wundt, who holds a genetic theory, psychological space is the resultant of a two-dimensional system of qualitative local signs multiplied into, or fused with, a one-dimensional intensive system of sensations aroused by movement. It is, primarily, tactual or visual. Psychological time, in the same way, is the resultant of qualitatively varied feelings multiplied into, or fused with, the same intensive system of sensations. The affective processes, in abstraction, are timeless; the primary sources of temporal ideas are audition and "internal touch." It follows that space and time, extent and duration, can be predicated only of formations, not of elements. Spatial arrangement (Wundt makes no distinction between "spatial arrangement" and "space" as "absolute contents") cannot "be an original attribute of the elements, analogous to the intensity or quality of sensations;" it "results from the bringing together of these elements," which means the "arising of new psychical conditions;" and the same thing is true of time. Opposed to this genetic theory is the nativistic view, represented for space, *e.g.*, by Stumpf, according to which every sensation has about it something of tridimensionality, a certain bigness or voluminousness, and every elemental process a certain duration.

It is, indeed, hardly possible to keep the psychological problem of space and time clear of epistemology, on the one hand, and of psychogenesis, on the other. It would, perhaps, be unwise to make any attempt to do so, in a work meant to serve the purpose of instruction; for the attempt would involve a total disregard of historical conditions. Nevertheless, there can be little doubt as to the anatomical facts. I am wholly unable to conceive of a sensation or affective process as timeless, as lacking duration; analysis of mind as it is leaves me, always, with a process-lasting-some-time. I am equally unable to conceive of a visual sensation or sensation of pressure as spaceless, punctual; analysis leaves me, always, with a process-spread-out. On the other hand, I feel no constraint to regard the spreading-out as tridimensional. Neither does the surface itself necessarily imply the depth perception, nor need the relation of the surface to the ideating subject be present in consciousness. And the other sensations, tones, tastes, etc., as well as the affections seem to be entirely devoid of space attributes. In mental morphology, the perfect element (say, a sensation of color) shows us quality, intensity, duration, and superficial extension.

A similar difficulty confronts us with regard to the attribute of clearness. Variation in degree of clearness of the constituent processes in ideas is the anatomical equivalent of what is functionally termed the "distribution of attention." Wundt places degree of clearness on the same level with spatial and temporal arrangement. "As these attributes [clearness and obscurity, distinctness and indistinctness] arise always and only from the interconnection of the various psychical formations, they cannot be considered as determinants of the psychical elements." Yet, on Wundt's own principle of relativity, the same thing would be true of sensation intensity; we cannot say anything of the intensity of a sensation unless a formation—at least two sensations, side by side—be there for "comparison." Moreover, we must exclude genetic arguments here as before. If we make analytic introspection the test, we cannot but admit that the ultimate sensation may be conceived of as clear or obscure.

I conclude, then, that the affective element is constituted of quality, intensity, and duration; the sense element (sensation or idea) of quality, intensity, duration, clearness, and (in some cases) extent. Quality is intrinsic and individual; intensity and clearness are "relative" characteristics; duration and extent are, very probably, extrinsic translations into structure of the lowest terms of a functional series. And the corollary is that the "elements" of the experimentalists, as they themselves have been the first to urge, are artifacts, abstractions, usefully isolated for scientific ends, but not found in experience save as connected with their like.

It is unnecessary to pursue further our examination of structural psychology. Just as morphology proper, passing beyond the cell, becomes a morphology of organs, so does structural psychology, passing beyond the elementary processes, become an anatomy of functional complexes. The experimental psychologies deal, as do the descriptive works, with the perceptions and emotions and actions handed down in popular and psychological tradition. Külpe, working out a distinction which was quite clearly drawn in the physiological psychology of the younger Mill, has reduced all the "higher" processes to two structural patterns: mixtures of intensities and qualities (fusions), and connections of spatial and temporal attributes (colligations). This reduction marks a decided step in advance; but its chief value lies in the suggestion of a plan of arrangement for the results gained by analysis of the basal functions. A discussion of these results themselves would far transgress the limits of the present paper.

What remains, now, is to assure ourselves that the various "unique" processes of current psychology, not recognized in the preceding analysis, are conceived of in terms of function, and not in terms of structure. There is no room for doubt of this, in the case of Stout's Analytic Psychology. The author's use of the phrase "mental functions," his constant reference to Brentano, his insistence upon mental "activity," are indications enough. In view of the similarity of standpoint, it may be interesting to compare his final classification with that of Brentano. The latter, as we have seen, ranks ideation, judgment, and interest as the fundamental functions of mind. Stout distinguishes two primary attitudes of consciousness: the cognitive and the volitional. Cognition includes thought and sentience as "fundamentally distinct mental functions," and thought, again, subdivides into simple apprehension and judgment. Volition, in its turn, includes "two fundamentally distinct modes of reference to an object," feeling and conation. We have, then, five "fundamental modes of consciousness," grouped under the two primary conscious attitudes. The difference between Brentano and Stout is at least as apparent as their agreement.

James' "fiat of the will," or "express consent to the reality of what is attended to," is also a functional process:

> This consent . . . seems a subjective experience *sui generis,* which we can designate but not define. We stand here exactly where we did in the case of belief. When an idea *stings* us in a certain way, makes as it were a certain electric connection with our self, we believe that it *is* a reality. When it stings us in another way, makes another connection with our self, we say *let it be* a reality. To the words "is" and "let it be" correspond peculiar attitudes of consciousness which it is vain to seek to explain.*

Lastly, I may refer in this connection to Dr. Irons' contention that emotion is an "irreducible" process, an "ultimate and primary aspect of mind." Dr. Irons has stated that the method of his enquiry is not genetic; and his definition of emotion as "feeling attitude" implies that it is not anatomical. But while his words are the words of function ("cognition," etc.), his criticism is very largely criticism of the morphologists. It would seem that he has not fully recognized the difference between the two standpoints. No one among the experimentalists has hitherto expressed a doubt—I venture to assert that no one ever will—as to the composite nature of the emotive process.

The burden of the argument has been that there is reasonable agreement, within the experimental camp, as to the postulates of a purely structural psychology, whereas there is pretty radical disagreement among the psychologists of function. Let it not be supposed, now, that this latter state of affairs is anything else than a disadvantage for psychology at large; above all, let it not be thought that the experimentalist rejoices at the lack of unanimity among his colleagues. It is a commonplace of the biological sciences that structure and function are correlative terms, and that advance in knowledge of the one conditions and is

---

* *Principles,* II, pp. 568, 569.

conditioned by advance in the understanding of the other. Only, in psychology, functional analysis—required by the living of our daily life—had been carried out to a degree sufficient for the successful prosecution of anatomical work, before the experimental method appeared. Structural psychology might proceed far on its way, even if the psychology of function had halted at Kant or, for that matter, at Aristotle. I believe that physiological psychology (in the sense of this paper) has a great future; and I subscribe fully to all that has been said of the critical subtlety of Brentano's discussions, of the delicacy of discrimination shown in Stout's recent book, of the genius of James' work. Nevertheless, I believe as firmly that the best hope for psychology lies to day in a continuance of structural analysis, and that the study of function will not yield final fruit until it can be controlled by the genetic and, still more, by the experimental method—in the form both of laboratory experimenting and of interpretation of that natural experiment which meets us in certain pathological cases.

•　•　•

Criticisms and Contributions of Structuralism

CRITICISMS OF INTROSPECTION

The most severe criticisms against structuralism have been leveled at the method of introspection. This method has been attacked on several grounds. One problem relates to the definition of introspection. Even Titchener seems to have had a difficult time defining introspection satisfactorily and apparently attempted to relate it to the particular experimental conditions. "The course that an observer follows will vary in detail with the nature of the consciousness observed, with the purpose of the experiment, with the instruction given by the experimenter. Introspection is thus a generic term, and covers an indefinitely large group of specific methodological procedures" (Titchener, 1912, p. 485). It is difficult to find similarities among the different uses of the term.

One point mentioned earlier relates to the question of precisely what introspecters were trained to do. An observer learning to introspect had to learn to ignore certain classes of words—the so-called meaning words—that had become an established part of his vocabulary. The phrase "I see a table" would have no scientific meaning to a structuralist, for the word "table" is a meaning word, based on previously established and generally agreed upon knowledge about the specific conglomeration of sensations we have learned to identify and label as "table." The observation "I see a table" told the structuralist nothing about the observer's conscious experience. The structuralist was interested not in the aggregate of sensations summarized in a meaning word, but in the specific elementary forms of the experience. An observer who said "table" was committing the stimulus error.

If these everyday, commonly agreed upon words were stricken from the vocabulary, how was the experience to be described? An introspective language or vocabulary had to be developed for the purpose. Since both Wundt and Titchener emphasized that the external conditions of the experiment must be carefully controlled so that the conscious contents could be precisely determined, then two observers should have the same experience and their results should serve to corroborate one another. Because of these highly similar experiences under controlled conditions, it seemed possible, theoretically at least, to develop a working vocabulary devoid of meaning words. It is, after all, because of commonalities of experience in everyday life that we are able to agree on a conventional meaning for the word "table" (or "house," or whatever).

Although the development of such a vocabulary is perhaps possible in principle, it was never realized in actuality. There was often disagreement among introspecters, even under carefully controlled conditions of observation. Introspecters at different laboratories obtained different results. Titchener nevertheless maintained that agreement would be reached eventually, but it never was. It is possible that, had there been sufficient agreement on introspective findings, structuralism might still be a vital force today.

There were other criticisms of the method of introspection. It was charged that introspection is, in reality, retrospection, because some period of time must elapse between the experience itself and the reporting of it. Since forgetting is particularly rapid immediately after an experience, it seems likely that some of the experience would be lost. The structuralists' answer to this criticism was to specify that the observers worked with very short time intervals. The structuralists also postulated the existence of a primary mental image that was alleged to maintain the experience for the observer until it could be reported.

Another difficulty is that the very act of minutely examining the experience in introspective fashion may radically change the experience. Consider the difficulty in introspecting the conscious state of anger. In the process of rationally attending to it and trying to dissect the experience into its elementary components, the anger may subside or disappear completely. Titchener believed, however, that the experienced, well-trained introspecter became unconscious of his observational task with continued practice.

A final criticism relates to the large and growing body of data that seemed to belong within the province of psychology, but which was decidedly not available to the introspecter. Animal psychologists, for example, were rapidly accumulating useful data, obviously without the use of introspection. The psychoanalysts were pointing to the importance of unconscious determinants of behavior, which were not accessible to the introspectionists.

ADDITIONAL CRITICISMS

The method of the structuralists was not the only subject of criticism. The movement has been accused of artificiality and sterility because of its attempt to analyze conscious processes into elements. Critics agree that the whole of an experience cannot be recovered by any synthesis or compounding of the elemental parts. Experience, they argue, does not come to man in sensory, imaginal, or affective elements, but in unified wholes. Something of the experience must inevitably be lost in what critics consider an artificial breakdown of the conscious experience.

The structuralists' narrow definition of psychology has also come under attack. Psychology was growing in a number of areas and the structuralists, in the person of Titchener, preferred to exclude these newer areas if they were not congruent with the structuralists' definition and method of psychology. Titchener regarded animal and child psychology as not really psychology at all—indeed, they were not his brand of psychology. His conception of psychology was simply too narrow to contain the growing body of data being accumulated by a rapidly increasing number of psychologists.

CONTRIBUTIONS OF STRUCTURALISM

There is no denying that structuralism made singularly important contributions to psychology. As Heidbreder (1933) stated, "It is a simple historical fact that it was the kind of psychology which Titchener taught, the enterprise which centered in the German laboratories, that first gained recognition for psychology as a science" (p. 148).

For the first time, psychology achieved a formal academic identity and stature clearly separate from philosophy and physiology. At that time, the structuralist approach to the study of the mind was probably the best available: philosophy and physiology did not seem to offer a better or more effective alternative.

The subject matter of the structuralists—conscious experience—was sharply defined. Their research methods were purely empirical in nature, involving as they did observation, experimentation, and measurement. Since consciousness was best perceived by the person having the conscious experience, then the best method for that subject matter was self-observation.

While the subject matter and aims of the structuralists are dead issues, introspection, if we define it as simply the giving of a verbal report based on experience, continues to be used in many areas of psychology.

Psychophysics, for example, asks a subject whether a second tone sounds louder or softer than the first. Also, verbal reports are rendered by the person describing his experiences in an unusual experimental environment, such as a sensory deprivation cubicle. Clinical reports from a patient and responses on personality tests or attitude scales are introspective in nature. These examples, and many more, involve a verbal report based on experience and are acceptable and legitimate forms of data collecting. Obviously, the current-day usage of introspection is not of the structuralists' sort, as the verbal reports are in the language of behavior, not that of the structuralists.

The final, and perhaps greatest, contribution of structuralism is its service as a target for criticism. It provided a very strong system of orthodoxy against which the newly developing functional, Gestalt, behavioristic, and to some extent, psychoanalytic movements could marshal their forces. These newer schools owed their existence in no small measure to their progressive reformulation of the psychology that the structuralists began. As we noted earlier, forward movement requires something against which to push. With the help of the structuralist position, psychology advanced far beyond its boundary.

SUGGESTED FURTHER READINGS

Titchener
Boring, E. G. The stimulus-error. *American Journal of Psychology*, 1921, **32**, 449–471.
Boring, E. G. Edward Bradford Titchener: 1867–1927. *American Journal of Psychology*, 1927, **38**, 489–506.

General
Bentley, M. The psychologies called "Structuralism": historical derivation. In C. Murchison (Ed.), *Psychologies of 1925*. Worcester, Mass.: Clark University Press, 1926. Pp. 383–393.
Bentley, M. The work of the structuralists. In C. Murchison (Ed.), *Psychologies of 1925*. Worcester, Mass.: Clark University Press, 1926. Pp. 395–404.
Boring, E. G. A psychological function is the relation of successive differentiations of events in the organism. *Psychological Review*, 1937, **44**, 445–461.

Introspection
Bakan, D. A reconsideration of the problem of introspection. *Psychological Bulletin*, 1954, **51**, 105–118.
Boring, E. G. A history of introspection. *Psychological Bulletin*, 1953, **50**, 169–186.
McKellar, P. The method of introspection. In J. Scher (Ed.), *Theories of the mind*. New York: Free Press, 1962. Pp. 619–644.

VI

FUNCTIONALISM: ANTECEDENT INFLUENCES

What Is Functionalism?

THE PAPER BY Titchener in Chapter V has introduced and defined the nature and scope of functional psychology, which, in striking contrast to structural psychology, is concerned with the mind as it functions or as it is used in the adaptation of the organism to its environment.

The structuralists were concerned with the description of nature and asked the questions: what happens and how does it happen? They did not deal with the question of why it happens. The functionalists, on the other hand, were involved with all three questions: the what, how, and why; and their basic emphasis was on the investigation of the functions that the mind must fulfill in adapting itself to the external world.

Functionalism was the first truly American system of psychology (we will discuss the interesting reasons for this in Chapter VII). It was the product of a rebellion by the "colonial" psychologists against the land of their origins, Germany, and the structuralist position it had fostered. It is interesting to note that it was the functionalists who applied the term "structuralism" to the initial school of thought in psychology. The structuralists themselves rarely called themselves structuralists—they were simply "psychologists."

Functionalism was never as rigid or as formally differentiated a systematic position as structuralism; hence, it cannot be described as neatly or precisely as the earlier school. Moreover, there has never existed a single functional psychology, as there was a single structural psychology. There were several functional psychologies, each differing somewhat from the others. All, however, shared an interest in the functions of consciousness. Because of this emphasis on the functioning of an organism in its environment, functionalism is vitally concerned with applied psychology, which developed rapidly with the supportive attitude of the American functional psychologist.

84

Historical Overview of Functionalism

Functionalism ranges over a very long period of time—from the mid-1850s to the present, at least in modified form. Its historical development, unlike that of structuralism, was influenced by a number of intellectual leaders with a variety of interests and backgrounds. It was probably at least partly because of this variegated background that functionalism did not stultify and decline, like structuralism.

This chapter considers the early antecedent influences on the movement, including the works of Charles Darwin, Sir Francis Galton, and early students of animal behavior. Interestingly, although these early sources of influence were all British, functionalism, as we have already mentioned, formally began and flourished in the United States (see Chapter VII).

Speaking in general terms, it may be said that American psychology today is functionalistic in its orientation and attitude. This is evident in psychology's current emphasis on testing, learning, perception, and other such functional processes that aid the organism in its adaptation and adjustment to the environment.

The Evolution Revolution: Charles Darwin

On the Origin of Species by Means of Natural Selection, written in 1859, is rightly considered one of the most important books in the history of Western civilization. The theory of evolution presented in this book served to free contemporary thinking men of restraining traditions and superstitions and ushered in the era of maturity and respectability of the so-called life sciences. Further, it "influenced the development of modern psychology as much as any other single event in the nineteenth century. It would be impossible to understand what psychologists today are trying to accomplish or why they go about it as they do unless one first understood something of the importance of evolutionary theory for our contemporary vision of man and his destiny" (Miller, 1962, p. 129).

The idea that living things change with time, which is the fundamental notion of evolution, was not introduced by Darwin. Intellectual anticipations of this general idea can be traced back to ancient times. For example, Erasmus Darwin (grandfather of Charles Darwin and Sir Francis Galton) had expressed the belief, toward the end of the eighteenth century, that all warm-blooded animals had evolved from one living filament that had been given animation by the Creator. In 1809, Chevalier de Lamarck had formulated a behavioral theory of evolution, emphasizing the modification of animal bodily form through the organism's efforts to adapt to its environment—modifications that were inherited by succeeding generations. For instance, the giraffe developed his long neck by generations of reaching up to higher and higher branches for food. In the mid-1800s, Lyell introduced the notion of evolution into geological theory, arguing that the earth had gone through various stages of development in evolving to its present structure.

It seems that the *Zeitgeist* was at work in the period 1750–1850, for men were beginning to think in evolutionary terms not only in biology but also in broader social spheres. As reflected in the Industrial Revolution and in various political revolutions, this was a time of rapid social change and development.

This changing intellectual and social climate rendered the notion of evolution scientifically respectable. There was, however, a great deal of speculating and theorizing, but little in the way of supporting evidence. *On the Origin of Species,* with its enormous and well-ordered masses of evidence, changed evolution from controversial speculation to controversial fact (Miller, 1962).

THE LIFE OF DARWIN (1809–1882)

Darwin was born in 1809 in England. His father was a physician and his grandfather, Erasmus, was noted as a philosopher, physician, and poet. After two years at Edinburgh, Darwin entered Cambridge, receiving his BA in 1831. One of his instructors, the noted botanist John Stevens Henslow, promoted Darwin's appointment as a naturalist aboard H.M.S. *Beagle,* which the British government was then preparing for a scientific voyage around the world. This famous voyage, lasting from 1831 to 1836, began in South American waters and proceeded to Tahiti and New Zealand, to return by way of Ascension Island and the Azores. The trip afforded a unique opportunity to observe and collect a wide variety of plant and animal life, and Darwin returned to England with an immense amount of data.

In 1837, his health forced him to retire to the country, where he was able to work only about four hours a day. He was in poor health for the remainder of his life but this did not prevent his writing numerous scientific papers and books.

One year before the publication of the *Origin of Species,* Darwin received a letter and a manuscript from a young English naturalist in the East Indies, Alfred Russel Wallace, who proposed essentially the same theory that Darwin had been patiently working on for 22 years —another instance of simultaneous discovery, as discussed in Chapter I. During an illness, Wallace had developed the main outlines of an evolutionary theory very similar to Darwin's, reportedly doing so in a few hours! In his letter he asked for Darwin's opinion of the theory and for help in getting it published. (One can imagine Darwin's feelings, after 22 years of diligent, laborious, and painstaking work.[1]) Darwin was in a difficult position, to say the least. It must be noted that Wallace's theory contained no great wealth of data such as Darwin had collected.

Darwin asked Lyell what he should do. At Lyell's suggestion, he read Wallace's paper and portions of his own forthcoming book at a meeting of the Linnean Society on July 1, 1858. After the presentation of this joint essay, Darwin's scientific colleagues eagerly awaited publication of the evolutionary doctrine in comprehensive form. Every one of the 1250 copies of the first printing of the *Origin* was sold on the day it was published. Excitement and controversy were generated immediately, and Darwin was subjected to much abuse and criticism from some quarters. (In some parts of the United States, the theory is still referred to as "evilution.")

THE WORKS OF DARWIN

The Darwinian theory of evolution is so well known that only an overview of the more fundamental points is presented here. Starting with the obvious fact of variability of individual members of the same species, Darwin reasoned that this spontaneous variability was inheritable. In nature there is a natural selection resulting in the survival of those organisms best fitted for their particular environments, and in the elimination of those that are not fitted. There is, he said, a continuing struggle for survival in nature and those forms that survive are the ones that have made successful adaptations or adjustments to the environmental difficulties to which they have been exposed; those who cannot successfully adapt do not survive.

Darwin formulated the notion of "struggle for survival" upon reading *Essay on the Principle of Population,* written by Thomas Malthus in 1789. Malthus had argued that the world's food supply increases arithmetically while the human population tends to increase geometrically. The inevitable result, which the Reverend Malthus described as having "a melancholy hue," is that a large portion of human beings invariably live under near-starvation conditions. Only the most forceful and cunning survive.

Darwin extended this principle to all living organisms and developed the concept of natural selection. Those forms that survive the struggle and reach maturity tend to transmit to their offspring the particular skills or advantages that allowed them to survive. Further, since variation

---

[1] Darwin developed his theory in absolute secrecy, revealing his thoughts to only one man, Dr. Joseph Hooker, in 1844, and that under an oath of silence.

is another general law of heredity, offspring will show variation among themselves, with some possessing the advantageous qualities developed to a higher level than their parents. These qualities in turn will tend to survive, and in the course of many such generations, great changes in form may develop. Indeed, these changes can be so great as to account for the differences between species as they exist today. Herrnstein and Boring (1965) noted that natural selection was not the only mechanism of evolution for Darwin. He also believed in the Lamarckian doctrine that changes in form brought about by experience during an animal's lifetime can be passed on to subsequent generations.

Many religionists saw the theory as a threat because they thought it inconsistent with the Biblical account of creation. White (1965) noted some of the following comments by distinguished clergymen of the time: "an attempt to dethrone God"; "a huge imposture from the beginning"; "If the Darwinian theory is true, Genesis is a lie, the whole framework of the book of life falls to pieces, and the revelation of God to man, as we Christians know it, is a delusion and a snare"; one said succinctly (and perhaps prophetically), "God is dead" (p. 93). The stormy controversy raged for many years.

Within a year of the book's publication, a most exciting debate took place at Oxford between Thomas Henry Huxley, defending Darwin and evolution, and Bishop Wilberforce, defending the Book of Genesis. As Miller (1962) noted, "Wilberforce asked Huxley whether it was through his grandmother or his grandfather that he claimed descent from an ape, thus phrasing the central issue in terms every man could understand. Huxley replied that an ape would be preferable to the Bishop as an ancestor, and with that the battle began. Science and religion were at it again" (p. 129).

Other books of interest to psychology followed the *Origin*. In 1871, Darwin's second major report on evolution, *The Descent of Man*, appeared. This work marshaled the evidence for the evolution of man from lower forms of life, emphasizing the similarity between the mental processes of animals and those of man, and stressing the importance of sexual selection as a factor in evolution.

Darwin made an intensive study of emotional expression in man and animals and suggested that the changes of gesture and posture that characterize the major emotions could be interpreted in evolutionary terms. This notion was published in 1872 in *The Expression of the Emotions in Man and Animals*. He argued that emotional expressions were remnants of movements that had, at one time, served some practical function.

Beginning in 1840, Darwin kept a diary of his infant son, recording facts of his development, and publishing it in a journal article, *Biographi-*

cal Sketch of an Infant, in 1877. This work, together with a similar study by Preyer, served as one of the early sources for modern child psychology.

The importance of mental factors in evolution was apparent in Darwin's theory, which frequently cited a number of conscious reactions in man and animals. Because of the role accorded consciousness in evolutionary theory, psychology was compelled to accept an evolutionary point of view.

THE INFLUENCE OF DARWIN UPON PSYCHOLOGY

As noted earlier, the impact of Darwin on psychology in the last quarter of the nineteenth century probably was as influential as any single factor in shaping psychology as it exists today. The theory raised the intriguing possibility of a basic continuity of mind between animals and man. The evidence demonstrating animal–man continuity was largely anatomical in nature, but it strongly suggested similar continuities in the development of behavior as well as mental processes. If the human mind has evolved from more primitive minds, then there may exist similarities in mentality between animals and man. The discrete gap between animals and man posited by Descartes was thus open to serious question. Therefore, many scientists turned to the investigation of the mental functioning of animals, introducing a new subject of study into the psychological laboratory. Animal psychology, a field with far-reaching implications for psychology (see Chapters IX, X), was the result.

Darwin's influence also brought about a pronounced change in the goal of psychology. The structuralists' focus, as we have seen, was on the analysis of conscious content. Darwin influenced some psychologists to consider the functions that consciousness might serve. This seemed to many a more important and basic task than determining the elements of consciousness. Thus, psychology came to be more and more concerned with the adaptation of the organism to its environment and, as a result, the detailed investigation of mental elements began to lose its appeal.

A third great effect of evolution on psychology was the notion of the importance of individual differences. The fact of variation among members of the same species was obvious to Darwin as a result of his five-year observation of so many species and forms. Evolution could not occur at all if each generation were identical with its forebears. Hence, variation was an important ingredient of any evolutionary theory. While the structuralists continued their search for general laws to encompass all minds, other psychologists, influenced by Darwin, began to search for all the many and varied ways in which individual minds could differ from one another. Thus, the study of individual differences began. The psychology of the structuralists had little room for the consideration of animal minds and individual differences. It remained for scientists of a more functionalistic persuasion to pursue these problems.

Individual Differences: Sir Francis Galton

Galton effectively brought the spirit of evolution to bear on psychology in his brilliant work on the problems of mental inheritance and individual differences in human capacity. Prior to Galton's efforts, the phenomenon of individual differences had not been considered a subject for serious study in psychology. Murphy (1949) suggested that this neglect was the most extraordinary blind spot in the previous history of psychology. Only a few isolated efforts existed before the time of Galton, notably those of Weber, Fechner, and Helmholtz, who had reported individual differences but had not investigated them systematically.

THE LIFE OF GALTON (1822–1911)

Possessed of a remarkably high degree of intelligence (an estimated IQ of 200) and a wealth of novel ideas, Galton is perhaps without equal in the history of modern psychology. His highly creative curiosity and genius attracted him to a variety of new problems, the details of which he left to be filled in by others. A few of the areas he investigated are fingerprints, fashions, geographical distribution of female beauty, weight lifting, the future of the race, and an experimental investigation of the efficacy of prayer. There was little that did not interest this versatile and inventive man.

Galton was born in 1822 near Birmingham, England, the last of nine children. His father was a prosperous banker whose wealthy and socially prominent family comprised important persons in all spheres of influence, including Members of Parliament, clergymen, and military leaders. Thus from an early age Galton was acquainted with many influential people through his family connections.

At the age of 16, at his father's insistence, Galton began the study of medicine by becoming a house pupil at the Birmingham General Hospital. He worked as an apprentice to the hospital physicians, dispensed pills, studied medical books, set broken bones, amputated fingers, pulled teeth, vaccinated children, and found diversion in reading Horace and Homer. It was, to say the least, not a very pleasant existence and apparently only the continued pressure from his father kept him there.

One amusing incident, reflecting his ever-present curiosity, took place during this medical apprenticeship. Wanting to learn for himself the effects of the various medicines in the pharmacy, he began taking small doses of each one, beginning in systematic fashion with those under the letter A. This scientific venture ceased toward the end of the letter C when he took a dose of croton oil—a very powerful purgative.

After he completed a year in the hospital, Galton continued his medical education at King's College in London. A year later he changed his plans and enrolled in Trinity College, Cambridge, where, a bust of Newton opposite his fireplace, he specialized in mathematics. Although his studies were interrupted by a severe mental breakdown, he did manage to graduate. He then returned briefly to the study of medicine, but the death of his father released him from this profession, which he had come to dislike intensely.

Travel and exploration claimed Galton's attention next. He traveled in the Sudan in 1845 and in Southwest Africa in 1850. In that same year, he invented a teletype printer. He published accounts of his travels and, in 1854, the Royal Geographic Society awarded him a medal for his exploration of Southwest Africa which was, at the time, a totally unknown land.

In the 1850s he had to stop his travels and exploration because of marriage and poor health (no cause-and-effect relationship intended), but he served on many committees, wrote a guide for explorers called *The Art of Travel,* organized expeditions for others, and gave lectures on camp life to soldiers as a part of their training for the Crimean War.

His spirited restlessness led him next to meteorology and the design of instruments with which to plot weather data. His meteorological findings were summarized in a book that is considered the first attempt to chart weather patterns on an extensive scale.

When his cousin Darwin published the *Origin of Species,* Galton immediately became vitally interested in the new theory. The biological aspect of evolution interested him at first and he investigated the effects of transfusing blood between rabbits to determine if acquired characteristics could be inherited. Although the genetic side of evolution did not interest him for very long, the social implications of the theory held his attention for quite some time. In the early 1860s, Galton began the work that was destined to have a profound influence on modern psychology.

THE WORKS OF GALTON

Mental Inheritance. Galton's first important work to influence psychology was *Hereditary Genius,* published in 1869. The book's purpose was to demonstrate that individual greatness or genius follows family lines with a frequency of occurrence too great to be explained on the basis of environmental influences—hence the thesis that eminent men have eminent sons. For the most part, the biographical studies reported in this book were investigations into the ancestries of famous scientists, physicians, jurists, and so on. Galton's data showed that in each case these men inherited not only genius but specific forms of genius. A great scientist, for example, was born of a family that had attained not only eminence, but eminence in science.

Galton's ultimate interest was in encouraging the productivity of the more eminent or fit, and discouraging the birth rate of the unfit. To help achieve this end, he founded the science of eugenics and argued that the human strain, like livestock, could be improved by artificial selection. He believed that if men and women of considerable talents were selected and mated generation after generation, a highly gifted race of people would be the eventual result.

In attempting to verify his eugenic thesis, Galton became very much involved in problems of measurement and statistics. In *Hereditary Genius,* he applied statistical notions to the problems of heredity and ranked the celebrated men in his sample into classes or categories, according to the frequency with which their level of ability appeared in the population. He found that eminent men have a higher probability of producing eminent sons than do average men. His main sample consisted of 977 noted men, each so outstanding as to be one in 4000. On a chance basis this group would be expected to have only one prominent relative; instead they had 332. The probability of eminence in certain families was high, but not high enough for Galton to consider seriously any possible influence of superior environment, education, and opportunity open to sons of outstanding families. For example, he considered his own education for the most part a waste of time.

However, he did not completely rule out the possibility of environmental influence. Later he made the first psychological research study of twins, in which he attempted to separate the effects of heredity and environment. His results demonstrated that twins had much more in common with each other, at least in terms of physical characteristics, than nontwin children of the same parents.

Galton followed his first book with *English Men of Science* (1874) and *Natural Inheritance* (1889), and between 30 and 40 papers on problems of inheritance. His interest in heredity grew in scope from the individual and the family to the race. He became more and more concerned with the possibility of improving the human race by selective breeding. To this end, in 1883, he formulated proposals for a science of heredity, eugenics, which resulted in the creation of the journal *Biometrika* in 1901, the establishment of the Eugenics Laboratory at University College, London, in 1904, and the founding of an organization for promoting the idea of racial improvement. All of these are still flourishing today.

Statistical Methods. Galton's interest in measurement and statistics has already been noted. Throughout his career, he never seemed fully satisfied with a problem until he had found some means of quantifying the data and statistically analyzing them. In addition to using statistical methods, he developed some of his own.

Adolph Quetelet (1796–1874), a Belgian astronomer, had made the first application of both statistical methods and the normal probability curve to biological and social data. The normal curve had been discovered earlier and used in work on the distribution of measurements and errors in scientific observation. The principle of normal distribution, however, had never been applied to human variability until Quetelet's demonstration that anthropometric measurements made on unselected samples of people typically yielded a normal curve. For example, he demonstrated that measures of stature of some 10,000 subjects approximated the normal curve of distribution, and he used the phrase *l'homme moyen* to express the finding that most individuals tend to cluster toward the average or center of the normal curve, with fewer and fewer cases found as one moves away from the center toward the two extremes.

Impressed by Quetelet's data, Galton assumed that the same results held true for mental as well as physical characteristics. He found, for instance, that the marks given on university examinations followed the same normal curve distribution as had Quetelet's physical measures. Because of the simplicity of this curve and its consistency over a number of traits, Galton proposed that an entire range of measurements could be meaningfully defined and summarized with just two numbers—the average value of the distribution and the dispersion or range of variation around this average value (essentially, the mean and standard deviation, in today's terms). Thus, a large set of measurements or values on human beings could be meaningfully reduced to these two numbers.

Galton's further work in statistics resulted in one of the most important measures in statistics, the correlation. The first report of what he called "co-relations" appeared in 1888. Modern sophisticated techniques for determining the validity and reliability of tests, and the factor analytic methods, are direct outgrowths of Galton's discovery of correlation, which resulted from his observation that inherited characteristics tend to regress toward the mean of the distribution of those characteristics. For instance, he noticed that tall men are, on the average, not as tall as their fathers, while the sons of very short men are, on the average, taller than their fathers. He devised the graphic means to represent the basic properties of the correlation coefficient and even developed a formula for its calculation, though it did not remain in use for long.

Galton applied his newfound method to variations in physical measurement demonstrating a correlation between body height and head length, for example. With Galton's encouragement, his student Karl Pearson developed the presently used mathematical formula for the precise calculation of the correlation coefficient: the Pearson product-moment coefficient of correlation (known and loved by generations of students). The traditional symbol for correlation coefficient, r, is taken from the first letter of the word "regression," in recognition of its origin in Galton's discovery of the tendency of regression toward mediocrity or averageness in the inheritance of human traits.

The notion of correlation continues to be fundamentally important in the social and behavioral sciences, as well as in engineering and the natural sciences. Many present-day statistical tools and techniques developed in large measure from this pioneering work of Galton.

Mental Tests. Galton was the first to develop certain specific mental tests; indeed, it may be said that he initiated the whole idea of mental tests (although the term itself came later). He began by assuming that intelligence could be measured in terms of one's level of sensory capacity. Thus, he believed that sensory ability is correlated with intelligence: the higher the intelligence, the higher the level of sensory discrimination.

He had to develop the apparatus for mental tests such that psychological measurements could be made quickly and accurately on large numbers of people. With characteristic ingenuity and enthusiasm, he devised a number of instruments to measure the senses. To measure the highest frequencies of sound that could be heard, he invented a whistle with which he tested animals as well as people. (He tested animals by walking through the streets and the Zoological Gardens with the whistle fixed to one end of a hollow walking stick that had a rubber bulb at the other end.) This "Galton Whistle," in improved form, became a standard piece of psychological equipment until it was displaced by more sophisticated electronic apparatus in the 1930s.

Other apparatus included: a photometer to measure how precisely a subject could match two spots of color; a calibrated pendulum to measure reaction time to sounds and lights; a series of weights to be arranged in order of heaviness to measure kinesthetic sensitivity; a bar with a variable distance scale to test estimation of visual extension; sets of bottles containing different substances to test olfactory discrimination. Most of his tests are prototypes for standard equipment used in psychological laboratories today.

Armed with his newly devised tests, Galton proceeded to collect data from large numbers of subjects. To accomplish this, he established the Anthropometric Laboratory in 1884 at the International Health Exhibition. Later moved to the South Kensington Museum in London, this laboratory remained active for six years, collecting a wide range of data from a total of 9337 people. Instruments for taking anthropometric and psychometric measurements were placed on a long table at one end of a long narrow room. For a threepence admission fee, a person passed along the table with an attendant who made the successive measurements and filled in the data on a card. Some of the measurements taken included height, weight, breathing power, strength of pull and squeeze, quickness of blow, hearing, seeing, and color sense.

The aim of this large-scale testing program was to determine the range of human capacities for a large number of attributes and abilities. Galton wanted to test the entire population of Great Britain so that the country would know, for the first time, the exact level of the mental resources of its people. Due to his development of mental tests and the establishment of his laboratory, Galton may properly be called the first practitioner of psychology.

Association. Galton worked on two problems of interest in the area of association: the study of the wide diversity of associations of ideas, and the study of the time it takes a person to produce associations.

Following his habit of counting whenever possible, one of Galton's methods for studying the diversity of associations was to walk 450 yards along Pall Mall and focus his attention on an object until it suggested one or two associated thoughts to him. The first time he did this, he was amazed at the large number of associations that developed with the nearly 300 objects seen. He found that many of these associations were in the form of recollections of past experiences, including many incidents long forgotten. Repeating the walk a few days later, he found considerable repetition of the associations that had occurred during the first walk. This greatly diminished his interest in this aspect of the study of associations, and he turned to his reaction time experiments, which produced more useful results.

Galton prepared a list of 75 words on individual slips of paper. After he had forgotten the words, he exposed them to his view, one at a time, using a chronometer to record the time necessary to produce two associations with each word. With this procedure, he was able to obtain an association reaction time for each word. Many of the associations were in the form of individual words, but several others appeared not as a single word but as an image or mental picture that required a number of words to describe.

The next task involved the determination of the origin of these associations. He found that a large number of these associative reactions could be traced back to experiences in his childhood and adolescence. This was one of the very first attempts to demonstrate the influence of early life experiences, particularly those of childhood, on the adult personality. It also demonstrated the amount of childish material that remains in adulthood.

Of greater importance, however, was the introduction of the experimental study of association. Galton's invention of the word association test marked the first attempt to subject association to laboratory experimentation. Wundt adapted the technique, limited the response to just one word, and used it at Leipzig.

Mental Imagery. Galton's investigation of mental imagery marks the first extensive psychological use of the questionnaire. Subjects were asked to imagine a scene, such as their breakfast table of that morning, and to try to elicit images of that scene. They were also to report whether the images were dim or clear, bright or dark, colored or not colored, and so on.

To Galton's amazement, his first group of subjects, scientific acquaintances, reported no clear imagery at all. Some were not even sure what Galton was talking about when he questioned them about their images. Further investigation, using subjects of more average ability, resulted in the reporting of clear and distinct images that were often full of detail and color. He found the imagery of women and children to be particularly concrete and detailed. As more and more subjects were investigated, it became clear that imagery is more or less normally distributed in the population.

Galton's work began a long line of research on imagery and, generally speaking, his results have been supported. As with most of his research, his interest in imagery was in the attempt to demonstrate hereditary similarities. He found, for example, that similarity in imagery is greater between siblings than between individuals who are not related.

Additional Studies. The areas of research discussed thus far constitute Galton's chief sources of influence on psychology. Since he performed many other studies, however, we will discuss a few of them to indicate further the richness and variety of his talent.

At one time, Galton tried to put himself into the state of mind of the insane by imagining that everything, human, animal, and inanimate, that he saw while walking was a spy. As Watson tells it, "By the end of the morning stroll, every horse seemed to be watching him either directly or, what was just as suspicious, they were disguising their espionage by elaborately paying no attention!" (1963, p. 286). He found that it took hours for this state of mind to wear off and that it was all too easy to reestablish.

As noted, the debate between evolution and theology was acute. With great scientific objectivity, Galton investigated the problem and concluded that there was no evidence that religious beliefs are valid just because large numbers of people believe in them intensely. For instance, in one of his books, he discussed the power or capability of prayer to produce results and concluded that it was of no use to physicians as a means of curing patients, or to meteorologists as a method of invoking weather changes, or to clergymen in conducting their worldly affairs! Galton firmly believed that there is little difference to be found between those who profess a belief in one of the many brands of religion and those who do not, in terms of their dealings with their fellow man or in their own emotional lives. He would have liked to give the world a new set of beliefs, structured in terms of science, as a substitute for religious dogma. He believed that evolutionary development of a finer and nobler race, through eugenics, should be man's goal, instead of heaven.

At one time, Galton wanted to understand the feeling that primitive man might have had for his God and so he pretended that the drawing of Punch was a divine being possessing the power to reward or punish. Apparently, he was successful in his efforts, since he reported that, for a long time thereafter, he retained the feeling toward the drawing that a savage might have for his idol.

Galton always seemed to be counting something. He occupied himself at lectures or at the theater by counting the yawns and fidgets of the audience per unit time, using the results as a measure of audience boredom. At one time, he decided to try to count by odors instead of numbers. Training himself to forget what the numbers 1, 2, 3, and so on, mean, he assigned number values for various odors such as camphor and peppermint. He found that he could add or subtract by thinking of odors instead of numbers. Out of this intellectual exercise came a paper entitled *Arithmetic by Smell.*

COMMENT

Galton spent only 15 years engaged in activities of a psychological nature, yet his efforts during this short period pointed the direction in which psychology was soon to go. He was not truly a psychologist, any more than he was truly a eugenicist or an anthropologist—he was, uniquely, Galton! Consider the areas which Galton initiated in which psychologists became interested: adaptation; heredity versus environment; comparison of species; studies of children; use of the questionnaire; statistical techniques; the broad question of individual differences; and the field of mental tests. Small wonder Galton is considered such a profound influence on psychology! As Flugel and West (1964) commented, "Never again in the history of the science up to the present time do we meet an investigator so brilliant, so versatile, so wide in his interests and abilities, so little bound by prejudice or preconception. Compared with him, all others (with the one exception perhaps of William James) are apt to appear a little ponderous and pedantic, a little blinkered in their outlook" (p. 111).

Herbert Spencer

Often called the philosopher of evolution, Spencer (1820–1903) was an evolutionist before Darwin's influential publications. This primarily self-taught Englishman had written on the topic of evolution as early as 1850, but his pre-Darwin publications attracted comparatively little attention.

When the *Origin of Species* was published, Spencer became associated with the movement and his own brand of more speculative evolutionism gained strength from Darwin's well-documented position. Darwin accepted Spencer as a member of the movement, calling him "our philosopher," and the two served to complement one another very well. Whereas Darwin was cautious about generalizing beyond his detailed data, Spencer was wont to draw out the implications of the theory and apply it universally over the wide spectrum of human knowledge and experience.

To accomplish this end, he created his "synthetic philosophy"—an all-encompassing system in which the master concept of evolution is applied to all human knowledge. He argued that development of all aspects of the universe (whether it be plants, humans, or social institutions) involves the process of differentiation, followed by integration. Any developing or growing thing is initially homogeneous and simple. In the later course of development, recognizably distinct parts emerge (differentiation). Still later comes integration, in which these separate and unique parts are joined in a new functioning whole. Growing and developing things always have a differentiation phase followed by an integration phase.

To Spencer, this notion of differentiation followed by integration, in which all things proceed from homogeneity to heterogeneity, was evolution. There is, thus, a unity to all things that exists in the evolutionary process; therefore, all existence is evolutionary. The implication of this viewpoint for psychology is that as the nervous system evolves to greater complexity, there is a corresponding increase in the richness and variety of experience to which an organism is exposed, and higher and higher integrations of function. According to Spencer, association is the mechanism of integration that makes possible more complex levels of experience. His position on association is, more appropriately, discussed in Chapter IX.

Successive volumes of *The System of Synthetic Philosophy* were published between 1862 and 1893. Spencer's more important work, in terms of his influence on psychology, is *The Principles of Psychology,* which appeared first in 1855, and then in 1870 and 1872 in two volumes. Spencer discussed, perhaps for the first time, the notion that the mind exists in its present form because of past (and continuing) efforts to adapt to different kinds of environments. He stressed the adaptive nature of nervous and mental processes, and said that increasing complexity of experiences, and hence behavior, is a part of the process of an organism's adaptation to its environment.

Spencer agreed with the notion that ability is inherited, but he maintained that social factors are also important in developing one's abilities. Thus, he believed that genius will not develop without favorable environmental conditions, no matter what the inherited ability.

Animal Psychology

The evolutionary theory of Darwin provided the impetus for animal psychology. Prior to the Darwinian theory, there was little reason for scientific interest in the animal mind. Descartes considered animals to be soulless automata with no point of similarity to or commonality with man.

Publication of the *Origin of Species* radically changed this notion, for it was made clear that no sharp break existed between the mind of man and that of animals. Instead, a continuity between all aspects of man and animals, mental as well as physical, was posited, since man was believed to be derived from animals by the evolutionary process of continuous change and development. If mind could be demonstrated to exist in animals, and if continuity of the animal mind with the human mind could be shown, such evidence would serve as a defense of Darwin's theory against the man–animal dichotomy espoused by Descartes. A great quest for evidence of mind in animals was begun.

Darwin himself actually undertook the defense of his theory in *Expression of the Emotions in Man and Animals,* the thesis of which is that emotional behavior in man results from the inheritance of behavior once useful to animals, but no longer of any use to man. One of Darwin's famous examples to demonstrate this point was man's curling of his lips in sneering. He held this to be a remnant of the baring of the canine teeth in rage by animals. Many such examples were cited to demonstrate a mental continuity between animals and man.

A more formal and direct approach to the question of mental evolution was made by a friend of Darwin's, George John Romanes (1848–1894). In 1883, Romanes published *Animal Intelligence,* generally considered to be the first book devoted to the field of comparative psychology. Romanes collected a large body of data on the behavior of fishes, birds, domestic animals, and monkeys. The method used in collecting these data is referred to in somewhat contemptuous terms as the anecdotal method—the utilization of observational, often rather casual, reports about animal behavior. For example, many of the reports used by Romanes came from uncritical and untrained observers. Such reports were open to the dangers of incorrect observation, careless description, and biased interpretation. These difficulties, together with Romanes' tendency to anthropomorphize, have caused his anecdotal method to be discarded by animal psychologists.

Romanes' work fell far short of modern scientific rigor. In fairness, however, it must be noted that he did employ certain rigid criteria for judging the reliability of the reports he used and he strictly adhered to them. Despite these precautions, the line between fact and subjective interpretation in his data is not made clear. Although there are deficiencies in his data and method, Romanes is respected for his pioneer efforts in stimulating the development of comparative psychology and preparing the way for the experimental approach to this area that followed. In many areas of science, reliance on observational data has preceded the development of refined experimental methodology, and it was Romanes who launched the observational stage of comparative psychology.

The weaknesses inherent in the use of the anecdotal method were recognized by C. Lloyd Morgan (1852–1936), who established his "law of parsimony" (often called "Lloyd Morgan's Canon") in an effort to counter the tendency to anthropomorphize. This principle states that an animal's behavior must not be interpreted as the outcome of a higher mental process, if it can be interpreted in terms of lower mental processes.

Morgan also introduced the first large-scale use of the experimental method in animal psychology. His experiments were not conducted under rigid laboratory conditions (as was later the case); rather, they involved careful and detailed observations of the behavior of animals in their natural environments, under special and artificially produced modifications. While not permitting the same degree of control as laboratory experiments, they were nonetheless a great advance over Romanes' anecdotal method.

Interest in animal psychology grew rapidly toward the end of the nineteenth century and served as an antecedent of both functional psychology and behaviorism.

Comparative psychology was an outgrowth of the excitement and controversy engendered by Darwin's notion of continuity. Perhaps comparative psychology would have begun without the theory of evolution, but most likely it would not have gotten such a sound start, nor would it have begun when it did.

A Final Note

A basic part of Darwin's theory of evolution is the notion of function—and the assertion that as a species evolves, its physical structure is determined by its own requirements for survival. This premise influenced biologists to look on each anatomical structure as a functioning element in a living, adapting, total system. When psychologists began to consider mental processes in the same manner, they created an entirely new movement—functionalism. The following two chapters consider the development of this new movement as it occurred in America.

SUGGESTED FURTHER READINGS

Darwin

Angell, J. R. The influence of Darwin on psychology. *Psychological Review,* 1909, **16,** 152–169.

Boring, E. G. The influence of evolutionary theory upon American psychological thought. In S. Persons (Ed.), *Evolutionary thought in America.* New Haven: Yale University Press, 1950. Pp. 267–298.

Galton

Galton, F. *Memories of my life.* London: Methuen, 1908.

Pearson, K. *The life, letters and labors of Francis Galton.* London: University of Cambridge Press, 1914–1924.

Animal Psychology, Romanes, Morgan

Warden, C. J. The historical development of comparative psychology. *Psychological Review,* 1927, **34,** 57–85; 135–168.

VII

FUNCTIONALISM: AMERICAN
PIONEERS

By the turn of the century, psychology in America had assumed a definite character. "It had inherited its physical body from German experimentalism, but it had got its mind from Darwin. American psychology was to deal with mind in use" (Boring, 1950, p. 506). Why did functional psychology develop and thrive in America, rather than in England, where the functional spirit originated? The answer seems to be in the *Zeitgeist*—America was ready to accept what the times had for it.

"Only in America"

Until the end of the nineteenth century, American psychology consciously imitated German experimental psychology. Americans went to Leipzig in rather large numbers to study under Wundt and brought back to this country at least the external features of Wundtian psychology. They taught their courses and developed their laboratories on the Wundtian model. Beneath the surface, however, a brand of psychology that resembled Galton's more than Wundt's was developing.

The American *Zeitgeist* radically altered the German psychology, for America during the latter part of the nineteenth century was still a pioneer country—rough, direct, highly practical, aggressively ambitious, and self-assured. Land was still freely available to those with the courage, readiness, and ability to take it and wrest a living from it. The principles of natural selection and survival of the fittest were vividly demonstrated in everyday life, where success, and sometimes raw survival, depended on how well one adapted to the demands of the environment.

The success philosophy so characteristic of America was based on individual ambition and taking advantage of opportunities, and it produced a sort of shirt-sleeves democracy, a strong pragmatic spirit, and

102

overall, a functional and practical attitude. American psychology, in its pioneering stages, quite naturally reflected these same qualities. Thus, America was more amenable to evolutionism than Germany or even England. American psychology became a functional psychology because evolutionism and its derived functional spirit were both in keeping with the basic temperament of America.

Anticipator of Functional Psychology: William James

James became the leading American antecedent of functional psychology, the pioneer of the new movement and its senior psychologist. Although this movement claimed to be scientific and experimental, James himself was not an experimentalist, neither in attitude nor in deed. There were times when he even denied that he was a psychologist and that there was a new psychology. He founded no formal system of psychology and had no disciples in the manner of Wundt. All this may sound paradoxical—and it is! And, the author feels, this adds to the unique fascination of the man. He did not found functional psychology, but wrote and thought most clearly and effectively in the functional atmosphere permeating American psychology at that time and, in so doing, influenced the functional movement through the inspiration he gave to subsequent psychologists.

THE LIFE OF JAMES (1842–1910)

James was born of a well-known and wealthy family, in a New York hotel, the Astor House. (His brother Henry became the eminent novelist.) Their father, wealthy enough to live on his income, devoted himself with great enthusiasm to the education of his five children, which alternated between Europe (because of his belief that American schools were too restricted in their outlook) and America (because of his equally strong belief that his children should be educated among their own countrymen). James's early formal education, often interrupted by travel, took place in France, England, Switzerland, Germany, Italy, and the United States. The father strongly encouraged intellectual independence among his children, whose family ties remained extremely strong throughout their lives.

The stimulating travel experiences of his youth made James quite literally a man of the world, exposing him to the intellectual and cultural advantages that England and Europe offered a perceptive young man. Frequent trips abroad characterized James's entire life, for his father's unique method of dealing with illness was to send the ailing member to Europe rather than a hospital. Since their health was seldom good, the family became great travelers.

In 1860, at the age of 18, James decided that he wanted to be an artist, so the family returned to America. (As Henry commented, "We went home to learn to paint.") Six months at the studio of William Morris Hunt convinced James that he lacked promise as an artist. In 1861, he enrolled in the Lawrence Scientific School at Harvard. He soon left his first choice, chemistry, apparently because he disdained the painstaking demands of laboratory work, and enrolled in medical school. He was not enthusiastic about the practice of medicine, however, for he commented in a letter to a cousin that "With the exception of surgery, in which something positive is sometimes accomplished, a doctor does more by the moral effect of his presence on the patient and family, than by anything else. He also extracts money from them."

James interrupted his medical studies for a year in 1865 to assist the famous zoologist Louis Agassiz during the Thayer Expedition to Brazil. On this trip he sampled another possible career, biology, but found he could not tolerate the precise and orderly collecting and categorizing that this field required. His reaction to chemistry and biology was perhaps prophetic of his subsequent personal distaste for experimentation in psychology.

Although medicine was no more attractive to him after the expedition than when he first studied it, James reluctantly resumed his medical studies since nothing else appealed to him. There was another interruption occasioned by his feeling that he did not have the stamina to continue the hard work, by a host of physical complaints (digestive disorders, insomnia, eye problems, a weak back), and by episodes of deep depression. As Miller (1962) noted:

> It was obvious to everyone that he was suffering from America; Europe was the only cure. In 1867 he went to Dresden and Berlin, where he took baths for his back, read widely in German and other literature, toyed with thoughts of suicide, displayed his loneliness and homesickness by the tremendous volume of his correspondence, and remained just as miserable as he had been at home (p. 70).

Returning again to the United States, he took his medical degree in 1869, but his depression deepened and his will to live was not very strong. In these dark months, he began to build a philosophy of life, compelled not so much by intellectual curiosity as by sheer desperation.

After reading a number of essays by Charles Renouvier on free will, James, persuaded of its existence, resolved that his first act of free will would be to believe in free will, and to believe that he could cure himself through belief in the efficacy of the will. He apparently succeeded, for in 1872 he felt well enough to accept a position at Harvard teaching physiology. After one year, he took a year off to travel to Italy, but then returned to teaching.

In 1875–1876, James taught his first course in psychology, called "The Relations Between Physiology and Psychology," the first American offering of the new experimental psychology. (James, by the way, had never received formal classroom instruction in psychology; the first psychology lecture he ever attended was his own.) Also in 1875, the year Wundt established his laboratory at Leipzig, James secured $300.00 from Harvard to purchase laboratory and demonstrational equipment for the course.

In 1878, two important events occurred: his marriage, which produced five children, and his signing of a contract with the publishing house of Henry Holt and Company, which resulted in one of the classic books in psychology. He initially felt that it would take him two years to write the book; it actually took twelve.

In 1880, James was made assistant professor of philosophy; he was promoted to professor in 1885; and his title was changed to professor of psychology in 1889. The work on his book was delayed by travel abroad, where he met many European psychologists of the day. He had little regard for the senior European psychologists, describing Wundt, for example, as "the finished example of how much *mere* education can do for a man."

The Principles of Psychology finally appeared in 1890 and was reviewed as an extremely important contribution to the field. One indication of the book's singular success is that it is often read by people who are not required to do so. (Paperbound editions are currently available.) Two years after the publication of this great book, discussed later in the chapter, James published a condensed version designed to serve as a textbook. For many years, this condensation was called "Jimmy" to distinguish it from the more comprehensive "James."

After the publication of the *Principles,* feeling that he had said all he knew about psychology, James turned to philosophy. No longer wanting to direct the psychological laboratory (for which, in 1890, he had raised $4000.00), James arranged for Hugo Münsterberg, then at the University of Freiburg in Germany, to become director of the Harvard laboratory and to teach courses in psychology. James was thus freed for his work as a philosopher. Münsterberg had been vehemently criticized by Wundt, and this was high praise indeed in James's eyes. Münsterberg, however, never fulfilled James's plan of acquiring a leader in experimental research for Harvard; he worked in a variety of fields, such as psychotherapy, legal psychology, and industrial psychology, and paid little attention to the laboratory after his first few years there.

As for James's attitude toward laboratory work in psychology, we have already mentioned that he was not an experimentalist, although he began and equipped the laboratory at Harvard. He was apparently never fully convinced of the value of laboratory work and certainly did not like it personally. "I naturally hate experimental work," he had written to Münsterberg. In 1894, he said that the United States had far too many laboratories, and in the *Principles* he commented that the results of laboratory work were not in proportion to the amount of painstaking effort involved. It is hardly surprising, then, that James contributed little of importance in the way of experimental work.

Having made his major contributions to psychology by 1892, James spent the last 20 years of his life rounding out his philosophical system. In fact, in the 1890s, he came to be recognized as America's leading philosopher. It cannot be said that he actually ceased being a psychologist, but he did move intellectually far from the field.

In 1899, he published *Talks to Teachers,* which developed from a series of public lectures given to teachers, and which helped to apply psychology to the classroom learning situation. *Varieties of Religious Experience* appeared in 1901–1902 and three other important books in philosophy were published in 1907 and 1909.

His health was still poor and he retired from Harvard in 1907. In 1898, while climbing in the Adirondack Mountains, he had been lost for 13 hours and the ordeal aggravated a heart lesion. The condition grew worse and eventually resulted in his death in 1910, two days after his return from a final trip abroad.

THE CONTRIBUTIONS OF JAMES

Since James was decidedly not an experimentalist, how did he exercise such a profound influence on psychology at a time when it was dominated by experimentation? Why is he often considered the greatest American psychologist? Boring (1950) suggested three reasons for his overwhelming stature and influence.

First is his personality, which is reflected to a considerable extent in his written work. He wrote with a brilliance and clarity extremely rare in psychology, or any science, then as well as now; magnetism, spontaneity, and charm pervade his writing.

The second reason for his influence is negative, in the sense in which all movements are negative. He opposed the very foundation of the then current Wundtian psychology; its introspective analysis of consciousness into elements. The third reason is positive: James offered an alternative way of looking at the mind—an approach congruent with the American functional approach to psychology. The times were ready for the acceptance of what James had to say.

The concept of functionalism is explicit in James's psychology, in which he presented what subsequently became the central tenet of American functionalism: the study of the living person as he adapts to his environment, as opposed to the discovery of elements of experience. The function of consciousness, he said, is to guide the organism to those ends required for survival. Consciousness is thus thought of as an organ, particularly appropriate to the needs of a complex organism in a highly complex environment, without which the process of evolution could not have occurred in man.

The Principles of Psychology

The publication of *The Principles* was hailed both at home and abroad as an event of the first magnitude in the psychological world. Not only was it a comprehensive survey of a new field of learning, not only was it a new synthesis of the facts of psychology; it was itself a contribution to psychology. From the first, it was recognized as more than a mere book about psychology. Because of its freshness and power, because of its definite attitudes and stimulating suggestions, it was itself an event in the history of psychology (Heidbreder, 1933, p. 197).

Perhaps the most striking characteristic of the book is that it explicitly treats psychology as a natural science; more specifically, as a biological science. Treating psychology as a science was nothing new in 1890, but in James's hands the science of psychology took a different direction from German orthodox psychology. James was concerned with conscious processes as activities of an organism that produced some difference in that organism's life. Mental processes were seen by James as useful activities to living creatures as they attempt to maintain and adapt themselves in the world of nature. This point of view had pronounced effects on American psychology, expressing as it did an attitude that became the first American school of psychology—functionalism.

A related attitude stressed throughout his entire book is James's emphasis on the nonrational aspect of human nature. Man, he noted, is a creature of action and emotion as well as thought and reason. Even when discussing purely intellectual processes themselves, he stressed the nonrational influencing factors. For instance, he carefully noted that intellect operates under the physiological influences of the body, that one's beliefs are determined by emotional factors, and that reason and the formation of concepts are influenced by various wants and needs. In short, James did not consider the human being a wholly rational creature by any means.

Let us briefly survey this influential book. The first six chapters of the first volume introduce to the reader certain biological foundations that James believed necessary in order to prepare a base for psychology itself. In them he discusses certain aspects of nervous system activity of importance to mental functioning. He felt that all of mental life is determined in large degree by the tendency of the nervous system to undergo modification by each individual action it makes, so that subsequently the organism will find it easier to perform similar responses.

James next discusses and criticizes all major philosophical conceptions of the relations between mind and body. He accepted states of consciousness (mind) and brain processes (body) as phenomena in the natural world, and noted a correspondence, term for term, between the succession of conscious states and the succession of brain processes.

The remainder of the first volume is concerned with psychology proper—the subject matter and methods of investigation for psychology. Here he develops fully his notion of consciousness and its characteristics (discussed later).

The second volume begins with a treatment of sensation, followed by chapters dealing with perception, belief, reasoning, instinct, and volition. The last two chapters, which are almost appendixes, deal with hypnosis and with psychogenesis (the problem of the development of the human species and of the individual). Following are several of James's major points, as expressed in the *Principles*.

Subject Matter for Psychology. James stated in the opening sentence of the book that "psychology is the Science of Mental Life, both of its phenomena and of their conditions." In terms of subject matter, the key words are "phenomena" and "conditions." Phenomena indicate that the subject matter is to be found in experience; conditions mean that the immediate conditions of mental life are found in the body, particularly the brain.

The physical substructures of consciousness, then, form an important part of psychology, according to James. He recognized the importance of considering consciousness, which was the focal point of his interest, in its natural setting—the physical human being. This awareness of biology, of the action of the brain on consciousness, is one of the most distinctive features of Jamesian psychology.

A New Look at Consciousness—A Revolt Against Wundt. James rebelled violently against what he considered the artificiality and narrowness of the structuralist position. His revolt led to the more general protest that the functionalists subsequently made. Experiences are simply what they are, he said, not groups or amalgamations of elements. The discovery of discrete elements through introspective analysis does not demonstrate that they exist independently of the observation. He argued that a psychologist reads into an experience what his systematic position in psychology tells him should be there. A teataster can train himself to discriminate various elements in a flavor that may not be perceived by the untrained individual. The latter, sipping tea, experiences a fusion of any alleged flavor elements, a total blend or taste not capable of analysis. Similarly, James argued, the fact that one person can analyze his conscious experiences does not mean that the resulting discrete elements are present in the consciousness of everyone else exposed to the same experience. James considered the making of such an assumption the "psychologists' fallacy."

More than merely a cleverly caustic critic of elementism, James outlined a new positive program for psychology. Mental life is a unity, he argued; a total experience that flows and changes. The basic point of James's conception of consciousness is that it "goes on"—is a stream—and he coined the famous phrase "stream of consciousness" to express this property. Since consciousness is a continuous flow, any attempt to subdivide it into temporally distinct elements or phases can only distort it.

Another characteristic of consciousness is that it is always changing, hence one can never have exactly the same state or thought twice. Objects in the environment can occur again and again, but not the same sensations or thoughts. It is true, he said, that we may think of an object on more than one occasion, but each time we think of it, we experience it in different fashion because of the effect of intervening experiences. Thus, consciousness is cumulative in nature and not recurrent.

The mind is also sensibly continuous, *i.e.*, there are no sharp breaks in the stream of consciousness. There may be gaps in time, as when a person is asleep, for example, but upon awakening the person has no difficulty in "reaching back" and making connection with the stream of consciousness that was ongoing prior to the interruption.

Still another characteristic of the mind is its selectivity: it chooses from among the many stimuli to which it is exposed. The mind is always accepting, rejecting, uniting, and separating stimuli (and parts of stimuli). We can attend to only a part, and a small part at that, of our experiential world, and the criterion of selection, according to James, is relevance. There is a selection of relevant stimuli in order that consciousness may operate in a logical manner and a series of ideas may arrive at a rational end. It is noteworthy that James anticipated the Würzburg concept of set and determining tendency with his notion of relevance.

Above all, James stressed the purpose of consciousness. He felt that consciousness must have some biological utility to the organism or it would not have survived. The purpose or function of consciousness is to better adapt man to his environment by enabling him to choose. He made a distinction between conscious choice and habit, the latter being involuntary and nonconscious. When the organism faces a new problem and needs a new mode of adjustment, consciousness comes into play. This emphasis on purposiveness reflects the influence of the new evolutionary theory.

The Methods of Psychology. The foregoing discussion on the subject matter of psychology provides some clues to James's methods of study in psychology. Since psychology deals with a highly personal consciousness, introspection must be a basic tool. James believed that it was eminently possible to discover states of consciousness by an examination of one's own mind. If consciousness is not capable of analysis, the Jamesian form of introspection could not be of the rigid type practiced by Wundt and Titchener. James considered introspection the exercise of a natural gift, consisting in "catching the very life of a moment as it passed, in a fixing and reporting of the fleeting event as it occurred in its natural setting. It was not the introspection of the laboratory, aided by brass instruments; it was the quick and sure arresting of an impression by a sensitive and acute observer" (Heidbreder, 1933, p. 171).

James was well aware of the difficulties and limitations of introspection and he accepted it as a possible but not infallible form of observation. He did believe, however, that introspective results could be verified by the use of appropriate checks and through comparison of the findings of different observers. Though not himself a devotee of the experimental method, James did believe in the use of the experimental method as another possible means to psychological knowledge.

Finally, to supplement the experimental and the introspective methods, James urged the use of the comparative method in psychology. By inquiring into the psychological functioning of animals, children, preliterate peoples, and the insane, James felt that variations in mental life could be usefully and meaningfully revealed.

On a higher level, over and above specific methods, James emphasized the value for psychology of pragmatism. The basic tenet of the pragmatic point of view is that the validity of an idea, or of any knowledge, must be tested only by its consequences. In more popular terms, the pragmatic viewpoint is usually stated as "anything is true if it works." The notion of pragmatism had been advanced in the 1870s by Charles S. Peirce, philosopher and lifelong friend of James. Peirce's work, however, remained largely ignored until James wrote his *Pragmatism*, one of his major contributions as a philosopher, in 1907.

Emotions. James's most famous theoretical contribution, dealing with emotions, illustrates his interest in the nervous system. His theory on emotions, published as an article in 1884 and six years later in the *Principles*, completely contradicted the then current way of thinking about emotions. It had previously been assumed that emotion precedes physical or bodily expression. For instance, the traditional example—we meet a bear, are frightened, and run—exemplifies the older notion that the emotion (being frightened) precedes the bodily expression (running).

James reversed this and stated that the arousal of the physical response precedes the appearance of the emotion. Thus for James the example would be—we see the bear, run, and are then afraid. In essence, the emotion is nothing else than the feeling of the bodily changes as they occur. As for supporting evidence, he appealed to the introspective observation that if the physiological symptoms, such as increased heartbeat, muscle tension, and so on, are taken away, nothing remains of the emotion. As another example of simultaneous discovery, we note that the Danish physiologist Carl Lange published an analogous theory in 1885. The similarity between the two led to the designation "James–Lange theory."

James's theory of emotion was the only specific theory to become influential and famous. It led to a great deal of discussion and controversy, stimulated much research, and is considered the starting point for much of modern theory on emotions.

Habit. The chapter dealing with habit is the most famous one in the *Principles*. In keeping with his awareness of physiological influences, James considered habit to involve the functioning of the nervous system. He posited that repeated actions serve to increase the plasticity of neural matter. As a result, the action becomes easier to perform on subsequent repetitions and, at the same time, requires less attention on the part of the individual. James also felt that habit had enormous social implications, as noted in this oft-quoted passage:

> Habit is thus the enormous fly-wheel of society, its most precious conservative agent. It alone is what keeps us all within the bounds of ordinance, and saves the children of fortune from the envious uprisings of the poor. It alone prevents the hardest and most repulsive walks of life from being deserted by those brought up to tread therein. It keeps the fisherman and the deck-hand at sea through the winter; it holds the miner in his darkness, and nails the countryman to his log-cabin and his lonely farm through all the months of snow; it protects us from invasion by the natives of the desert and the frozen zone. It dooms us all to fight out the battle of life upon the lines of our nurture or our early choice, and to make the best of a pursuit that disagrees, because there is no other for which we are fitted, and it is too late to begin again. It keeps different social strata from mixing. Already at the age of twenty-five you see the professional mannerism settling down on the young commercial traveller, on the young doctor, on the young minister, on the young counsellor-at-law. You see the little lines of cleavage running through the character, the tricks of thought, the prejudices, the ways of the

"shop," in a word, from which the man can by-and-by no more escape than his coat-sleeve can suddenly fall into a new set of folds. On the whole, it is best he should not escape. It is well for the world that in most of us, by the age of thirty, the character has set like plaster, and will never soften again (p. 79).

COMMENT

Our coverage of James cannot hope to encompass the scope and brilliance of his form of psychology. The publication of the *Principles* is of major importance and, as mentioned earlier, can legitimately be acclaimed as a great event in the history of psychology.

Miller (1962) suggested that it is an easier task to appreciate William James than to attempt to evaluate him. "If one points to the thousands of students who read his books, to the inspiration he provided for Dewey and the functional psychologists . . . to the sensitivity with which he exposed to view a rich world of inner experience, to the intelligence of his arguments, and the beauty of his prose, it is obvious that he was and still is, the foremost American psychologist" (pp. 77–78).

G. Stanley Hall

Although William James was the first truly great American psychologist, the tremendous growth of psychology in the United States between 1875 and 1900 was hardly the work of James alone. Another remarkable figure in the history of American psychology, and a worthy and influential contemporary of James, was Granville Stanley Hall.

Hall had one of the most interesting and varied careers of any psychologist. He worked in bursts of great energy and enthusiasm in a number of areas, leaving the details to be investigated by others. He did not directly contribute to the formal founding of functionalism, but his contributions to new fields and activities had a pronounced functional flavor.

American psychology owes Hall a great debt because of his outstanding record of "firsts." His was the first American doctorate in psychology, and he was the first American student in the first year of the first psychology laboratory (Wundt's). He began what is often considered the first psychological laboratory in the United States, as well as the first American journal in psychology. He was the first president of Clark University, and the organizer and first president of the American Psychological Association. Also, as Boring (1950) noted, Hall was "forever 'founding' ideas, that is to say, he would . . . bring together certain new ideas that were not original with himself, [and] add to them a supporting mass of other ideas drawn from his omnivorous reading" (p. 518).

THE LIFE OF HALL (1844–1924)

Born on a farm in Massachusetts, Hall began at an early age to develop a succession of intense interests that became characteristic of him in later life. In 1863, he entered Williams College, where he investigated many fields, including the theory of evolution. By the time of his graduation, he had won a number of honors and had developed an enthusiasm for philosophy and evolution.

In 1867, he enrolled in the Union Theological Seminary in New York City, without too much in the way of a "call" to prepare for the ministry. His interest in evolution was not exactly to his advantage in the seminary and he was not noted for his religious orthodoxy. The story has often been told that when Hall gave his trial sermon to the faculty and students, the faculty member whose job it was to criticize such trial sermons instead knelt and prayed for Hall's soul.

On the advice of the famous preacher Henry Ward Beecher, Hall went to Germany to study. After studying philosophy and theology in Bonn, he went to Berlin, where, in addition to theology and philosophy, he worked in physiology and physics. This phase of his education was supplemented by some romantic escapades and the frequenting of beer gardens and the theater.

He returned home in 1871 with no degree, heavily in debt, and 27 years old. He then took his degree in divinity and preached in a country church for all of ten weeks. After tutoring in a private family for more than a year, he secured a teaching appointment at Antioch College in Ohio. Besides teaching English literature, French and German language and literature, and philosophy, during his three years at Antioch he served as librarian, led the choir, and even preached! In 1874, his interest in the new psychology was aroused on reading Wundt's *Physiological Psychology*.

He immediately decided to return to Germany to study with Wundt. He finally set out in 1876 but got no farther than Cambridge, Massachusetts, where lack of funds forced him to accept an offer of a tutorship in English at Harvard. In spite of the monotonous and time-consuming work of teaching sophomore English, Hall managed to conduct research at the Medical School. In 1878, he presented his dissertation on the muscular perception of space, for his doctorate, the first degree in the new psychology awarded in America. While at Harvard, Hall got to know James very well. The two were close in age, but far apart in temperament. Boring (1950) noted that "Hall was a comet, caught for the moment by James' influence, but presently shooting off into space never to return" (p. 519).

Immediately after receiving his degree, Hall left for Europe, first studying physiology at Berlin and then moving to Leipzig, where he became Wundt's first American student. The anticipation of studying with Wundt was apparently greater than the reality. Although he attended Wundt's lectures and dutifully served as a subject in the laboratory, Hall's own research was more along physiological lines. He later commented in a letter to James that he had been disappointed with Wundt, and his career demonstrates that he was little influenced by the great man.

When Hall returned to America in 1880 he had neither a job nor any prospect of one. Fortunately, President Eliot of Harvard invited him to give a series of Saturday morning talks on education. These well-received lectures brought Hall much favorable publicity and, in 1881, an invitation to lecture at the Johns Hopkins University (which had begun only five years earlier as the first graduate school in America).

His lectures at Johns Hopkins were also successful and he was given a professorship in 1884. During his years there, he began what is usually considered to be the first American psychology laboratory, in 1883, and taught a number of students who later became prominent psychologists, among them Cattell and Dewey. In 1887, Hall began the *American Journal of Psychology*, the very first journal of psychology in America and still an important one today. Unlike Wundt's journal, Hall's was connected with no single laboratory or systematic position, but was open to papers from any quarter. This journal provided not only a platform for theoretical and experimental contributions, but also a sense of solidarity and independence for the new American psychology.

In 1888, Hall accepted the invitation to become the first president of the new Clark University. He aspired to make Clark a graduate scientific institute along the lines of Hopkins and the German universities, *i.e.*, with primary emphasis on research, not teaching. Unfortunately, the founder, wealthy merchant Jonas Gilman Clark, had different ideas and did not provide as much money as Hall had been led to expect. Upon Clark's death in 1900, the endowment was largely devoted to the founding of an undergraduate college, opposed by Hall, but long advocated by Clark.

Hall was professor of psychology as well as president, and continued to teach in the graduate school for a number of years. In spite of what must have been a taxing role as president of a new university, he founded another journal, the *Pedagogical Seminary* (now the *Journal of Genetic Psychology*) in 1891, at his own expense, to serve as an outlet for research in child study and educational psychology.

In 1892, the American Psychological Association was founded mainly through the efforts of Hall. At his invitation some 10 to 18 psychologists met in his study to plan the organization, and elected him the first president. The organization has grown from these humble beginnings to a membership of over 26,000.

Hall founded the *Journal of Religious Psychology* (1904), which ceased publication after a decade. In 1915, he founded the currently active *Journal of Applied Psychology*. By this time, there were already 15 other psychology journals in America.

Psychology prospered at Clark under Hall; during his 36 years there, some 81 doctorates were awarded in psychology. Perhaps the best known of these students is Lewis Terman, the American leader in testing and individual differences. At one time it was said that the majority of American psychologists had been associated with Hall, at either Clark or Hopkins, though he was not the primary source of inspiration for them all. Perhaps reflecting the personal influence of Hall is the fact that one third of his doctoral students eventually went into administration, as he had done.

Hall was one of the first Americans to become interested in psychoanalysis, and was in great part responsible for its becoming known in America. To celebrate the twentieth anniversary of Clark University in 1909, Hall invited Freud and Jung to participate in a series of conferences. This was Freud's only visit to the United States. Hall's invitation was a courageous step at that time because of the suspicion with which many American psychologists viewed psychoanalysis.

Hall continued his writing after retiring from Clark in 1920. He died four years later, a few months after his election as president of the American Psychological Association for the second time.

THE WORKS OF HALL

Hall's intellectual endeavors were characterized by enthusiasm for fresh objects and ideas, rather than by the Wundtian form of concentrated devotion to a single cause. A guiding theme, however, pervaded his intellectual wanderings: evolutionary theory. His work on a wide variety of psychological topics was governed by the conviction that the normal growth of the mind involves a series of evolutionary stages. Hall used the theory of evolution effectively as a framework for his broad theoretical speculations.

On the whole, Hall contributed more to educational psychology than to experimental psychology. Only the early phases of his productive career involved experimental psychology for, although he was always favorable toward it, he became impatient of its limitations. Laboratory work in the new psychology proved too narrow for Hall's broad goals and efforts. He adopted the approach he called "synthetic psychology," and sometimes "psychogenesis," which was an eclectic view with a very wide range. It consisted of a monumental application of facts designed to support a single hypothesis. Underneath this encyclopedic method, however, ran the constant reiteration of the genetic theme. Thus, Hall is often called a genetic psychologist—a psychologist and evolutionist whose concern was with human and animal development, and all the many secondary problems of adaptation and development.

At Clark, Hall's geneticism led him to the psychological study of the child and, later, of adolescence. In his child studies he made extensive use of questionnaires, a procedure he had learned in Germany. By 1915, Hall and his students had developed and used 194 questionnaires covering a wide variety of topics. So extensive was his use of questionnaires that, for a time, the method came to be associated in America with Hall's name, even though the technique had been used earlier by Galton.

These early studies of the child created great public enthusiasm and led to the so-called child study movement, which, although it disappeared in a few years because of poorly executed studies, served to establish the importance of the empirical study of the child and the concept of psychological development.

Hall's most important and influential work is the lengthy (about 1300 pages) two-volume *Adolescence: Its Psychology, and Its Relations to Physiology, Anthropology, Sociology, Sex, Crime, Religion, and Education,* published in 1904. It was not only an encyclopedia of useful material, but also contained the most complete statement of Hall's recapitulation theory of development. He believed that the child in his individual development repeats the life history of the race. When the child plays cowboys and Indians, for example, he is repeating the level of preliterate man. The book contained much material of interest to child psychologists and educators and went through several printings, one 20 years after publication.

Hall's interest in religion culminated in the publication of a book that presented a psychological analysis of Jesus—*Jesus, The Christ, in the Light of Psychology* (1917). The rather unorthodox expressions therein were not well received by his former colleagues of the clergy.

As Hall grew older, and could become a subject or observer for his own self-investigation, his genetic inquiry broadened. He investigated the psychology of old age and in 1922 published (appropriately, at the age of 78) the two-volume *Senescence,* the first large-scale geriatric survey of a psychological nature in any language. He also wrote two books of an autobiographical nature in the last few years of his life: *Recreations of a Psychologist* (1920) and *The Life and Confessions of a Psychologist* (1923).

COMMENT

G. Stanley Hall was once introduced to an audience as "the Darwin of the Mind." It was a characterization that evidently pleased him very much and vividly expressed his aspirations and the basic attitude that flavored his work. Throughout his amazing career he remained extremely versatile and agile in his works. He was so intent on his pioneering and founding role that he had to leave to others the task of detailed investigation into the areas he explored. His seemingly limitless enthusiasm was bold and nontechnical and it is perhaps this characteristic that made him so stimulating and spread his influence so far. He once said of himself that, in a sense, all his active conscious life had been made up of a series of fads. Hall once noted that Wundt would rather have been commonplace than brilliantly wrong. Watson (1963) suggested that Hall would have reversed that statement for himself.

James McKeen Cattell

In many ways, the functionalist spirit of American psychology is best represented in the life and works of Cattell, another contemporary of James. He is generally credited with strongly influencing the impressive movement in American psychology in the direction of a very practical test-oriented approach to the study of mental processes. His psychology was concerned with human abilities rather than with conscious content and, in this respect, he comes close to being a functionalist, though, like Hall and James, he was never formally associated with the movement. He did, of course, represent the American functionalistic spirit in his emphasis on mental processes in terms of their utility to the organism.

THE LIFE OF CATTELL (1860–1944)

Born in Easton, Pennsylvania, Cattell received his bachelor's degree in 1880 from Lafayette College, where his father was president. Following the custom of going to Europe for graduate studies, he went to Göttingen and then to Leipzig and Wundt. A paper in philosophy won for him a fellowship at Johns Hopkins at the very time Hall was beginning his laboratory. While at Hopkins, Cattell began research on the time required for different mental activities and this work reinforced his desire to become a psychologist.

His return to Wundt in 1883 is the subject of one of the most famous anecdotes in the history of psychology. As reported by Boring (1929), Cattell appeared at the Leipzig Laboratory and boldly announced, "Herr Professor, you need an assistant, and I will be your assistant." Thus,

Cattell became Wundt's first assistant! In yet another indication of Cattell's spirit of bold independence, he made it clear to Wundt that he would choose his own research project, on the psychology of individual differences. (We have noted earlier that the great man assigned topics of his own choosing to his graduate students.) Wundt is said to have characterized both Cattell and his project as *ganz Amerikanisch* (typically or completely American). Wundt's remark was not only justified but prophetic, for the interest in individual differences, a natural outcome of an evolutionary point of view, has since been a feature of American and not German psychology.

There are indications that the relationship between Cattell and Wundt became somewhat strained, though there was certainly never an open break. Apparently, the highly formal Wundt was too rigid and strict for Cattell. There was, for instance, an edict restricting the number of hours a student could spend in the laboratory. If a student wanted to extend the time, the work would have to be carried on at home. Cattell found it difficult to accept such restrictions.

He also firmly believed that the method of Wundtian introspection (fractionating the reaction time into various activities, such as perception or choice), was something he personally could not do. Indeed, he questioned the validity of the method for anyone's use. This attitude did not exactly ingratiate him with Wundt, who did not allow in his laboratory subjects who were unable to benefit from his method. Consequently, Cattell conducted some of his research in his own room.

In spite of these disagreements, Wundt and Cattell did agree on the value of studying reaction time. Cattell believed it to be especially useful for the study of the time necessary for various mental operations, particularly for research on individual differences. Many of the classic studies on reaction time were carried out by Cattell during his three years at Leipzig, and he published over a half-dozen articles on reaction time and individual differences before leaving there.

After obtaining his degree in 1886, Cattell lectured in psychology at Bryn Mawr and the University of Pennsylvania for one year. He then became lecturer at Cambridge University, where he met Galton and assisted him for a few months at the South Kensington Museum. They shared similar interests and views on individual differences and Galton, then at the zenith of his fame, served to broaden Cattell's horizons. In addition to admiring Galton's versatility and wide-ranging interests, Cattell seems to have been deeply impressed by his emphasis on measurement and statistics. As a result, Cattell became one of the first American psychologists to stress quantification, ranking, and ratings.

In 1888, Cattell was appointed professor of psychology at the University of Pennsylvania. This appointment has great significance because, as the first professorship of psychology anywhere in the world, it represented formal recognition of psychology's separate status. Earlier academic appointments of psychologists had been in departments of philosophy.

Leaving Pennsylvania in 1891, Cattell became professor of psychology and head of the department at Columbia University, where he remained for 26 years. Due to his dissatisfaction with Hall's *American Journal of Psychology*, Cattell began a new journal, *The Psychological Review*, in 1894, with another psychologist, J. Mark Baldwin. In 1895 he acquired from Alexander Graham Bell the weekly journal *Science*, which was ceasing publication for lack of funds. Five years later, it became the official journal of the American Association for the Advancement of Science. Cattell began, in 1906, a series of reference works: *American Men of Science, Leaders in Education,* and *The Directory of American Scholars.* He had started *Popular Science Monthly* in 1900; after selling the first name in 1915, he continued to publish the journal as *Scientific Monthly.* Another weekly, *School and Society,* was started in 1915. As can well be imagined, this truly phenomenal organizing and editing record required a great deal of time and, not surprisingly, Cattell's research productivity declined.

During Cattell's career at Columbia, more doctorates in psychology were awarded there than at any other school in the United States. Cattell stressed the importance of independent work and gave his students considerable freedom to do research on their own. He firmly believed that a professor should be equally independent; that his time need not be devoted exclusively to the university and students, so long as he was working in his discipline. To emphasize this point and make a reality of it, he lived some 40 miles from the campus and even set up a laboratory and editorial office at his home. He came to the university only certain days each week and thus was able to avoid the many inane distractions and interruptions so common to academic life.

This independence did not endear Cattell to the university administrators, and relations became somewhat strained. To further "charm" the administration, he actively urged increased faculty participation in university affairs, arguing that many decisions should be made by faculty and not by administrators. Toward this end, he helped to found the American Association of University Professors and became all the more unpopular with Columbia's administration.

The final blow came during World War I, when Cattell wrote to Congress protesting the practice of sending conscientious objectors into combat. It was a most unpopular position to take at that time but Cattell, with characteristic determination, remained adamant. He was dismissed from Columbia in 1917 on the grounds that he had been disloyal to his country. His reaction was to sue the university for libel, and although he was awarded a large annuity, he was not reinstated.

Cattell never returned to academic life. Instead, he devoted himself with even greater zest to his publications, the American Association for the Advancement of Science, and other learned societies. These efforts of a promotional nature, in which he served as a spokesman for psychology to other sciences, tended to give psychology a higher standing in the scientific community.

In 1921, Cattell realized one of his great ambitions—the promotion of the application of psychology. He organized the Psychological Corporation on the basis of stock purchased by members of the American Psychological Association at $10.00 a share. This corporation, providing psychological services to industry and the public, has grown considerably.

Cattell remained very active in his roles as editor and spokesman for psychology until his death in 1944. One final aspect of his life that deserves mention is his extremely rapid rise in American psychology. He was professor at the University of Pennsylvania at 28, chairman of the department at Columbia at 31, president of the American Psychological Association at 35, and the first psychologist elected to the National Academy of Sciences, at 40.

THE WORKS OF CATTELL

We have already mentioned Cattell's early work on reaction time and his interest in the study of individual differences. An indication of the scope of his work was provided in 1914, when a group of his students gathered together his original work, which had been published in numerous short papers. There were five main areas in addition to reaction time: reading and perception; association; psychophysics; the order of merit method; and individual differences.

Without denying the importance of these other works, we note that Cattell influenced psychology most through his work on individual differences and mental tests. In fact, the central theme of all his research is the problem of individual differences. By the time he went to Columbia in 1891, his interest in the development and promotion of mental tests had become paramount. A few years earlier, while still at Pennsylvania, he had administered a series of tests to students and, in a paper in 1890, had coined the term "mental tests." He continued the testing program at Columbia and collected a large body of data from several entering classes of students.

It is instructive to look at the kinds of tests Cattell used to try to measure the range and variability of human capacity. As distinguished from the later development of intelligence tests, which utilized more complex tasks of mental ability, Cattell's tests (like Galton's) dealt with more elementary bodily or sensory-motor measures. Cattell's basic tests included: dynamometer pressure; rate of movement (how quickly the hand can be moved 50 cm.); sensation areas using the two-point threshold; pressure causing pain (amount of pressure on the forehead necessary to cause pain); just noticeable differences in weight; reaction time for sound; time for naming colors; bisection of a 50-cm. line; judgment of a 10-second period of time; and the number of letters that can be remembered after one presentation.

By 1901, enough data had been collected to correlate the test scores with the subjects' academic performance. The correlations proved disappointingly low, as did intercorrelations among individual tests themselves. Similar results using sensory-motor tests had also appeared from Titchener's laboratory, and it seemed that tests of this type were not very valid predictors of intellectual ability.

As every student of psychology knows, the French psychologist Alfred Binet, together with Henri and Simon, developed an intelligence test using much more complex measures of higher mental abilities. These men published their first test in 1905. This approach provided a much more effective measure of intelligence and marked the beginning of the phenomenal growth of intelligence testing.

Cattell's influence was felt strongly in supporting and promoting the mental test movement. His student, E. L. Thorndike (Chapter IX) was a leader in the psychology of mental tests in America, and Columbia was the leading university in the testing movement for years.

Continuing the tradition of Galton's earlier work, Cattell undertook a series of studies to investigate the nature and origin of scientific ability, using a much improved technique, the method of order of merit, which he developed in 1902. With this method, stimuli ranked by a number of judges are placed in a final rank order by calculating the average rating given to each stimulus item. The method was applied to eminent American scientists by having competent men in each of the scientific fields rank, in order, a number of their outstanding colleagues. The source book *American Men of Science* emerged from this work.

COMMENT

Cattell's influence on the American psychological scene was actually much greater than the quantity of his scientific output. His force was exerted in more personal ways, for instance, through his 26-year tenure at Columbia, where more students came under his influence than was the case with any other psychologist in America. In addition, he possessed a high-level administrative ability and was actively involved in many psychological and scientific matters.

It must be noted that Cattell might not have been so influential if, like Titchener, he had been out of step with the times instead of so ably reflecting the ongoing American trend. That American psychology wanted and needed what Cattell had to say does not, of course, diminish his stature.

Ganz Amerikanisch

As we noted at the beginning of this chapter, evolutionary doctrine readily and rapidly took hold in America. And evolution meant, for psychology, an emphasis on individual differences and the techniques with which to measure them. An interest in individual differences began in England but did not flourish there. John Dewey noted, in 1899, that a psychology of individual differences can flourish only in a democracy, as the findings of a psychology of individual differences never support the notion of innate class differences.

A psychology of individual differences tends to be highly practical and we have already noted America's practical spirit and functional orientation. This country wanted a practical shirt-sleeves form of psychology and, through the efforts of James, Hall, Cattell, and other American pioneers, it was to have and use it most effectively, in the *ganz Amerikanisch* direct, bold, and aggressive fashion.

The exciting, vibrant, and dynamic development of American psychology is one of the most striking events in science during the period 1880–1900. In 1880 there were no laboratories; by 1895 there were 24. In 1880 there were no journals; by 1895 there were three. There was also a flourishing scientific society by 1895. Psychology's growth was much more rapid in America than in Europe.

After two chapters of anticipations and antecedents of the functionalist school, our discussion now turns to the formal founding of functionalism.

SUGGESTED FURTHER READINGS

Early Psychology in America
Jastrow, J. American psychology in the '80s and '90s. *Psychological Review,* 1943, **50,** 65–67.

Influence of Evolution on American Psychology
Boring, E. G. The influence of evolutionary theory upon American psychological thought. In S. Persons (Ed.), *Evolutionary thought in America.* New Haven: Yale University Press, 1950. Pp. 267–298.

James
Allen, G. W. *William James.* New York: Viking Press, 1967.
Allport, G. W. The productive paradoxes of William James. *Psychological Review,* 1943, **50,** 95–120.

Allport, G. W. William James and the behavioral sciences. *Journal of the History of the Behavioral Sciences*, 1966, **2**, 145–147.

Harper, R. S. The first psychological laboratory. *Isis*, 1950, **41**, 158–161.

Perry, R. B. *The thought and character of William James: as revealed in unpublished correspondence and notes, together with his published writings.* Vol. 1, *Inheritance and vocation;* Vol. 2, *Philosophy and psychology.* Boston: Little, Brown, 1935.

Hall

Burnham, W. H. The man, G. Stanley Hall. *Psychological Review*, 1925, **32**, 89–102.

Dennis, W., & Boring, E. G. The founding of APA. *American Psychologist*, 1952, **7**, 95–97.

Hall, G. S. *Life and confessions of a psychologist.* New York: Appleton, 1923.

Pruette, L. G. *Stanley Hall: A biography of a mind.* New York: Appleton, 1926.

Cattell

Poffenberger, A. T. (Ed.) *James McKeen Cattell—man of science.* Vol. 1, *Psychological research;* Vol. 2, *Addresses and formal papers.* Lancaster, Penna.: Science Press, 1947.

Woodworth, R. S. J. McKeen Cattell, 1860–1944. *Psychological Review*, 1944, **51**, 201–209.

VIII

FUNCTIONALISM: FORMAL
DEVELOPMENT

IN THE LAST CHAPTERS we discussed the nature of functionalism; we now focus on the major themes of this movement. Functionalism is concerned with the operation and processes of conscious phenomena, not with their structure. Further, its interest is with the utility or purpose of mental processes. Consciousness is considered useful to the living organism in its continuing attempts to adapt to its environment. Mental processes are regarded as activities leading to practical consequences, not as elements in some kind of composition. Functionalism's practical cast inevitably led to an interest in the application of science to the affairs of the world. Thus, applied psychology, disdained by Wundt and Titchener, was well accepted and practiced by the functionalists.

The Chicago School

In 1894, John Dewey and James Angell came to the newly organized University of Chicago. The combined influence of the two men was largely responsible for the university's becoming a leading center of psychology, particularly of functionalism. The functionalist school provided the first organized stand against the orthodox structuralist position in America.

JOHN DEWEY (1859–1952)

When functionalism is considered as a distinct school of psychology, rather than as an orientation or attitude, John Dewey is usually credited with sparking the development of that school. Paradoxically, though, it could almost be said that Titchener "founded" functional psychology for, as noted earlier, he adopted the word *structural* as opposed to *functional* in his 1898 paper reprinted in Chapter V. "What Titchener was

124

attacking was in fact nameless until he named it; hence he thrust the movement into high relief and did more than anyone else to get the term *functionalism* into psychological currency" (Harrison, 1963, p. 395). An 1896 paper by Dewey is generally considered the most important landmark in the formal establishment of functionalism. He exerted a great influence on this school although his years of active contribution to psychology were few.

Born in Vermont, Dewey had a rather undistinguished early life and showed no great intellectual promise until his junior year at the University of Vermont. After graduation, he taught high school for a few years and studied philosophy on his own, publishing several scholarly articles. He went to graduate school at Johns Hopkins and received his doctorate in 1884, in philosophy, after which he taught at the University of Michigan and the University of Minnesota. In 1886, he published the first American textbook in psychology (called, appropriately, *Psychology*), which became very popular, though it was soon eclipsed by James's *Principles*.

In 1894, Dewey was invited to the University of Chicago, where he remained for ten years, during which time he became a moving force in psychology. At Chicago he also began his experimental or laboratory school, which at the time was a radical innovation in education. It served as the cornerstone for the modern progressive education movement, which made him quite famous and controversial.

In 1904, he left Chicago for Columbia University, where he remained until his retirement in 1930, no longer working in psychology proper but applying psychology to the educational and philosophical problems with which he was then concerned.

Dewey's short paper, *The reflex arc concept in psychology* (1896) was the point of departure for the new movement. In this, his most important (and, unfortunately, last) contribution to psychology proper, Dewey attacked the psychological molecularism, elementism, and reductionism of the reflex arc with its distinction between stimulus and response. He argued that the behavior involved in a reflex response cannot be meaningfully reduced to its basic sensory-motor elements any more than consciousness can be meaningfully analyzed into its elementary components. When this form of artificial analysis and reduction of behavior is undertaken, the behavior loses all meaning: all that is left are abstractions that exist only in the minds of the psychologists performing the dissection. Dewey said that behavior should not be treated as an artificial scientific construct, but rather in terms of its significance to the organism in adapting to the environment. Hence, Dewey argued that the proper subject matter for psychology is the study of the total organism functioning in its environment.

Dewey was very strongly influenced by the theory of evolution and his philosophy was based on the notion of social change. He was against things remaining static, and for progress gained through the struggle of man's intellect with reality. In this struggle for survival, both consciousness and activity function for the organism, with consciousness bringing about the appropriate activity that enables the organism to survive and progress. A function is a total coordination of an organism toward achieving an end—survival. Functional psychology is thus the study of the organism "in use."

Dewey's philosophical position has had greater influence than his psychological studies. As a social philosopher, Dewey was greatly concerned with the welfare of man and his physical, social, and moral adjustment. He considered man's psychological processes, such as thinking and learning, to be of paramount importance in his adjustment to life. Thinking, he said, was a tool used by man to meet the exigencies of life: man thinks in order to live.

Dewey argued that the human effort to survive results in knowledge, and knowledge is also a weapon in the fight for survival, a tool in the adjustment process. Since life is learning, he regarded the problem of learning as the most important issue in psychology.

Unfortunately, the time Dewey spent in psychology was all too short. In keeping with his functional orientation, he devoted most of his efforts to education. His program for the progressive education movement is spelled out in a paper, *Psychology and social change*, given in 1900 on his retirement as president of the American Psychological Association. He remained titular head of the progressive education movement for the rest of his life. More than anyone else, Dewey is responsible for the application of a pragmatic spirit to education. He believed strongly that education is equivalent to life itself, and that teaching should be oriented toward the student rather than the subject matter.

Dewey's significance for psychology lies in his stimulation of others and his development of the philosophical framework for functionalism. When he left Chicago, the torch of functionalism was passed to James Rowland Angell.

JAMES ROWLAND ANGELL (1867–1949)

Angell molded the functionalist movement into a working school and, in the process, made the psychology department at Chicago the most important and influential one of the day. Chicago became the major training ground for functional psychologists.

Angell was born in Vermont into an academic family. His grandfather had been president of Brown University and his father president of the University of Vermont, and later of the University of Michigan.

He did his undergraduate work at Michigan, where he studied under Dewey; he then worked under James for a year at Harvard, receiving his MA in 1892. He continued his graduate work at Halle, in Germany, but did not obtain his PhD. His thesis was accepted, subject to revision (rendering it into better German), but to undertake this task he would have had to remain at Halle without remuneration. He chose instead to accept an appointment at the University of Minnesota, where the salary, though small, was sufficient for him to marry. It is interesting to note that although he did not earn his PhD, he was instrumental in the granting of many doctorates to others and, in the course of his career, was awarded some 23 honorary doctoral degrees!

After one year at Minnesota, Angell went to Chicago, where he remained for 25 years. Following in the family tradition, he became president of Yale (the first non-Yale man to do so) and helped to develop the Institute of Human Relations there. In 1906, he was elected the fifteenth president of the American Psychological Association. After his retirement from academic life, he served as an officer of the National Broadcasting Company.

Angell published a text in 1904 that embodied the functionalist approach to psychology. The book was so successful that it went through four editions by 1908. In it he maintained that the basic function of consciousness is to improve the adaptive activities of the organism, and that psychology must study how the mind aids this adjustment of the organism to its environment. A more important contribution to functional psychology was his presidential address to the American Psychological Association in 1906, which clearly spelled out the functionalist position. Since this paper is considered the best exposition of functionalism, it is reprinted here.

• • •

THE PROVINCE OF FUNCTIONAL PSYCHOLOGY[1]

Functional psychology is at the present moment little more than a point of view, a program, an ambition. It gains its vitality primarily perhaps as a protest against the exclusive excellence of another starting point for the study of the mind, and it enjoys for the time being at least the peculiar vigor which commonly attaches to Protestantism of any sort in its early stages before it has become respectable and orthodox. The time seems ripe to attempt a somewhat more precise characterization of the field of functional psychology than has as yet been offered.

[1] By James Rowland Angell. Delivered in substantially the present form as the president's annual address before the American Psychological Association at its fifteenth annual meeting held at Columbia University, New York City, December 27, 28, and 29, 1906. Reprinted in part from the *Psychological Review*, 1907, **14**, 61–91, by permission of the American Psychological Association.

What we seek is not the arid and merely verbal definition which to many of us is so justly anathema, but rather an informing appreciation of the motives and ideals which animate the psychologist who pursues this path. His status in the eye of the psychological public is unnecessarily precarious. The conceptions of his purposes prevalent in non-functionalist circles range from positive and dogmatic misapprehension, through frank mystification and suspicion up to moderate comprehension. Nor is this fact an expression of anything peculiarly abstruse and recondite in his intentions. It is due in part to his own ill-defined plans, in part to his failure to explain lucidly exactly what he is about. Moreover, he is fairly numerous and it is not certain that in all important particulars he and his confrères are at one in their beliefs. The considerations which are herewith offered suffer inevitably from this personal limitation. No psychological council of Trent has as yet pronounced upon the true faith. But in spite of probable failure it seems worth while to hazard an attempt at delineating the scope of functionalist principles. I formally renounce any intention to strike out new plans; I am engaged in what is meant as a dispassionate summary of actual conditions.

I

There is to be mentioned first the notion which derives most immediately from contrast with the ideals and purposes of structural psychology so-called. This involves the identification of functional psychology with the effort to discern and portray the typical *operations* of consciousness under actual life conditions, as over against the attempt to analyze and describe its elementary and complex *contents*. The structural psychology of sensation, *e.g.*, undertakes to determine the number and character of the various unanalyzable sensory materials, such as the varieties of color, tone, taste, etc. The functional psychology of sensation would on the other hand find its appropriate sphere of interest in the determination of the character of the various sense activities as differing in their *modus operandi* from one another and from other mental processes such as judging, conceiving, willing and the like.

In this its older and more pervasive form functional psychology has until very recent times had no independent existence. No more has structural psychology for that matter. It is only lately that any motive for the differentiation of the two has existed and structural psychology— granting its claims and pretensions of which more anon—is the first, be it said, to isolate itself. But in so far as functional psychology is synonymous with descriptions and theories of mental action as distinct from the materials of mental constitution, so far it is everywhere conspicuous in psychological literature from the earliest times down.

It must be obvious to any one familiar with psychological usage in the present year of grace that in the intent of the distinction herewith described certain of our familiar psychological categories are primarily structural—such for instance as affection and image—whereas others immediately suggest more explicit functional relationships—for example, attention and reasoning. As a matter of fact it seems clear that so long as we adhere to these meanings of the terms structural and functional every mental event can be treated from either point of view, from the standpoint of describing its detectable contents and from the standpoint of characteristic mental activity differentiable from other forms of mental process. In the practice of our familiar psychological writers both undertakings are somewhat indiscriminately combined.

The more extreme and ingenuous conceptions of structural psychology seem to have grown out of an unchastened indulgence in what we may call the "states of consciousness" doctrine. I take it that this is in reality the contemporary version of Locke's "idea." If you adopt as your material for psychological analysis the isolated "moment of consciousness," it is very easy to become so absorbed in determining its constitution as to be rendered somewhat oblivious to its artificial character. The most essential quarrel which the functionalist has with structuralism in its thoroughgoing and consistent form arises from this fact and touches the feasibility and worth of the effort to get at mental process as it *is* under the conditions of actual experience rather than as it *appears* to a merely postmortem analysis. It is of course true that for introspective purposes we must in a sense always work with vicarious representatives of the particular mental processes which we set out to observe. But it makes a great difference even on such terms whether one is directing attention primarily to the discovery of the way in which such a mental process operates, and what the conditions are under which it appears, or whether one is engaged simply in teasing apart the fibers of its tissues. The latter occupation is useful and for certain purposes essential, but it often stops short of that which is as a life phenomenon the most essential, *i.e.*, the *modus operandi* of the phenomenon.

As a matter of fact many modern investigations of an experimental kind largely dispense with the usual direct form of introspection and concern themselves in a distinctly functionalistic spirit with a determination of what work is accomplished and what the conditions are under which it is achieved. Many experiments in memory and association, for instance, are avowedly of this character.

The functionalist is committed *vom Grunde auf* to the avoidance of that special form of the psychologist's fallacy which consists in attributing to mental states without due warrant, as part of their overt constitution in the moment of experience, characteristics which subsequent reflective analysis leads us to suppose they must have possessed. When this precaution is not scrupulously observed we obtain a sort of *pâte de foie gras* psychology in which the mental conditions portrayed contain more than they ever naturally would or could hold.

It should be added that when the distinction is made between psychic structure and psychic function, the anomalous position of structure as a category of mind is often quite forgotten. In mental life the sole appropriateness of the term structure hinges on the fact that any moment of consciousness can be regarded as a complex capable of analysis, and the terms into which our analyses resolve such complexes are the analogues—and obviously very meager and defective ones at that—of the structures of anatomy and morphology.

The fact that mental contents are evanescent and fleeting marks them off in an important way from the relatively permanent elements of anatomy. No matter how much we may talk of the preservation of psychical dispositions, nor how many metaphors we may summon to characterize the storage of ideas in some hypothetical deposit chamber of memory, the obstinate fact remains that when we are not experiencing a sensation or an idea it is, strictly speaking, non-existent. Moreover, when we manage by one or another device to secure that which we designate the same sensation or the same idea, we not only have no guarantee that our second edition is really a replica of the first, we have a good bit of presumptive evidence that from the content point of view the original never is and never can be literally duplicated.

Functions, on the other hand, persist as well in mental as in physical life. We may never have twice exactly the same idea viewed from the side of sensuous structure and composition. But there seems nothing whatever to prevent our having as often as we will contents of consciousness which *mean* the same thing. They function in one and the same practical way, however discrepant their momentary texture. The situation is rudely analogous to the biological case where very different structures may under different conditions be called on to perform identical functions; and the matter naturally harks back for its earliest analogy to the instance of protoplasm where functions seem very tentatively and imperfectly differentiated. Not only then are general functions like memory persistent, but special functions such as the memory of particular events are persistent and largely independent of the specific conscious contents called upon from time to time to subserve the functions.

When the structural psychologists define their field as that of mental *process*, they really preëmpt under a fictitious name the field of function, so that I should be disposed to allege fearlessly and with a clear conscience that a large part of the doctrine of psychologists of nominally structural proclivities is in point of fact precisely what I mean by one essential part of functional psychology, *i.e.*, an account of psychical operations. Certain of the official exponents of structuralism explicitly lay claim to this as their field and do so with a flourish of scientific rectitude. There is therefore after all a small but nutritious core of agreement in the structure-function apple of discord. For this reason, as well as because I consider extremely useful the analysis of mental life into its elementary forms, I regard much of the actual work of my structuralist friends with highest respect and confidence. I feel, however, that when they use the term structural as opposed to the term functional to designate their scientific creed they often come perilously near to using the enemy's colors.

Substantially identical with this first conception of functional psychology, but phrasing itself somewhat differently, is the view which regards the functional problem as concerned with discovering how and why conscious processes are what they are, instead of dwelling as the structuralist is supposed to do upon the problem of determining the irreducible elements of consciousness and their characteristic modes of combination. I have elsewhere defended the view that however it may be in other sciences dealing with life phenomena, in psychology at least the answer to the question "what" implicates the answer to the questions "how" and "why."

Stated briefly the ground on which this position rests is as follows: In so far as you attempt to analyze any particular state of consciousness you find that the mental elements presented to your notice are dependent upon the particular exigencies and conditions which call them forth. Not only does the affective coloring of such a psychical moment depend upon one's temporary condition, mood and aims, but the very sensations themselves are determined in their qualitative texture by the totality of circumstances subjective and objective within which they arise. You cannot get a fixed and definite color sensation for example, without keeping perfectly constant the external and internal conditions in which it appears. The particular sense quality is in short functionally determined by the necessities of the existing situation which it emerges to meet. If you inquire then deeply enough what particular sensation you have in a given case, you always find it necessary to take account of the manner in which, and the reasons why, it was experienced at all. You may of course, if you will, abstract from these considerations, but in so far as you do so, your analysis and description is manifestly partial and incomplete. Moreover, even when you do so abstract and attempt to describe certain isolable sense qualities, your descriptions are of necessity couched in terms not of the experienced quality itself, but in terms of the conditions which produced it, in terms of some other quality with which it is compared, or in terms of some more overt act to which the sense stimulation led. That is to say, the very description itself is functionalistic and must be so. The truth of this assertion can be illustrated and tested by appeal to any situation in which one is trying to reduce sensory complexes, e.g., colors or sounds, to their rudimentary components.

II

A broader outlook and one more frequently characteristic of contemporary writers meets us in the next conception of the task of functional psychology. This conception is in part a reflex of the prevailing interest in the larger formulae of biology and particularly the evolutionary hypotheses within whose majestic sweep is nowadays included the history of the whole stellar universe . . . .

The functional psychologist . . . in his modern attire is interested not alone in the operations of mental process considered merely of and by and for itself, but also and more vigorously in mental activity as part of a larger stream of biological forces which are daily and hourly at work before our eyes and which are constitutive of the most important and most absorbing part of our world. The psychologist of this stripe is wont to take his cue from the basal conception of the evolutionary movement, i.e., that for the most part organic structures and functions possess their present characteristics by virtue of the efficiency with which they fit into the extant conditions of life broadly designated the environment. With this conception in mind he proceeds to attempt some understanding of the manner in which the psychical contributes to the furtherance of the sum total of organic activities, not alone the psychical in its entirety, but especially the psychical in its particularities—mind as judging, mind as feeling, etc.

This is the point of view which instantly brings the psychologist cheek by jowl with the general biologist. It is the presupposition of every philosophy save that of outright ontological materialism that mind plays the stellar rôle in all the environmental adaptations of animals which possess it. But this persuasion has generally occupied the position of an innocuous truism or at best a jejune postulate, rather than that of a problem requiring, or permitting, serious scientific treatment. At all events, this was formerly true.

This older and more complacent attitude toward the matter is, however, being rapidly displaced by a conviction of the need for light on the exact character of the accommodatory service represented by the various great modes of conscious expression. Such an effort if successful would not only broaden the foundations for biological appreciation of the intimate nature of accommodatory process, it would also immensely enhance the psychologist's interest in the exact portrayal of conscious life. It is of course the latter consideration which lends importance to the matter from our point of view. Moreover, not a few practical consequences of value may be expected to flow from this attempt, if it achieves even a measurable degree of success. Pedagogy and mental hygiene both await the quickening and guiding counsel which can only come from a psychology of this stripe. For their purposes a strictly structural psychology is as sterile in theory as teachers and psychiatrists have found it in practice.

As a concrete example of the transfer of attention from the more general phases of consciousness as accommodatory activity to the particularistic features of the case may be mentioned the rejuvenation of interest in the quasi-biological field which we designate animal psychology. This movement is surely among the most pregnant with which we meet in our own generation. Its problems are in no sense of the merely theoretical and speculative kind, although, like all scientific endeavor, it possesses an intellectual and methodological background on which such problems loom large. But the frontier upon which it is pushing forward its explorations is a region of definite, concrete fact, tangled and confused and often most difficult of access, but nevertheless a region of fact, accessible like all other facts to persistent and intelligent interrogation.

That many of the most fruitful researches in this field have been achievements of men nominally biologists rather than psychologists in no wise affects the merits of the case. A similar situation exists in the experimental psychology of sensation where not a little of the best work has been accomplished by scientists not primarily known as psychologists.

It seems hardly too much to say that the empirical conceptions of the consciousness of the lower animals have undergone a radical alteration in the past few years by virtue of the studies in comparative psychology. The splendid investigations of the mechanism of instinct, of the facts and methods of animal orientation, of the scope and character of the several sense processes, of the capabilities of education and the range of selective accommodatory capacities in the animal kingdom, these and dozens of other similar problems have received for the first time drastic scientific examination, experimental in character wherever possible, observational elsewhere, but observational in the spirit of conservative non-anthropomorphism as earlier observations almost never were. In most cases they have to be sure but shown the way to further and more precise knowledge, yet there can be but little question that the trail which they have blazed has success at its farther end.

One may speak almost as hopefully of human genetic psychology which has been carried on so profitably in our own country. As so often in psychology, the great desideratum here, is the completion of adequate methods which will insure really stable scientific results. But already our general psychological theory has been vitalized and broadened by the results of the genetic methods thus far elaborated. These studies constantly emphasize for us the necessity of getting the longitudinal rather than the transverse view of life phenomena and they keep immediately in our field of vision the basic significance of growth in mental process. Nowhere is the difference more flagrant between a functional psychology and the more literal minded type of structural psychology. . . .

The assertions which we have permitted ourselves about genetic psychology are equally applicable to pathological psychology. The technique of scientific investigation is in the nature of the case often different in this field of work from that characteristic of the other ranges of psychological research. But the attitude of the investigator is distinctly functionalistic. His aim is one of a thoroughly vital and generally practical kind leading him to emphasize precisely those considerations which our analysis of the main aspects of functional psychology disclose as the goal of its peculiar ambitions.

It is no purpose of mine to submerge by sheer *tour de force* the individuality of these various scientific interests just mentioned in the regnant personality of a functional psychology. But I am firmly convinced that the spirit which gives them birth is the spirit which in the realms of general psychological theory bears the name functionalism. I believe, therefore, that their ultimate fate is certain, still I have no wish to accelerate their translation against their will, nor to inflict upon them a label which they may find odious.

It should be said, however, in passing, that even on the side of general theory and methodological conceptions, recent developments have been fruitful and significant. One at least of these deserves mention.

We find nowadays both psychologists and biologists who treat consciousness as substantially synonymous with adaptive reactions to novel situations. In the writings of earlier authorities it is often implied that accommodatory activities *may be* purely physiological and non-psychical in character. From this view-point the mental type of accommodatory act supervenes on certain occasions and at certain stages in organic development, but it is no indispensable feature of the accommodatory process.

It seems a trifle strange when one considers how long the fundamental conception involved in this theory has been familiar and accepted psychological doctrine that its full implication should have been so reluctantly recognized. If one takes the position now held by all psychologists of repute, so far as I am aware, that consciousness is constantly at work building up habits out of coördinations imperfectly under control; and that as speedily as control is gained the mental direction tends to subside and give way to a condition approximating physiological automatism, it is only a step to carry the inference forward that consciousness immanently considered is *per se* accommodation to the novel. Whether conscious processes have been the precursors of our present instinctive equipment depends on facts of heredity upon which a layman may hardly speak. But many of our leaders answer strongly in the affirmative, and such an answer evidently harmonizes with the general view now under discussion.

To be sure the further assertion that no real organic accommodation to the novel ever occurs, save in the form that involves consciousness, requires for its foundation a wide range of observation and a penetrating analysis of the various criteria of mentality. But this is certainly a common belief among biologists to-day. Selective variation of response to stimulation is the ordinary external sign indicative of conscious action. Stated otherwise, consciousness discloses the form taken on by primary accommodatory process.

It is not unnatural perhaps that the frequent disposition of the functional psychologist to sigh after the flesh-pots of biology should kindle the fire of those consecrated to the cause of a pure psychology and philosophy freed from the contaminating influence of natural science. As a matter of fact, alarms have been repeatedly sounded and the faithful called to subdue mutiny. But the purpose of the functional psychologist has never been, so far as I am aware, to scuttle the psychological craft for the benefit of biology. Quite the contrary. Psychology is still for a time at least to steer her own untroubled course. She is at most borrowing a well-tested compass which biology is willing to lend and she hopes by its aid to make her ports more speedily and more surely. If in use it prove treacherous and unreliable, it will of course go overboard.

This broad biological ideal of functional psychology of which we have been speaking may be phrased with a slight shift of emphasis by connecting it with the problem of discovering the fundamental utilities of consciousness. If mental process is of real value to its possessor in the life and world which we know, it must perforce be by virtue of something which it does that otherwise is not accomplished. Now life and world are complex and it seems altogether improbable that consciousness should express its utility in one and only one way. As a matter of fact, every surface indication points in the other direction. It may be possible merely as a matter of expression to speak of mind as in general contributing to organic adjustment to environment. But the actual contributions will take place in many ways and by multitudinous varieties of conscious process. The functionalist's problem then is to determine if possible the great types of these processes in so far as the utilities which they present lend themselves to classification.

The search after the various utilitarian aspects of mental process is at once suggestive and disappointing. It is on the one hand illuminating by virtue of the strong relief into which it throws the fundamental resemblances of processes often unduly severed in psychological analysis. Memory and imagination, for example, are often treated in a way designed to emphasize their divergences almost to the exclusion of their functional similarities. They are of course functionally but variants on a single and basal type of control. An austere structuralism in particular is inevitably disposed to magnify differences and in consequence under its hands mental life tends to fall apart; and when put together again it generally seems to have lost something of its verve and vivacity. It appears stiff and rigid and corpse-like. It lacks the vital spark. Functionalism tends just as inevitably to bring mental phenomena together, to show them focalized in actual vital service. The professional psychologist, calloused by long apprenticeship, may not feel this distinction to be scientifically important. But to the young student the functionalistic stress upon community of service is of immense value in clarifying the intricacies of mental organization. On the other hand the search of which we were speaking is disappointing perhaps in the paucity of the basic modes in which these conscious utilities are realized.

III

The third conception which I distinguish is often in practice merged with the second, but it involves stress upon a problem logically prior perhaps to the problem raised there and so warrants separate mention. Functional psychology, it is often alleged, is in reality a form of psychophysics. To be sure, its aims and ideals are not explicitly quantitative in the manner characteristic of that science as commonly understood. But it finds its major interest in determining the relations to one another of the physical and mental portions of the organism.

It is undoubtedly true that many of those who write under functional prepossessions are wont to introduce frequent references to the physiological processes which accompany or condition mental life. Moreover, certain followers of this faith are prone to declare forthwith that psychology is simply a branch of biology and that we are in consequence entitled, if not indeed obliged, to make use where possible of biological materials. But without committing ourselves to so extreme a position as this, a mere glance at one familiar region of psychological procedure will disclose the leanings of psychology in this direction.

The psychology of volition affords an excellent illustration of the necessity with which descriptions of mental process eventuate in physiological or biological considerations. If one take the conventional analysis of a voluntary act drawn from some one or other of the experiences of adult life, the descriptions offered generally portray ideational activities of an anticipatory and deliberative character which serve to initiate immediately or remotely certain relevant expressive movements. Without the execution of the movements the ideational performances would be as futile as the tinkling cymbals of Scripture. To be sure, many of our psychologists protest themselves wholly unable to suggest why or how such muscular movements are brought to pass. But the fact of their occurrence or of their fundamental import for any theory of mental life in which consciousness is other than an epiphenomenon, is not questioned.

Moreover, if one considers the usual accounts of the ontogenesis of human volitional acts one is again confronted with intrinsically physiological data in which reflexes, automatic and instinctive acts are much in evidence. Whatever the possibilities, then, of an expurgated edition of the psychology of volition from which should be blotted out all reference to contaminating physiological factors, the actual practice of our representative psychologists is quite otherwise, and upon their showing volition cannot be understood either as regards its origin or its outcome without constant and overt reference to these factors. It would be a labor of supererogation to go on and make clear the same doctrine as it applies to the psychology of the more recondite of the cognitive processes; so intimate is the relation between cognition and volition in modern psychological theory that we may well stand excused from carrying out in detail the obvious inferences from the situation we have just described.

This disposition to go over into the physiological for certain portions of psychological doctrine is represented in an interesting way by the frequent tendency of structural psychologists to find explanation in psychology substantially equivalent to physiological explanation. Professor Titchener's recent work on *Quantitative Psychology* represents this position very frankly. It is cited here with no intent to comment disparagingly upon the consistency of the structuralist position, but simply to indicate the wide-spread feeling of necessity at certain stages of psychological development for resort to physiological considerations.

It is not clear that the functional psychologist because of his disposition to magnify the significance in practice of the mind-body relationships is thereby committed to any special theory of the character of these relationships, save as was said a moment since, that negatively he must seemingly of necessity set his face against any epiphenomenalist view. He might conceivably be an interactionist, or a parallelist or even an advocate of some wholly outworn creed. As a matter of fact certain of our most ardent functionalists not only cherish highly definite articles of faith as regards this issue, they would even go so far as to test functional orthodoxy by the acceptance of these tenets. This is to them the most momentous part of their functionalism, their holy of holies. It would display needless temerity to attempt within the limitations of this occasion a formulation of doctrine wholly acceptable to all concerned. But I shall venture a brief reference to such doctrine in the effort to bring out certain of its essentials.

The position to which I refer regards the mind-body relation as capable of treatment in psychology as a methodological distinction rather than a metaphysically existential one. Certain of its expounders arrive at their view by means of an analysis of the genetic conditions under which the mind-body differentiation first makes itself felt in the experience of the individual. This procedure clearly involves a direct frontal attack on the problem.

Others attain the position by flank movement, emphasizing to begin with the insoluble contradictions with which one is met when the distinction is treated as resting on existential differences in the primordial elements of the cosmos. Both methods of approach lead to the same goal, however, i.e., the conviction that the distinction has no existence on the genetically lower and more naif stages of experience. It only comes to light on a relatively reflective level and it must then be treated as instrumental if one would avoid paralogisms, antinomies and a host of other metaphysical nightmares. Moreover, in dealing with psychological problems this view entitles one to reject as at least temporarily irrelevant the question whether mind *causes* changes in neural action and conversely. The previous question is raised by defenders of this type of doctrine if one insists on having such a query answered. They invite you to trace the lineage of your idea of causality, insisting that such a searching of one's intellectual reins will always disclose the inappropriateness of the inquiry as formulated above. They urge further that the profitable and significant thing is to seek for a more exact appreciation of the precise conditions under which consciousness is in evidence and the conditions under which it retires in favor of the more exclusively physiological. Such knowledge so far as it can be obtained is on a level with all scientific and practical information. It states the circumstances under which certain sorts of results will appear.

One's view of this functionalistic metaphysics is almost inevitably colored by current philosophical discussion as to the essential nature of consciousness. David Hume has been accused of destroying the reality of mind chiefly because he exorcised from it relationships of various kinds. If it be urged, as has so often been done, that Hume was guilty of pouring out the baby with the bath, the modern philosopher makes good the disaster not only by pouring in again both baby and bath, but by maintaining that baby and bath, mind and relations, are substantially one. Nor is this unity secured after the manner prescribed by the good Bishop Berkeley. At all events the metaphysicians to whom I refer are not fond of being called idealists. But the psychological functionalist who emphasizes the instrumental nature of the mind-body distinction and the metaphysician who regards mind as a relation are following roads which are at least parallel to one another if not actually convergent.

Whether or not one sympathizes with the views of that wing of the functionalist party to which our attention has just been directed it certainly seems a trifle unfair to cast up the mind-body difficulty in the teeth of the functionalist as such when on logical grounds he is no more guilty than any of his psychological neighbors. No courageous psychology of volition is possible which does not squarely face the mind-body problem, and in point of fact every important description of mental life contains doctrine of one kind or another upon this matter. A literally pure psychology of volition would be a sort of hanging-garden of Babylon, marvelous but inaccessible to psychologists of terrestrial habit. The functionalist is a greater sinner than others only in so far as he finds necessary and profitable a more constant insistence upon the translation of mental process into physiological process and conversely.

IV

If we now bring together the several conceptions of which mention has been made it will be easy to show them converging upon a common point. We have to consider (1) functionalism conceived as the psychology of mental operations in contrast to the psychology of mental elements; or, expressed otherwise, the psychology of the how and why of consciousness as distinguished from the psychology of the what of consciousness. We have (2) the functionalism which deals with the problem of mind conceived as primarily engaged in mediating between the environment and the needs of the organism. This is the psychology of the fundamental utilities of consciousness; (3) and lastly we have functionalism described as psychophysical psychology, that is the psychology which constantly recognizes and insists upon the essential significance of the mind-body relationship for any just and comprehensive appreciation of mental life itself.

The second and third delineations of functional psychology are rather obviously correlated with each other. No description of the actual circumstances attending the participation of mind in the accommodatory activities of the organism could be other than a mere empty schematism without making reference to the manner in which mental processes eventuate in motor phenomena of the physiological organism. The overt accommodatory act is, I take it, always sooner or later a muscular movement. But this fact being admitted, there is nothing for it, if one will describe accommodatory processes, but to recognize the mind-body relations and in some way give expression to their practical significance. It is only in this regard, as was indicated a few lines above, that the functionalist departs a trifle in his practice and a trifle more in his theory from the rank and file of his colleagues.

The effort to follow the lead of the natural sciences and delimit somewhat rigorously—albeit artificially—a field of inquiry, in this case consciousness conceived as an independent realm, has led in psychology to a deal of excellent work and to the uncovering of much hidden truth. So far as this procedure has resulted in a focusing of scientific attention and endeavor on a relatively narrow range of problems the result has more than justified the means. And the functionalist by no means holds that the limit of profitable research has been reached along these lines. But he is disposed to urge in season and out that we must not forget the arbitrary and self-imposed nature of the boundaries within which we toil when we try to eschew all explicit reference to the physical and physiological. To overlook this fact is to substitute a psychology under injunction for a psychology under free jurisdiction. He also urges with vigor and enthusiasm that a new illumination of this preëmpted field can be gained by envisaging it more broadly, looking at it as it appears when taken in perspective with its neighboring territory. And if it be objected that such an inquiry however interesting and advantageous is at least not psychology, he can only reply; psychology is what we make it, and if the correct understanding of mental phenomena involves our delving in regions which are not at first glance properly mental, what recks it, provided only that we are nowhere guilty of untrustworthy and unverifiable procedure, and that we return loaded with the booty for which we set out, and by means of which we can the better solve our problem?

In its more basal philosophy this last conception is of course intimately allied to those appraisals of mind which emphasize its dominantly social characteristics, its rise out of social circumstances and the pervasively social nature of its constitutive principles. In our previous intimations of this standpoint we have not distinguished sharply between the physical and the social aspect of environment. The adaptive activities of mind are very largely of the distinctly social type. But this does not in any way jeopardize the genuineness of the connection upon which we have been insisting between the psychophysical aspects of a functional psychology and its environmental adaptive aspects.

It remains then to point out in what manner the conception of functionalism as concerned with the basal operations of mind is to be correlated with the other two conceptions just under discussion. The simplest view to take of the relations involved would apparently be such as would regard the first as an essential propaedeutic to the other two. Certainly if we are intent upon discerning the exact manner in which mental process contributes to accommodatory efficiency, it is natural to begin our undertaking by determining what are the primordial forms of expression peculiar to mind. However plausible in theory this conception of the intrinsic logical relations of these several forms of functional psychology, in practice it is extremely difficult wholly to sever them from one another.

Again like the biological accommodatory view the psychophysical view of functional psychology involves as a rational presupposition some acquaintance with mental processes as these appear to reflective consciousness. The intelligent correlation in a practical way of physiological and mental operations evidently involves a preliminary knowledge of the conspicuous differentiations both on the side of conscious function and on the side of physiological function.

In view of the considerations of the last few paragraphs it does not seem fanciful nor forced to urged that these various theories of the problem of functional psychology really converge upon one another, however divergent may be the introductory investigations peculiar to each of the several ideals. Possibly the conception that the fundamental problem of the functionalist is one of determining just how mind participates in accommodatory reactions, is more nearly inclusive than either of the others, and so may be chosen to stand for the group. But if this vicarious duty is assigned to it, it must be on clear terms of remembrance that the other phases of the problem are equally real and equally necessary. Indeed the three things hang together as integral parts of a common program.

The functionalist's most intimate persuasion leads him to regard consciousness as primarily and intrinsically a control phenomenon. Just as behavior may be regarded as the most distinctly basic category of general biology in its functional phase so control would perhaps serve as the most fundamental category in functional psychology, the special forms and differentiations of consciousness simply constituting particular phases of the general process of control. At this point the omnipresent captious critic will perhaps arise to urge that the knowledge process is no more truly to be explained in terms of control than is control to be explained in terms of knowledge. Unquestionably there is from the point of view of the critic a measure of truth in this contention. The mechanism of control undoubtedly depends on the cognitive processes, to say nothing of other factors. But if one assumes the vitalistic point of view for one's more final interpretations, if one regards the furtherance of life in breadth and depth and permanence as an end in itself, and if one derives his scale of values from a contemplation of the several contributions toward this end represented by the great types of vital phenomena, with their apex in the moral, scientific and aesthetic realms, one must certainly find control a category more fundamental than the others offered by psychology. Moreover, it may be urged against the critic's attitude that even knowledge itself is built up under the control mechanism represented by selective attention and apperception. The basic character of control seems therefore hardly open to challenge.

One incidental merit of the functionalist program deserves a passing mention. This is the one method of approach to the problem with which I am acquainted that offers a reasonable and cogent account of the rise of reflective consciousness and its significance as manifested in the various philosophical disciplines. From the vantage point of the functionalist position logic and ethics, for instance, are no longer mere disconnected items in the world of mind. They take their place with all the inevitableness of organic organization in the general system of control, which requires for the expression of its immanent meaning *as psychic* a theoretical vindication of its own inner principles, its modes of procedure and their results. From any other point of view, so far as I am aware, the several divisions of philosophical inquiry sustain to one another relations which are almost purely external and accidental. To the functionalist on the other hand they are and must be in the nature of the case consanguineous and vitally connected. It is at the point, for example, where the good, the beautiful and the true have bearing on the efficacy of accommodatory activity that the issues of the normative philosophical sciences becomes [*sic*] relevant. If good action has no significance for the enriching and enlarging of life, the contention I urge is futile, and similarly as regards beauty and truth. But it is not at present usually maintained that such is the fact.

These and other similar tendencies of functionalism may serve to reassure those who fear that in lending itself to biological influences psychology may lose contact with philosophy and so sacrifice the poise and balance and sanity of outlook which philosophy undertakes to furnish. The particular brand of philosophy which is predestined to functionalist favor cannot of course be confidently predicted in advance. But anything approaching a complete and permanent divorce of psychology from philosophy is surely improbable so long as one cultivates the functionalist faith. Philosophy cannot dictate scientific method here any more than elsewhere, nor foreordain the special facts to be discovered. But as an interpreter of the psychologist's achievements she will always stand higher in the functionalist's favor than in that of his colleagues of other persuasions, for she is a more integral and significant part of his scheme of the cosmos. She may even outgrow under his tutelage that "valiant inconclusiveness" of which the last of her long line of lay critics has just accused her.

A sketch of the kind we have offered is unhappily likely to leave on the mind an impression of functional psychology as a name for a group of genial but vaguer ambitions and good intentions. This, however, is a fault which must be charged to the artist and to the limitations of time and space under which he is here working. There is nothing vaguer in the program of the functionalist when he goes to his work than there is in the purposes of the psychologist wearing any other livery. He goes to his laboratory, for example, with just the same resolute interest to discover new facts and new relationships, with just the same determination to verify and confirm his previous observations, as does his colleague who calls himself perhaps a structuralist. But he looks out upon the surroundings of his science with a possibly greater sensitiveness to its continuity with other ranges of human interest and with certainly a more articulate purpose to see the mind which he analyzes as it actually is when engaged in the discharge of its vital functions. If his methods tempts him now and then to sacrifice something of petty exactitude, he is under no obligation to yield, and in any case he has for his compensation the power which comes from breadth and sweep of outlook.

So far as he may be expected to develop methods peculiar to himself—so far, indeed, as in genetic and comparative psychology, for example, he has already developed such—they will not necessarily be iconoclastic and revolutionary, nor such as flout the methods already devised and established on a slightly different foundation. They will be distinctly complementary to all that is solid in these. Nor is it in any way essential that the term functionalism should cling to this new-old movement. It seems at present a convenient term, but there is nothing sacrosanct about it, and the moment it takes unto itself the pretense of scientific finality its doom will be sealed. It means to-day a broad and flexible and organic point of view in psychology. The moment it becomes dogmatic and narrow its spirit will have passed and undoubtedly some worthier successor will fill its place.

• • •

COMMENT

In this classic paper, Angell brought together the three conceptions of functionalism that he considered acceptable.

1. Functional psychology is the psychology of mental operations in contrast to the psychology of mental elements, as in structuralism. The Wundtian and Titchenerian elementism was still quite strong and Angell promoted functionalism in direct and open opposition to it. The task of functionalism is to discover how a mental process operates, what it accomplishes, and under what conditions it appears. Angell argued that a mental function, unlike a given moment of consciousness studied by the structuralists, is not a momentary perishable thing. Rather, it persists and endures in the same manner as do biological functions. Just as a physiological function may operate through different structures, a mental function may operate through ideas that are markedly different in their context.

2. Functionalism is the psychology of the fundamental utilities of consciousness. Consciousness, viewed in this utilitarian spirit, serves an end: it mediates between the needs of the organism and the demands of its environment. Thus, functionalism studies mental processes not as isolated and independent events, but as an active ongoing part of the larger biological activity and, indeed, as part of the larger movement of organic evolution. Structures and functions of the organism exist as they are because by adapting the organism to the conditions of its environment they have enabled it to survive. Angell believed that since consciousness has survived, it too, must perform an essential service that the organism could not otherwise accomplish. Functionalism had to discover precisely what this service is, for consciousness as well as for more specific mental processes, such as judging, and willing.

3. Functional psychology is the psychology of psychophysical relations concerned with the total relationship of the organism to the environment. Thus, functionalism includes all mind-body functions. This point leaves open the study of nonconscious or habitual behavior. Functionalism assumes some sort of interrelationship between the mental and the physical, an interplay of the same sort as occurs in the relation between forces in the physical world. Functionalism finds no real palpable distinction between the mind and the body, considering them not as two different entities but as belonging to the same order, and assuming an easy transfer from one to the other.

Angell's address was given at a time when the spirit of functionalism was already an established force that had attained considerable popularity and influence. Angell shaped this force into an active, visible endeavor with a laboratory, an impressive body of data, a vital and enthusiastic staff of teachers, and a core of graduate students. In guiding functionalism to the status of a formal school, he gave it the centralization necessary to make it effective.

Interestingly enough, Angell insisted that functionalism did not really constitute a school and should not be identified with the psychology taught at Chicago. He believed that the movement was much too broad in scope to be encompassed adequately within the framework of any one school. Further, he felt that the principles of functionalism had always been a part of psychology, and that it was structuralism that had broken away from the mainstream of psychology. Despite Angell's protestations, the school of functionalism flourished and was definitely associated with the kind of psychology practiced at Chicago.

HARVEY A. CARR (1873–1954)

The work of Carr represents functionalism when it ceased to be a crusade against structuralism, but had become a recognized school. Carr received his doctorate at Chicago in 1905 and succeeded Angell as chairman of the psychology department from 1919 to 1938, awarding some 150 doctorates during that time. Under Carr, Chicago functionalism reached its zenith as a formally defined system. He took the position that functional psychology is the American psychology. The work being done at Chicago was considered the psychology of the time, and as such had little need for a highly developed systematic formulation.

Alternative approaches to psychology, such as behaviorism, Gestalt psychology, and psychoanalysis, were regarded as needlessly exaggerated developments operating on more limited aspects of psychology. It was thought that these other schools had little to add to the all-encompassing functionalist psychology.

Because Carr's *Psychology* (1925) is an expression of the finished form of functionalism, it is instructive for us to consider two of its major points. Carr defined the subject matter of psychology as mental activity, *i.e.*, processes such as memory, perception, feeling, imagination, judgment, and will. The function of mental activity is to acquire, fixate, retain, organize, and evaluate experiences, and to use these experiences in the determination of action. Carr called the specific form of action in which mental activities appear adaptive or adjustive behavior.

Thus, we see a by now familiar emphasis, not on elements and the content of consciousness, but rather on mental processes. And we see a description of mental activity in terms of what it accomplishes in enabling the organism to adapt or adjust to its environment. It is significant that by 1925 these points were discussed dispassionately as statements of fact, not as matters for argument.

Discussing the methods of studying mental activity, Carr recognized the validity of both introspective and objective observation. He noted that the experimental method is the more highly desirable but admitted that adequate experimental control of the mind is a virtual impossibility. Carr also felt that the study of cultural products, such as literature, art, language, or social and political institutions, can provide information on the kind of mental activities that produced them. He also recognized the value of knowledge of the physiological processes involved in mental activity.

Obviously then, functionalism did not adhere to any one method of study, as had structuralism. In actual practice, however, there was a marked emphasis on objectivity in the functionalists' research. A great deal of the research undertaken at Chicago did not use introspection, and in those cases where it was used, it was checked as much as possible by objective controls. It is important to note that animal as well as human studies were carried out at Chicago.

Functionalism at Columbia

ROBERT SESSIONS WOODWORTH (1869–1962)

We have discussed Cattell's work, with its functionalistic orientation, while he was at Columbia University. E. L. Thorndike conducted research on learning, also of a functionalistic nature, at Columbia (see Chapter IX). A third functional psychologist working at Columbia during this period was Robert S. Woodworth.

At the outset it must be noted that this remarkable and influential man did not belong formally to the functionalist school in the tradition of Angell and Carr. Indeed, Woodworth expressed great dislike for the constraints imposed by membership in any school of thought. As he said in 1930, the kind of psychology that he developed "does not aspire to be a school. That is the very thing it does not wish to be. Personally, I have always balked on being told, as we have been told at intervals for as long as I can remember, what our marching orders are—what as psychologists we ought to be doing, and what in the divine order of the sciences psychology must be doing" (p. 327). Thus we cannot label Woodworth as a strict functionalist. Yet his work is appropriately discussed in a chapter on American functionalism because he did express and reflect a very broad, free form of functionalism that was, and still is, characteristic of American psychology. Much of what Woodworth had to say about psychology is in the functionalist spirit, but he added an important new ingredient to it.

Woodworth was active in psychology for over 70 years as a researcher, beloved teacher, writer, and editor. After receiving his BA from Amherst, he taught high school science for two years, and then mathematics in a small college for two more years, before beginning his graduate work. He received his MA from Harvard, and PhD from Columbia under

Cattell in 1899. He taught physiology in New York City hospitals for three years, and then spent a year with the famous physiologist Sherrington at Liverpool. In 1903, he returned to Columbia, where he remained until his first retirement in 1945. In 1958, at the age of 89, he retired from Columbia a second time, having continued to lecture to large classes since his first retirement!

Woodworth's list of publications is lengthy and his work greatly influenced several generations of students. His position is put forth in a number of journal articles and given fuller treatment in *Dynamic Psychology* (1918) and *Dynamics of Behavior* (1958). In 1911 he revised Ladd's *Physiological Psychology*, then wrote an introductory text, *Psychology*, that first appeared in 1921 and went through five editions by 1947. This book was so popular that it outsold every other psychology text for 25 years (Boring, 1950). His *Experimental Psychology*, written in 1938 and revised in 1954 with Harold Schlosberg, is a classic in that area. In 1931, he wrote *Contemporary Schools of Psychology*, revised in 1948 and again in 1964 with Mary Sheehan (appearing posthumously). The last two books are standard texts in many colleges and universities today.

In 1956, Woodworth received the first Gold Medal Award of the American Psychological Foundation and was cited as having made "unequaled contributions to shaping the destiny of scientific psychology," and as an "integrator and organizer of psychological knowledge" (American Psychological Foundation, 1956, p. 58).

Woodworth introduced into functionalism a dynamic psychology that seemed, in a way, a continuation of the teachings of James and Dewey. The word "dynamic" had been used as early as 1884 by Dewey and 1908 by James (Roback, 1942). The concept of a dynamic psychology (*i.e.*, a psychology concerned with change and with the interpretation of the causal factors in change) represents an interest in motivation. Woodworth had said, in 1897, that he wanted to develop a "motivology."

The first expression of Woodworth's systematic position is in his *Dynamic Psychology* of 1918, a plea for a functional kind of psychology but with the area of motivation added to it. Although there are many similarities between Woodworth's position and that of the Chicago functionalists, Woodworth more heavily stressed the physiological events underlying behavior. His dynamic psychology or motivology is concerned with cause and effect relationships though, he was quick to point out, his interest was not in ultimate causes of man's conduct, but in more immediate causes. He believed that psychology's real interest should be in determining why people behave as they do; why they feel and act in certain ways. Hence, his primary concern is with the so-called driving forces that activate the organism.

He argued that when psychology considers only the stimulus and the response in attempting to explain behavior, it is missing perhaps the most important element of all—the living organism itself. The stimulus, he said, is not the complete cause of a particular response; the organism, with its varying energy levels, its current and past experience, etc., also acts to determine the response.

> Even in a machine like a loaded gun, the action is not determined solely by the stimulus (the blow of the trigger); the structure of the gun and its stored energy (the gunpowder) must also be taken into account. In the human organism, as in the loaded gun, a stimulus, corresponding to the blow of the trigger, is necessary to start action; but the nature of the action is determined quite as much by the structure and condition of the organism itself as by the stimulus that initiates it (Heidbreder, 1933, p. 300).

Thus, according to Woodworth, psychology must consider the organism itself as interpolated between the stimulus and response. It follows that the subject matter for psychology must be both consciousness and behavior. The external stimulus as well as the overt response are both discovered by objective observation of behavior, but what happens inside the organism can best be known through introspection. Woodworth, therefore, accepted introspection as a useful, but certainly not the only legitimate, method for psychology. He also made full use of observation and experimentation.

In discussing causal sequences in behavior, Woodworth distinguished two kinds of events: mechanisms and drives. A mechanism is concerned with how a task is performed, such as the mechanical aspects of a physical movement. A drive is concerned with the question of why the task was performed. Mechanisms and drives are, however, essentially alike in that they are both responses of an organism. Mechanisms may become drives and vice versa.

This brief discussion of Woodworth's position indicates his eclectic viewpoint in psychology. He did not want to adhere to any single system, nor did he want to develop a rigid system or school of his own. His position was built not on protest but rather on growth, elaboration, and synthesis. He sought out the best features of each system of thought, and found in them common interests and goals.

Criticisms of Functionalism

Functionalism was criticized because of its rather vague definition. In 1913, C. A. Ruckmich, a student of Titchener's, examined 15 general psychology textbooks to determine how function was defined by the various writers. The two most common usages were an activity or process, and a service to other processes or to the whole organism. In the first usage, function is essentially the same as activity; for instance, remembering and perceiving are functions. In the second case, function is defined in reference to the utility of some activity to the organism, such as the function of digestion or breathing. Ruckmich suggested that the functionalists sometimes used the word function to describe an activity, and at other times to refer to the utility of an activity. It followed that one could speak of the function of an activity, or the function of a function.

It was some years before this charge of inconsistent and ambiguous definition was answered. Carr (1930) argued that the two different usages were not really inconsistent and that the same two uses are found in biology. He believed that both kinds of definition really referred to the same processes. Functionalism was interested in a particular activity for its own sake (as in the first definition) as well as in the relationship of the activity to other conditions or activities (as in the second).

It is instructive to note that Carr's analysis of this problem came considerably after the fact. As Heidbreder (1933) noted, "Functionalism used the concept first and defined it later; and this sequence of events is characteristic of the movement. . . . functionalism has never been disposed to place definition and systematization in the foreground" (p. 228).

Another criticism, particularly from Titchener, related to the definition of psychology itself. The structuralists held that functionalism was not really psychology at all, for it was not restricted to the subject matter and methodology of structuralism. Anything other than introspective analysis of the mind into elements simply was not psychology for those who followed Titchener. Of course, it was this very definition of psychology that the functionalists were questioning. To criticize functionalism because it did not follow the system it had purposely discarded seems to be a point not worth pursuing.

Other critics found fault with the functionalists' interest in activities of a practical or applied nature, stirring up the old rivalry between pure and applied science. The structuralists, we noted, did not look favorably on the application of psychology. The functionalists, however, were never really concerned with remaining "pure" and certainly never apologized for their practical interests. Carr suggested that rigorous scientific procedures can be adhered to in both pure and applied psychology; that equally valid research can be performed in an industrial setting and in a university laboratory. In the final analysis, Carr noted, it is the method and not the subject matter that determines how "scientific" a field of inquiry is. This controversy between pure and applied science no longer exists in such an extreme form in contemporary American psychology. Indeed, this aspect of functionalism might be seen today as a positive feature of the school, and not as a point of criticism.

Functionalists have sometimes been criticized for their eclecticism. They certainly were not as dogmatic as the structuralists; rather, they consistently made use of any theoretical or methodological approach considered appropriate to the solution of the problem at hand. Many see virtue in this more flexible approach to psychology, particularly since it coexisted with tough-minded insistence on proper scientific control and methodology. It is difficult to see why their more open-minded eclecticism made them any less scientifically respectable than the more close-minded structuralists.

Contributions of Functionalism

As an attitude or general viewpoint, functionalism was so successful that it became part of the mainstream of psychology. Its early vigorous opposition to structuralism was of immense value to American psychology at a time when the new science was beginning to develop. The long-range consequences of the shift in emphasis from structure to function were extremely important. One result was that the rapidly increasing research on animal behavior became a vitally important part of psychology. Animal research was in accord with a functional psychology, but was irrelevant to structural psychology, for which introspection was the indispensable tool. It was, after all, difficult to get animals to report on their experiences.

In addition to studies of animals, the functionalists' broadened definition of psychology was able to incorporate studies of children, the mentally retarded, and the insane. It also allowed psychologists to supplement the method of introspection with other ways of securing data, such as physiological research, mental tests, questionnaires, and objective descriptions of behavior. All of these methods, which were anathema to the structuralists, became respectable sources of information to psychology.

By the time Wundt died in 1920, his purely introspective form of psychology had been overshadowed by the broader, more practical approach of the functional school. The functionalist victory was undeniably complete by 1930, and in the United States today, psychology remains definitely functional in orientation.

SUGGESTED FURTHER READINGS

Dewey

Boring, E. G. John Dewey: 1859–1952. *American Journal of Psychology*, 1953, **66**, 145–147.

Angell
Miles, W. James Rowland Angell, 1869–1949, psychologist—educator. *Science,* 1949, **110**, 1–4.

Woodworth
Poffenberger, A. T. Robert Sessions Woodworth: 1869–1962. *American Journal of Psychology,* 1962, **75**, 677–692.

General
Angell, J. R. *Psychology: an introductory study of the structure and function of the human consciousness.* New York: Holt, 1904.
Carr, H. A. Functionalism. In C. Murchison (Ed.), *Psychologies of 1930.* Worcester, Mass.: Clark University Press, 1930. Pp. 59–78.
Harrison, R. Functionalism and its historical significance. *Genetic Psychology Monographs,* 1963, **68**, 387–423.
James, W. The Chicago school. *Psychological Bulletin,* 1904, **1**, 1–5.

IX

ASSOCIATIONISM

What Is Associationism?

ASSOCIATIONISM CANNOT BE as neatly categorized as the other systematic positions in the history of psychology. It is not really a school in the sense in which we have been using the term. Rather, it is more of a principle—a principle that stemmed from epistemological questions posed by philosophers from Plato and Aristotle onward.

Associationism attempts to explain man's complicated higher-order mental experiences as resulting from combinations (or associations) of simpler mental elements. The empiricist philosophers held that knowledge is derived through the senses. But what about the higher-level mental processes (thoughts, abstractions, and so on), which are not directly sensed? It was believed that these higher-level complex ideas derived from the association of simple ideas. This was the first rule of associationism. In essence, the earlier philosophical concept of associationism presaged the more sophisticated and detailed learning theories that were subsequently developed by experimental psychology. Because associationism deals with learning, its influence has extended into contemporary psychology, and associationistic ideas in one form or another were adopted by most of the schools.

Historical Overview

"Associationism of some kind is probably the oldest factor in psychological theory which has persisted to the present day" (Brett, 1930, p. 39). We find a number of philosophers discussing this notion of connections between ideas. The first attempt at formalization of the notion (in the broad sense of a "school") occurred in the eighteenth and early nineteenth centuries with the work of the British empiricists and associationists (discussed in Chapter II). This early speculative and philosophical, albeit empirical, approach helped to set the stage for the experimental attack on the problem.

152

In 1885 experimental studies of association or learning that were carried out by the German psychologist Hermann Ebbinghaus brought about a profound shift in associationism and became a milestone in the history of scientific psychology.

The great Russian physiologist, Ivan Pavlov also exerted a profound influence on the study of association by changing the kind of associations studied from ideas, which are subjective in nature and difficult to control with precision in the laboratory, to the highly objective stimulus–response (S-R) connections. He also introduced the study of the formation of associations in animals.

The first formal and experimentally based system (or, as some might prefer, miniature system) of learning was offered by the American psychologist E. L. Thorndike. His system, which influenced the development of learning theory for at least a half century, was transitional in nature insofar as it was characterized by its associationistic foundations on the one hand and by its behavior-oriented approach to experimentation on the other.

Thus, in the history of associationism as in the history of psychology as a whole, two distinct phases or eras, the philosophical and the experimental, are evident.

The Philosophical Phase

It has often been noted that Aristotle's principles of association became the foundation of the British school of associationism. Actually the concept of the association of ideas appeared first in Plato, who, in a passage from the *Phaedo*, exemplified the principles of contiguity and similarity. This passage seems to have been generally forgotten, however, and it has become traditional to begin the history of association with Aristotle's essay on *Memory*, where the fundamental point is made that one thing is apt to remind a person of another. In effect, Aristotle asked: if A reminds one of B, what is the relation between A and B; why does A remind one of B? Aristotle felt that there were three possible relations that explained association: contiguity, similarity, and contrast. Thus, A may remind one of B because they are so much alike (similarity), or because they are so vastly different (contrast), or because the two have occurred together (contiguity). The British empiricists and associationists called these three principles or relations the laws of association.

It was pointed out in Chapter II that one of the major implications of British empiricism for psychology was the creation of a need for a theory of association to account for the combining of simple elements to form more complicated structures. The development of associative processes was a topic of prime importance to the British empiricists and associationists, who attempted, with some success, to reduce Aristotle's three laws of association to the single law of contiguity. They argued that similarity and contrast alone are not sufficient conditions for the formation of associations: contiguity must also be present. There were many variations, points of disagreement, and ramifications of English associationism, but the detailing of the specific positions is not necessary in order to appreciate the overall influence of the school. In their attempts to reduce the complexities of mind to associations, the associationists developed the foundation for modern learning theory. They asked the right questions (at least in broad terms) and left it to scientific experimental psychology to phrase those questions more precisely and objectively and to find more adequate answers.

Herbert Spencer, an Englishman who was not formally allied with associationism, nevertheless influenced its prescientific phase. In Chapter VI we noted Spencer's advocacy of evolutionary principles on a broader scale than Darwin. As part of his program, he made association an evolutionary doctrine. He argued that associations that are often repeated will develop an hereditary tendency so that offspring will be likely to inherit associations that have been learned by their forebears. Thus, Spencer maintained that acquired associations can be inherited: what is learned in one generation may then be instinctive in succeeding generations.

The Newer Associationists: The Scientific Approach

Hermann Ebbinghaus

Ebbinghaus was the first psychologist to study learning and memory systematically. His work was new and important not only because it was experimental in nature but also because it studied the formation of associations—the learning process. Prior to Ebbinghaus, it was customary to start with already formed associations and "work backward," i.e., to attempt to determine how the associations had been formed. Ebbinghaus began at a different starting point, the study of the development of associations. In this way, it was possible to control the conditions under which the associations were formed and thus to make the study of learning more objective.

Considered one of the truly great manifestations of original genius in experimental psychology, Ebbinghaus successfully investigated the higher mental processes—a task that Wundt had considered impossible. Moreover, Ebbinghaus' investigation of learning and forgetting was the first venture of experimental psychology into a truly psychological problem area; one that was not simply a part of physiology. As Murphy (1949) noted, the bulk of Wundt's experimental procedure was borrowed from physiologists. "The field of experimental psychology changed immediately as Ebbinghaus entered it; his conceptions and methods soon came to be as characteristic of the 'new psychology' as were those of Wundt" (p. 175).

HIS LIFE (1850–1909) AND WORK

Born near Bonn in 1850, Ebbinghaus undertook his university studies first at Bonn in history and philology and then at Halle and Berlin. In the course of his academic training his interests shifted to philosophy, in which he received his degree in 1873, following military service during the Franco-Prussian War. The next seven years were devoted to independent study in Berlin, England, and France, where his interests shifted toward science. About 1876, Ebbinghaus bought a secondhand copy of Fechner's *Elemente der Psychophysik* at a bookstall in Paris. This chance encounter profoundly influenced him, and shortly, the new psychology. Fechner's mathematical approach to psychological phenomena was an exciting disclosure to the young Ebbinghaus, and he resolved to do for the study of memory what Fechner had done for psychophysics, through rigid systematic measurements. He wanted to apply the experimental methods to the higher mental processes and decided, probably as a result of the influence of the English associationists, to make the attempt in the field of memory.

Consider the scope of Ebbinghaus' course of action in the light of the status of the problem he chose and his own personal situation. Learning and memory had never been studied experimentally; only a few years before, the eminent Wundt had stated, in *Physiological Psychology*, that experimental methods could not be applied to the higher mental processes. Boring (1950) notes that Ebbinghaus must surely have known of this work. Further, he had no academic appointment, no university setting in which to conduct his work, no teacher, and no laboratory. Nevertheless, he carried out alone, over a period of five years, a long series of carefully controlled and thorough studies, using himself as the only subject. For the basic measure of learning he adapted a technique from the English associationists, who had gradually been emphasizing the principle of frequency of associations as a condition of recall. He reasoned that the difficulty of learning material could be measured by simply counting the number of repetitions needed to learn the material to a criterion of one perfect reproduction.

In addition to using similar (though not identical) materials to be learned, Ebbinghaus insisted upon repetition of the same task so as to be assured of the accuracy of his results. In order to cancel out variable errors from trial to trial, Ebbinghaus used, as had Fechner, the same procedure over and over again, changing only the content to be learned. Then he was able to take an average measure. So systematic was Ebbinghaus in his experimentation that he even regulated his own personal habits, keeping them as constant as possible and following the same rigid daily pattern, always learning the material at exactly the same time each day.

For the subject matter of his research, the material to be learned, Ebbinghaus invented the nonsense syllable. He recognized an inherent difficulty in using prose or poetry: meanings or associations are already attached to words by those who know the language. These already formed associations can facilitate the learning of material and, since they exist at the time of experimentation, cannot be meaningfully controlled. Ebbinghaus therefore sought material that would be uniformly unassociated, completely homogeneous, and equally unfamiliar, material with which there could not be any past associations. Nonsense syllables, formed of two consonants with a vowel in between, as in *lef, bok,* or *yat,* satisfied these criteria. He put all possible combinations of consonants and vowels on separate cards, giving him a supply of 2300 syllables from which to draw at random those to be learned.

Ebbinghaus designed a number of experiments to determine the influence of various conditions on both learning and retention. One of his earliest studies investigated the difference between his speed in memorizing lists of nonsense syllables and in memorizing meaningful materials. To determine this difference, he memorized stanzas of Byron's *Don Juan,* each stanza having 80 syllables. He found that it required about nine readings to memorize one stanza. He then memorized a list of 80 nonsense syllables and found that this task required almost 80 repetitions. He concluded that meaningless material is approximately nine times as hard to learn as meaningful material. He also investigated the effect of the length of the material to be learned on the number of repetitions necessary for a perfect reproduction, and found that longer material required more repetitions and, consequently, more time to learn. He found, further, that the average time per syllable was markedly increased by lengthening the number of syllables to be learned. These results, of course, are predictable enough in a general way; the more we have to learn, the longer it will take us. The great significance of the work is in his very careful control of conditions, his quantitative analysis of the data, and the finding that both total learning time and time per syllable increase with longer lists.

Ebbinghaus went on to investigate a number of other variables thought to influence learning and retention, such as the effect of overlearning (repeating the lists more times than necessary for one perfect reproduction), near and remote associations within lists, effect of repeated learning or review, and influence of the passage of time between learning and recall.

His research on the influence of the passage of time produced the famous Ebbinghaus curve of forgetting. This curve, as every psychology student knows, demonstrates that material is forgotten very rapidly in the first few hours after learning, and more and more slowly thereafter.

In 1880, Ebbinghaus received an academic appointment at Berlin, where he continued his research on memory, repeating and verifying his earlier studies. He published the results of all of his research in the important *Über das Gedächtnis* (*On Memory*) in 1885. "It was epoch-making, not merely because of its scope and style, although these features must have helped, but because it was seen at once to be a breach by experimental psychology in the barrier about the 'higher mental processes.' Ebbinghaus had opened up a new field . . ." (Boring, 1950, p. 388).

This book represents what is perhaps the most brilliant single investigation in the history of experimental psychology. In addition to beginning a whole new field of study (which is still vital today), it provided a striking example of great technical skill, perseverance, and ingenuity. It is not possible to find, in the entire history of psychology, any other single investigator working alone who subjected himself to such a rigid regime of experimentation. His research was so exacting, thorough, and systematic that it is still cited in modern textbooks.

Ebbinghaus did not continue research on memory but instead let others develop the field and extend and refine the methodology. Actually, he published relatively little in any area after 1885. In 1886, he was promoted to assistant professor at Berlin. He founded a laboratory and a journal (the latter with Arthur König), the *Zeitschrift für Psychologie und Physiologie der Sinnesorgane* (*Journal of Psychology and Physiology of the Sense Organs*) in 1890. A new journal was needed in Germany because Wundt's *Studien,* as the exclusive organ of the Leipzig Laboratory, could not present all the research being conducted at that time.

Apparently because of his lack of publications, Ebbinghaus was not promoted again at Berlin. In 1894, when someone else was advanced to full professor "over Ebbinghaus' head," he moved to a lesser post in the university hierarchy at Breslau, where he remained until 1905. There he developed a completion test, apparently the first successful test of the so-called higher mental capacities, a modified form of which is used in many modern-day tests of general intelligence.

In 1902, Ebbinghaus published in complete form his highly successful general text, *Die Grundzüge der Psychologie* (*The Principles of Psychology*), and in 1908 there appeared an even more popular text, *Abriss der Psychologie* (*A Summary of Psychology*). Both books went through several editions and were revised several times by others after Ebbinghaus' death. Ebbinghaus left Breslau for Halle in 1905 and died suddenly of pneumonia four years later at the age of 59.

COMMENT

Throughout his career, Ebbinghaus published relatively little, though what he did write was extremely important. He did not make any theoretical or systematic contributions to psychology; indeed, he had no formal system, no disciples of importance to psychology. He did not found a school, nor did he seem to want to. Yet, he is of great importance not only to the study of learning and memory, which he began, but also to experimental psychology as a whole. Boring commented that he was influential "because he helped to make articulate and effective the spirit of the times that called for an emancipation of psychology from philosophy" (1950, p. 392). Perhaps the clearest indication of his influence and importance to psychology is that his research findings have withstood the test of time and are still relevant to contemporary psychology.

George Elias Müller

A physiologist and philosopher by training, Müller (1850–1934) also had a strong interest in psychology. Although he did considerable work on color and extensively criticized and elaborated on Fechner's work in psychophysics, it is his research on learning that is noteworthy. He was one of the very first to work in the area begun by Ebbinghaus—the experimental study of learning and memory—and his careful research verified and extended many of Ebbinghaus' findings. Ebbinghaus' approach had been strictly objective; that is, he had not recorded any introspections about his mental processes while engaged in his learning tasks. Müller felt that Ebbinghaus' reports tended to make learning appear as too much of a mechanical or automatic process. He believed that the mind is more actively involved in the learning process, and so, while he used the objective methods of Ebbinghaus, Müller added introspective report. His results indicated that the learning of his subjects was not proceeding mechanically, that the subjects were quite actively involved in learning. They seemed to be consciously organizing and grouping the material, and even finding meanings in the nonsense syllables.

On the basis of this research, Müller concluded that association by contiguity alone cannot adequately account for learning because the subjects seemed to be actively searching for relations among the stimuli to be learned. He suggested that there is a set of mental phenomena, such as readiness, hesitation, and doubt (the so-called "conscious attitudes"), that actively influence learning. Similar findings soon followed from the work of the Würzburg laboratory.

One final contribution of Müller to the study of learning deserves mention. Along with Friedrich Schumann, Müller developed the memory drum, a revolving drum that makes possible the uniform presentation of the material to be learned. Used since in many studies of learning (and by now a familiar piece of laboratory equipment), this innovation is of importance because it increased precision and objectivity in learning research.

Ivan Petrovitch Pavlov

The influence of Ivan Pavlov is keenly felt in many areas of contemporary psychology. His work in the area of association or learning completed the shift of associationism from its traditional application to subjective ideas to completely objective and quantifiable glandular secretions and muscular movements. This change in viewpoint also served as an important antecedent to American behaviorism (see Chapter X).

THE LIFE OF PAVLOV (1849–1936)

The son of a village priest, Pavlov was born in a provincial town in central Russia. He initially attended a local theological seminary, intending to prepare for the priesthood. He changed his mind, however, and in 1870 went to the University of St. Petersburg, where he specialized in animal physiology. Miller (1962) commented that because of the university training, Pavlov joined the newly emerging third class in Russian society—the intelligentsia:

> . . . too well-educated and too intelligent for the peasantry from which he came, but too common and too poor for the aristocracy into which he could never rise. These social conditions often produced an especially dedicated intellectual, one whose entire life was centered on the intellectual pursuits that justified his existence. And so it was with Pavlov, whose almost fanatic devotion to pure science and to experimental research was supported by the energy and simplicity of a Russian peasant. Those traits characterized the man and his work throughout his life (p. 177).

He obtained his degree in 1875, completed medical training in 1883, studied in Germany for two years, and then returned to St. Petersburg for several hard years as a laboratory research assistant. In 1890, at the age of 41, he became professor of pharmacology at the Military Medical Academy of St. Petersburg and, five years later, was advanced to professor of physiology.

Pavlov's dedication to research was of paramount importance in his life. His single-mindedness of purpose was not distracted by practical issues such as salary, clothes, and living conditions. Luckily, his wife devoted her entire life to protecting him from mundane matters. (Characteristic of his indifference to practical affairs is the story that his wife often had to remind him when it was time to collect his salary.)

In his relations with others, he was given to explosive emotional tirades most often directed at his research assistants. The anecdote is told, for example, that during the Russian revolution Pavlov bitterly chastised one of his assistants for being ten minutes late for an experiment; pitched battles in the streets were not to interfere with research (Miller, 1962). Usually, however, these outbursts were quickly forgotten. His students always knew exactly what was expected of them for Pavlov never hesitated to tell them. He was always completely honest and direct, if not always considerate, in his dealings with other people.

His relations with the Soviet regime were complicated and difficult, as he was openly critical of the revolution and the Soviet government. He wrote dangerously strong, angry letters of protest to Stalin and even boycotted Russian scientific meetings to demonstrate his disapproval of the government. By 1933, he finally accepted the government and acknowledged that it had achieved some success in uniting the Russian people. For the last three years of his life he lived in peace with the government of which he had been so critical for 16 years.

Moreover, despite Pavlov's attitude, he received generous government support throughout his career for all his research, and he apparently worked in complete freedom with no pressure from the government.

PAVLOV'S RESEARCH

During his distinguished and productive career, Pavlov worked on only three research problems. The first problem was concerned with the function of the nerves of the heart and the second with the primary digestive glands. This brilliant research on digestion won for him both world-wide recognition and, in 1904, the Nobel Prize. His third research area, the one for which he is best known, was the functions of the higher nervous centers in the brain. He pursued this study with characteristic energetic determination and devotion from 1902 until his death in 1936. In his attack on this problem he made use of conditioning, which was his greatest scientific achievement. Instead of dwelling on those aspects of Pavlov's classical conditioning with which every student of psychology is familiar, we will discuss how Pavlov developed this technique, which completely changed the direction of his own career and profoundly influenced the development of psychology.

The notion of conditioned reflexes originated (as have so many scientific breakthroughs) in an accidental discovery. In his work on digestive glands, Pavlov used the method of surgical exposure of the subjects (dogs) to permit the collection and measurement of the digestive secretions at the surface of the body. The surgical operations necessary to divert the secretion of a particular gland through a tube to the outside of the body without in any way damaging the nerves and the blood supply were extremely difficult. Pavlov's amazing ingenuity and technical skill in performing these operations became legendary among physiologists.

One aspect of his work dealt with the function of saliva, which would be involuntarily secreted when food was placed in the dog's mouth. But Pavlov observed that sometimes saliva would be secreted before the food was given to the animal; there was, in other words, an anticipatory saliva flow. The dogs salivated when they saw the food or the man who regularly fed them, and even when they heard his footsteps! The reflex of secretion with its unlearned response of salivation had somehow become attached to, or conditioned to, stimuli that had previously been associated with feeding. These "psychic" reflexes (as Pavlov originally called them) were aroused in the animal by stimuli other than the original one (food), and Pavlov realized that this happened because these other stimuli (sight and sound of the attendant, etc.) had so often been associated with the ingestion of food. The associationists called this phenomenon association by frequency of occurrence.

After a long period of doubt and indecision as to whether he should follow up this observation because of its psychical nature, Pavlov decided in 1902 to investigate these psychic reflexes, and became completely absorbed in the new research. His first experiments were quite simple. Pavlov showed a dog a piece of bread in his hand before giving it to the dog to eat. In time, salivation began as soon as the dog saw the bread. The dog's response of salivation at the placing of the bread in his mouth is a natural reflexive response of the digestive system—no learning is necessary for it to occur. Accordingly, Pavlov called this an inborn or unconditioned reflex. Salivation at the sight of food, however, is not a reflexive response but rather one that must be learned. This response he called a conditional reflex (having dropped the too mentalistic term "psychic reflex") because it was conditional on the formation of an association between the sight of food and the subsequent consumption of food.

Pavlov soon discovered that any stimulus could produce the conditioned salivary response so long as it was capable of attracting the animal's attention without arousing fright or anger. He variously used such stimuli as a bell, buzzer, light, and the tick of a metronome. His typical thoroughness and precision are evidenced by the elaborate and sophisticated technique he used to collect saliva. A rubber tube was connected to the fistula; saliva flowed through this tube and onto a very delicate platform resting on a sensitive spring. As each drop struck the platform, it caused a movement that was recorded by a delicate marker on a revolving drum. This arrangement, which made it possible to record the exact number of drops as well as the precise moment at which each drop fell, is but one example of Pavlov's painstaking efforts to standardize experimental conditions, use rigid controls, and eliminate sources of error.

In addition to studying the formation of conditioned responses, Pavlov and his associates investigated a number of other well-known phenomena: reinforcement, extinction, spontaneous recovery, generalization, discrimination, and higher-order conditioning (all household words in the language of psychology today). Some 200 collaborators came to work with Pavlov and the research program extended over a longer period of time and involved more people than anything since Wundt. The conditioning situation itself was quite simple but it generated so many specific questions about its nature that answers could come only through years of patient and thorough experimentation. Pavlov gave a preliminary report on his findings in 1923, after 20 years of research. In 1926, at the age of 77, he published a more systematic account of his work. This long interval between the beginning of his research and the two reports of his findings testifies not only to the enormous scope of the problem but also to Pavlov's scientific integrity. He wanted to be certain of the accuracy and validity of his findings before making them generally known.

COMMENT

With Pavlov, more and more objective measures and terminology were introduced in the study of association or learning. Thus the area became more precise and scientifically respectable. Also, Pavlov demonstrated that higher mental processes could be effectively studied in physiological terms and with the use of animal subjects. Thus, he influenced psychology's shift to greater objectivism in subject matter and methodology. The effects of this shift are seen most strikingly in the development of behaviorism (Chapter X).

It seems quite ironic that Pavlov's greatest influence has been on psychology, a field toward which his attitude has been described as one of "pessimistic skepticism" (Watson, 1963). He believed that psychology would never achieve the status of an independent science. He completely excluded psychology from his own work, and even fined workers in his laboratory when he found them using psychological rather than physiological terminology. Woodworth and Sheehan (1964) noted that in his lectures Pavlov often made such remarks as:

In conclusion we must count it as an uncontested fact that the physiology of the highest part of the nervous system of higher animals cannot be successfully studied, unless we utterly renounce the untenable pretensions of psychology (p. 77).

When he was invited to attend the International Congress of Psychology in 1929, Pavlov replied that he did not believe psychologists would really be interested in what he had to say! This attitude did not prevent psychology from making very effective use of his work. At first, psychologists used the conditioned response to measure sensory discrimination in animals (it is still used for that purpose today). During the 1920s it began to be used, primarily in America, as the foundation for learning theories. Since then, it has generated much experimentation and theory as well as controversy.

Pavlov's immense contributions to science are widely recognized and respected, but the social and philosophical implications of his research and its effects on the conception of human nature have often been sharply attacked. "Many people have been frightened by grim visions of a brave, new world where machines will condition every child into submissive uniformity" (Miller, 1962, p. 191). Miller went on to note that "Pavlov angered the nonscientists whose preconceived notions were threatened by his discoveries. But such anger is the way we pay our greatest men. It is a special tribute reserved for those whose work is truly significant" (p. 192).

Vladimir M. Bekhterev

Another important figure in the shift of associationism from subjective ideas toward objectively observed overt behavior is Vladimir Bekhterev (1857–1927). Though generally less well known than Pavlov, this Russian physiologist, neurologist, and psychiatrist pioneered a number of important research areas. He was a contemporary and rival of Pavlov in the opening years of this century and became interested in conditioning independently of Pavlov.

Bekhterev received his degree from the Military Medical Academy in St. Petersburg in 1881. He studied abroad in Leipzig, Berlin, and Paris, and then returned to Russia to the chair of mental diseases at the University of Kazan. In 1893, he returned to the Military Medical Academy in St. Petersburg to the chair of mental and nervous diseases, and he organized a mental hospital. In 1907, he founded the Psychoneurological Institute, where he conducted a great deal of neurological research.

While Pavlov's conditioning research had been conducted almost exclusively on glandular secretions, Bekhterev was interested in the motor conditioning response, a concern that thus extended the Pavlovian conditioning principle to striped muscles. His prime concept was the "associated reflex" as revealed through the study of motor responses. He found that reflexive movements, such as withdrawing a finger from electric shock, could be elicited not only by the unconditioned stimulus (electric shock) but also by stimuli that had become associated with the original response-eliciting stimulus. For instance, the visual and auditory cues present at the time the reflex occurred soon elicited the response by themselves.

The associationists explained such connections in terms of the operation of some sort of mental process. Bekhterev, however, considered such reactions reflexive in nature. He felt that higher-level behaviors of greater complexity could be explained in the same way as a compounding of the low-level motor reflexes. To Bekhterev, thought processes themselves were of the same character in that they depended on inner activities of the speech musculature. He argued for a completely objective approach to psychological phenomena and against the use of mentalistic terms and concepts. His stand is expressed in *Objective Psychology,* published in 1907 and translated into German and French in 1913. A third edition was published in English in 1932 and called *General Principles of Human Reflexology.*

Edward Lee Thorndike

Thorndike developed a highly systematic stimulus-response form of psychology that represented a purely associationistic system. Beginning his research career with the study of learning in animals, he soon switched to human learning and developed an interest in social and educational psychology as well. Throughout his research he maintained an associationistic mode of thinking and applied associationism to a wide range of psychological phenomena.

The work of Thorndike and Pavlov is an example of simultaneous independent discovery (see Chapter I). Pavlov's law of reinforcement was developed in 1902 and Thorndike's law of effect in 1898, though it was many years before the great degree of similarity between the two was recognized.

THE LIFE OF THORNDIKE (1874–1949)

Thorndike's interest in psychology began (as for so many others) when he read James's *Principles* while an undergraduate at Wesleyan University. He later studied under James at Harvard and began his investigations of animal learning. His initial research was with chicks, which he trained to run through mazes that he improvised by placing books on end. The story is often told of Thorndike's difficulties in finding room for his chicks. Since his landlady took a dim view of his raising chicks in his bedroom, he turned to James for help. James was unsuccessful in finding space in either the laboratory or the museum, so he took Thorndike and chicks into the basement of his home, apparently to the delight of the James children.

Offered a fellowship by Cattell at Columbia, Thorndike went to New York, taking his two best-trained chicks with him. He continued his animal research at Columbia, working with cats and dogs and using puzzle boxes of his own design. He was awarded his doctorate in 1898. His thesis, *Animal Intelligence; An experimental study of the associative processes in animals,* was subsequently published along with other research on associative learning in chicks, fish, and monkeys. This classic article is reprinted in part on pages 166–178.

Thorndike became an instructor in psychology at Teachers College, Columbia, in 1899, and remained there for the rest of his career. At Cattell's suggestion, Thorndike applied his animal research techniques to children and young people; thereafter, he worked more and more with human subjects. Most of the rest of his career was spent in the areas of human learning, education, and mental testing, and he is considered a leader in the mental testing movement.

Thorndike was very prolific and his 50 years at Columbia are among the most productive ever recorded for one man. His bibliography includes 507 items, many of which are lengthy books and monographs. He "retired" in 1939, but continued working quite actively until his death ten years later.

THORNDIKE'S CONNECTIONISM

Thorndike created an experimental brand of associationism, which he called connectionism and which included several important departures from the more classical tradition. In 1931, he said that if he were to analyze man's entire mind he would:

> . . . find connections of varying strength between (a) situations, elements of situations, and compounds of situations and (b) responses, readinesses to respond, facilitations, inhibitions, and directions of responses. If all these could be completely inventoried, telling what the man would think and do and what would satisfy and annoy him, in every conceivable situation, it seems to me that nothing would be left out. . . . Learning is connecting. The mind is man's connection-system (Thorndike, 1931, p. 122).

This associationistic position was a direct descendant of the older philosophical associationism with one significant difference. Instead of talking about associations or connections between ideas, Thorndike talked about connections between situations and responses. Thus, he was able to incorporate a physiological frame of reference into his psychological theory. His study of learning also differed from classical associationism in that his subjects were animals rather than men; this method had become acceptable as an aftermath of the Darwinian notion of continuity of species.

Thorndike's conclusions were derived through the use of new research apparatus, the "puzzle box." An animal placed in the box had to learn to operate a latch in order to escape. As a measure of learning, Thorndike used the decreasing time taken by the animal to escape in successive confinements in the box. His extensive research with cats is perhaps the best known. It involved placing the cat, which had been deprived of food, in the slatted puzzle box, outside of which food had been placed as a reward for escaping. This experiment is discussed in Thorndike's classic article, *Animal Intelligence*, which follows.

•   •   •

ANIMAL INTELLIGENCE; AN EXPERIMENTAL STUDY OF THE
ASSOCIATIVE PROCESSES IN ANIMALS[1]

This monograph is an attempt at an explanation of the nature of the process of association in the animal mind. Inasmuch as there have been no extended researches of a character similar to the present one either in subject-matter or experimental method, it is necessary to explain briefly its standpoint.

Our knowledge of the mental life of animals equals in the main our knowledge of their sense-powers, of their instincts or reactions performed without experience, and of their reactions which are built up by experience. Confining our attention to the latter we find it the opinion of the better observers and analysts that these reactions can all be explained by the ordinary associative processes without aid from abstract, conceptual, inferential thinking. These associative processes then, as present in animals' minds and as displayed in their acts, are my subject-matter. Any one familiar in even a general way with the literature of comparative psychology will recall that this part of the field has received faulty and unsuccessful treatment. The careful, minute, and solid knowledge of the sense-organs of animals finds no counterpart in the realm of associations and habits. We do not know how delicate or how complex or how permanent are the possible associations of any given group of animals. And although one would be rash who said that our present equipment of facts about instincts was sufficient or that our theories about it were surely sound, yet our notion of what occurs when a chick

[1] By E. L. Thorndike. Reprinted in part from the *Psychological Review Monograph Supplements*, 1898, **2** (4), Whole No. 8, by permission of the American Psychological Association.

grabs a worm are [sic] luminous and infallible compared to our notion of what happens when a kitten runs into the house at the familiar call. The reason that they have satisfied us as well as they have is just that they are so vague. We say that the kitten associates the sound "kitty kitty" with the experience of nice milk to drink, which does very well for a commonsense answer. It also suffices as a rebuke to those who would have the kitten ratiocinate about the matter, but it fails to tell what real mental content is present. Does the kitten feel "*sound of call, memory-image of milk in a saucer in the kitchen, thought of running into the house, a feeling, finally, of 'I will run in'?*" Does he perhaps feel only the sound of the bell and an impulse to run in, similar in quality to the impulses which make a tennis player run to and fro when playing? The word association may cover a multitude of essentially different processes, and when a writer attributes anything that an animal may do to association his statement has only the negative value of eliminating reasoning on the one hand and instinct on the other. His position is like that of a zoölogist who should today class an animal among the "worms." To give to the word a positive value and several definite possibilities of meaning is one aim of this investigation.

The importance to comparative psychology in general of a more scientific account of the association-process in animals is evident. Apart from the desirability of knowing all the facts we can, of whatever sort, there is the especial consideration that these associations and consequent habits have an immediate import for biological science. In the higher animals the bodily life and preservative acts are largely directed by these associations. They, and not instinct, make the animal use the best feeding grounds, sleep in the same lair, avoid new dangers and profit by new changes in nature. Their higher development in mammals is a chief factor in the supremacy of that group. This, however, is a minor consideration. The main purpose of the study of the animal mind is to learn the development of mental life down through the phylum, to trace in particular the origin of human faculty. In relation to this chief purpose of comparative psychology the associative processes assume a rôle predominant over that of sense-powers or instinct, for in a study of the associative processes lies the solution of the problem. Sense-powers and instincts have changed by addition and supersedence, but the cognitive side of consciousness has changed not only in quantity but also in quality. Somehow out of these associative processes have arisen human consciousnesses with their sciences and arts and religions. The association of ideas proper, imagination, memory, abstraction, generalization, judgment, inference, have here their source. And in the metamorphosis the instincts, impulses, emotions and sense-impressions have been transformed out of their old natures. For the origin and development of human faculty we must look to these processes of association in lower animals. Not only then does this department need treatment more, but promises to repay the worker better.

Although no work done in this field is enough like the present investigation to require an account of its results, the *method* hitherto in use invites comparison by its contrast and, as I believe, by its faults. In the first place, most of the books do not give us a psychology, but rather a *eulogy*, of animals. They have all been about animal *intelligence*, never about animal *stupidity*. Though a writer derides the notion that animals have reason, he hastens to add that they have marvelous capacity of forming associations, and is likely to refer to the fact that human beings only rarely reason anything out, that their trains of ideas are ruled mostly by association, as if, in this latter, animals were on a par with them. The history of books on animals' minds thus furnishes an illustration of the well-nigh universal tendency in human nature to find the marvelous wherever it can. We wonder that the stars are so big and so far apart, that the microbes are so small and so thick together, and for much the same reason wonder at the things animals do. They used to be wonderful because of the mysterious, God-given faculty of instinct, which could almost remove mountains. More lately they have been wondered at because of their marvelous mental powers in profiting by experience. Now imagine an astronomer tremendously eager to prove the stars as big as possible, or a bacteriologist whose great scientific desire is to demonstrate the microbes to be very, very little! Yet there has been a similar eagerness on the part of many recent writers on animal psychology to praise the abilities of animals. It cannot help leading to partiality in deductions from facts and more especially in the choice of facts for investigation. How can scientists who write like lawyers, defending animals against the charge of having no power of rationality, be at the same time impartial judges on the bench? Unfortunately the real work in this field has been done in this spirit. The level-headed thinkers who might have won valuable results have contented themselves with arguing against the theories of the eulogists. They have not made investigations of their own.

In the second place the facts have generally been derived from anecdotes. Now quite apart from such pedantry as insists that a man's word about a scientific fact is worthless unless he is a trained scientist, there are really in this field special objections to the acceptance of the testimony about animals' intelligent acts which one gets from anecdotes. Such testimony is by no means on a par with testimony about the size of a fish or the migration of birds, etc. For here one has to deal not merely with ignorant or inaccurate testimony, but also with prejudiced testimony. Human folk are as a matter of fact eager to find intelligence in animals. They like to. And when the animal observed is a pet belonging to them or their friends, or when the story is one that has been told as a story to entertain, further complications are introduced. Nor is this all. Besides commonly misstating what facts they report, they report only such facts as show the animal at his best. Dogs get lost hundreds of times and no one ever notices it or sends an account of it to a scientific magazine. But let one find his way from Brooklyn to Yonkers and the fact immediately becomes a circulating anecdote. Thousands of cats on thousands of occasions sit helplessly yowling, and no one takes thought of it or writes to his friend, the professor; but let one cat claw at the knob of a door supposedly as a signal to be let out, and straightway this cat becomes the representative of the cat-mind in all the books. The unconscious distortion of the facts is almost harmless compared to the unconscious neglect of an animal's mental life until it verges on the unusual and marvelous. It is as if some denizen of a planet where communication was by thought-transference, who was surveying humankind and reporting their psychology, should be oblivious to all our inter-communication save such as the psychical-research society has noted. If he should further misinterpret the cases of mere coincidence of thoughts as facts comparable to telepathic communication, he would not be more wrong than some of the animal psychologists. In short, the anecdotes give really the *abnormal* or *supernormal* psychology of animals.

Further, it must be confessed that these vices have been only ameliorated, not obliterated, when the observation is first-hand, is made by the psychologist himself. For as men of the utmost skill have failed to prove good observers in the field of spiritualistic phenomena, so biologists and psychologists before the pet terrier or hunted fox often become like Samson shorn. They, too, have looked for the intelligent and unusual and neglected the stupid and normal.

Finally, in all cases, whether of direct observation or report by good observers or bad, there have been three other defects. Only a single case is studied, and so the results are not necessarily true of the type; the observation is not repeated, nor are the conditions perfectly regulated; the previous history of the animal in question is not known. Such observations may tell us, if the observer is perfectly reliable, that a certain thing takes place, but they cannot assure us that it will take place universally among the animals of that species, or universally with the same animal. Nor can the influence of previous experience be estimated. All this refers to means of getting knowledge about what animals *do*. The next question is, *"What do they feel?"* Previous work has not furnished an answer or the material for an answer to this more important question. Nothing but carefully designed, crucial experiments can. In abandoning the old method one ought to seek above all to replace it by one which will not only tell more accurately *what they do,* and give the much-needed information *how they do it,* but also inform us *what they feel* while they act.

To remedy these defects experiment must be substituted for observation and the collection of anecdotes. Thus you immediately get rid of several of them. You can repeat the conditions at will, so as to see whether or not the animal's behavior is due to mere coincidence. A number of animals can be subjected to the same test, so as to attain typical results. The animal may be put in situations where its conduct is especially instructive. After considerable preliminary observation of animals' behavior under various conditions, I chose for my general method one which, simple as it is, possesses several other marked advantages besides those which accompany experiment of any sort. It was merely to put animals when hungry in enclosures from which they could escape by some simple act, such as pulling at a loop of cord, pressing a lever, or stepping on a platform. (A detailed description of these boxes and pens will be given later.) The animal was put in the enclosure, food was left outside in sight, and his actions observed. Besides recording his general behavior, special notice was taken of how he succeeded in doing the necessary act (in case he did succeed), and a record was kept of the time that he was in the box before performing the successful pull, or clawing, or bite. This was repeated until the animal had formed a perfect association between the sense-impression of the interior of that box and the impulse leading to the successful movement. When the association was thus perfect, the time taken to escape was, of course, practically constant and very short.

If, on the other hand, after a certain time the animal did not succeed, he was taken out, but *not fed.* If, after a sufficient number of trials, he failed to get out, the case was recorded as one of complete failure. Enough different sorts of methods of escape were tried to make it fairly sure that association in general, not association of a particular sort of impulse, was being studied. Enough animals were taken with each box or pen to make it sure that the results were not due to individual peculiarities. None of the animals used had any previous acquaintance with any of the mechanical contrivances by which the doors were opened. So far as possible the animals were kept in a uniform state of hunger, which was practically utter hunger. That is, no cat or dog was experimented on when the experiment involved any important question of fact or theory, unless I was sure that his motive was of the standard strength. With chicks this is not practicable, on account of their delicacy. But with them dislike of loneliness acts as a uniform motive to get back to the other chicks. Cats (or rather kittens), dogs and chicks were the subjects of the experiments. All were apparently in excellent health, save an occasional chick.

By this method of experimentation the animals are put in situations which call into activity their mental functions and permit them to be carefully observed. One may, by following it, observe personally more intelligent acts than are included in any anecdotal collection. And this actual vision of animals in the act of using their minds is far more fruitful than any amount of histories of what animals have done without the history of how they did it. But besides affording this opportunity for purposeful and systematic observation, our method is valuable because it frees the animal from any influence of the observer. The animal's behavior is quite independent of any factors save its own hunger, the mechanism of the box it is in, the food outside, and such general matters as fatigue, indisposition, etc. Therefore the work done by one investigator may be repeated and verified or modified by another. No personal factor is present save in the observation and interpretation. Again, our method gives some very important results which are quite uninfluenced by *any* personal factor in any way.

DESCRIPTION OF APPARATUS

The shape and general apparatus of the boxes which were used for the cats is shown by the accompanying drawing [Fig. 2] of box K. Unless special figures are given, it should be understood that each box is approximately 20 inches long by 15 broad by 12 high. Except where mention is made to the contrary, the door was pulled open by a weight attached to

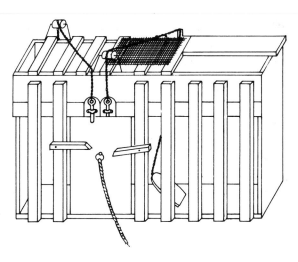

Figure 2

a string which ran over a pulley and was fastened to the door, just as soon as the animal loosened the bolt or bar which held it. Especial care was taken not to have the widest openings between the bars at all near the lever, or wire-loop, or what not, which governed the bolt on the door. For the animal instinctively attacks the large openings first, and if the mechanism which governs the opening of the door is situated near one of them the animal's task is rendered easier. You do not then get the association process so free from the helping hand of instinct as you do if you make the box without reference to the position of the mechanism to be set up within it. These various mechanisms are so simple that a verbal description will suffice in most cases. The facts which the reader should note are the nature of the movement which the cat had to make, the nature of the object at which the movement was directed, and the position of the object in the box. In some special cases attention will also be called to the force required. In general, however, that was very slight (20 to 100 grams if applied directly). The various boxes will be designated by capital letters.

A. A string attached to the bolt which held the door ran up over a pulley on the front edge of the box, and was tied to a wire loop (2½ inches diameter) hanging 6 inches above the floor in front center of box. Clawing or biting it, or rubbing against it even, if in a certain way, opened the door. We may call this box A *"O at front."*

B. A string attached to the bolt ran up over a pulley on the front edge of the door, then across the box to another pulley screwed into the inside of the back of the box 1¼ inches below the top, and passing over it ended in a wire loop (3 inches in diameter) 6 inches above the floor in back center of box. Force applied to the loop or *to the string* as it ran across the top of the box between two bars would open the door. We may call B *"O at back."*

B1. In B1 the string ran outside the box, coming down through a hole at the back, and was therefore inaccessible and invisible from within. Only by pulling the loop could the door be opened. B1 may be called *"O at back 2nd."*

C. A door of the usual position and size [as in Fig. 2] was kept closed by a wooden button 3½ inches long, ⅞ inch wide, ½ inch thick. This turned on a nail driven into the box ½ inch above the middle of the top edge of the door. The door would fall inward as soon as the button was turned from its vertical to a horizontal position. A pull of 125 grams would do this if applied sideways at the lowest point of the button 2¼ inches below its pivot. The cats usually clawed the button round by downward pressure on its top edge, which was 1¼ inches above the nail. Then, of course, more force was necessary. C may be called *"Button."*

D. The door was in the extreme right of the front. A string fastened to the bolt which held it ran up over a pulley on the top edge and back to the top edge of the back side of the box (3 inches in from the right side) and was there firmly fastened. The top of the box was of wire screening and arched over the string ¾ inch above it along its entire length. A slight pull on the string anywhere opened the door. This box was 20 × 16, but a space 7 × 16 was partitioned off at the left by a wire screen. D may be called "*String.*"

D1 was the same box as B, but had the string fastened firmly at the back instead of running over a pulley and ending in a wire loop. We may call it "*String 2nd.*"

E. A string ran from the bolt holding the door up over a pulley and down to the floor outside the box, where it was fastened 2 inches in front of the box and 1½ inches to the left of the door (looking from the inside). By poking a paw between the bars and pulling this string inward the door would be opened. We may call E "*String outside.*"

EXPERIMENTS WITH CATS

In these various boxes were put cats from among the following. I give approximately their ages while under experiment.

No. 1. 8–10 months	No. 7. 3–5 months
No. 2. 5–7 months	No. 8. 6–6½ months
No. 3. 5–11 months	No. 10. 4–8 months
No. 4. 5–8 months	No. 11. 7–8 months
No. 5. 5–7 months	No. 12. 4–6 months
No. 6. 3–5 months	No. 13. 18–19 months

The behavior of all but 11 and 13 was practically the same. When put into the box the cat would show evident signs of discomfort and of an impulse to escape from confinement. It tries to squeeze through any opening; it claws and bites at the bars or wire; it thrusts its paws out through any opening and claws at everything it reaches; it continues its efforts when it strikes anything loose and shaky; it may claw at things within the box. It does not pay very much attention to the food outside, but seems simply to strive instinctively to escape from confinement. The vigor with which it struggles is extraordinary. For eight or ten minutes it will claw and bite and squeeze incessantly. With 13, an old cat, and 11, an uncommonly sluggish cat, the behavior was different. They did not struggle vigorously or continually. On some occasions they did not even struggle at all. It was therefore necessary to let them out of some box a few times, feeding them each time. After they thus associate climbing out of the box with getting food, they will try to get out whenever put in. They do not, even then, struggle so vigorously or get so excited as the rest. In either case, whether the impulse to struggle be due to an instinctive reaction to confinement or to an association, it is likely to succeed in letting the cat out of the box. The cat that is clawing all over the box in her impulsive struggle will probably claw the string or loop or button so as to open the door. And gradually all the other non-successful impulses will be stamped out and the particular impulse leading to the successful act will be stamped in by the resulting pleasure, until, after many trials, the cat will, when put in the box, immediately claw the button or loop in a definite way.

The starting point for the formation of any association in these cases, then, is the set of instinctive activities which are aroused when a cat feels discomfort in the box either because of confinement or a desire for food. This discomfort, plus the sense-impression of a surrounding, confining wall, expresses itself prior to any experience, in squeezings, clawings, bitings, etc. From among these movements one is selected by success. But this is the starting point only in the case of the first box experienced. After that the cat has associated with the feeling of confinement certain impulses which have led to success more than others and are thereby strengthened. A cat that has learned to escape from A by clawing has when put into C or G a greater tendency to claw at things than it instinctively had at the start, and a less tendency to squeeze through holes. A very pleasant form of this decrease in instinctive impulses was noticed in the gradual cessation of howling and mewing. However, the useless instinctive impulses die out slowly, and often play an important part even after the cat has had experience with six or eight boxes. And what is important in our previous statement, namely, that the activity of an animal when first put into a new box is not directed by any appreciation of *that* box's character, but by certain general impulses to acts, is not affected by this modification. Most of this activity is determined by heredity; some of it, by previous experience.

My use of the words *instinctive* and *impulse* may cause some misunderstanding unless explained here. Let us . . . understand by instinct any reaction which an animal makes to a situation *without experience*. It thus includes unconscious as well as conscious acts. Any reaction, then, to totally new phenomena, when first experienced, will be called instinctive. Any impulse then felt will be called an instinctive impulse. Instincts include whatever the nervous system of an animal, as far as inherited, is capable of. My use of the word will, I hope, everywhere make clear what fact I mean. If the reader gets the fact meant in mind it does not in the least matter whether he would himself call such a fact instinct or not. Any one who objects to the word may substitute "hocus-pocus" for it wherever it occurs. The definition here made will not be used to prove or disprove any theory, but simply as a signal for the reader to imagine a certain sort of fact.

The word *impulse* is used against the writer's will, but there is no better. Its meaning will probably become clear as the reader finds it in actual use, but to avoid misconception at any time I will state now that *impulse* means the consciousness accompanying a muscular innervation *apart* from *that feeling of the act which comes from seeing oneself move, from feeling one's body in a different position, etc.* It is the *direct feeling of the doing* as distinguished from the *idea of the act done* gained through eye, etc. For this reason I say "impulse *and* act" instead of simply "act." Above all, it must be borne in mind that by impulse I never mean the *motive* to the act. In popular speech you may say that hunger is the impulse which makes the cat claw. That will never be the use here. The word *motive* will always denote that sort of consciousness. Any one who thinks that the act ought not to be thus subdivided into impulse and deed may feel free to use the word *act* for *impulse* or *impulse and act* throughout, if he will remember that the act in this aspect of being felt as to be done or as doing is in animals the important thing, is the thing which gets associated, while the act as done, as viewed from outside, is a secondary affair. I prefer to have a separate word, impulse, for the former, and keep the word act for the latter, which it commonly means.

Starting, then, with its store of instinctive impulses, the cat hits upon the successful movement, and gradually associates it with the sense-impression of the interior of the box until the connection is perfect, so that it performs the act as soon as confronted with the sense-impression. The formation of each association may be represented graphically by a time-curve. In these curves lengths of one millimeter along the abscissa represent successive experiences in the box, and heights of one millimeter above it each represent ten seconds of time. The curve is formed by joining the tops of perpendiculars erected along the abscissa 1 mm. apart (the first perpendicular coinciding with the y line), each perpendicular representing the time the cat was in the box before escaping. Thus, in Fig. [3] . . . the curve marked 12 in A shows that, in 24 experiences or trials in box A, cat 12 took the following times to perform the act, 160 sec., 30 sec., 90 sec., 60, 15, 28, 20, 30, 22, 11, 15, 20, 12, 10, 14, 10, 8, 8, 5, 10, 8, 6, 6, 7. A short vertical line below the abscissa denotes that an interval of approximately 24 hours elapsed before the next trial. Where the interval was longer it is designated by a figure 2 for two days, 3 for three days, etc. If the interval was shorter

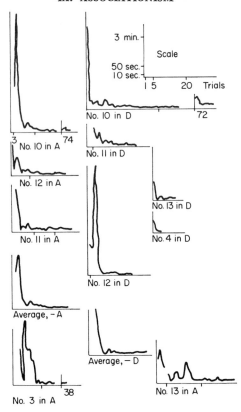

Figure 3

the number of hours is specified by 1 hr., 2 hrs., etc. In many cases
the animal failed in some trial to perform the act in ten or fifteen minutes
and was then taken out by me. Such failures are denoted by a break
in the curve either at its start or along its course. In some cases there
are short curves after the main ones. These, as shown by the figures
beneath, represent the animal's mastery of the association after a very
long interval of time, and may be called memory curves.

CONCLUSION

I do not think it is advisable here, at the close of this paper, to
give a summary of its results. The paper itself is really only such a
summary with the most important evidence, for the extent of territory
covered and the need of brevity have prevented completeness in explanation or illustration. If the reader cares here, at the end, to have the
broadest possible statement of our conclusions and will take the pains

to supply the right meaning, we might say that our work has described a method, crude but promising, and has made the beginning of an exact estimate of just what associations, simple and compound, an animal can form, how quickly he forms them, and how long he retains them. It has described the method of formation, and, on the condition that our subjects were representative, has rejected reason, comparison or inference, perception of similarity, and imitation. It has denied the existence in animal consciousness of any important stock of free ideas or impulses, and so has denied that animal association is homologous with the association of human psychology. It has homologized it with a certain limited form of human association. It has proposed, as necessary steps in the evolution of human faculty, a vast increase in the number of associations, signs of which appear in the primates, and a freeing of the elements thereof into independent existence. It has given us an increased insight into various mental processes. It has convinced the writer, if not the reader, that the old speculations about what an animal could do, what it thought, and how what it thought grew into what human beings think, were a long way from the truth, and *not on the road to it*.

Finally, I wish to say that, although the changes proposed in the conception of mental development have been suggested somewhat fragmentarily and in various connections, that has not been done because I think them unimportant. On the contrary, I think them of the utmost importance. I believe that our best service has been to show that animal intellection is made up of a lot of specific connections, whose elements are restricted to them, and which subserve practical ends *directly*, and to homologize it with the intellection involved in such human associations as regulate the conduct of a man playing tennis. The fundamental phenomenon which I find presented in animal consciousness is one which can harden into inherited connections and reflexes, on the one hand, and thus connect naturally with a host of the phenomena of animal life; on the other hand, it emphasizes the fact that our mental life has grown up as a mediation between stimulus and reaction. The old view of human consciousness is that it is built up out of elementary sensations, that very minute bits of consciousness come first and gradually get built up into the complex web. It looks for the beginnings of consciousness to *little* feelings. This our view abolishes and declares that the progress is not from little and simple to big and complicated, but from direct connections to indirect connections in which a stock of isolated elements plays a part, is from "pure experience" or undifferentiated feelings, to discrimination, on the one hand, to generalizations, abstractions, on the other. If, as seems probable, the primates display a vast increase of associations, and a stock of free-swimming ideas, our view gives to the line of descent a meaning which it never could have so long as the question was the vague one of more or less "intelligence." It will, I hope, when supported by an investigation of the mental life of the primates and of the period in child life when these directly practical associations become overgrown by a rapid luxuriance of free ideas, show us the real history of the origin of human faculty. It turns out apparently that a modest study of the facts of association in animals has given us a working hypothesis for a comparative psychology.

•   •   •

COMMENT

Thorndike speaks of the "stamping in" or "stamping out" of a response tendency by its favorable or unfavorable results. He noted that all the nonsuccessful response tendencies (those that do nothing to get the cat out of the box) are stamped out over a number of trials. On the other hand, response tendencies that do lead to success are stamped in after a number of trials. After many trials, the cat, when placed in the box, immediately performs the correct responses leading to escape. Thorndike called this kind of learning "trial and error learning."

This stamping in or out of a response tendency was formalized in 1905 as Thorndike's famous law of effect.

> Any act which in a given situation produces satisfaction becomes associated with that situation, so that when the situation recurs the act is more likely than before to recur also. Conversely, any act which in a given situation produces discomfort becomes disassociated from that situation, so that when the situation recurs the act is less likely than before to recur (Thorndike, 1905, p. 203).

A companion law is the law of exercise or of use or disuse, which says that any response made in a particular situation becomes associated with the situation. The more the response is used in the situation, the more strongly it becomes associated with it. Conversely, prolonged disuse of the response tends to weaken the association. In other words, sheer repetition of any response in the situation tends to strengthen that response. Thorndike's later research convinced him that sheer repetition of a response is relatively ineffective compared to the reward consequences of the response.

In the early 1930s, Thorndike further examined his law of effect in an extensive program of research using human subjects. The results revealed that rewarding a response did indeed strengthen that response but punishment of a response did not produce a comparable negative effect. He revised the law of effect in the light of these results, placing a much greater emphasis on reward than on punishment.

Thorndike's pioneer investigations into the fields of human and animal learning are among the greatest in the history of psychology. His theory of associationism or learning served to herald the rapid rise of learning theory to its present prominent position. Although new learning theories and models have appeared since Thorndike's work, the significance of his contributions remains secure. His influence declined with the advent of more sophisticated learning systems, but his work remains a cornerstone of associationism.

Associationism and the Zeitgeist

Herrnstein and Boring (1965) noted that the early investigations that set the pattern for most subsequent research on learning were undertaken within a period of less than 20 years (1885–1904). How can we explain this emergence of experimentation on association and the whole new field that it spawned?

It could not have been due to a suddenly awakened interest in the learning process, for as we have seen, speculative inquiry into associative processes had been going on for centuries. Nor could it have been the result of technical advances, for the basic methods used in these early learning studies were simple enough to have been devised much earlier.

The answer seems to lie, as usual, in the *Zeitgeist*. We have discussed the growing emphasis on and confidence in science in general and scientific experimental psychology in particular. This increasing awareness of and interest in the application of scientific method to the mind seems to have encouraged men to begin experimental investigation of problems of learning. The many resulting scientific successes have "stamped in" this behavior not only in the study of learning but also in other areas of psychology.

Criticisms of Associationism

Two points of criticism leveled against associationism in general are concerned with its elementism and mechanistic determinism, as noted by Marx and Hillix (1963). Associationism, from the British philosophers to the present day, is indeed an elementistic position, and those who oppose the analysis of behavior into elements are thus opposed to associationism. Those who want psychology to concern itself with the totality of human behavior argue that the attempt to reduce behavior to elements, such as stimulus-response connections, produces a highly artificial view of behavior. (Behaviorism is opposed by the same critics for the same reason.) The validity of this criticism cannot yet be answered. Although the elemental or molecular approach to the study of behavior has provided a great deal of useful data, supporters of the global or molar approach make the same claim. These contrasting and often conflicting approaches are examined later in our discussions of behaviorism and Gestalt psychology. History will make its judgment in time.

The other point of criticism, that of mechanistic determinism, is also made against behaviorism. The feeling is widespread among nonscientists that a mechanistic scientific psychology, such as Thorndike's brand of associationism or Pavlov's conditioning, degrades and perhaps even destroys human values. These critics take offense at the notion that man's behavior is the product of specific antecedent conditions, which, once known, can be used to anticipate and control (or at least attempt to determine) his behavior. The deterministic viewpoint, of course, is in direct opposition to the tradition that regards man as a free agent.

Thorndike countered this charge, in his *Selected Writings from a Connectionist's Psychology* (1949), by arguing that the only way in which man can improve himself and his social order is by discovering "causal" sequences of his behavior and being able to describe his world as one where the same cause consistently produces the same result. Man "can determine the fate of the world and his own best, not by prayers or threats, but by treating it and himself by the method of science as phenomena, determined, as far as he can see, by their past history" (p. 347). In one of the most effective passages ever addressed to this question, he wrote:

> Thus, at last, man may become ruler of himself as well as of the rest of nature. For strange as it may sound man is free only in a world whose every event he can understand and foresee. Only so can he guide it. We are captains of our own souls only in so far as they act in perfect law so that we can understand and foresee every response which we will make to every situation. Only so can we control our own selves. It is only because our intellects and morals—the mind and spirit of man—are a part of nature, that we can be in any significant sense responsible for them, proud of their progress, or trustful of their future (Thorndike, 1949, p. 362).

Since the problem of mechanistic determinism is one of the key issues in the continuing battle between science and its opponents, we will touch on the point again.

Contemporary Status of Associationism

The primary task of both associationism and science involves the search for functional relationships between variables. Actually, associationism shares this goal with functionalism; indeed, the two movements have been closely associated, at least in this country.

Associationism, however, is a special kind of functionalism, for one could certainly be, like James and Dewey, a functionalist and not an associationist. By the same token, one could be an associationist and accept nothing but the common methodological orientations from functionalism. Also, most associationists deal with a restricted range of behavior (learning), whereas functionalists are generally not so constrained.

Associationism today has been almost completely absorbed into psychology; at least as a technique, if not as a formal systematic position. The issue of exactly what is to be associated remains important, however, and has been attacked by several more refined varieties of associationism of more recent origin. Some of these newer developments along behavioristic lines are discussed in Chapters X and XI.

The general notion of association has been accorded an important role in psychology and it is noteworthy that such an old and basic notion has persisted for such a long period of time. This longevity is dramatic evidence of the vitality of the concept of mind as a "connection-system."

SUGGESTED FURTHER READINGS

Ebbinghaus
Shakow, D. Hermann Ebbinghaus. *American Journal of Psychology*, 1930, **42**, 505–518.

Müller
Boring, E. G. Georg Elias Müller, 1850–1934. *American Journal of Psychology*, 1935, **47**, 344–348.

Pavlov
Babkin, B. P. *Pavlov: a biography*. Chicago: University of Chicago Press, 1949.
Pavlov, I. P. *Selected works*. Trans. S. Belsky. Moscow: Foreign Languages Publishing House, 1955.
Pavlov, I. P. *Lectures on conditioned reflexes*. Trans. W. H. Gantt. New York: Liveright, 1928.
Pavlov, I. P. *Conditioned reflexes*. Trans. G. V. Anrep. London and New York: Oxford University Press, 1927.

Thorndike
Postman, L. The history and present status of the Law of Effect. *Psychological Bulletin*, 1947, **44**, 489–563.

General
Warren, H. C. *A history of the association psychology*. New York: Scribner's, 1921.

Contemporary Learning Theory
Bugelski, B. R. *The psychology of learning*. New York: Holt, 1956.
Deese, J. *The psychology of learning*. New York: McGraw-Hill, 1958.
Hilgard, E. R. *Theories of learning*. (2nd ed.) New York: Appleton-Century-Crofts, 1956.

X

BEHAVIORISM: THE BEGINNING

Introduction

DURING THE PERIOD when structuralism was at its height and the two decades when functionalism developed to maturity, a revolt directed in part against both these schools was being formulated. The revolution formally began in 1913 with the publication of an article by John B. Watson, the 35-year-old founder of the new psychology: behaviorism.

Watson's article, the manifesto of the new movement, was a broad, slashing attack on the existing systems of psychology. The old order, it stated, was a failure and had to give way to behaviorism if psychology were to advance. In relatively little time, the older views were largely abandoned, and behaviorism became the most influential (and controversial) American system of psychology. Moreover, it assumed a prominent role in the cultural and social life of the times.

The boldly simple tenets of Watson's behaviorism included one main positive point and one main negative point. On the positive side, Watson argued for a totally objective psychology—the science of behavior—dealing only with observable behavioral acts that were to be objectively described in such terms as stimulus and response. He wanted to apply to human beings the experimental procedures and principles of animal psychology, a field in which he had been active.

Watson's positive interest sheds light on what he wanted to discard. If behavioristic psychology were to be an objective science, all mentalistic concepts and terms would have to be rejected. Such terms as "image," "mind," and "consciousness," carry-overs from mental philosophy, were meaningless, and the technique of introspection, which assumed the existence of conscious processes, was irrelevant. After examining the antecedents of behaviorism, we will discuss Watson's life and system, including his original article on behaviorism.

182

Historical Overview

Watsonian behaviorism grew out of three major trends: (*a*) the philosophical tradition of objectivism, (*b*) functionalism, and (*c*) animal psychology. Watson's insistence on the need for increased objectivity in psychology was by no means new. The movement has a long history, beginning perhaps with Descartes, whose attempts at mechanistic explanations of the body and mind were among the first steps in the direction of greater objectivity.

More important in the history of objectivism is Auguste Comte (1798–1857), founder of the movement called *positivism*, which emphasized positive knowledge, the truth of which is not debatable, as discussed in Chapter II. According to Comte, the only valid knowledge is that which is social in nature and objectively observable. These criteria rule out introspection, which depends on a private consciousness that cannot be objectively observed. Comte vigorously protested against mentalism and subjective methodology.

The second antecedent of behaviorism is functionalism. Although functional psychology is not totally objective, in Watson's day it represented an increase in objectivity over its predecessors. Cattell and other functionalists who moved in the direction of emphasizing behavior and more objective methods had expressed some dissatisfaction with introspection. The various applied areas of interest to the functionalists paid little attention to consciousness and introspection and were essentially an objective functional psychology.

James Angell, perhaps the most forward-looking functionalist, foresaw that American psychology, already functional, was ready to move further in the direction of objectivity. In 1910, for example, he commented that it seemed highly possible that the term "consciousness" would disappear from psychology much as had the term "soul." In 1913, shortly before Watson's manifesto, Angell elaborated on this point, suggesting that it would be profitable if the "possible existence" of consciousness were forgotten and that animal and human behavior be described objectively instead.

Probably the most important single antecedent to the development of Watson's program was animal psychology, which, as we know, grew out of evolutionary theory and led to attempts to demonstrate the presence of mind in lower organisms and the continuity between the human and animal minds.

We discussed the work of two pioneer animal psychologists, George Romanes and C. Lloyd Morgan (see Chapter VI). An influential animal researcher who worked mainly in this country was the German zoologist and physiologist Jacques Loeb (1859–1924). Loeb developed an explanatory theory of animal behavior based on the concept of *tropism* or forced movement. According to tropistic theory, the animal's response is a direct function of the stimulus. In this sense, the behavior is forced and does not require any explanation in terms of consciousness. Loeb became the leader of the mechanistic movement and his work emphasized experimental methods and deemphasized the role of consciousness.

At the beginning of the twentieth century, the study of animal behavior within a biological framework was becoming widespread. During this same time, experimental animal psychology (*e.g.*, the work of Thorndike) developed rapidly. Robert Yerkes began animal studies in 1900 and his work, using a wide range of animals, greatly strengthened the position and influence of comparative psychology. Also in 1900, the rat maze was introduced by W. S. Small, and the white rat and the maze became the standard means of studying learning.

Laboratories of comparative psychology were being established and many universities began offering courses in the area. In 1911, the *Journal of Animal Behavior*, which later became the *Journal of Comparative Psychology*, was begun. At the same time, the work of Pavlov, which greatly supported objective psychology in general and Watson's behaviorism in particular, was becoming known in the United States.

There is one additional, and more subtle, influence on the development of behaviorism—the *Zeitgeist*: American psychology was indeed ready for behaviorism.

> That American psychology was ready for such a program had been made abundantly plain by the hospitality it had shown functionalism. For the same conditions that ensured for functionalism an interested hearing paved the way for behaviorism's more spectacular victory. Practically, behaviorism did what functionalism did, and did it more dramatically. It cut the Gordian knot, which functionalism had merely loosened to give psychology a wider tether. . . . The simple fact is that American psychologists had grown restive under conventional restraints. They were finding the old problems lifeless and thin, they were "half sick of shadows," and turning gladly toward something that seemed more alive and substantial, they welcomed a plain, downright revolt. For behaviorism was far more satisfactory than functionalism as a release from repression. It called upon its followers to fight an enemy who must be utterly destroyed, not merely to parley with one who might be induced to modify his ways (Heidbreder, 1933, p. 239).

The Founding of Behaviorism: John B. Watson

Behaviorism was officially launched in 1913 when John B. Watson began his vigorous campaign against introspection and for an objective psychology.

Watson was born on a farm outside of Greenville, South Carolina, where his early education was conducted in a one-room schoolhouse. The Watsons later moved into Greenville and 12-year-old John attended public schools. His family was very religious and he was originally intended for the ministry. Watson described himself as being somewhat lazy and insubordinate and as never earning more than just passing grades. His teachers remember him as indolent, argumentative, and not easily controlled. He grew up in what Bakan (1966) described as a state of semidelinquency. He fought a great deal and was twice arrested, once for shooting firearms within the city limits. It was not exactly a promising beginning! Nevertheless, he entered Furman University in Greenville at age 16 and obtained an MA in five years.

An interest in philosophy led Watson to pursue graduate study at the University of Chicago under John Dewey. He reported that he found Dewey "incomprehensible" and his enthusiasm for philosophy rather quickly diminished, though he did continue it as a minor. Watson became interested in psychology under the influence of Angell and he took a second minor in neurology; in addition, he studied biology and physiology under Jacques Loeb. Besides his courses, he worked at various jobs, such as a waiter in a fraternity house, a rat caretaker, and an assistant (!) janitor. Toward the end of his graduate studies he suffered a breakdown during which he experienced acute attacks of anxiety and an inability to sleep without a light on, among other symptoms.

In 1903, he received his PhD, married, and remained at the University of Chicago as an instructor until 1908. In his years at Chicago as both student and instructor, Watson engaged in much research, demonstrating early his preference for animal subjects. As he stated in his autobiographical sketch:

> I never wanted to use human subjects. I hated to serve as a subject. I didn't like the stuffy, artificial instructions given to subjects. I always was uncomfortable and acted unnaturally. With animals I was at home. I felt that, in studying them, I was keeping close to biology with my feet on the ground. More and more the thought presented itself: Can't I find out by watching their behavior everything that the other students are finding out by using O's [observers]? (J. B. Watson, 1936, p. 276).

In 1908, Watson was eligible for an assistant professorship at Chicago when he was offered a full professorship at Johns Hopkins University. He was reluctant to leave Chicago but the opportunity to direct the laboratory, the increase in rank, and the substantial increase in salary offered by Hopkins left him little choice. He remained at Hopkins until 1920 and these twelve years were his most productive in psychology.

Watson said that he began thinking about a more objective approach to psychology around 1903. His thoughts on the subject were expressed publicly for the first time in 1908 in a lecture at Yale University. In 1912, he again spoke on the subject in a series of lectures at Columbia University. The following year saw the publication of his famous position paper, and behaviorism was officially launched.

Watson's first book, *Behavior: An Introduction to Comparative Psychology*, appeared in 1914. It argued strongly for the acceptance of animal psychology and stressed the advantages of using animals as subjects in psychological research. Watsonian behaviorism appealed to many younger psychologists who felt that Watson was cleansing the polluted atmosphere of psychology by casting off the long-standing mysteries and uncertainties carried over from philosophy. The rapid acceptance of his position was evidenced by his election to the presidency of the American Psychological Association in 1915—just two years after his paper appeared. He was then 37 years of age.

Watson's professional activities were interrupted by his tour in the Army Aviation Service as a major during World War I. After the war, in 1918, Watson conducted research on young children, one of the earliest attempts at experimental work on human infants. His second book, *Psychology from the Standpoint of a Behaviorist*, appeared in 1919.

Watson's highly promising academic career had lasted only 17 years when it ended, abruptly, in 1920. The sensationalized nationwide publicity accorded divorce proceedings brought against him resulted in his being asked to resign from Johns Hopkins, and he never returned to a full-time university position. In that same eventful year he married his former laboratory assistant, who had worked with him in the earlier studies of infant behavior (including the famous "Albert" study of conditioned fear). In 1921, he undertook an entirely different professional career in the field of advertising. He joined the J. Walter Thompson agency, worked in every department, and made house-to-house surveys, sold coffee, and clerked in Macy's in order to learn about the business world. With characteristic enterprise and success, Watson was made vice-president only three years later. In 1936, he joined another advertising agency where he remained as vice-president until his retirement in 1945.

He maintained contact with psychology for a while through popular articles in such magazines as *Collier's*, *McCall's*, and *Harper's*, and through two more books. He lectured at the New School for Social Research in New York and out of these lectures came his semipopular book, *Behaviorism* (1925), which contained a positive program for the improvement of society. This book attracted considerable attention, both favorable and unfavorable, from the lay public. In 1928, he published a book on child care (*Psychological Care of the Infant and Child*), in which he presented a regulatory, as opposed to a permissive, system of child-rearing in keeping with his strong environmentalistic position. This was "a book he later publicly regretted" (Skinner, 1959, p. 198). In 1930, he revised *Behaviorism*—his last professional activity in psychology. He died in 1958 after a long illness.

WATSON'S BEHAVIORISM

There is probably no better starting point for a discussion of Watson's behaviorism than the article that began the movement.

• • •

PSYCHOLOGY AS THE BEHAVIORIST VIEWS IT[1]

Psychology as the behaviorist views it is a purely objective experimental branch of natural science. Its theoretical goal is the prediction and control of behavior. Introspection forms no essential part of its methods, nor is the scientific value of its data dependent upon the readiness with which they lend themselves to interpretation in terms of consciousness. The behaviorist, in his efforts to get a unitary scheme of animal response, recognizes no dividing line between man and brute. The behavior of man, with all of its refinement and complexity, forms only a part of the behaviorist's total scheme of investigation.

It has been maintained by its followers generally that psychology is a study of the science of the phenomena of consciousness. It has taken as its problem, on the one hand, the analysis of complex mental states (or processes) into simple elementary constituents, and on the other the construction of complex states when the elementary constituents are given. The world of the physical objects (stimuli, including here anything which may excite activity in a receptor), which forms the total phenomena of the natural scientist, is looked upon merely as means to an end. That end is the production of mental states that may be "inspected" or "observed." The psychological object of observation in the case of an emotion, for example, is the mental state itself. The problem in emotion is the determination of the number and kind of elementary constituents present, their loci, intensity, order of appearance, etc. It is agreed that introspection is the method *par excellence* by means of which mental states may be manipulated for purposes of psychology. On this assumption, behavior data (including under this term everything which goes under the name of comparative psychology)

[1] By John B. Watson. Reprinted in part from the *Psychological Review*, 1913, **20**, 158–177, by permission of the American Psychological Association.

have no value *per se*. They possess significance only in so far as they may throw light upon conscious states. Such data must have at least an analogical or indirect reference to belong to the realm of psychology.

Indeed, at times, one finds psychologists who are sceptical of even this analogical reference. Such scepticism is often shown by the question which is put to the student of behavior, "what is the bearing of animal work upon human psychology?" I used to have to study over this question. Indeed it always embarrassed me somewhat. I was interested in my own work and felt that it was important, and yet I could not trace any close connection between it and psychology as my questioner understood psychology. I hope that such a confession will clear the atmosphere to such an extent that we will no longer have to work under false pretences. We must frankly admit that the facts so important to us which we have been able to glean from extended work upon the senses of animals by the behavior method have contributed only in a fragmentary way to the general theory of human sense organ processes, nor have they suggested new points of experimental attack. The enormous number of experiments which we have carried out upon learning have likewise contributed little to human psychology. It seems reasonably clear that some kind of compromise must be effected: either psychology must change its viewpoint so as to take in facts of behavior, whether or not they have bearings upon the problems of "consciousness"; or else behavior must stand alone as a wholly separate and independent science. Should human psychologists fail to look with favor upon our overtures and refuse to modify their position, the behaviorists will be driven to using human beings as subjects and to employ methods of investigation which are exactly comparable to those now employed in the animal work.

Any other hypothesis than that which admits the independent value of behavior material, regardless of any bearing such material may have upon consciousness, will inevitably force us to the absurd position of attempting to *construct* the conscious content of the animal whose behavior we have been studying. On this view, after having determined our animal's ability to learn, the simplicity or complexity of its methods of learning, the effect of past habit upon present response, the range of stimuli to which it ordinarily responds, the widened range to which it can respond under experimental conditions,—in more general terms, its various problems and its various ways of solving them,—we should still feel that the task is unfinished and that the results are worthless, until we can interpret them by analogy in the light of consciousness. Although we have solved our problem we feel uneasy and unrestful because of our definition of psychology: we feel forced to say something about the possible mental processes of our animal. We say that, having no eyes, its stream of consciousness cannot contain brightness and color sensations as we know them,—having no taste buds this stream can contain no sensations of sweet, sour, salt and bitter. But on the other hand, since it does respond to thermal, tactual and organic stimuli, its conscious content must be made up largely of these sensations; and we usually add, to protect ourselves against the reproach of being anthropomorphic, "if it has any consciousness." Surely this doctrine which calls for an analogical interpretation of all behavior data may be shown to be false: the position that the standing of an observation upon behavior is determined by its fruitfulness in yielding results which are interpretable only in the narrow realm of (really human) consciousness.

This emphasis upon analogy in psychology has led the behaviorist somewhat afield. Not being willing to throw off the yoke of consciousness he feels impelled to make a place in the scheme of behavior where the rise of consciousness can be determined. This point has been a shifting one. A few years ago certain animals were supposed to possess "associative memory," while certain others were supposed to lack it. One meets this search for the origin of consciousness under a good many disguises. Some of our texts state that consciousness arises at the moment when reflex and instinctive activities fail properly to conserve the organism. A perfectly adjusted organism would be lacking in consciousness. On the other hand whenever we find the presence of diffuse activity which results in habit formation, we are justified in assuming consciousness. I must confess that these arguments had weight with me when I began the study of behavior. I fear that a good many of us are still viewing behavior problems with something like this in mind. More than one student in behavior has attempted to frame criteria of the psychic—to devise a set of objective, structural and functional criteria which, when applied in the particular instance, will enable us to decide whether such and such responses are positively conscious, merely indicative of consciousness, or whether they are purely "physiological." Such problems as these can no longer satisfy behavior men. It would be better to give up the province altogether and admit frankly that the study of the behavior of animals has no justification, than to admit that our search is of such a "will o' the wisp" character. One can assume either the presence or the absence of consciousness anywhere in the phylogenetic scale without affecting the problems of behavior by one jot or one tittle; and without influencing in any way the mode of experimental attack upon them. On the other hand, I cannot for one moment assume that the paramecium responds to light; that the rat learns a problem more quickly by working at the task five times a day than once a day, or that the human child exhibits plateaux in his learning curves. These are questions which vitally concern behavior and which must be decided by direct observation under experimental conditions.

This attempt to reason by analogy from human conscious processes to the conscious processes in animals, and *vice versa:* to make consciousness, as the human being knows it, the center of reference of all behavior, forces us into a situation similar to that which existed in biology in Darwin's time. The whole Darwinian movement was judged by the bearing it had upon the origin and development of the human race. Expeditions were undertaken to collect material which would establish the position that the rise of the human race was a perfectly natural phenomenon and not an act of special creation. Variations were carefully sought along with the evidence for the heaping up effect and the weeding out effect of selection; for in these and the other Darwinian mechanisms were to be found factors sufficiently complex to account for the origin and race differentiation of man. The wealth of material collected at this time was considered valuable largely in so far as it tended to develop the concept of evolution in man. It is strange that this situation should have remained the dominant one in biology for so many years. The moment zoölogy undertook the experimental study of evolution and descent, the situation immediately changed. Man ceased to be the center of reference. I doubt if any experimental biologist today, unless actually engaged in the problem of race differentiation in man, tries to interpret his findings in terms of human evolution, or ever refers to it in his thinking. He gathers his data from the study of many species of plants and animals and tries to work out the laws of inheritance in the particular type upon which he is conducting experiments. Naturally, he follows the progress of the work upon race differentiation in man and in the descent of man, but he looks upon these as special topics, equal in importance with his own yet ones in which his interests will never be vitally engaged. It is not fair to say that all of his work is directed toward human evolution or that it must be interpreted in terms of human evolution. He does not have to dismiss certain of his facts on the inheritance of coat color in mice because, forsooth, they have little bearing upon the differentiation of the *genus homo* into separate races, or upon the descent of the *genus homo* from some more primitive stock.

In psychology we are still in that stage of development where we feel that we must select our material. We have a general place of discard for processes, which we anathematize so far as their value for psychology is concerned by saying, "this is a reflex"; "that is a purely physiological fact which has nothing to do with psychology." We are not interested (as psychologists) in getting all of the processes of adjustment which the animal as a whole employs, and in finding how these various responses are associated, and how they fall apart, thus working out a systematic scheme for the prediction and control of response in general. Unless our observed facts are indicative of consciousness, we have no use for them, and unless our apparatus and method are designed to throw such facts into relief, they are thought of in just as disparaging a way. I shall always remember the remark one distinguished psychologist made as he looked over the color apparatus designed for testing the responses of animals to monochromatic light in the attic at Johns Hopkins. It was this: "And they call this psychology!"

I do not wish unduly to criticize psychology. It has failed signally, I believe, during the fifty-odd years of its existence as an experimental discipline to make its place in the world as an undisputed natural science. Psychology, as it is generally thought of, has something esoteric in its methods. If you fail to reproduce my findings, it is not due to some fault in your apparatus or in the control of your stimulus, but it is due to the fact that your introspection is untrained. The attack is made upon the observer and not upon the experimental setting. In physics and in chemistry the attack is made upon the experimental conditions. The apparatus was not sensitive enough, impure chemicals were used, etc. In these sciences a better technique will give reproducible results. Psychology is otherwise. If you can't observe 3–9 states of clearness in attention, your introspection is poor. If, on the other hand, a feeling seems reasonably clear to you, your introspection is again faulty. You are seeing too much. Feelings are never clear.

The time seems to have come when psychology must discard all reference to consciousness; when it need no longer delude itself into thinking that it is making mental states the object of observation. We have become so enmeshed in speculative questions concerning the elements of mind, the nature of conscious content (for example, imageless thought, attitudes, . . . etc.) that I, as an experimental student, feel that something is wrong with our premises and the types of problems which develop from them. There is no longer any guarantee that we all mean the same thing when we use the terms now current in psychology. Take the case of sensation. A sensation is defined in terms of its attributes. One psychologist will state with readiness that the attributes of a visual sensation are *quality, extension, duration,* and *intensity.* Another will add *clearness.* Still another that of *order.* I doubt if any one psychologist can draw up a set of statements describing what he means by sensation which will be agreed to by three other psychologists of different training. Turn for a moment to the question of the number of isolable sensations. Is there an extremely large number of color sensations—or only four, red, green, yellow and blue? Again, yellow, while psychologically simple, can be obtained by superimposing red and green spectral rays upon the same diffusing surface! If, on the other hand, we say that every just noticeable difference in the spectrum is a simple sensation, and that every just noticeable increase in the white value of a given color gives simple sensations, we are forced to admit that the number is so large and the conditions for obtaining them so complex that the concept of sensation is unusable, either for the purpose of analysis or that of synthesis. Titchener, who has fought the most valiant fight in this country for a psychology based upon introspection, feels that these differences of opinion as to the number of sensations and their attributes; as to whether there are relations (in the sense of elements) and on the many others which seem to be fundamental in every attempt at analysis, are perfectly natural in the present undeveloped state of psychology. While it is admitted that every growing science is full of unanswered questions, surely only those who are wedded to the system as we now have it, who have fought and suffered for it, can confidently believe that there will ever be any greater uniformity than there is now in the answers we have to such questions. I firmly believe that two hundred years from now, unless the introspective method is discarded, psychology will still be divided on the question as to whether auditory sensations have the quality of "extension," whether intensity is an attribute which can be applied to color, whether there is a difference in "texture" between image and sensation and upon many hundreds of others of like character.

The condition in regard to other mental processes is just as chaotic. Can image type be experimentally tested and verified? Are recondite thought processes dependent mechanically upon imagery at all? Are psychologists agreed upon what feeling is? One states that feelings are attitudes. Another finds them to be groups of organic sensations possessing a certain solidarity. Still another and larger group finds them to be new elements correlative with and ranking equally with sensations.

My psychological quarrel is not with the systematic and structural psychologist alone. The last fifteen years have seen the growth of what is called functional psychology. This type of psychology decries the use of elements in the static sense of the structuralists. It throws emphasis upon the biological significance of conscious processes instead of upon the analysis of conscious states into introspectively isolable elements. I have done my best to understand the difference between functional psychology and structural psychology. Instead of clarity, confusion grows upon me. The terms sensation, perception, affection, emotion, volition are used as much by the functionalist as by the structuralist. The addition of the word "process" ("mental act as a whole," and like terms are frequently met) after each serves in some way to remove the corpse of "content" and to leave "function" in its stead. Surely if these concepts are elusive when looked at from a content standpoint, they are still more deceptive when viewed from the angle of function, and especially so when function is obtained by the introspection method. It is rather interesting that no functional psychologist has carefully distinguished between "perception" (and this is true of the other psychological terms as well) as employed by the systematist, and "perceptual process" as used in functional psychology. It seems illogical and hardly fair to criticize the psychology which the systematist gives us, and then to utilize his terms without carefully showing the changes in meaning which are to be attached to them. I was greatly surprised some time ago when I opened Pillsbury's book and saw psychology defined as the "science of behavior." A still more recent text states that psychology is the "science of mental behavior." When I saw these promising statements I thought, now surely we will have texts based upon different lines. After a few pages the science of behavior is dropped and one finds the conventional treatment of sensation, perception, imagery, etc., along with certain shifts in emphasis and additional facts which serve to give the author's personal imprint.

I believe we can write a psychology, define it as Pillsbury, and never go back upon our definition: never use the terms consciousness, mental states, mind, content, introspectively verifiable, imagery, and the like. . . . It can be done in terms of stimulus and response, in terms of habit formation, habit integrations and the like. Furthermore, I believe that it is really worth while to make this attempt now.

The psychology which I should attempt to build up would take as a starting point, first, the observable fact that organisms, man and animal alike, do adjust themselves to their environment by means of hereditary and habit equipments. These adjustments may be very adequate or they may be so inadequate that the organism barely maintains its existence; secondly, that certain stimuli lead the organisms to make the responses. In a system of psychology completely worked out, given the response the stimuli can be predicted; given the stimuli the response can be predicted. Such a set of statements is crass and raw in the extreme, as all such generalizations must be. Yet they are hardly more raw and less realizable than the ones which appear in the psychology texts of the day. I possibly might illustrate my point better by choosing an everyday problem which anyone is likely to meet in the course of his work. Some time ago I was called upon to make a study of certain species of birds. Until I went to Tortugas I had never seen these birds alive. When I reached there I found the animals doing certain things: some of the acts seemed to work peculiarly well in such an environment, while others seemed to be unsuited to their type of life. I first studied the responses of the group as a whole and later those of individuals. In order to understand more thoroughly the relation between what was habit and what was hereditary in these responses, I took the young birds and reared them. In this way I was able to study the order of appearance of hereditary adjustments and their complexity, and later the beginnings of habit formation. My efforts in determining the stimuli which called forth such adjustments were crude indeed. Consequently my attempts to control behavior and to produce responses at will did not meet with much success. Their food and water, sex and other social relations, light and temperature conditions were all beyond control in a field study. I did find it possible to control their reactions in a measure by using the nest and egg (or young) as stimuli. It is not necessary in this paper to develop further how such a study should be carried out and how work of this kind must be supplemented by carefully controlled laboratory experiments. Had I been called upon to examine the natives of some of the Australian tribes, I should have gone about my task in the same way. I should have found the problem more difficult: the types of responses called forth by physical stimuli would have been more varied, and the number of effective stimuli larger. I should have had to determine the social setting of their lives in a far more careful way. These savages would be more influenced by the responses of each other than was the case with the birds. Furthermore, habits would have been more complex and the influences of past habits upon the present responses would have appeared more clearly. Finally, if I had been called upon to work out the psychology of the educated European, my problem would have required several lifetimes. But in the one I have at my disposal I should have followed the same general line of attack. In the main, my desire in all such work is to gain an accurate knowledge of adjustments and the stimuli calling them forth. My final reason for this is to learn general and particular methods by which I may control behavior. My goal is not "the description and explanation of states of consciousness as such," nor that of obtaining such proficiency in mental gymnastics that I can immediately lay hold of a state of consciousness and say, "this, as a whole, consists of gray sensation number 350, of such and such extent, occurring in conjunction with the sensation of cold of a certain intensity; one of pressure of a certain intensity and extent," and so on *ad infinitum*. If psychology would follow the plan I suggest, the educator, the physician, the jurist and the business man could utilize our data in a practical way, as soon as we are able, experimentally, to obtain them. Those who have occasion to apply psychological principles practically would find no need to complain as they do at the present time. Ask any physician or jurist today whether scientific psychology plays a practical part in his daily routine and you will hear him deny that the psychology of the laboratories finds a place in his scheme of work. I think the criticism is extremely just. One of the earliest conditions which made me dissatisfied with psychology was the feeling that there was no realm of application for the principles which were being worked out in content terms.

What gives me hope that the behaviorist's position is a defensible one is the fact that those branches of psychology which have already partially withdrawn from the parent, experimental psychology, and which are consequently less dependent upon introspection are today in a most flourishing condition. Experimental pedagogy, the psychology of drugs, the psychology of advertising, legal psychology, the psychology of tests, and psychopathology are all vigorous growths. These are sometimes wrongly called "practical" or "applied" psychology. Surely there was never a worse misnomer. In the future there may grow up vocational bureaus which really apply psychology. At present these fields are truly scientific and are in search of broad generalizations which will lead to the control of human behavior. For example, we find out by experimentation whether a series of stanzas may be acquired more readily if the whole is learned at once, or whether it is more advantageous to learn each stanza separately and then pass to the succeeding. We do not attempt to apply our findings. The application of this principle is purely voluntary on the part of the teacher. In the psychology of drugs we may show the effect upon behavior of certain doses of caffeine. We may reach the conclusion that caffeine has a good effect upon the speed and accuracy of work. But these are general principles. We leave it to the individual as to whether the results of our tests shall be applied or not. Again, in legal testimony, we test the effects of recency upon the reliability of a witness's report. We test the accuracy of the report with respect to moving objects, stationary objects, color, etc. It depends upon the judicial machinery of the country to decide whether these facts are ever to be applied. For a "pure" psychologist to say that he is not interested in the questions raised in these divisions of the science because they relate indirectly to the application of psychology shows, in the first place, that he fails to understand the scientific aim in such problems, and secondly, that he is not interested in a psychology which concerns itself with human life. The only fault I have to find with these disciplines is that much of their material is stated in terms of introspection, whereas a statement in terms of objective results would be far more valuable. There is no reason why appeal should ever be made to consciousness in any of them. Or why introspective data should ever be sought during the experimentation, or published in the results. In experimental pedagogy especially one can see the desirability of keeping all of the results on a purely objective plane. If this is done, work there on the human being will be comparable directly with the work upon animals. For example, at Hopkins, Mr. Ulrich has obtained certain results upon the distribution of effort in learning—using rats as subjects. He is prepared to give comparative results upon the effect of having an animal work at the problem once per day, three times per day, and five times per day. Whether it is advisable to have the animal learn only one problem at a time or to learn three abreast. We need to have similar experiments made upon man, but we care as little about his "conscious processes" during the conduct of the experiment as we care about such processes in the rats.

I am more interested at the present moment in trying to show the necessity for maintaining uniformity in experimental procedure and in the method of stating results in both human and animal work, than in developing any ideas I may have upon the changes which are certain to come in the scope of human psychology. Let us consider for a moment the subject of the range of stimuli to which animals respond. I shall speak first of the work upon vision in animals. We put our animal in a situation where he will respond (or learn to respond) to one of two monochromatic lights. We feed him at the one (positive) and punish him at the other (negative). In a short time the animal learns to go to the light at which he is fed. At this point questions arise which I may phrase in two ways: I may choose the psychological way and say "does the animal see these two lights as I do, *i.e.*, as two distinct colors, or does he see them as two grays differing in brightness, as does the totally color blind?" Phrased by the behaviorist, it would read as follows: "Is my animal responding upon the basis of the difference in intensity between the two stimuli, or upon the difference in wave-lengths?" He nowhere thinks of the animal's response in terms of his own experiences of colors and grays. He wishes to establish the fact whether wave-length is a factor in that animal's adjustment. If so, what wave-lengths are effective and what differences in wave-length must be maintained in the different regions to afford bases for differential responses? If wave-length is not a factor in adjustment he wishes to know what difference in intensity will serve as a basis for response, and whether that same difference will suffice throughout the spectrum. Furthermore, he wishes to test whether the animal can respond to wave-lengths which do not affect the human eye. He is as much interested in comparing the rat's spectrum with that of the chick as in comparing it with man's. The point of view when the various sets of comparisons are made does not change in the slightest.

However we phrase the question to ourselves, we take our animal after the association has been formed and then introduce certain control experiments which enable us to return answers to the questions just raised. But there is just as keen a desire on our part to test man under the same conditions, and to state the results in both cases in common terms.

The man and the animal should be placed as nearly as possible under the same experimental conditions. Instead of feeding or punishing the human subject, we should ask him to respond by setting a second apparatus until standard and control offered no basis for a differential response. Do I lay myself open to the charge here that I am using introspection? My reply is not at all; that while I might very well feed my human subject for a right choice and punish him for a wrong one and thus produce the response if the subject could give it, there is no need of going to extremes even on the platform I suggest. But be it understood that I am merely using this second method as an abridged behavior method. We can go just as far and reach just as dependable results by the longer method as by the abridged. In many cases the direct and typically human method cannot be safely used. Suppose, for example, that I doubt the accuracy of the setting of the control instrument, in the above experiment, as I am very likely to do if I suspect a defect in vision? It is hopeless for me to get his introspective report. He will say: "There is no difference in sensation, both are reds, identical in quality." But suppose I confront him with the standard and the control and so arrange conditions that he is punished if he responds to the "control" but not with the standard. I interchange the positions of the standard and the control at will and force him to attempt to differentiate the one from the other. If he can learn to make the adjustment even after a large number of trials it is evident that the two stimuli do afford the basis for a differential response. Such a method may sound nonsensical, but I firmly believe we will have to resort increasingly to just such a method where we have reason to distrust the language method.

There is hardly a problem in human vision which is not also a problem in animal vision: I mention the limits of the spectrum, threshold values, absolute and relative, flicker, Talbot's law, Weber's law, field of vision, the Purkinje phenomenon, etc. Every one is capable of being worked out by behavior methods. Many of them are being worked out at the present time.

I feel that all the work upon the senses can be consistently carried forward along the lines I have suggested here for vision. Our results will, in the end, give an excellent picture of what each organ stands for in the way of function. The anatomist and the physiologist may take our data and show, on the one hand, the structures which are responsible for these responses, and, on the other, the physico-chemical relations which are necessarily involved (physiological chemistry of nerve and muscle) in these and other reactions.

The situation in regard to the study of memory is hardly different. Nearly all of the memory methods in actual use in the laboratory today yield the type of results I am arguing for. A certain series of nonsense syllables or other material is presented to the human subject. What should receive the emphasis are the rapidity of the habit formation, the errors, peculiarities in the form of the curve, the persistence of the habit so formed, the relation of such habits to those formed when more complex material is used, etc. Now such results are taken down with the subject's introspection. The experiments are made for the purpose of discussing the mental machinery involved in learning, in recall, recollection and forgetting, and not for the purpose of seeking the human being's way of shaping his responses to meet the problems in the terribly complex environment into which he is thrown, nor for that of showing the similarities and differences between man's methods and those of other animals.

The situation is somewhat different when we come to a study of the more complex forms of behavior, such as imagination, judgment, reasoning, and conception. At present the only statements we have of them are in content terms. Our minds have been so warped by the fifty-odd years which have been devoted to the study of states of consciousness that we can envisage these problems only in one way. We should meet the situation squarely and say that we are not able to carry forward investigations along all of these lines by the behavior methods which are in use at the present time. In extenuation I should like to call attention to the paragraph above where I made the point that the introspective method itself has reached a *cul-de-sac* with respect to them. The topics have become so threadbare from much handling that they may well be put away for a time. As our methods become better developed it will be possible to undertake investigations of more and more complex forms of behavior. Problems which are now laid aside will again become imperative, but they can be viewed as they arise from a new angle and in more concrete settings.

Will there be left over in psychology a world of pure psychics, to use Yerkes' term? I confess I do not know. The plans which I most favor for psychology lead practically to the ignoring of consciousness in the sense that that term is used by psychologists today. I have virtually denied that this realm of psychics is open to experimental investigation. I don't wish to go further into the problem at present because it leads inevitably over into metaphysics. If you will grant the behaviorist the right to use consciousness in the same way that other natural scientists employ it—that is, without making consciousness a special object of observation—you have granted all that my thesis requires.

In concluding, I suppose I must confess to a deep bias on these questions. I have devoted nearly twelve years to experimentation on animals. It is natural that such a one should drift into a theoretical position which is in harmony with his experimental work. Possibly I have put up a straw man and have been fighting that. There may be no absolute lack of harmony between the position outlined here and that of functional psychology. I am inclined to think, however, that the two positions cannot be easily harmonized. Certainly the position I advocate is weak enough at present and can be attacked from many standpoints. Yet when all this is admitted I still feel that the considerations which I have urged should have a wide influence upon the type of psychology which is to be developed in the future. What we need to do is to start work upon psychology, making *behavior,* not *consciousness,* the objective point of our attack. Certainly there are enough problems in the control of behavior to keep us all working many lifetimes without ever allowing us time to think of consciousness *an sich.* Once launched in the undertaking, we will find ourselves in a short time as far divorced from an introspective psychology as the psychology of the present time is divorced from faculty psychology.

• • •

COMMENT

As indicated, this attack on the old psychology and the call for a dramatic "new" approach was a stirring appeal to many psychologists. Consider the major points. Psychology is to be the science of behavior (and not the introspective study of consciousness)—a purely objective experimental branch of natural science. Both human and animal behavior will be investigated. The new psychology will discard all mentalistic concepts, and use only behavior concepts such as stimulus and response. The goal of psychology is the prediction and control of behavior.

It is important to note that these points were not new with Watson. As discussed earlier, objective experimental methods had been employed for some time and functional concepts had certainly been highly influential, indeed, dominant, in America. Research on animal learning had begun to yield information applicable to human learning and objective tests had been developed and used with some success to predict and control behavior. Even Watson's definition of psychology as the science of behavior had been anticipated—by the English psychologist, William McDougall, in 1908. Many psychologists had already begun to think in terms of this broader definition by 1913.

Thus, Watson's positive points were not totally novel. What was unique and provocative about his program was his pronounced negative emphasis—drop mind and consciousness, do away with mentalistic concepts, stop speculating about what might be occurring in the brain, and stop using introspection. He was "a breath of fresh air, clearing away the musty accumulation of the centuries" (R. I. Watson, 1963, p. 401).

THE METHODS OF BEHAVIORISM

As should be apparent by now, only objective methods of study are admissible in the behavioristic laboratory. Watson stated quite explicitly the methods to be used in research: (a) observation, with and without the use of instruments, (b) the conditioned reflex method, (c) the verbal report method, and (d) testing methods.

The method of observation, self-explanatory and fundamental, is a necessary basis for the other methods. Objective tests were already in use but Watson proposed that test results be treated as samples of behavior, and used to determine special abilities as well as more general aspects of behavior. Also, as we have seen, conditioning methods were in use before the advent of behaviorism, although their use in America had been limited and Watson was largely responsible for their subsequent widespread application in American psychological research.

The verbal report method is unique in Watson's system and therefore deserves special attention. Watson was, as noted, violently opposed to introspection; in view of this opposition, his admission of verbal reporting into the laboratory was regarded by some as a compromise whereby he admitted introspection at the back door after having vigorously thrown it out the front. His system was particularly sensitive to this criticism.

Let us first consider why Watson was so opposed to introspection. That introspection could not be used by those who performed research on animals obviously caused Watson to look upon it with disfavor. He also distrusted the accuracy of introspection. If even the most highly trained introspectionists could not agree on what they observed, Watson asked, how was psychology to progress? More fundamental was the objection that a behaviorist could not tolerate in his laboratory anything that could not be objectively observed. Watson wanted to deal only with tangibles and objected strongly to the introspectionists' pretensions of reporting on occurrences within an organism, which could not be verified through objective observation.

In spite of his opposition to introspection, Watson felt he could not rule out all the work in psychophysics, which made use of introspection. He posited that speech reactions are, after all, objectively observable and hence are as meaningful to the behaviorist as any other type of motor reaction:

> Now what can we observe? Well, we can observe *behavior—what the organism does or says*. And let me make this fundamental point at once: that *saying* is doing—that is, *behaving*. Speaking overtly or to ourselves (thinking) is just as objective a type of behavior as baseball (J. B. Watson, 1925, p. 6).

The use of verbal report in the methodology of behaviorism was a concession that was much debated by Watson's critics, who contended that, in this respect, Watson was asking for mere verbal changes, not a genuine alteration of research procedures. It is noted that Watson (1914) considered verbal report to be an "inexact" method and not a satisfactory substitute for more objective methods of observation. He wanted to limit the use of verbal report to those situations in which it was totally accurate and capable of verification, as for example in observing differences in tones. Unverifiable verbal reports, such as imageless thoughts or comments about feeling states, were ruled out. While indicating that he would severely restrict the use of verbal report, he never said exactly how he would do so.

Initially, Watson's arguments for the use of only objective methods (the so-called "methodological behaviorism") seemed to many to be a major advance. Calmer retrospective analysis, however, suggests that the behaviorists actually contributed little that was positive, "for the excellent reason that objective methods had been a major concern of psychology since it began to be experimental" (Woodworth, 1948, p. 76). For example, studies in psychophysics, memory, and conditioning were already using objective methods. Therefore, it is suggested that the contributions of the behaviorists were extensions and refinements of methods, rather than origination. This "latter-day" conclusion does not, of course, detract from the impact of Watson's pronouncements at the time they were made.

THE SUBJECT MATTER OF BEHAVIORISM

In the long run, Watson's "conceptual behaviorism" has proved to be of greater importance for psychology than his methodological behaviorism. The primary subject matter or data must always be items of behavior—muscular movements or glandular secretions. Watson said that these responses constitute evidence of the organism's ability to react in discriminate fashion to its environment. Psychology, as the science of behavior, must deal only with acts that can be described objectively in terms of stimulus and response, habit formation, habit integration, etc. All human and animal behavior can be described in these terms without employing mentalistic concepts and terminology. Through the objective study of behavior, behavioristic psychology can fulfill its aim of predicting the response given to the stimulus, and predicting the antecedent stimulus given the response. Human and animal behavior can be effectively understood, predicted, and controlled by reducing the behavior to the stimulus-response level.

Despite this reduction of behavior to stimulus-response units, behaviorism deals with the behavior of the whole organism. While a response can be something as simple and low-level as a knee jerk or other reflex, it can also be much more complex, in which case the term "act" is applied. For example, Watson considered response acts to include such things as taking of food, writing a book, playing baseball, or building a house. Thus, an act involves the organism's response through movement in space such as talking, walking, etc. Watson seemed to have thought of a response in terms of accomplishing some result in the environment, rather than as an assemblage of muscular elements, *i.e.*, in more molar than molecular terms.

Nevertheless, these behavioral acts, no matter how complex, can be reduced to lower-level motor or glandular responses. Responses are classified in two ways: learned or unlearned, and explicit or implicit. Watson considered it important for behaviorism to distinguish between innate responses and those that are learned, and to discover for the latter the laws of learning.

Explicit responses are overt and therefore directly observable. Implicit responses, such as visceral movements, glandular secretions, and nerve impulses, take place inside the organism. Though such movements are not overt, they are nonetheless items of behavior. In introducing this notion of implicit behavior, Watson modified somewhat his initial requirement that all the subject matter of psychology must be *actually* observable and said instead that everything must be *potentially* observable (Woodworth, 1948, p. 75). The movements or responses occurring within the organism are theoretically observable through the use of instrumentation.

The exciting stimuli, like the responses with which the behaviorist deals, may be complex. A stimulus may, of course, be something relatively simple, such as light waves striking the retina, but it can also be a physical object in the environment or total situations (or constellations of specific stimuli). Just as the constellation of responses involved in an act can be reduced to particular responses, so the "stimulus situation" can be resolved into its component specific stimuli.

Thus, behaviorism deals with the behavior of the whole organism in relation to its environment. Specific laws of behavior can be worked out through the analysis of the total stimulus and response complexes into their more elemental stimulus and response segments. This analysis was not to be as minute and detailed as that performed by the physiologist in determining the structure and organization of the central nervous system. Because of the inaccessibility of the "mystery box" (Watson's term for the brain), he had little interest in cortical functioning. Behavior, to Watson, is concerned with the total organism and cannot be restricted to the nervous system alone. Watson focused on larger units of behavior—the whole response of the organism to a given situation.

In both subject matter and methodology, the new psychology of John B. Watson was an attempt to provide a real science that was completely free of mentalistic notions and subjective methods. As Chaplin and Krawiec (1960) noted, behaviorism is "as objective as chemistry or physics. And, in keeping with its new status as a natural science, it is forever free and independent of its philosophical ancestry" (p. 51).

We now consider Watson's treatment of some of the traditional topics in psychology: instinct, learning, emotion, and thinking.

SPECIFIC VIEWS AND CONCEPTS

Like all systematic theorists, Watson developed his psychology in accordance with his fundamental theses. All areas of behavior, emotions, feelings, thought, etc., are to be treated in objective stimulus-response terms.

Instinct and Learning. Watson's position on the role of instinct in behavior changed from an initial acceptance of instincts to a categorical denial of their existence in humans—the latter position announced in 1925. All those aspects of human behavior that seem instinctive, Watson argued, are in reality socially conditioned responses. With his position that learning is the key to understanding the development of human behavior, Watson became an extreme environmentalist. He went beyond just denying instincts and refused to admit that there were inherited capacities, temperaments, or talents of any kind. This excessive emphasis on environmentalism won him great popular appeal and influence outside of psychology.

Watson's views on learning showed a progressive change in the direction of the incorporation of conditioning as a basic part of his system. In his 1913 article there is no mention of conditioning, and his first book, *Comparative Psychology* (1914), gives but slight emphasis to Pavlov's conditioning experiments, even expressing doubt that the method can be used with primates.

In his 1915 presidential address to the American Psychological Association, however, he suggested that the conditioned reflex method should displace introspection. From then on it was one of the chief methods of the behaviorists. Watson never completely developed a satisfactory theory of learning and conceptually seemed to belong with the pre-

Thorndikian associationists. He rejected Thorndike's law of effect and relied primarily on the older laws of contiguity, frequency, and recency. He maintained that the correct response was the most recent one and that it occurred more and more frequently during the process of learning.

In spite of his enthusiasm for classical conditioning, Watson failed to recognize the importance of Pavlov's law of reinforcement and its similarity to Thorndike's law of effect. Thus, while accepting conditioning principles and using them in his research, he continued to cling to a law of exercise and to emphasize frequency and recency as primary factors of learning.

Emotion. Emotions, to Watson, are nothing more than bodily responses to specific stimuli. The stimulus (the presence of danger, for instance) produces internal body changes and the appropriate learned overt responses. This notion, of course, implies no conscious perception of the emotion nor any mass of sensations from the internal organs. Each separate emotion involves its particular pattern of changes in the general body mechanism, particularly in the visceral and glandular systems. Although Watson recognized that all emotional responses involve overt movements, *e.g.*, of the arms and legs, the internal responses predominate in his concept. Emotion, then, is a form of implicit behavior in which the hidden visceral responses are evident, at least to some extent, as changes in pulse and breathing, blushing, etc.

Watson's theory of emotion is much simpler than that of James, discussed earlier. In James's theory, the bodily changes follow immediately upon the perception of the exciting stimulus, and the feeling of these bodily changes is the emotion. Watson was highly critical of this position, saying that "James gave the psychology of the emotions a setback from which it has only recently begun to recover" (1925, p. 108).

Watson discarded the conscious processes of perception of the situation and the feeling state and said simply that emotions can be understood in terms of the objective stimulus situation, the overt bodily response, and the internal visceral changes.

A famous study of Watson is his investigation of the stimuli that produced emotional responses in infants. He found what he believed to be the three fundamental emotions: fear, rage, and love. Fear is produced by loud sounds and sudden loss of support, rage by hampering of body movement, and love by stroking the skin, rocking, and patting. He also found characteristic reaction patterns to these stimuli.

Watson believed that fear, rage, and love are the only unlearned emotional responses. All the remaining human emotional responses are built up from these basic three through the process of conditioning. He felt that the basic emotional responses may become attached, through conditioning, to a variety of environmental stimuli that were not originally capable of eliciting them.

Watson experimentally demonstrated this in his study, mentioned earlier, of Albert, who at 11 months of age was conditioned to fear a white rat that he had not feared prior to the conditioning trials. The fear was established quite easily by presenting a very loud noise (striking a steel bar with a hammer) behind Albert's head when he touched the rat. In a short time, just the sight of the rat produced signs of fear and discomfort in the child. Watson went on to demonstrate that this conditioned fear could be generalized to other somewhat similar stimuli, such as a rabbit, a white fur coat, and Santa Claus whiskers. Watson suggested that many adult fears, aversions, and anxieties may well have been conditioned in like manner in early childhood.

Having demonstrated that fears could be conditioned, Watson then turned to the problem of eliminating them. Several rather common techniques, such as disuse and verbal appeal, and frequent application of the fear stimulus, were tried but proved unsuccessful. Success was reached through the use of the unconditioning or reconditioning technique. The subject was a child (not Albert) who showed a fear of rabbits that had not been conditioned in the laboratory. While the child was eating, the fear stimulus was presented, but at a distance great enough so as to not elicit the fear response. Thereafter, the rabbit was brought progressively closer to the child, always while the latter was eating. The point was finally reached where the child could handle the rabbit without fear. Watson also found that generalized fear responses to other similar objects could be eliminated by this procedure.

Watson's behavioristic approach to the emotions and his interest in the physiological changes that accompany emotional behavior stimulated a great deal of research on emotional development in children and on the specific reaction patterns for the specific emotions.

Thought. Prior to the advent of behaviorism, the traditional point of view with regard to thought processes was the "centralist" theory of thinking, which held that thought processes occurred in the brain, "so faintly that no neural impulse passes out over the motor nerve to the muscle, hence no response takes place in the muscles and glands" (J. B. Watson, 1925, p. 192). According to this view, thought processes, because they occur in the absence of muscular movements, are not considered accessible to observation and experimentation. Hence, thought is regarded as intangible and uncorporeal; something exclusively mental in nature with no physical referents. The concept of image, as used by the structuralists, is an example of this conception of thought.

Watson's "peripheral theory of thinking," perhaps his most famous theory, takes issue with this older notion and attempts to reduce thinking to implicit motor behavior. Thinking, he argued, must be, like all other aspects of human functioning, sensorimotor behavior of some sort. He reasoned that the behavior of thinking must be implicit speech movements. Verbal thinking, then, is reduced to subvocal talking involving muscular habits learned in overt speech. These muscular habits become inaudible as the child grows up, as described by Watson (1925):

> The child talks incessantly when alone . . . . At three he even plans the day aloud, as my own ear placed outside the keyhole of the nursery door has very often confirmed. Aloud he voices (may I use literary terms and not psychological ones?) his wishes, his hopes, his fears, his annoyances, his dissatisfactions with his nurse or his father. Soon society in the form of nurse and parents steps in. "Don't talk aloud—daddy and mother are not always talking to themselves." Soon the overt speech dies down to whispered speech and a good lip reader can still read what the child thinks of the world and of himself. Some individuals never even make this concession to society. When alone they talk aloud to themselves. A still larger number never go beyond even the whispering stage when alone. Watch people reading on the street car; peep through the keyhole some time when individuals not too highly socialized are just sitting and thinking. But the great majority of people pass on to the third stage under the influence of social pressure constantly exerted. "Quit whispering to yourself," and "Can't you even read without moving your lips?" and the like are constant mandates. Soon the process is forced to take place behind the lips. Behind these walls you can call the biggest bully the worst name you can think of without even smiling. You can tell the female bore how terrible she really is and the next moment smile and overtly pay her a verbal compliment (p. 193).

After we learn to talk by conditioning, thought becomes nothing more than talking silently to ourselves. Watson suggested that the foci for much of this implicit behavior are the muscles of the larynx and the tongue. In fact, Watson's equivalent term for thinking is "laryngeal habits," and, initially, the larynx was considered to be the "organ of thought." In addition to these laryngeal habits, language or thought is also mediated by gestures, frowns, shrugs, etc., which symbolize more overt reactions to situations.

One obvious source of evidence supporting Watson's hypothesis is that most of us are aware that we often talk to ourselves while thinking. This is inadmissible, however, since it is purely introspective, and Watson could hardly use introspection to corroborate a tenet of behaviorism. Behaviorism required objective evidence of these implicit speech movements, and attempts were made to record movement in the tongue and larynx during thought. Such measurements revealed slight movements part (not all) of the time that the subjects were thinking. Similarly, measurements taken from the hands and fingers of deaf mutes revealed movement some of the time during thought. In spite of the inability to always secure positive results in these studies, Watson was convinced that implicit speech movements existed and that their clear demonstration awaited only the development of more sophisticated instrumentation.

An oft-quoted passage from Watson's *Behaviorism* (1925) indicates his extreme environmentalistic position:

> Give me a dozen healthy infants, well-formed, and my own specified world to bring them up in and I'll guarantee to take any one at random and train him to become any type of specialist I might select—doctor, lawyer, artist, merchant-chief and, yes, even beggar-man and thief, regardless of his talents, penchants, tendencies, abilities, vocations, and race of his ancestors (p. 82).

There is little room for heredity as an explanation of human behavior in such a statement. Watson's conditioning experiments, such as the study of Albert, convinced him that emotional disturbances in adults cannot be traced back to sex alone, as Freud held. Instead, Watson argued, these adult disturbances can be traced to conditioned and transferred responses established in infancy and youth. If such disturbances are a function of faulty conditioning in childhood, then a proper program of childhood conditioning should prevent their emergence. Watson believed that such practical control of infant behavior (and hence of the later adult) is quite possible. Toward this end, he developed a plan for social improvement—a program of "experimental ethics" based on the principles of behaviorism.

No one gave him "a dozen healthy infants" so that he might test his claim, and he admitted that in making the claim he was going beyond the known facts. He noted, however, that those who believe in the predominance of heredity had been arguing their case for thousands of years and still had no real evidence to support their claims.

The following passage from the end of *Behaviorism* reveals some of the fervor with which Watson described his program for saner living under the banner of behaviorism:

> I think behaviorism does lay a foundation for saner living. It ought to be a science that prepares men and women for understanding the first principles of their own behavior. It ought to make men and women eager to rearrange their own lives, and especially eager to prepare themselves to bring up their own children in a healthy way. I wish I had time more fully to describe this, to picture to you the kind of rich and wonderful individual we should make of every healthy child if only we could let it shape itself properly and then provide for it a universe in which it could exercise that organization—a universe unshackled by legendary folk lore of happenings thousands of years ago; unhampered by disgraceful political history; free of foolish customs and conventions which have no significance in themselves, yet which hem the individual in like taut steel bands (1925, p. 248).

WATSON'S POPULAR APPEAL

Watson's bold pronouncements won him a large following not only among psychologists, but among the lay public as well. Why this public acclaim? Surely the nonscientific public was not distressed because some psychologists practiced introspection, whereas others refuted its use; or because some psychologists pretended to be conscious while others joyously proclaimed that psychology had finally lost its mind; or whether thinking took place in the head or in the neck. While these issues aroused comment and controversy among psychologists they would hardly concern the general public.

What did stir the public was Watson's call for a "brave new world" based on scientifically shaped and controlled behavior, free from myths, customs, and conventions. This appeal offered hope to many people who had become disenchanted with the older guiding creeds. In fervor and faith it had some aspects of religion and, indeed, to many "It was a religion to take the place of religion" (Woodworth, 1948, p. 94). Some of the excitement generated by Watson's appeal can be appreciated from the newspaper reviews of *Behaviorism*. The *New York Times* said dramatically, "It marks an epoch in the intellectual history of man" (August 2, 1925); the *New York Herald Tribune* commented, "Perhaps this is the most important book ever written. One stands for an instant blinded with a great hope" (Woodworth, 1948, p. 93). This "great hope" remained only a hope on Watson's part, for his program of experimental ethics to replace the older speculative ethics based on religion was never carried out. He outlined his plan in rather brief terms and left it as a framework for future research. Unfortunately (or fortunately, to many) such a social system based on scientifically shaped behavior remains little more than a plan.

A FINAL NOTE

Although Watson's productive career in psychology lasted less than twenty years, he profoundly influenced the course of psychology. In fact, his impact compels us to count him among psychology's great men. As noted earlier, Watson was an effective agent of the *Zeitgeist,* and the times were changing not only in psychology but in general scientific attitudes as well. The nineteenth century had produced magnificent advances in every branch of science. It was thought that perhaps science was capable of finding an answer to everything, if given enough time. It was an era in which tender-minded idealism was rapidly yielding to a spirit of tough-minded realism. Thus, Watson's behavioristic crusade helped American psychology in its ongoing transition from concentration on consciousness and subjectivism to materialism and objectivism in the study of behavior.

While Watson's program did not realize his ambitious goals, the behavioristic orientation in general remains a strong and active force in modern psychology. One can only wonder what heights Watson might have reached had he remained active in professional psychological endeavors.

Criticisms of Watsonian Behaviorism

Any systematic program that so blatantly attacks the existing order of things (indeed, suggests the complete discarding of the earlier version of the truth) and proposes such radical and sweeping revisions is bound to come under criticism. As we have seen, American psychology was already moving in the general direction of increased objectivity when Watsonian behaviorism formally began, but not all psychologists were pleased at the extreme form of objectivity that Watson proposed. Many, including some who generally supported the objective movement, felt that important components of psychology, such as sensory and perceptual processes, were being left out.

One of Watson's outstanding opponents was William McDougall (1871–1938), the English psychologist who came to this country in 1920. McDougall is probably most important for his espousal of an instinct theory of behavior; a theory that stated that all human action results from innate tendencies to thought and action. He is also well known for the impetus his most influential book, *Social Psychology,* gave to that area. This book, published in 1908, went through 14 editions by 1921.

McDougall's instinct theory enjoyed considerable initial success among social scientists but rapidly lost ground when behaviorism came to the fore. In addition to his instinct theory, McDougall was an ardent supporter of a number of unpopular causes, such as freedom of the will, Nordic superiority, and psychic research.

By 1925 Watson had rejected the notion of instincts and on this issue a pitched battle was joined between Watson and McDougall. The debate reached such proportions that much of it was published in 1929 in *The Battle of Behaviorism,* by Watson and McDougall. Most of the criticisms that follow were made by McDougall—although he was not alone.

Mention has already been made of the criticism directed at Watson's damaging admission of verbal reports as a method of research. Watson's use of verbal report only when it was accurate and verifiable was precisely the point of the whole behavioristic movement—to use only accurate and verifiable data.

Another point of criticism relates to Watson's attempts at translation of some of the older mentalistic concepts into the more objective language of behaviorism. Heidbreder (1933), for instance, felt that Watson tended to regard a translation as an explanation, and commented that we add little to our knowledge of thoughts, for example, by calling them language mechanisms.

This may well be true, but the point has been made (Marx & Hillix, 1963) that such translations ought to be regarded only as starting points in the direction of more total objectification. The mentalistic terms as used before Watson had no objective meaning at all and therefore his translations were indeed definitions. This is not to say that after translation the particular concept was fully explained, but it was made more "workable," *i.e.*, it was given a meaning that was useful within the framework of natural science.

These are but a few of the attacks on the methodology of behaviorism. Watson's denial of the mind is, of course, subject to much criticism. He felt it necessary to drop the mind in order to free psychology from the continuing futility of attempting to study this presumed, unobservable entity. Psychology could hardly become a natural science if it continued to be burdened with a carry-over from philosophy. A concept of mind that is useful to science has yet to be developed. Scientific issues must be based on matters of demonstrable fact and it is not yet possible even to ask scientifically meaningful questions regarding mind, much less to offer any solutions. Therefore, Watson's concentration on behavior to the exclusion of mind is a great service to the advancement of psychology.

A general criticism of behaviorism involves the long-standing opposition between advocates of determinism and free will, a controversy mentioned in our discussion of associationism. Science accepts a strictly determined natural world, while theology and some philosophies accept "freedom of the will." Watson, of course, belongs in the determinist camp. Since all behavior is interpretable in physical terms, all acts of behavior must be physically determined in advance. Watson did not believe that people are personally responsible for their actions in terms of having a free will. This belief has important social implications, particularly in the treatment of criminals, who, according to Watson, should not be punished for their actions but rather should be reconditioned.

This basic disagreement remains unresolved and we can do little more than note that Watson's position on the issue is representative of the position of science generally. We recall, however, Thorndike's statements on the issue (Chapter IX)—that we are free only if determined, and we can determine and shape people's behavior, and so produce a better society, only if that behavior is lawfully determined.

The determinist-behaviorists would argue that their critics' claim to be in favor of freedom is false; that what they actually espouse is not true freedom but simply a different kind of determinism. For example, devotees of free will who are of a fundamentalistic religious persuasion believe in "a determination by some divine force: the individual is free only in order that he can accept the fully determined rule of God" (Marx & Hillix, 1963, p. 163).

Contributions of Watsonian Behaviorism

Watson's primary contribution was his advocacy of a completely objective science of behavior. He exerted an enormous influence in rendering psychology more objective, in both methods and terminology. Methodological behaviorism is so much a part of American psychology today that it "has conquered itself to death. It . . . has become a truism. Virtually every American psychologist, whether he knows it or not, is nowadays a methodological behaviorist" (Bergmann, 1956, p. 270).

Although his positions on specific topics have stimulated a great deal of research, Watson's original formulations are no longer of use. Behaviorism as a separate school has not lasted but has been replaced by newer forms of psychological objectivism that built upon it. Boring said in 1929 that behaviorism was already past its prime as a movement. Since movements depend on protest for their strength and very existence, it is a most effective tribute to Watsonian behaviorism that only 16 years after its inception, it no longer needed to protest. Objective methodology and terminology have largely become the American psychology, and behaviorism died, as have other successful movements, by being incorporated into the main body of thought.

To some degree, the acceptance of Watsonian behaviorism is a function of the clarity and force of the man himself. R. I. Watson commented that "his appeal was enhanced by characteristics he manifested—the youthful optimism, the tough mindedness, and a trenchant, self-confident style of writing—all of which contributed to his great effect upon psychology" (1963, p. 401). Add to these characteristics his boldness and his scorn of tradition, mystery, and the older versions of psychology—and note the spirit of the times in which he spoke—and we find summated the characteristics of the great man.

SUGGESTED FURTHER READINGS

Antecedents to Behaviorism
Diserens, C. M. Psychological objectivism. *Psychological Review*, 1925, **32**, 121–152.

Early Animal Psychology
Warden, C. J., & Warner, L. H. The development of animal psychology in the U. S. during the past three decades. *Psychological Review*, 1927, **34**, 196–205.

Watson

Bergmann, G. The contributions of John B. Watson. *Psychological Review,* 1956, **63,** 265–276.

Skinner, B. F. John Broadus Watson, behaviorist. *Science,* 1959, **129,** 197–198.

Woodworth, R. S. John Broadus Watson: 1878–1958. *American Journal of Psychology,* 1959, **72,** 301–310.

General

Harrell, W., & Harrison, R. The rise and fall of behaviorism. *Journal of General Psychology,* 1938, **18,** 367–421.

Roback, A. A. *Behaviorism and psychology.* Cambridge, Mass.: University Bookstore, 1923.

XI

BEHAVIORISM: AFTER
THE FOUNDING

Early Behaviorists

IN THE EARLY 1920s behaviorism seemed to capture the attention and imagination of all American psychologists except those who remained loyal to Titchener. However, not everyone in this new generation of behaviorists adopted the Watsonian viewpoint intact; some developed their own approaches and were more receptive to divergent views than Watson had been. Although Watson was both the founder of behaviorism and its most effective spokesman for a time, other psychologists had reached the same general point of view simultaneously with him, but had attempted to move in somewhat different directions. We will discuss several of these men and then consider the work of more contemporary psychologists, who might appropriately be called neobehaviorists.

Edward B. Holt

Holt (1873–1946) received his PhD at Harvard in 1901 and spent his academic career there and at Princeton. His main line of influence was in terms of the philosophical framework that he provided for behaviorism. His was a rather unorthodox view of behaviorism, probably because he was, as Boring (1950) noted, half an experimentalist and half a philosopher. Holt did not agree with Watson's complete rejection of consciousness and mental phenomena. Rather, he suggested that consciousness should be related to epistemological realism, according to which objects exist as perceived even when we are not perceiving them. Consciousness meant, to Holt, "an adjustment of the sensorimotor apparatus to the perceived object; it is a sort of photographic lens which reflects the correct picture of the reflected object" (Wolman, 1960, p. 86).

Holt believed that consciousness was simply a label given to the pro-

213

cess of sensorimotor adjustment to a physical object. Thus, to be conscious of an object involved the relation of the sensorimotor aspects of the organism to that object, such as the oculomotor movements necessary to focus clearly on an object. Physical objects in the environment, then, have essentially similar qualities to those within consciousness, according to Holt. There were, therefore, physical referents for what was called conscious experiencing.

Holt agreed with Watson on the relative unimportance of heredity in shaping human behavior. He believed that an individual's behavior patterns are developed in two ways. The primary way is through learning, which occurs in response to what Holt called inner or outer motivation. Outer motivation refers to external forms of stimulation, whereas inner motivation refers to inner needs or drives, such as hunger, thirst, and so on. The latter point anticipated the development of Hull's learning theory with its emphasis on internal drive reduction as a necessary condition for learning. The second way in which behavior patterns are acquired is through the preservation in adulthood of childhood patterns of behavior.

Holt did not believe that psychology should attempt to reduce behavior to elemental units, whether stimulus-response connections or anything else. He wanted to deal with responses on a more molar level, i.e., as wholes accomplishing some end. He was concerned with behavior on a larger scale, behavior that had both a unity and a purpose, concepts that Watson could not allow in his system.

Holt's unorthodox form of behaviorism enabled him to use a great variety of sources and to take an interest in problems outside the mainstream of American behaviorism. For instance, in one of his books, *The Freudian Wish and Its Place in Ethics* (1915), he attempted to synthesize the major features of behaviorism and psychoanalysis. Probably his greatest single influence is, as we shall see, his role as a stimulus for a later behaviorist, E. C. Tolman.

Albert P. Weiss

Born in Germany, Weiss (1879–1931) came to the United States when he was very young, received his PhD in 1916 at the University of Missouri, and pursued his career as a behaviorist, studying primarily child development at Ohio State University. His book, *A Theoretical Basis of Human Behavior* (1925), outlines his program of unabashed behaviorism. He strongly believed that psychology must operate as a natural science. All reference to conscious and mental phenomena had to be eliminated along with the subjective method of introspection; anything not accessible to a natural science had no place in psychology.

Weiss's behaviorism stressed an extreme reductionism that urged psychology to deal only with the elements of matter with which physics deals. Thus, all behavior was seen as capable of analysis and reduction to physical-chemical entities. Weiss believed that psychology was actually a branch of physics and, as such, should not claim a nonphysical entity (*i.e.*, consciousness) as its subject matter. Thus, we see in Weiss's system a strong emphasis on biological components of behavior, which in turn are reducible to physical elements. If this were his complete system, we might reasonably label him a physiologist, not a psychologist. But there was more: man is not only biological, but social as well; Weiss argued that man is a product of both forces and he coined the term "biosocial" to denote this.

The organism is a solely biological entity only during early infancy. As it matures and develops, its behavior is shaped and modified by social forces encountered in its interaction with other people. The importance of biological forces does not diminish, however; behavior is just as capable of reduction to physical-chemical units whether the individual is alone or influenced by other people. Weiss believed that psychology must study both physiological and social processes and that its primary task is to understand how the infant develops into a social adult. He outlined a program of research on child development and learning that, because of his early death, was unfortunately never implemented.

Karl Lashley

A prominent physiological psychologist, Lashley (1890–1958) was a student of Watson's at Johns Hopkins University, where he received his PhD in 1915. His productive career took him to the universities of Minnesota and Chicago, then to Harvard, and finally to the Yerkes Laboratory of Primate Biology. An ardent supporter of behaviorism, Lashley vigorously championed increased objectivism in psychology and opposed the study of consciousness through introspection.

His own thorough research produced some results that differed from Watson's position on certain points. Specifically, he believed that S-R connections developed through conditioning are not the most effective approach to the analysis of behavior. However, Lashley's adherence to the basic tenets of behavioristic psychology never wavered; only his attitude toward some of Watson's secondary points changed.

Lashley is perhaps best known for his work involving brain extirpation of rats and other animals. He devoted many years to patient research on the role of the brain in the learning process. His initial studies were conducted with his former teacher, S. I. Franz, who, with Thorndike, had studied under Cattell.

Conceptually, the basic research procedure followed by Lashley and Franz is a simple one. After an animal had successfully learned a certain behavior, such as escaping from puzzle boxes of the type used by Thorndike, different parts of the brain were extirpated to determine the effect on the learned behavior. Would the animal be able to retain and perform the behavior with portions of the cortex no longer operative?

The results of this program were surprising and somewhat disturbing because they were at variance with the then accepted views on localization of function within the cortex. Earlier investigators had demonstrated specific sensory and motor areas in the cortex. Lashley's research showed that, even though destruction of large cortical areas resulted in slower learning, it seemed not to matter which specific cortical area was destroyed. That is, animals were able to learn just as well with one part of the cortex as with another. This perplexing finding seemed to indicate that other cortical centers were capable of taking over the functions performed by destroyed centers. Lashley thus concluded that the brain must function as a whole.

Lashley summarized his research findings in *Brain Mechanisms and Intelligence* (1929), in which he plotted errors in learning against (a) amount of cortical tissue destroyed, and (b) the difficulty of the learning task. His results led him to postulate two famous principles: mass action and equipotentiality. The law of mass action states that the efficiency of learning is a function of the total mass of the cortex left intact. In other words, the more cortical tissue available, the better the learning.

Thus, learning depends on the amount of cortex left functioning rather than on the integrity of a particular part; or, expressed as Lashley's principle of equipotentiality, one part of the cortex is essentially equal to another in terms of its contribution to tasks such as maze learning. There are, however, some exceptions to this principle: visual perception of a shape or pattern, for instance, requires that a certain part of the cortex be intact, though within that specific cortical area, the subparts are to a large degree equal in potential.

Lashley had expected to find in his research specific pathways and connections between sensory and motor apparatus with definite points of localization in the cortex. Such findings would have supported the primacy of the reflex arc as an elemental unit of behavior. His results, however, challenged the Watsonian notion of a simple point-to-point connection in reflexes, according to which the brain merely serves to switch incoming sensory nerve impulses into outgoing motor impulses. Lashley's results suggested that the brain has a more active role in learning and questioned Watson's assumption that behavior is compounded bit by bit through conditioned reflexes.

Thus, while discrediting a basic point of Watson's system, Lashley's work did not weaken the behaviorists' fundamental contention that only completely objective methods should be used. Quite the contrary, his work is an excellent demonstration of the tremendous value of objective methods in psychological research.

More Recent Behaviorists

A burst of growth occurred in behaviorism around 1925–1930, when new behavioristic systems as well as new people appeared on the scene. The movement began to branch out into distinct subsystems, generating much controversy that has continued up to the present day, particularly with regard to theories of learning.

The increasingly dominant behavioristic movement in American psychology was further strengthened by the development of the principle of operationism. Actually, the relationship between this principle and behaviorism was somewhat circular: on the one hand, as just noted, behaviorism was fortified by operationism, while on the other, the increasingly objective framework of behavioristic psychology had prepared the way for the acceptance of operationism.

The Influence of Operationism

Operationism is more of an attitude (indeed, it is a way of life to many) than a formal school in the sense in which we have been using the term. Its purpose is to render the language and terminology of science more objective and precise and to rid science of those problems (the so-called pseudo-problems) that are not actually observable or physically demonstrable. Briefly, operationism holds that the validity of a given scientific finding or theoretical construct is dependent on the validity of the operations used in arriving at that finding or construct.

The operationist viewpoint was championed by the well-known Harvard physicist Percy W. Bridgman, who wrote *The Logic of Modern Physics* (1927). In this book, which quickly captured the attention of many psychologists, Bridgman proposed that physical concepts must be defined in more precise and rigid terms and that all concepts lacking physical referents must be promptly discarded. Bridgman's own terms are perhaps more precise:

> The new attitude toward a concept is entirely different. We may illustrate by considering the concept of length: what do we mean by the length of an object? We evidently know what we mean by length if we can tell what the length of any and every object is, and for the physicist nothing more is required. To find the length of an object, we have to perform certain physical

operations. The concept of length is therefore fixed when the operations by which length is measured are fixed: that is, the concept of length involves as much as and nothing more than a set of operations; *the concept is synonymous with the corresponding set of operations* (1927, p. 5).

Thus, a physical concept is the same as the set of operations or procedures by which it is determined. Many psychologists quickly found this principle to be of great use in the science of psychology and some applied it with great eagerness. But as promptly as it was accepted by some psychologists, it provoked opposition from others.

Bridgman's concern with pseudo-problems, or questions that defy answer by any known objective test, is especially noteworthy. Notions or propositions that cannot be put to experimental test are meaningless for science. An example of a pseudo-problem is the problem of the existence and nature of the soul. What is this thing "soul"? Can it be observed in the laboratory? Can it be measured and manipulated under controlled conditions to determine its effects on behavior? If it cannot be so observed, measured, manipulated, etc., it has absolutely no use, no meaning, and no relevance for science. It follows that the concept of an individual and private consciousness is a pseudo-problem in psychology, for neither its existence nor its characteristics can be determined or investigated through objective methods. Consciousness, therefore, has no place in a scientific psychology.

It can be argued that operationism is not really new; that it is little more than a formal statement of methods that had already been used in psychology when the meanings of words or concepts were defined in terms of their physical referents. We have already noted the trend in American psychology toward an increasing objectification of methods and subject matter. Thus, it can be said that the spirit of operationism— as a basic attitude and as the framework within which to conduct research and formulate theories—had already been in use by a number of American psychologists for some years before the publication of Bridgman's book in 1927. Since the time of Wundt, however, physics had been the paragon of scientific respectability for the newer psychology and when physics favored operationism, psychology quickly followed suit.

As we mentioned earlier, operationism did not win universal recognition in psychology, nor is it universally accepted even today. Controversy continues about the relative utility or futility of limiting psychology's subject matter to that which has empirical reference. The important point about operationism for our present purpose is that the generation of behaviorists that came of age in the late 1920s characteristically included operationism in their approach to psychology. We now turn the discussion to these neo-behaviorists.

Edward Chace Tolman

One of the very early adherents to behaviorism, Tolman (1886–1959) originally studied engineering at the Massachusetts Institute of Technology. He then changed to psychology and studied under Holt at Harvard, where he received his PhD in 1915. In his last year of graduate work, while being trained in the Wundt–Titchener tradition, Tolman became acquainted with Watsonian behaviorism. Already questioning the scientific usefulness of introspection while still a graduate student, Tolman said in his *Autobiography* (1952) that Watson's behaviorism came as a "tremendous stimulus and relief."

After receiving his degree, Tolman became an instructor at Northwestern University until 1918, when he went to the University of California at Berkeley. It was at Berkeley, where he taught comparative psychology and conducted research on learning with rats, that he definitely became a behaviorist, though of a different sort than Watson.

There were two interruptions to his career at Berkeley. During World War II, he served in the Office of Strategic Services (1944–1945), and from 1950 to 1953, he was a leader in the spirited and commendable faculty opposition to the California state loyalty oath. During this time he taught at Harvard and the University of Chicago.

TOLMAN'S PURPOSIVE BEHAVIORISM

The most definitive statement of Tolman's position is presented in his first and most important book, *Purposive Behavior in Animals and Men*, published in 1932. His system of purposive behaviorism might appear, at first glance, to be a curious blending of two contradictory terms: purpose and behavior. Attributing purpose to an organism seems to imply consciousness. Surely such a mentalistic concept can have no place in a behavioristic system.

Tolman made it clear, however, both in this book and in his careful research, that he was very much the behaviorist in both subject matter and methodology, and that he was not urging a return to consciousness for psychology. He vigorously rejected introspection of the structuralist sort. Like Watson, Tolman had no interest in assumed internal experiences that were not accessible to objective observation. Any reference to conscious processes in Tolman's system was phrased in terms of cautious inferences from observed behavior.

It is equally clear, however, that Tolman was not a Watsonian behaviorist, for the two differed in at least two important respects. First, Tolman was not interested in studying behavior at the molecular level, *i.e.*, in terms of stimulus-response connections. Thus, unlike Watson, he was not concerned with elemental units of behavior—activities of the nerves, muscles, and glands. His focus was molar behavior—the total response actions of the whole organism. In this respect, his system is actually behavioristic and Gestalt (see Chapter XII) at the same time.

The major point of difference between Watson and Tolman, however, and the major tenet of Tolman's system, is the introduction of the notion of purposive behavior. Purposiveness in behavior, Tolman said, can be defined in very objective behavioral terms without appeal to introspection and to how the organism might "feel" about the experience. It seemed obvious to Tolman that all behavior is goal directed; the cat tries to get out of the puzzle box, the rat learns a difficult maze, the human studies music. Behavior, he said, "reeks of purpose." All behavior is oriented toward achieving some goal object, learning the means to an end. The rat persistently goes through a maze, making fewer errors, getting to the goal faster and faster each time. In other words, the rat is learning, and the very fact of learning, in a rat or a man, is highly objective behavioral evidence of purpose. Note that Tolman is dealing with the response of the organism and that his measures are in terms of the response behavior changing as a function of learning.

Watsonian behaviorists were quick to criticize this attribution of purpose to behavior for, they argued, did this not rest on the assumption of consciousness in the organism? Tolman's answer was that it made no difference to him whether the animal was conscious or not. What the conscious experience (if any) was associated with purposing did not in any way influence the behavioral responses of the organism; only the overt response behavior concerned Tolman.

If there is a conscious awareness of the goal, Tolman said, this is a private matter within each individual organism and not available to the objective tools of science. Anything that is internal and cannot be observed from outside the organism is not within the realm of science. Woodworth (1948) described Tolman's argument in the following fashion.

> If I try to describe to you my sensation of the color red, I find it cannot be done. I can point to a red object, I can say that red is somewhat like orange or purple, and very different from green and blue, quite a gay, stimulating color, very nice for a tie but a little too gay for a professor's overcoat—I can put red in many such relations but I cannot describe the sensation itself. I should have the same difficulty in trying to describe my feelings of pleasantness. . . . Only to the extent that private experience can be *reported*, made public, can it have any place in science (p. 106).

INTERVENING VARIABLES

As a behaviorist, Tolman believed that the initiating causes of behavior, and the final resulting behavior itself, must be capable of being objectively observed and operationally defined. He felt that the initiating causes of behavior consist of five independent variables: the environmental stimuli (S), physiological drive (P), heredity (H), previous training (T), and age (A). Behavior, then, is a function of these independent variables:

$$B = f_x (S, P, H, T, A)$$

Between these observable independent variables and the final response measure (the observable dependent variable), Tolman postulated a set of inferred and nonobserved factors, the intervening variables, which are the actual determinants of behavior. They are the internal processes that connect the antecedent stimulus situation with the observed response. The statement S-R must now read S-O-R. The intervening variable, then, is what is going on within O (the organism) that brings about a given response in reaction to a given stimulus.

This intervening variable cannot be objectively observed and therefore can be of no use to science unless it can be clearly related to both the experimental (independent) variable and the behavior (dependent) variable. The classic example is the intervening variable of hunger, which cannot be seen, as such, in another person or in a rat. Hunger can, however, be precisely and objectively related to an objective experimental variable—the length of time since the organism last had food. It can also be objectively and precisely related to an objective response variable such as the amount of food or how rapidly it is consumed. Thus, this unobservable inferred variable can be given precise empirical referents and is subject to quantification and experimental manipulation.

Tolman originally proposed two kinds of intervening variables: demand variables and cognitive variables. The demand variables are essentially motives and include, e.g., sex, hunger, and demand for safety in the face of danger. The cognitive (or "know-how") variables are abilities and include perception of objects, motor skills, and the like. In 1951, Tolman revised his intervening variables and proposed three main categories: (a) need systems—the physiological deprivation or drive situation at a given moment in time; (b) belief-value motives— these represent the intensity of preference for certain goal objects and the relative strengths of these goal objects in satisfying needs; and (c) behavior-spaces—behavior takes place in the behavior-space of the individual. In this behavior-space, some objects attract (have a positive valence), whereas others repel (have a negative valence).

Tolman's concept of the intervening variable has been useful to many psychologists, though it has certainly not gone uncriticized. Intervening variables appear to be of value in developing an acceptable theory of behavior so long as they are empirically related to both experimental and behavior variables. Doing this comprehensively and completely, however, is a monumental task.

THEORY OF LEARNING

Tolman felt that all animal and human behavior (with the exception of tropisms and simple reflexes) is capable of modification through experience. Hence, learning is a very important part of his system. He rejected Thorndike's law of effect, saying that reward or reinforcement plays little, if any, role in learning. In its place, he proposed a cognitive theory of learning in which the continued performance of a task builds up *sign Gestalts,* which are learned relationships between cues in the environment and the organism's expectations. The animal, he said, gets to know some of his environment.

Let us follow Tolman's system as we watch a hungry rat placed in a maze. The animal moves about in the maze, sometimes in correct alleys and sometimes in blind alleys. Eventually, he discovers the food. In subsequent trials in the maze, Tolman argued, purpose and direction are given to the rat's behavior by the goal. At each choice point, expectations are established. The rat comes to expect that certain cues associated with the choice point will lead on to food. If the rat's expectancy is confirmed (if he gets food), the *sign Gestalt* of cue expectancy associated with that choice point is strengthened. Over all the choice points in the maze, there is established an entire pattern of *sign Gestalts,* which Tolman called a "cognitive map." This pattern, according to Tolman, is what the animal learns—a cognitive map of the maze, not a set of motor habits. In a sense, then, the rat establishes a comprehensive "knowledge" of the maze or of any familiar environment. Something like a field map is developed in its brain, enabling it to go from one spot in the environment to another without being restricted to a fixed series of bodily movements.

A great deal of research was conducted in Tolman's laboratory relating to the question of cognitive learning. For example, in studies of latent learning, rats demonstrated evidence of learning a maze in the absence of food or any other obvious reinforcement.

COMMENT

Tolman exercised considerable influence on psychology, particularly in the area of learning, for a period of more than 40 years; moreover, his influence is still felt in psychology today. He has been criticized for his failure to develop a fully integrated theoretical system, and many feel that he failed to adequately relate behavior to the more covert functioning, such as cognitive states. A further and more obvious point of attack relates to his language, which many feel is too subjective and mentalistic.

On the positive side, Tolman initiated many important research topics in learning and introduced the concept of the intervening variable to psychology. One point of general significance is Tolman's strong support of the use of the rat as an appropriate subject for psychological study. An essay written in 1945 clearly and delightfully states his position on this issue:

What . . . can we now say as to the contributions of us rodent psychologists to human behavior? What is it that we rat runners still have to contribute to the understanding of the deeds and the misdeeds, the absurdities and the tragedies of our friend, and our enemy—*homo sapiens?* The answer is that, whereas man's successes, persistences, and socially unacceptable divagations . . . are all ultimately shaped and materialized by specific cultures, it is still true that most of the formal underlying laws of intelligence, motivation, and instability can still be studied in rats as well as, and more easily than, in men.

And, as a final peroration, let it be noted that rats live in cages; they do not go on binges the night before one has planned an experiment; they do not kill each other off in wars; they do not invent engines of destruction, and, if they did, they would not be so inept about controlling such engines; they do not go in for either class conflicts or race conflicts; they avoid politics, economics, and papers on psychology. They are marvelous, pure, and delightful. And, as soon as I possibly can, I am going to climb back again out on that good old phylogenetic limb and sit there, this time right side up and unashamed, wiggling my whiskers at all the silly, yet at the same time far too complicated, specimens of *homo sapiens,* whom I shall see strutting and fighting and messing things up, down there on the ground below me (p. 166).

Edwin Ray Guthrie

After receiving his PhD in 1912 from the University of Pennsylvania, Guthrie (1886–1959) began his academic career in 1914 at the University of Washington, where he remained until his retirement in 1956. While in graduate school, he became an ardent convert to a behavioristic approach to psychology, an approach from which he never wavered. He strongly believed that science must deal only with objectively observable conditions and events. So extreme an empiricist was Guthrie that he opposed the practice of attempting to relate behavioral events to what he considered the invisible brain and nervous system. Although his basic orientation is definitely that of behaviorism, he cannot be described as a Watsonian behaviorist.

His most important influence on psychology is his formulation of an extremely simple learning theory. Variously described as the most persistent advocate of conditioning (Wolman, 1960) and the most radical of all the associationists (Woodworth & Sheehan, 1964), Guthrie remained for several decades a forceful proponent of a theory of learning based on only one principle—contiguity. In accounting for the strengthening of learned responses, he rejected Thorndike's laws of effect and frequency as well as Pavlovian reinforcement. He relied, instead, on what he called simultaneous conditioning, which he considered the most general law in psychology.

To Guthrie, all learning or behavior modification depends solely on the contiguity of stimulus and response. Thus, if a stimulus just once elicits a response, then the S-R association is established. It is, in essence, a *one-trial learning* situation, which is his most famous principle. Repetition and reinforcement form no essential part of his system. His primary, and actually his only, formal law of learning states that: "A combination of stimuli which has accompanied a movement will on its recurrence tend to be followed by that movement" (1935, p. 26). Note that there is no mention of internal drive states, of repetitions of the stimulus-response pairings, or of any form of reinforcement. One pairing of the stimulus and the resulting movement serves to establish the association: the behavior is learned.

Note that the law refers to movements, which Guthrie carefully distinguished from acts. He defined a movement as a pattern of motor and glandular responses or actions. An act, on the other hand, is a movement or series of movements that brings about end results. Although an act is a movement, a movement is not an act. The latter is on a larger scale: hitting a basket with a ball is an act composed of a number of separate movements. Guthrie believed that in measuring learning, the performance of the complete act is usually taken as the criterion of learning, whereas it is the movements that are actually conditioned as responses.

He considered this focus on the movements as a major distinguishing feature of his theory. He argued that Thorndike, for instance, was concerned with the total act, with the acquisition of a skill that is a function of a number of individual muscular movements. These individual movements are developed or acquired in single trials, but learning of the total act calls for repeated practice. The movements, or individual parts of the learned act, are the basic raw data in Guthrie's system. Because they are smaller, these movements are more difficult to observe in a learning situation, which (he explained) is why they are often overlooked.

Just as the response of the organism is composed of a number of separate components, so too is the stimulation to which the organism is exposed. Since the stimulus and response comprise so many components it is necessary to have a large number of pairings of the total stimulus and response situations in order to achieve any degree of consistency in the behavior under question. So, practice is necessary to bring about improvement of the total constellation of movements (the act), but each component movement is learned after just one pairing with the stimulus.

COMMENT

During his active career, Guthrie seemed to prefer writing and argumentation to experimentation. He believed strongly in the importance of theory for the development of psychology, and had commented that theories, not facts, endure. His several books contain evidence of an anecdotal (albeit persuasive) nature, and comparatively little in the way of experimental evidence. There is, however, empirical support for his theory, mainly his own research involving stereotypy in the behavior of the cat in a puzzle box, and the research of a number of others. Compared to some other theoretical positions in neo-behavioristic psychology, however, there is relatively little empirical support. Much of the appeal of Guthrie's system probably rests upon its consistency over the years and its great simplicity. It is indeed a system that is quite easy to understand when compared to other more complex learning theories.

Thus, the inherent simplicity of the system elicits praise from some but it also provides a point of criticism for others. For instance, it has been suggested that the simplicity has been maintained as a result of Guthrie's failure to deal explicitly with certain major problems in learning that might defy explanation within his framework. Mueller and Schoenfeld (1954) noted, for example, that "It is undoubtedly true that many reviews of Guthrie in the literature have mistaken incompleteness for simplicity" (p. 368). Such critics suggest that a number of additional constructs and assumptions are necessary to encompass the major problem areas of learning.

Nevertheless, Guthrie was able to successfully maintain his theoretical position and stature as a leading learning theorist. His system is still a subject for serious consideration in contemporary psychology. The value of his contributions received formal recognition in 1958 when the American Psychological Foundation presented him with their Gold Medal Award. Finally, it is noted that the recent appearance of statistical models of learning are based largely on the Guthrian scheme.

Clark Leonard Hull

First and foremost a behaviorist, Hull (1884–1952) has achieved a highly respected position in contemporary psychology. Perhaps no previous psychologist had been so consistently and keenly devoted to the problems inherent in scientific method. "Few psychologists have had such a mastery of mathematics and formal logic as Hull had. Hull applied the language of mathematics to psychological theory in a manner used by no other psychologist" (Wolman, 1960, p. 105).

Hull was troubled with very poor health as a child and poor eyesight throughout his life, but he nevertheless diligently pursued his academic career. Initially intending to be a mining engineer, he changed to psychology and received his PhD in 1918 from the University of Wisconsin, where he remained for ten years. His early research presaged his lifelong emphasis on objective methods and functional laws. He investigated concept formation and the effects of tobacco on behavioral efficiency, and surveyed the literature on tests and measurements, publishing an important early text in that area in 1928. He also worked on the development of practical methods of statistical analysis and even invented a machine for calculating correlations.

Hull devoted ten years to the study of hypnosis and suggestibility, publishing 32 papers and a book, *Hypnosis and Suggestibility* (1933), that summarized the research. In 1929, he became a research professor at Yale, where he developed his final major research interest: a theory of behavior based on Pavlov's laws of conditioning. He had first read Pavlov in 1927 and became greatly interested in the problem of conditioned reflexes and learning.

Hull believed there were four methods that can be useful to science. Three methods then in current use included: (*a*) simple observation, (*b*) systematic controlled observation, and (*c*) experimental testing of hypotheses. While not altogether denying their utility, Hull argued for strict adherence to the *hypothetico-deductive method,* which utilizes rigorous deduction from a set of formulations that are determined in a priori fashion. The method involves establishing postulates from which experimentally testable conclusions can be deduced. These conclusions are then submitted to experimental test: failure results in revision; passing allows for their incorporation into the body of science. Hull believed that if psychology was to be an objective science on the order of other natural sciences (in accord with the behavioristic program), then the only appropriate method was the hypothetico-deductive one. Universal generalizability can be achieved only through quantitative and formal-logical statements.

The primary focus in Hull's system is Pavlov's conditioned reflex and the concept of reinforcement, which Hull held to be fundamental to all learning and very amenable to the experimental method. In the 1930s he wrote a number of articles on conditioning that argued that complex higher-order behaviors could be explained in terms of the basic principles of conditioning. In 1940 he published, with five colleagues, a difficult book, *Mathematico-Deductive Theory of Rote Learning: A Study in Scientific Methodology.* Though it was considered a notable achievement in the development of scientific psychology, it was "seldom read, less often understood, and unproductive of research. . . . an idealized but relatively fruitless model of psychological theory construction" (Marx & Hillix, 1963, p. 244).

Hull's next major publication, *Principles of Behavior* (1943), was considerably less difficult to read. In it, he outlined, in great detail and with characteristic precision, a theoretical framework so comprehensive as to include all behavior. With the publication of this book, Hull's system assumed a position of paramount importance and influence in the area of learning in this country, a position it still commands today. A tremendous amount of research was generated by the book and Hull soon became the most frequently cited psychologist in the field. His system underwent revision in a number of journal articles and the final revision appeared in *A Behavior System* (1952). Hull had been ill for a number of years, and he died before reading the galley proofs of this book.

HULL'S SYSTEM: THE FRAME OF REFERENCE

Hull believed that human behavior involves a continuing interaction between the organism and the environment. The objective stimuli provided by the environment and the objective behavioral responses provided by the organism are, of course, observable facts. This interaction takes place, however, within a much larger context that cannot be totally defined in observable stimulus-response terms.

This broader context or frame of reference is the biological adaptation of the organism to its unique environment. The survival of the organism is aided by this biological adaptation. Whenever survival is in jeopardy, Hull considered the organism to be in a state of need. Thus, need involved a situation in which the biological requirements for survival were not being met. When in a state of need, the organism behaves in a manner designed to reduce that need. The behavior, therefore, serves to reinstate the optimal biological conditions necessary for survival.

Hull's concern with biological survival grew out of his interest in certain aspects of evolutionary theory. It is also quite consistent with the functionalists' emphasis on adaptation to the environment. Hull was, however, totally committed to a behavioristic or objective psychology, allowing no place in his system for consciousness, purpose, or any other mentalistic notion.

DRIVES

As we have seen, Hull considered bodily need arising from a deviation from optimal biological conditions as the basis of motivation. However, rather than introduce the concept of biological need as such directly into his system, he postulated the intervening variable of drive. Drive was posited as a stimulus (S_D) that arises from a state of tissue need and that functions to arouse or activate behavior. The strength of the drive, Hull noted, can be empirically determined in terms of either the length of deprivation, or the intensity, strength, or energy expenditure of the resulting behavior. He considered the duration of deprivation a rather imperfect index, and he placed greater emphasis on behavior strength.

There are two major kinds of drives in Hull's system: primary and secondary. The primary drives are associated with the biological need states and are directly and intimately involved with the organism's survival. These drives arise from a state of tissue need and include hunger, thirst, air, temperature regulation, defecation, urination, sleep, activity, sexual intercourse, relief from pain, etc. These are basic innate processes of the organism and vitally necessary for survival.

Hull recognized that both humans and animals are motivated by forces other than the basic primary drives. Accordingly, he postulated the secondary or learned drives. The secondary drive concept refers to situations (or other stimuli in the environment) that are associated with the reduction of primary drives and that may, as a result, become drives themselves. This means that previously neutral stimuli assume drive characteristics because they are capable of eliciting responses that are similar to those aroused by the original need state or primary drive. A simple example involves being burned by a stove. The painful burn (tissue damage) produces a primary drive (relief from pain). Other stimuli associated with this primary drive, such as the sight of the stove, may lead to the withdrawing of the hand when the visual stimulus is perceived. Thus, the sight of the stove may become the stimulus for the learned drive of fear. These secondary drives or motivating forces develop on the basis of the primary drives.

Since Hull postulated learned drives, learning obviously plays a key part in his system.

LEARNING

It is important to note that Hull's system is basically and primarily concerned with motivation. This may surprise those who first heard of Hull in discussions of learning. Certainly he focused great attention on problems of learning but, as Cofer and Appley (1964) noted, "learning was, in the last analysis, only an instrumentality that permitted an organism to extend the range and variety of its efforts to satisfy its needs . . ." (p. 469). In the course of developing his system, Hull became less concerned with learning and more concerned with other factors capable of influencing behavior, although he is best known and most frequently studied in terms of his theory of learning.

Probably the most important part of Hull's theory is his attempt to integrate, or at least reconcile, Thorndike's law of effect with Pavlovian conditioning. He believed that learning could not be adequately explained by the principles of recency and frequency. Instead, the major focus of his learning theory is on the principle of reinforcement, which is essentially Thorndike's effect principle.

Hull's famous law of primary reinforcement states that if a stimulus-response relationship is followed by a reduction in need, then on subsequent occasions, the probability is high that the same stimulus will evoke the same response. Note that reward or reinforcement is defined not in terms of Thorndike's notion of satisfaction but rather in terms of reduction of a primary need. Thus, primary reinforcement, referring to the reduction of a primary drive, is the cornerstone of Hull's system of learning. Just as his system contains secondary drives, it also deals with secondary reinforcement. If a secondary or learned drive brings about a reduction in the intensity of the stimulus, it will act as a secondary reinforcement. As Hull stated it:

> It follows that any stimulus consistently associated with a reinforcement situation will through that association acquire the power of evoking the conditioned inhibition, *i.e.*, reduction in stimulus intensity, and so of itself producing the resulting reinforcement. Since this indirect power of reinforcement is acquired through learning, it is called *secondary reinforcement* (1951, pp. 27–28).

Hull believed that the stimulus-response connection is strengthened by the number of reinforcements that have taken place. He called the strength of the S-R connection habit strength, which refers to the persistence of the conditioning and is a function of reinforcement.

Learning cannot take place in the absence of reinforcement that is necessary to bring about a reduction of the drive. Because of this emphasis on reinforcement, Hull's system is called a need-reduction theory, as opposed to Guthrie's contiguity theory and Tolman's cognitive theory.

Hull's system is presented in terms of highly specific and detailed postulates and corollaries, all of which are phrased in difficult verbal and mathematical form. In his last presentation (*A Behavior System,* 1952) there are 18 postulates and 12 corollaries. Though the system was based originally upon conditioning principles, Hull believed that his fundamental position could be elaborated upon to include complex processes such as problem solving, social behavior, and forms of learning other than conditioning. He lived to see only a portion of this ambition realized.

COMMENT

This overview of Hull's system is, of course, far too brief to encompass the enormous scope of his work. It is important, however, to understand the way in which contemporary systems, such as Hull's, derive from or grow out of older ways of thinking. There is a continuity of development in psychology, and brief mention of contemporary derivatives of past systems should give the student an appreciation of the relevance of the past for the present.

Hull's system has remained in a continuous state of development and even after his death cannot be considered "finished." His students and his students' students are still actively engaged in research. The older systems we have discussed are finished in the sense that proponents of them are no longer conducting research. Such systems *qua* systems are extinct (though, in some cases, their spirit lingers on). It remains for future books on the history of psychology to attempt to evaluate whether Hull's program, as last presented, will have made lasting contributions to psychological theory. It is not yet history.

The system has, however, achieved a position of such prominence that it has generated a great deal of criticism since its inception. This, in itself, constitutes evidence of its wide influence in psychology. A few of the more general points of criticism are noted.

As a leading exponent of neo-behaviorism, Hull is subject to the same general kinds of criticism aimed at Watson and others who followed the behavioristic tradition. Thus, those who oppose a behavioristic approach to psychology on methodological and theoretical grounds include Hull among those in the "enemy camp."

A specific criticism of Hull's system is its lack of generalizability. It has been asserted that, in his attempt to define his variables with total precision in quantitative terms, he operated too specifically, functioning at times on a miniature system basis. His approach was, in other words, extremely particularistic, in that he often formulated his postulates from results of single experimental situations. Many opponents argue that generalization to all behavior on the basis of such extremely specific experimental demonstrations is questionable.

As Hilgard (1956) stated the problem:

> Surely a set of laws of mammalian behavior ought not reflect in the constants of its basic postulates such specialized information as the most favorable interval for human eyelid conditioning (Postulate 2), . . . the weight in grams of food needed to condition a rat (Postulate 7), . . . or the amplitude in millimeters of galvanometer deflection in human conditioning (Postulate 15) (p. 181).

While such precise quantification is certainly necessary and commendable in a natural science approach to psychology, it does tend to reduce the range of applicability of the findings.

Thus, we see that Hull's adherence to a mathematical and formal system of theory building is open to both praise and criticism at the same time. Wolman (1960) suggested that "Hull became, to a certain extent, a victim of his zest for mathematics. . . . Whenever the opportunity came, he quantified his statements, sometimes pursuing the issue *ad absurdum* . . ." (p. 124). His system is so thoroughly and minutely developed in quantitative terms that incomplete or inaccurate formulations are relatively easy to spot. Gaps and inconsistencies in a theory expressed in ordinary verbal terms can be easily filled in with appropriate illustrative examples. Some critics have found such gaps in Hull's system and argue that at least some parts of Hull's formulations are not as tightly constructed as was originally thought.

Damaging though the criticisms are, Hull's enormous influence on contemporary psychology cannot be minimized. We have already mentioned the great amount of research occasioned by Hull's work; this alone constitutes a major contribution to psychology. He provided an objective terminology that was not only well accepted but that represented a new approach to psychological data rather than a simple relabeling of older concepts.

Marx and Hillix (1963) suggest that no other psychologist has had such a pronounced and extensive effect on the professional motivation of so many other psychologists. He defended, extended, and expounded the strictly objective behavioristic approach as had never been done before.

Perhaps it is true that Hull's contribution to systematic psychological theory building in general is greater than his own theory, but as noted earlier, it is still too close in time to fully determine this. While many psychologists question parts or all of Hull's theory, there is general respect and admiration for the rigorous methods used to develop it. It is also a tribute to the greatness of the man to note a few of today's leading psychologists who are his disciples and followers: Dollard, Hovland, Kimble, Miller, Mowrer, and Spence; and whose names should be familiar.

Burrhus Frederick Skinner

Although much younger than both Hull and Tolman, Skinner (1904–   ) was their active contemporary in the new birth of behaviorism in the 1930s. Both Hull and Skinner are behaviorists, but there are marked differences between their approaches to psychology. Whereas Hull stressed the importance of theory, Skinner favors a strictly empirical system with no theoretical framework within which to conduct his research. Where Hull's work consisted of postulating theory on an a priori basis and then checking the deduced conclusions against experimental evidence, Skinner avoids theory completely and practices instead a strict brand of positivism. Skinner begins with empirical data and then proceeds very carefully and slowly (if at all) toward tentative generalizations. Hull represents the deductive method; Skinner represents the inductive method.

Skinner received his PhD from Harvard in 1931. His dissertation provides an early glimpse of his point of view toward psychology, to which he has successfully and consistently adhered throughout his career. His major proposition is that a reflex is the correlation between stimulus and response and nothing more. To Skinner, there are no intervening links between S and R, either physiological or theoretical.

Following several years of postdoctoral fellowships, Skinner taught at the University of Minnesota from 1936 to 1945 and Indiana University from 1945 to 1947. In 1947 he returned to Harvard, where he is still active. His career is remarkable for the great variety and scope of his interests and the ingenuity with which he conducts his research. His diverse contributions to psychology have been concerned with "an analysis of verbal learning, with missile-guiding pigeons, with teaching machines, and with the control of behavior by scheduled reinforcement. The ingenious apparatus to his credit includes an automatized baby-tending device, used with one of his own children and later marketed commercially. . . . Skinner has even managed to write a novel on a utopian theme, *Walden two*" (Marx & Hillix, 1963, p. 256).

SKINNER'S POSITION

In a number of important respects, Skinner's position represents a renewal of the older Watsonian behaviorism. As MacLeod stated, "Watson's spirit is indestructible. Cleaned and purified, it breathes through the writings of B. F. Skinner" (1959, p. 34).

Skinner's is an exclusively descriptive kind of strict behaviorism that is devoted to the study of responses and is atheoretical in nature. Thus, his concern is with describing behavior rather than explaining it. He deals only with observable behavior and believes that the task of scientific inquiry is to establish functional relations between the antecedent experimenter-controlled stimulus conditions and the subsequent response of the organism. Skinner is not at all concerned with theorizing or speculating about what might be going on inside the organism. His program includes no reference to any presumed internal entities, whether described as intervening variables or as physiological processes. Whatever might occur between the stimulus and the response does not represent objective data for a behaviorist, according to Skinner. This purely descriptive behaviorism has, with good reason, been called the "empty-organism approach."

In opposition to much of contemporary psychology, Skinner does not believe in the use of large numbers of subjects and statistical comparisons between mean responses of groups. Instead, he has focused on the intense and thorough investigation of a single subject:

> A prediction of what the *average* individual will do is often of little or no value in dealing with a particular individual. . . . a science is helpful in dealing with the individual only insofar as its laws refer to individuals. A science of behavior which concerns only the behavior of groups is not likely to be of help in our understanding of the particular case (Skinner, 1953, p. 19).

Skinner believes that truly valid replicable results can be obtained without the use of statistical analysis if a large body of data is collected from a single subject under very well-controlled experimental conditions. In 1958, the Skinnerians established their *Journal for the Experimental Analysis of Behavior,* because of the unwritten requirements of the existing journals concerning subject sample size and statistical analysis.

The student is no doubt aware of the Skinner box and of Skinner's emphasis on operant as opposed to respondent behavior. In the Pavlovian conditioning situation, a known stimulus is paired with a response under conditions of reinforcement. The behavioral response is elicited by a specific observable stimulus situation and is called, by Skinner, a respondent behavior.

Operant behavior, on the other hand, occurs without any observable external stimuli. The organism's response is seemingly spontaneous in that it is not related to any known observable stimulus. This is not to say that there is definitely no stimulus eliciting the response, but rather that no stimulus is detected when the response occurs. Thus, as far as the experimenter is concerned, there is no stimulus because he has not applied any and cannot see any.

Operant behavior also operates on the organism's environment; respondent behavior does not. The harnessed dog in Pavlov's laboratory can do nothing but respond when the experimenter presents the stimulus. The dog cannot act "on his own" to secure the stimulus. The operant behavior of the rat in the Skinner box, however, is instrumental in securing the stimulus (food): when the rat presses the bar, it secures food. Skinner feels that operant behavior is much more representative of the real-life human learning situation. Hence, since behavior is mostly of the operant variety, the most effective approach to a science of behavior, according to Skinner, is the study of the conditioning and extinction of operant behaviors.

Skinner's classic experimental demonstration involved bar pressing in the Skinner box that was especially constructed to eliminate all extraneous stimuli. In this experiment, a rat that had been deprived of food was placed in the box and allowed to explore. In the course of this general exploratory behavior the rat sooner or later, and by accident, depressed a lever activating a food magazine that released a food pellet into a tray. After a few reinforcements, conditioning was usually very rapid. Note that the rat's behavior operated on the environment (pressed the lever) and was instrumental in securing food.

From this basic experiment, Skinner derived his law of acquisition, which states that the strength of an operant is increased when that operant is followed by presentation of a reinforcing stimulus. Although practice is important in the establishment of high rates of bar pressing, the key variable is reinforcement. Practice by itself will not increase the rate; all it does is provide the opportunity for additional reinforcement to occur.

Skinner's law of acquisition differs from the positions of Thorndike and Hull on learning. First, Skinner does not speak in terms of any pleasure-pain consequences of reinforcement, as did Thorndike. In opposition to Hull, Skinner makes no attempt to interpret reinforcement in terms of drive reduction. Whereas the systems of Thorndike and Hull are explanatory, Skinner's is descriptive. Skinner does not view drive as a stimulus or a physiological state. Rather, he considers drive as simply a set of operations that influence response behavior in a certain way. He defines drive quite objectively in terms of number of hours of deprivation.

Skinner and his followers conducted a great deal of research on numerous problems in learning. Their studies included the role of punishment in the acquisition of responses, the effect of different schedules of reinforcement, extinction of operant response, secondary reinforcement, and generalization, among others.

In recent years, Skinner has worked with animals other than rats, as well as with human subjects, using the same basic approach as the Skinner box. With pigeons, the operant behavior involves pecking at a spot with food as a reinforcement. The operant behavior for human subjects involves problem solving reinforced by verbal approval or by knowledge of having given the correct answer.

Skinner has effectively demonstrated the extremely wide range of applicability of operant conditioning. In *Science and Human Behavior* (1953), he extended his system into broader areas, such as social behavior, religion, psychotherapy, education, and the effective control of behavior. In *Verbal Behavior* (1957), he deals with language as a verbal behavior, considering it basically similar to other forms of behavior.

Skinner has also noted the ethical problem of controlling behavior. His own research clearly demonstrates that it is possible to control an individual's behavior without his awareness. In his writings he discusses quite dispassionately the alternatives of individual freedom in the traditional sense as opposed to man controlled by science. He spells out the far-reaching social and ethical implications of operant conditioning for human life in a novel, *Walden Two* (1948), which describes a scientifically shaped utopian society.

COMMENT

The foregoing treatment does not do justice to the thoroughness of Skinner's research program and the wide range and variety of his interests. As with Hull, Skinner's system is active and influential in contemporary psychology and should, therefore, already be familiar.

Perhaps the most frequent criticism of Skinner is directed at his extreme brand of positivism and its accompanying opposition to theory. Opponents argue that it is impossible to eliminate all theorizing, as Skinner would have it. Since the details of an experiment are planned in advance of the actual situation, this advance planning in itself, critics claim, is evidence of theorizing, however simple. Chaplin and Krawiec (1960) note that Skinner's acceptance of the basic principles of conditioning as the framework for his research constitutes some degree of theorizing. Further, it has been argued that his willingness to extrapolate beyond his basic data, particularly in regard to his proposals about complex human problems, is also inconsistent with his antitheory stand. Skinner has made very confident assertions about economic, social, political, and religious affairs of human conduct that apparently are derived from his own system. Marx and Hillix (1963) suggest that this is in violation of a major tenet of his approach to psychology, *i.e.*, a strict adherence to observable fact.

Assuming that these criticisms are valid, the amount of theorizing possibly extant in Skinner's system is hardly on the order of that found in a system such as Hull's. Skinnerians do not actually oppose the use of theory in psychology for all time. Rather, they oppose "unripe theorizing," positing that the data in psychology are not yet complete enough to allow its ordering in theoretical terms. There have also been criticisms addressed to specific technical points in Skinner's system.

Skinner's influence on contemporary psychology is reflected in the work of an enthusiastic and highly active band of Skinnerians. Final evaluation of Skinner's position, however, must be deferred, because the system is still developing. Skinner's significance as the incontestable leader and champion of a behavioristic psychology has been formally recognized. Contemporary psychology has noted the magnitude of his contribution and, in 1958, the American Psychological Association granted him their Distinguished Scientific Contribution Award, with the following citation.

An imaginative and creative scientist, characterized by great objectivity in scientific matters and by warmth and enthusiasm in personal contacts. Choosing simple operant behavior as subject matter, he has challenged alternative analyses of behavior, insisting that description take precedence over hypotheses. By careful control of experimental conditions, he has produced data which are relatively free from fortuitous variation. Despite his antitheoretical position, he is considered an important systematist and has developed a self-consistent description of behavior which has greatly increased our ability to predict and control the behavior of organisms from rat to man. Few American psychologists have had so profound an impact on the development of psychology and on promising younger psychologists (APA Committee on APA Distinguished Scientific Contribution Awards, 1958, p. 735).

Concluding Commentary

Behaviorism, like all the other systematic positions, has a very long past. It can be traced back to Descartes, who considered man's body as a complex machine. Watson gave voice to the changing climate of the times in American psychology, revolted against its mentalistic background, and formally established a completely objective science of behavior. This vigorous Watsonian revolt marked the beginning of the positivistic era in American psychology, which seems to have grown stronger with each passing year. There have followed, immediately and up to the present day, highly enthusiastic formulations of many different forms of behaviorism, and the general American acceptance of operationism.

Although behaviorism as a formal school is dead, the neo-behavioristic spirit still flourishes, albeit as a general point of view or attitude rather than as a formal school; for behaviorism has evolved into the American tradition in experimental psychology. No psychologist today calls himself a behaviorist—it is no longer necessary to do so. To the extent that American experimental psychology is today objective, empirical, reductionistic, and (to some degree) environmentalistic, the spirit, if not the letter, of Watsonian behaviorism lives on. Fifty years after the publication of Watson's article, which formally began behaviorism, Skinner celebrated the anniversary with his article, *Behaviorism at Fifty* (1963), in which he noted that the tremendous progress in experimental psychology in America has been due primarily to the influence of behaviorism.

In recent years, however, a small but vocal group of psychologists has begun to question the behavioristic point of view. Their numbers appear to be growing and they may represent the beginning of a disinclination to view psychology wholly as a science of behavior. It is still too early to assess this so-called humanistic movement (indeed, perhaps too early to call it a movement), but it does exist, and is discussed in Chapter XV.

SUGGESTED FURTHER READINGS

Lashley

Beach, F. A., Hebb, D. O., Morgan, C. T., & Nissen, H. W. (Eds.) *The Neuropsychology of Lashley.* New York: McGraw-Hill, 1960.

Carmichael, L. Karl Spencer Lashley, experimental psychologist. *Science,* 1959, **129**, 1409–1412.

Operationism

Bergmann, G. Sense and nonsense in operationism. *Scientific Monthly,* 1954, **79**, 210–214.

Bridgman, P. W. Remarks on the present state of operationism. *Scientific Monthly,* 1954, **79**, 224–226.

Margenau, H. On interpretations and misinterpretations of operationalism. *Scientific Monthly,* 1954, **79**, 209–210.

Stevens, S. S. The operational basis of psychology. *American Journal of Psychology,* 1935, **47**, 323–330.

Tolman

MacCorquodale, K., & Meehl, P. E. Edward C. Tolman. In W. Estes *et al.* (Eds.), *Modern learning theory.* New York: Appleton-Century-Crofts, 1954. Pp. 177–266.

Tolman, E. C. Principles of purposive behavior. In S. Koch (Ed.), *Psychology: a study of a science.* Vol. 2. New York: McGraw-Hill, 1959. Pp. 92–157.

Guthrie

Guthrie, E. R. *The psychology of learning.* New York: Harper, 1935. (Rev. ed., 1952.)

Mueller, C. G., Jr., & Schoenfeld, W. N. Edwin R. Guthrie. In W. Estes *et al.* (Eds.), *Modern learning theory.* New York: Appleton-Century-Crofts, 1954. Pp. 345–379.

Hull

Hull, C. L. Mind, mechanism and adaptive behavior. *Psychological Review,* 1937, **44**, 1–32.

Koch, S. Clark L. Hull. In W. Estes *et al.* (Eds.), *Modern learning theory.* New York: Appleton-Century-Crofts, 1954. Pp. 1–176.

Skinner

Bixenstine, V. E. Empiricism in latter-day behaviorial science. *Science,* 1964, **145**, 464–467.

Skinner, B. F. A case history in scientific method. In S. Koch (Ed.), *Psychology: a study of a science.* Vol. 2. New York: McGraw-Hill, 1959. Pp. 359–379.

Skinner, B. F. *Cumulative record.* (Rev. ed.) New York: Appleton-Century-Crofts, 1961.

Contemporary Learning Theory

Bugelski, B. R. *The psychology of learning.* New York: Holt, 1956.

Deese, J. *The psychology of learning.* New York: McGraw-Hill, 1958.

Hilgard, E. R. *Theories of learning.* (2nd ed.) New York: Appleton-Century-Crofts, 1956.

General

Blanshard, B. Critical reflections on behaviorism. *Proceedings of the American Philosophical Society,* 1965, **109,** 22–28.

Boring, E. G. The trend toward mechanism. *Proceedings of the American Philosophical Society,* 1964, **108,** 451–454.

Hebb, D. O. The American revolution. *American Psychologist,* 1960, **15,** 735–745.

Skinner, B. F. Behaviorism at fifty. *Science,* 1963, **140,** 951–958.

Spence, K. W. The methods and postulates of behaviorism. *Psychological Review,* 1948, **55,** 67–78.

Wann, T. W. (Ed.) *Behaviorism and phenomenology: contrasting bases for modern psychology.* Chicago: University of Chicago Press, 1964.

XII

GESTALT PSYCHOLOGY

Introduction

THE FOREGOING discussions of the development of functionalism and behaviorism may have created the impression that psychology after Wundt was concentrated wholly in America. Although these two important schools were certainly American in both temperament and formal pronouncement and growth, another movement was developing in Europe at the same time—Gestalt psychology.

Around 1912—the year described by Woodworth and Sheehan (1964) as a "time of troubles" for the old theory of psychology—behaviorism was beginning its violent attack against the old Wundtian order of things, as well as against the newer functionalism. The updated associationism of Thorndike and Pavlov had been on the rise for a decade. Thorndike's first full statement of his position was made in 1911–1913 and the significance for psychology of the Pavlovian conditioned reflex was being acknowledged. Another fresh approach, psychoanalysis, was already over a decade old.

The Gestalt psychologists' attack on structuralism in Europe was simultaneous with, although independent of, the American movement. At the outset, both movements opposed Wundtian structuralism, although later they came to oppose each other. There were marked differences between the Gestaltists and the behaviorists: the former accepted the value of consciousness but disallowed the attempt to analyze consciousness into elements, whereas the latter refused to do anything at all with consciousness, even acknowledge it.

Gestalt psychologists referred to the Wundtian approach (with a sneer) as the "brick-and-mortar psychology," with the elements (the bricks) held together by the mortar of the process of association. They argued that a person when looking out a window sees immediately the trees and the sky, not the various alleged sensory elements (bright-

239

nesses, hues, etc.) that might constitute the perception of the sky and the trees according to the Wundtians.

Wundtians claimed that perception of objects consists in the accumulation of elements into groups or collections (Gestaltists called this the "bundle hypothesis"). The Gestalt psychologists maintained that when sensory elements are brought together, something new is formed. Put together a number of individual musical notes and something new (a melody) emerges from their combination, something that did not exist in any of the individual notes. Put simply and succinctly, "the whole is more than the sum of its parts." This was the keynote of the Gestalt opposition to Wundtian structuralism.

Miller[1] described an imaginary visit to a psychological laboratory around this time, in which the basic difference between the Gestalt and structural approaches to perception is disclosed. As you walk into the laboratory, a psychologist asks you what you see on the table:

"A book."

"Yes, of course, it is a book," he agrees, "but what do you *really* see?"

"What do you mean, 'What do I *really* see'?" you ask, puzzled. "I told you that I see a book. It is a small book with a red cover."

The psychologist is persistent. "What is your perception *really?*" he insists. "Describe it to me as precisely as you can."

"You mean it isn't a book? What is this, some kind of trick?"

There is a hint of impatience. "Yes, it is a book. There is no trickery involved. I just want you to describe to me *exactly* what you can see, no more and no less."

You are growing very suspicious now. "Well," you say, "from this angle the cover of the book looks like a dark red parallelogram."

"Yes," he says, pleased. "Yes, you see a patch of dark red in the shape of a parallelogram. What else?"

"There is a grayish white edge below it and another thin line of the same dark red below that. Under it I see the table—" He winces. "Around it I see a somewhat mottled brown with wavering streaks of lighter brown running roughly parallel to one another."

"Fine, fine." He thanks you for your cooperation.

As you stand there looking at the book on the table you are a little embarrassed that this persistent fellow was able to drive you to such an analysis. He made you so cautious that you were not sure any longer what you really saw and what you only thought you saw. You were, in fact, as suspicious as the New England farmer who would admit only that, "It looks like a cow on this side." In your caution you began talking about what you saw in terms of sensations, where just a moment earlier you were quite certain that you perceived a book on a table.

Your reverie is interrupted suddenly by the appearance of a psychologist who looks vaguely like Wilhelm Wundt. "Thank you, for helping to confirm once more my theory of perception. You have proved," he says, "that the book

---

[1] From pp. 103–105, *Psychology*, by George A. Miller. Copyright 1962 by George A. Miller. Reprinted by permission of Harper & Row.

you see is nothing but a compound of elementary sensations. When you were trying to be precise and say accurately what it was you really saw, you had to speak in terms of color patches, not objects. It is the color sensations that are primary, and every visual object is reducible to them. Your perception of the book is constructed from sensations just as a molecule is constructed from atoms."

This little speech is apparently a signal for battle to begin. "Nonsense!" shouts a voice from the opposite end of the hall. "Nonsense! Any fool knows that the *book* is the primary, immediate, direct, compelling, perceptual fact!" The psychologist who charges down upon you now bears a faint resemblance to William James, but he seems to have a German accent, and his face is so flushed with anger that you cannot be sure. "This reduction of a perception into sensations that you keep talking about is nothing but an intellectual game. An object is not just a bundle of sensations. Any man who goes about seeing patches of dark redness where he ought to see books is sick!"

As the fight begins to gather momentum you close the door softly and slip away. You have what you came for, an illustration that there are two different attitudes, two different ways to talk about the information that our senses provide.

Thus, the Gestalt psychologists feel there is more to perception than meets the eye (so to speak); that our perception somehow goes beyond the basic physical data provided to the sense organs. As with other movements, the basic notion of the Gestaltist protest has its historical roots in antiquity. After examining these antecedent influences, we shall discuss the formal founding of the Gestalt movement.

Antecedent Influences

The basis of the Gestalt position—the focus on the unity of perception—can be traced to the German philosopher Immanuel Kant (1724–1804). This eminent man, who never ventured more than 60 miles from his place of birth, dominated philosophical thinking for more than a generation. Although less extensive than his contribution to philosophy, his contribution to psychology is important.

Kant influenced psychology through his stress on the unity of a perceptual act. He argued that when we perceive objects (or what we call objects), we encounter mental states that might seem to be composed of bits and pieces (the sensory elements of which the associationists spoke). However, these elements are meaningfully organized in a priori fashion and not through the process of association. The mind, in the process of perception, forms or creates a unitary experience, an object within a meaningful context. According to Kant, perception is not a passive impression and combination of sensory elements, but an active organization of these elements into a unitary and coherent experience. The raw material of perception is thus given form and organization by the mind. This position obviously attacks the very heart of associationism.

To Kant, some of the forms imposed on experience by the mind are innate, such as space, time, and causality. That is, time and space are not derived from experience, but exist innately in the mind as a priori forms of perception; they are intuitively knowable.

As was the case with functionalism and behaviorism, Wundt, in his role as a target for criticism, was a precursor of Gestalt psychology. He was also a more direct influence, however, in that his principle of creative synthesis (very similar to John Stuart Mill's mental chemistry) recognized that new characteristics might emerge when elements are combined into wholes. Wundt made little of this notion, however.

Franz Brentano, discussed in Chapter IV, anticipated the formal Gestalt movement through his insistence that psychology study the process or act of experiencing rather than the content of experience (elementary sensations). He considered the Wundtian method of introspection to be highly artificial and favored a less rigid and more direct observation of experience as it occurs, like the later Gestalt method.

A physicist, Ernst Mach (1838–1916), provided a more direct influence on the Gestalt revolution. In his book, *The Analysis of Sensations* (1885), Mach spoke of sensations of space-form and time-form, considering spatial patterns (such as geometrical figures) and temporal patterns (such as melodies) as sensations. These space-form and time-form sensations he considered independent of their elements. For example, a circle might be white or black, or large or small, and lose absolutely nothing of its quality of circularity.

This notion was expanded by Christian von Ehrenfels (1859–1932), who is often considered the immediate intellectual antecedent of the Gestalt movement (although Gestalt psychologists denied this). Von Ehrenfels suggested that there are qualities of experience that cannot be explained in terms of combinations of the traditional kinds of sensations. He called these qualities *Gestalt qualitäten,* or form qualities, and they are perceptions based on something over and above the individual sensations. A melody, for example, will sound the same even when transposed to different keys. Thus, a melody is independent of the particular sensations it provides. To von Ehrenfels, and the Austrian School of *Gestalt qualität* that was founded at Graz, form itself was an element (not a sensation), a new element created by the action of the mind operating on the sensory elements. Thus, the mind creates form out of the elementary sensations.

Mach and von Ehrenfels were not true Gestalt psychologists but were actually carrying on the elementistic position of the structuralists. Rather than opposing the very notion of elementism, as the Gestalt psychologists did, they simply added new elements. As Marx and Hillix (1963) noted, "They pointed out the problem but gave an entirely wrong solution. They complicated rather than simplified" (p. 174); we can see why Gestalt psychology denies any direct connection with the two.

In America, an antecedent of Gestalt psychology is found in William James's opposition to psychological elementism. James regarded elements of consciousness as purely artificial abstractions and noted that we see objects, not bundles of sensations.

One very important early influence is the phenomenological movement in German philosophy and psychology. As a methodological tool, phenomenology refers to a free and unbiased description of immediate experience just as it occurs. It is an "uncorrected" kind of observation in which an experience is accepted as it is (*i.e.*, is not analyzed into elements or otherwise artificially abstracted). It involves the almost naïve experience of common sense rather than experience as reported by a trained introspector with a special systematic orientation.

The phenomenological tradition in psychology is generally assumed to have begun with Goethe and its active use can be traced to a number of scholars in psychology as well as other disciplines. A particularly active group of phenomenological psychologists were at G. E. Müller's laboratory at Göttingen in the years 1909–1915. Three men, Erich R. Jaensch, David Katz, and Edgar Rubin, conducted extensive phenomenological research that was supportive of, indeed anticipated, the formal Gestalt school.

Not to be neglected among antecedent influences of Gestalt psychology is the *Zeitgeist*. In nineteenth-century science, distrust of the primacy of elements and atoms, and of the method of analyzing physical phenomena into irreducible bits, was growing. The study of electromagnetism led to consideration of regions or fields as new structural entities, not as summations of effects generated by individual particles. The era of atomism that so profoundly influenced Wundt's thinking was ending, and the growing tendency in physical science to think in terms of fields and organic wholes was reflected in psychology in the Gestalt position.

The Founding of Gestalt Psychology

The formal movement known as Gestalt psychology grew out of a research study conducted by the German psychologist Max Wertheimer, the primary founder of the new school. While on a train on his vacation, Wertheimer had an idea for an experiment on the seeing of motion. Promptly forgetting his vacation, he left the train at Frankfurt am Main, bought a toy stroboscope,[2] and verified his insight in a preliminary way in his hotel room. He later carried out more formal research at the University of Frankfurt, which provided a tachistoscope for his use. In Frankfurt at that time were two other young German psychologists who, some years earlier, had been students with Wertheimer at the University of Berlin: Kurt Koffka and Wolfgang Köhler. Each had been working productively in psychology and they shortly embarked on a joint crusade against Wundtian elementism.

Wertheimer's research problem, on which Koffka and Köhler served as subjects, involved the perception of apparent movement; *i.e.*, the perception of motion or movement when no actual physical movement has taken place. Using the tachistoscope, Wertheimer projected light through two slits, one vertical and the other 20 or 30 degrees from the vertical. If light was shown through one slit and then the other, with a long interval in between (over 200 msec.), the subjects saw two successive lights, first at one slit and then at the other. If the interval between the lights was very short, the subjects saw both lights on continuously. With an optimal interval (about 60 msec.) between the lights, however, the subjects saw the line of light actually move from one place to the other and back again. These findings might seem trivial and straightforward since this phenomenon, after all, had been known for many years. It might even be considered a matter of common sense.

But according to the prevailing psychological (*i.e.*, structuralist) viewpoint, all conscious experience could be analyzed into its sensory elements. Yet how could this perception of apparent movement be explained in terms of a summation of individual sensory elements? Can one stationary stimulus be added to another to produce a sensation of movement? This is precisely the point of Wertheimer's brilliantly simple demonstration: it defied explanation by the prevailing Wundtian system!

Wertheimer believed that the phenomenon verified in his laboratory was, in its own way, as elementary as a sensation, yet it obviously differed from a sensation or even a succession of sensations. Wertheimer gave the phenomenon a name befitting its unique status: the phi phenomenon.

We may reasonably ask how Wertheimer explained this phi phenomenon if the traditional introspective structuralism could not. His answer was as simple and ingenious as the verifying experiment itself: *apparent movement did not need explaining;* it simply existed and could not be reduced to anything simpler.

---

[2] The stroboscope, invented about 80 years earlier by Plateau, was a forerunner of the motion-picture camera; it is an instrument that rapidly projects a series of different pictures on the eye, producing apparent motion.

According to Wundt, introspection of the stimulus would produce two successive lines and nothing else. But, no matter how rigorously one might try to introspect the two exposures, the experience of a single line in motion persisted. Any attempt at analysis was a failure. The whole (the movement) was indeed greater than the sum of its parts! The traditional associationist–structuralist psychology, dominant for so many years, had been challenged—and it was a challenge it could not meet.

Wertheimer's results were published in 1912 in an article, *Experimental Studies of the Perception of Movement,* that is often considered to mark the beginning of the new school.

After considering the lives of the three key figures in this movement, we shall examine the basic principles of the Gestalt school.

MAX WERTHEIMER (1880–1943)

Wertheimer was the oldest of the three original Gestalt psychologists and the intellectual leader of the movement. Koffka and Köhler served to promote Wertheimer's more prominent position. Born in Prague, Wertheimer attended the local gymnasium until the age of 18 and then studied law for two and one-half years at the university there. He later shifted to philosophy and attended the lectures of von Ehrenfels, among others. He then studied philosophy and psychology at Berlin and finally took his degree in 1904 at Würzburg under Külpe.

Very little is known about the years between 1904 and his arrival at Frankfurt, though it has been established that he spent his time variously at Prague, Vienna, and Berlin. He lectured at Frankfurt from 1912 until 1916, when he returned to Berlin. In 1929, he received a professorship at Frankfurt. During World War I, he participated in research of military value dealing with listening devices for submarines and harbor fortifications. Wertheimer did not write a great deal, at least not as much as Koffka and Köhler, but a paper on creative thinking was published in 1920, and in 1923 he wrote an influential article on perceptual grouping.

In 1921 the three primary Gestaltists, together with Goldstein and Gruhle, founded the journal *Psychologische Forschung,* which became the official organ of the Gestalt school. It published 22 volumes before its suspension in 1938 under the Hitler regime.

Wertheimer was among the first group of refugee scholars from Germany to arrive in New York in 1933. In 1934, he became associated with the New School for Social Research in New York City, where he remained until his death in 1943. Though his years in the United States were busy, he published little, due to increasing exhaustion and the burden of adapting to a new language and culture. His research was conducted rather informally and was communicated to his friends and to meetings.

KURT KOFFKA (1886–1941)

Koffka was considered the most productive of the triumvirate.[3] He received his education at Berlin, his place of birth. During his early years he developed a strong interest in science and philosophy that was strengthened during a year at Edinburgh (1903–1904). After returning to Berlin, he studied psychology and received his degree in 1909 under Stumpf. A number of research positions followed until 1910, when in Frankfurt he began his long and productive association with Wertheimer and Köhler. In 1911, he went to the University of Giessen, some 40 miles from Frankfurt, and remained there until 1924. At Giessen he conducted a good deal of research, and during World War I he worked with brain-damaged and aphasic patients at the psychiatric clinic.

After the war, American psychology was becoming vaguely aware of the school developing in Germany and Koffka was persuaded to write an article on the new movement for the *Psychological Bulletin*. This article, *Perception: An Introduction to Gestalt-Theorie*, appeared in 1922 and presented the basic concepts along with the results and implications of much research.

In 1921, Koffka published *The Growth of the Mind*, a book in developmental child psychology that became a great success in Germany and America. He was a visiting professor first at Cornell and later at Wisconsin in 1924, and in 1927 was appointed professor at Smith College, where he remained until his death in 1941.

In 1932, Koffka accompanied an expedition to study the people of Central Asia. While recovering from recurrent fever contracted on this expedition, he began work on his *Principles of Gestalt Psychology*, published in 1935. It was an extremely difficult book and did not become the definitive treatment of Gestalt psychology it was intended to be.

WOLFGANG KÖHLER (1887–1967)

The youngest of the three, Köhler was the spokesman for the Gestalt movement and became the best known (Boring, 1950). His books, written with great care and precision, became the definitive works on certain aspects of Gestalt psychology. Born in the Baltic provinces, Köhler was five years old when his family moved to northern Germany. His university education was at Tübingen, Bonn, and Berlin, where he received

---

[3] Boring (1950) suggested that "the originality of these three men varied inversely with their productivity" (p. 594).

his degree in 1909 under Stumpf. He then went to Frankfurt, arriving just before Wertheimer and his stroboscope.

In 1913 Köhler, at the invitation of the Prussian Academy of Science, went to the Spanish island of Tenerife in the Canary Islands to study chimpanzees. Six months after his arrival, World War I began and he was unable to leave. For the next seven years he studied learning in chimpanzees and produced the classic volume *Mentality of Apes* (1917). The book appeared in a second edition in 1924, and was then translated into English (1925) and French (1928). This work is discussed later.

In 1920, Köhler returned to Germany and in 1922 succeeded Stumpf at Berlin, where he remained until 1935. The apparent reason for his appointment to this coveted position was the publication in 1920 of *Static and Stationary Physical Gestalts,* a difficult book that won critical acclaim for its high level of scholarship.

Köhler lectured at Clark and Harvard Universities in 1925–1926, and in 1929 published, in English, *Gestalt Psychology,* the most definitive and thorough argument for the Gestalt movement. In 1934–1935, Köhler gave the William James lectures at Harvard, and in 1935 he left Germany for good since he was in continual conflict with the Nazi regime. He went to Swarthmore College, where he remained until his retirement. His later books include *The Place of Value in a World of Facts* (1938), *Dynamics in Psychology* (1940), and *Figural After-Effects* (1944), the latter with Hans Wallach. In 1956, he received the Distinguished Contribution Award from the American Psychological Association and in 1959 was elected president of that organization.

The Nature of the Gestalt Revolt

The Gestalt principles were in full and direct opposition to most of the academic tradition of psychology in Germany. Behaviorism was less of an immediate revolution because functionalism had already brought about some change in American psychology. No such tempering effect paved the way for the Gestalt revolt in Germany; the pronouncements of the Gestaltists were nothing short of heresy to the German structuralist tradition. Consider the basic points of Gestalt psychology in the light of Wundt's brand of psychology: (*a*) complex mental experience can have an existence of its own, (*b*) the primary data of perception are not elements but significantly structured forms, (*c*) it is acceptable when introspecting to use simple descriptive words; *i.e.,* it is acceptable to say, "I see a book"!

The initiators of the Gestalt movement realized, as they began their revolt, that they were taking on a powerful and rigid tradition; that they were striking at the very foundation of psychology. Like most revolutionary movements, the Gestalt school demanded a complete revision of the old order. After the study of apparent movement, they were quick to seize upon other perceptual phenomena to support their position. The experience of perceptual constancies afforded ample corroboration. For example, if we stand directly in front of a window, it projects a rectangular image in the retina. But if we stand off to one side and look at the window, the retinal image becomes a trapezoid, yet we still perceive the window as rectangular. Thus, our perception of the window remains unchanged even though the sensory datum (the image projected on the retina) has changed.

The same thing occurs with brightness and size constancy: the actual sensory elements can change radically, yet our perception does not. There are many similar examples in everyday experience. In these cases, as with apparent movement, the perceptual experience has a quality of wholeness that is not found in any of the parts. There can exist, then, a difference between the character of the actual perception and the character of the sensory stimulation. Thus, the perception cannot be explained as a collection of sensory elements or as the mere sum of the parts.

> The perception itself shows a character of totality, a form, a *Gestalt*, which in the very attempt at analysis is destroyed; and this experience, as directly given, sets the problem for psychology. It is this experience that presents the raw data which psychology must explain, and which it must never be content to explain away. To begin with elements is to begin at the wrong end; for elements are products of reflection and abstraction, remotely derived from the immediate experience they are invoked to explain. *Gestalt* psychology attempts to get back to naïve perception, to immediate experience "undebauched by learning"; and it insists that it finds there not assemblages of elements, but unified wholes; not masses of sensations, but trees, clouds, and sky. And this assertion it invites any one to verify simply by opening his eyes and looking at the world about him in his ordinary everyday way (Heidbreder, 1933, p. 331).

Boring (1950) commented that the word "Gestalt" has caused some difficulty because it does not clearly indicate what the movement stands for (like functionalism or behaviorism), and it has no exact English counterpart. Several "equivalents" are in common use (*e.g.,* form, shape, configuration), and in modern usage Gestalt has become part of the English language.

In Köhler's *Gestalt Psychology* of 1929, it is noted that the word "Gestalt" was used in two ways in German. One usage involved the denoting of shape or form as a property of objects. In this sense the word refers to general properties that would be expressed in such terms as "angular" or "symmetrical." It describes characteristics such as triangularity (in geometrical figures) or temporal sequences (in a melody).

The second usage denoted an entity that is concrete and has as one of its attributes a specific shape or form. In this sense, the word refers to triangles, rather than, as in the first usage, the notion of triangularity. Thus, the word is used in reference to objects rather than to the characteristic forms of these objects. In this sense, Gestalt refers to any segregated whole.

Finally, the use of the term is not restricted to the visual field or even to the total sensory field.

> In fact, the concept "Gestalt" may be applied far beyond the limits of sensory experience. According to the most general functional definition of the term, the processes of learning, of recall, of striving, of emotional attitude, of thinking, acting, and so forth, may have to be included. . . . "Gestalt" in the meaning of shape is no longer the center of the Gestalt Psychologist's attention (Köhler, 1947, pp. 178–179).

And it is in this larger sense of the term that the Gestalt psychologists wanted to deal with the whole province of psychology—in terms of "Gestalten."

Wertheimer's Principles of Organization

Perhaps the best known of all the propositions put forward by the Gestaltists are Wertheimer's principles of perceptual organization, presented in a paper in 1923. Wertheimer took the position that a person perceives objects in the same direct and unified manner in which he perceives apparent motion—as unified wholes, not as clusters of individual sensations. These principles, which may be found in most general psychology texts today, are essentially rules or laws by which a person organizes his perceptual world.

A basic premise of Wertheimer's principles is that in perception, organization occurs whenever we see (or hear) different shapes or patterns. Parts of the perceptual field become connected and these groups or collections of parts unite to form segregated structures distinct from the background. This perceptual organization is spontaneous and inevitable whenever an organism looks about its environment. We do not have to learn to so organize, as the structuralists and associationists claimed.

According to Gestalt theory, the primary brain process in visual perception is not a collection of small separate activities, but is, instead, a dynamic system. The visual area of the brain does not respond in terms of separate elements of visual input, with these elements being connected by a principle of association. Rather, the brain is a dynamic system in which all those elements active at a given time interact. Elements that are similar or close together tend to combine; elements that are dissimilar or far apart do not tend to combine.

Several of the principles of organization are listed here, and examples are given in Figure 4.

1. Proximity: Parts that are close together in time or space tend to be perceived together. For example, in Figure 4a the circles are seen in three groups or units.

2. Similarity: Similar parts tend to be seen together as forming a group (Figure 4b). Since the circles and the dots appear to "belong" together, we tend to perceive rows instead of columns.

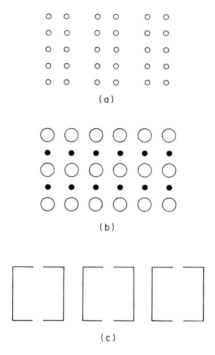

Figure 4. Examples of perceptual organization.

3. Closure: There is a tendency in our perception to complete incomplete figures—to fill in gaps. In Figure 4c we perceive three squares even though the figures are incomplete.

4. *Prägnanz:* There is a tendency to see a figure as being as "good" as possible under the stimulus conditions. A "good" figure is one that is symmetrical, simple, and stable, and that cannot be made simpler or more orderly.

These organizing factors do not depend on the higher mental processes of the individual nor on his past experience, but are present in the stimuli themselves. While stressing these "peripheral" factors, Wertheimer did recognize that "central" factors (*i.e.*, factors within the organism) can also influence perception. For example, the factors of familiarity and set or attitude (higher mental processes) can influence perception. In general, however, the Gestaltists tend to concentrate on the more direct and primitive peripheral factors of perceptual organization, rather than on the role of learning.

Gestalt Principles of Learning

As we have seen, perception is the primary focus of interest to the Gestalt psychologists, and they take the position that learning plays only a small role in perceptual processes. It is certainly not correct, however, to imply that the topic of learning, considered independently of perception, received no attention from the Gestalt psychologists. Some of the most significant experiments in the history of psychology, experiments still cited in contemporary psychology books, are those Köhler devised to study problem solving in apes. It seems true, however, that learning, although certainly not neglected, played a role subordinate to perception in Gestalt psychology.

From its very beginning, Gestalt psychology opposed the Thorndikian trial-and-error learning and, later, the Watsonian stimulus-response learning. In fact, the members of the Gestalt school have felt that one of their most important contributions to psychology is their consistent criticism of associationistic and S-R theories of learning. To illustrate the Gestalt view of learning, we discuss Köhler's work on apes and Wertheimer's work on productive thinking in humans.

THE MENTALITY OF APES: KÖHLER

Mention was made earlier of Köhler's confinement on the island of Tenerife during World War I, during which time he investigated the intelligence of chimpanzees as shown in their solving of problems. These studies were conducted in and around the animals' cages and involved simple props, such as the bars of the cages themselves (to block access), bananas, sticks for drawing the bananas into the cage, and boxes for climbing.

Congruent with the Gestalt view of perception, Köhler interpreted the results of his animal studies in terms of the whole situation and relations between the various stimuli found therein. He considered problem solving a matter of restructuring the perceptual field. In one of his studies, a banana was placed outside the cage with an attached string leading into the cage. The apes pulled the banana into the cage with little hesitation. Köhler said that in this situation the problem was easily grasped as a whole by the animal. However, if several strings led from the cage in the general direction of the banana, the ape would not clearly recognize at first which string to pull. To Köhler, this indicated that the problem could not be envisioned clearly all at once.

A perhaps more explicit example involved placing an unattached banana just beyond the ape's reach. Now, if a stick was placed near the bars of the cage (facing the banana), the stick and the banana would be seen as parts of the same situation and the ape would readily use the stick to pull in the banana. If the stick was placed at the back of the cage, however, the two objects would be less readily perceived as parts of the same situation. In the latter case, a restructuring of the perceptual field was necessary in order to solve the problem.

Another example involved placing a banana outside the cage, beyond reach, and placing several hollow bamboo sticks, each by itself too short to reach the banana, inside the cage. In order to solve this problem, two sticks would have to be pushed together (the end of one inserted in the end of the other) to produce a stick of sufficient length to reach the banana. Thus, the animal had to perceive an entirely new relationship between the sticks.

Sultan, Köhler's brightest ape, failed when initially confronted with this problem. He first tried to get the banana with one stick; next, he pushed a stick out as far as he could, then pushed it farther with a second stick until the first one touched the banana (an interesting attempt). Sultan did not succeed during a one-hour trial.

Immediately after this trial, however, while playing with the sticks, Sultan solved the problem, as reported by his keeper:

> Sultan first of all squats indifferently on the box, which has been left standing a little back from the railings; then he gets up, picks up the two sticks, sits down again on the box and plays carelessly with them. While doing this, it happens that he finds himself holding one rod in either hand in such a way that they lie in a straight line; he pushes the thinner one a little way into the opening of the thicker, jumps up and is already on the run towards the railings, to which he has up to now half turned his back, and begins to draw a banana towards him with the double stick. I call the master: meanwhile, one of the animal's rods has fallen out of the other, as he has pushed one of them only a little way into the other; whereupon he connects them again (Köhler, 1927, p. 127).

In later trials, Sultan solved the problem without any difficulty, even when some of the sticks provided would not fit together. Köhler reported that Sultan did not even attempt to join these nonfitting sticks.

Studies such as these were interpreted by Köhler as evidence of insight—the apparently spontaneous seeing of relations.

> The solutions of such problems, when they came, appeared to come suddenly, as though a new "configuration," embracing the whole complicated means to

the desired end, had suddenly sprung up in the animal's consciousness; it was exactly as though the appropriate action followed on a "flash of insight," and, as in the case of all insightful behavior, the insight remained a permanent possession, enabling its possessor to act at once appropriately on a subsequent occasion (Flugel & West, 1964, p. 206).

This viewpoint differed dramatically from the trial-and-error learning of Thorndike and others. Köhler became a highly vocal critic of Thorndike's work, arguing that his experimental arrangements were artificial and allowed only blind, random, trial-and-error behavior on the part of the animal. Köhler suggested that the cats in Thorndike's puzzle box, for instance, could not survey the entire release mechanism (all the elements pertaining to the whole), and thus could engage in nothing but trial-and-error behavior. In the Gestalt view, the organism must be able to see the relationship among the various parts of the problem before insight can occur.

These famous studies of insight were used to support the Gestalt molar conception of behavior (as opposed to the molecular elementistic view of the associationists and behaviorists) and the Gestalt notion that learning involves a reorganization or restructuring of the psychological environment.

PRODUCTIVE THINKING: WERTHEIMER

Wertheimer's posthumous *Productive Thinking* (1945) applied the Gestalt learning principles to human creative thinking and suggested that such thinking should be done in terms of wholes. Not only must the learner regard the situation as a whole; the teacher must also present the situation as a whole, not (like Thorndike) hiding the solution and thus, in a sense, requiring the person to make errors.

The case material in this book ranged from the study of children solving geometrical problems to the study of Einstein's thought processes leading to the theory of relativity. At all ages and levels of problem difficulty Wertheimer found evidence to support his notion that the whole problem must dominate the parts. He believed that the detailed aspects of the problem should be considered only in relation to the structure of the total situation, and that problem solving should proceed from the whole problem downward to the parts, not the reverse.

Wertheimer demonstrated that if a teacher arranged problems so that elements of classroom exercises were organized into meaningful wholes, then insight would occur. He also demonstrated that once the principle of a problem's solution had been grasped, it readily transferred to other situations.

Wertheimer also attacked the traditional educational practice of mechanical drill and rote learning, which derived from the associationistic theory of learning. Blind repetition is rarely productive, he argued, and cited as evidence the student's inability to solve a variation of a problem when the solution had been learned by rote rather than by insight. He did agree, however, that some material, such as names and dates, must be learned in rote fashion through association strengthened by repetition. Thus, he felt that repetition is useful to a point, but that its habitual use can produce habits of strictly mechanical behavior, resulting in robotlike performance rather than truly creative or productive thinking.

The Principle of Isomorphism

Having established that perceptions are organized wholes, the Gestalt psychologists turned to the problem of the cortical mechanisms involved in perception and attempted to develop a theory of the underlying neurological correlates of perceived *Gestalten*. Brief mention was made earlier of the Gestalt view of the cortex as a dynamic system in which the elements active at a given time interact. This view is in sharp contrast to the so-called "machine" conception of the nervous system, which likens nervous activity to a telephone switchboard that mechanically connects the sensory elements received via associationistic principles. In the latter view, the brain functions passively and is not capable of actively organizing or modifying the sensory elements received. Also, this view of the brain implies a one-to-one correspondence between the perception and its neurological counterpart.

In his original research on apparent movement, Wertheimer suggested that cortical activity is a configural whole process. Since apparent and actual motion are experienced identically, he argued, the cortical processes for actual and apparent motion must be similar. On the assumption that these two kinds of movement are identical, there must be corresponding brain processes. In order to account for the phi phenomenon, there must be a correspondence between the psychological experience and the underlying "brain experience."

This point of view has been called isomorphism, which says that "*Experienced order in space is always structurally identical with a functional order in the distribution of underlying brain processes*" (Köhler, 1947, p. 61). Thus, the correspondence is topological in nature but not topographical. According to this principle of isomorphism, there is no one-to-one correspondence between the stimulus and the perception. It is the form of the perceptual experience that corresponds to the form of the stimulus. Thus, *Gestalten* are indeed "true" representations of the real world, but are not perfect reproductions of it. A percept is not a literal copy of the stimulus, just as a map is not a literal copy of the terrain it represents. The percept, however, like the map, is identical (*iso*) in form or shape (*morphic*) to that which it represents, so that it does serve as a reliable guide to the perceived real world. The view has been supported by the three principal Gestaltists and is definitely associated with the Gestalt school.

The position was extended and elaborated upon by Köhler in his book, *Static and Stationary Physical Gestalts*, in 1920. Köhler considered that cortical processes behave in a manner similar to fields of electrical force. He suggested that, like the behavior of an electromagnetic field of force around a magnet, fields of neuronal activity may be established by electromechanical processes in the brain in response to sensory impulses. He conducted an extensive research program investigating various aspects of the concept of isomorphism and cortical brain fields. To Köhler, the notion of isomorphism was but one phase of a much more ambitious undertaking to demonstrate that physics, chemistry, biology, and astronomy all involve *Gestalten*.

The Reaction in America

The Gestalt movement gained momentum rather quickly in Germany as there were many who were dissatisfied with the artificiality and sterility of the older Wundtian psychology. In the United States, where it met with less enthusiastic and more varied response, its progress was comparatively slow, for several excellent reasons. In the first place, American psychology had already advanced beyond structuralism. Behaviorism was already the second phase of American opposition to structuralism; hence America was much further removed from Wundtian elementism than Europe was at that time. As far as American psychologists were concerned, the Gestaltists were fighting a dead issue. There was also a language barrier which delayed dissemination of the Gestalt principles. Third, behaviorism was at a peak of popularity in American psychology at that time.

Thus the Gestaltists came to America protesting something that was no longer a vital concern. This is a dangerous situation when we remember that movements need something to oppose—something to push against—in order to survive.

When the Gestaltists became familiar with the trend in America, however, they perceived a new target: behaviorism, with its reductionistic and atomistic tendencies. The Gestaltists argued that behaviorism, like structuralism, dealt with artificial abstractions. It makes little difference, they said, whether analysis is in terms of introspective reduction to elements (Wundt) or objective reduction to conditioned reflexes (Watson): the end result is the same.

The Gestaltists also took issue with the behaviorists' denial of the validity of introspection and their elimination of consciousness. Although the Gestaltists did not use Wundtian introspection, they favored the study of direct conscious experience.

Later Developments

THE SPREAD OF GESTALT PSYCHOLOGY AFTER THE FOUNDING

By the mid-1930s, the Gestalt movement was a respectable point of view, well established primarily in Germany and the United States. Its doctrines and principles were being used in such areas as child psychology, applied psychology, psychiatry, education, anthropology, and sociology. After about 1933 and the beginning of the Nazi regime, the three principle proponents of the movement, along with other adherents, left Germany, mostly for the United States. They brought the message of Gestalt psychology more forcefully to this country and a good deal of research began within the Gestalt framework. Also, many clinical psychologists began to combine the Gestalt approach with that of psychoanalysis.

By the late 1930s and early 1940s, with the appearance in American journals of Gestalt doctrines and the results of Gestalt-oriented research, Gestalt psychology became a vital part of American psychology. In the country of its birth, it suffered seriously from the departure of its leaders and the effects of the Hitler regime. In addition to the general anti-intellectual orientation of the Nazi era, Gestalt psychology was reduced to a minor position in the German academic system of the day. Some work in the Gestalt tradition went on, but it was of a rather diluted variety. Various areas of applied psychology using theories of wholeness, such as graphology (the study of handwriting), did play a role in clinical assessment. Also, personality testing based on derivatives of Gestalt theory was used extensively in German psychological warfare. On the whole, however, the years of Nazi domination were sterile for German psychology in general. Woodworth and Sheehan (1964) report that Gestalt psychology has shown a renewed vitality since the 1950s as a part of a general resurgence of interest in psychology in West Germany.

According to Murphy (1949), the general tendency in the United States has been to consider the principles of Gestalt psychology interesting and potentially useful but certainly not the basis of an all-encompassing system. He also notes that American psychology has attempted to demonstrate that both elemental and organized responses occur, and that both are useful.

FIELD THEORY: KURT LEWIN

The growing tendency of nineteenth-century science was to think in terms of field relationships, and to move away from an atomistic and elementistic framework. As we have seen, Wertheimer and Gestalt psychology reflected this trend. The concept of field theory arose within psychology as an analogy to the concept of fields of force in physics.

In psychology, the term "field theory" has come to refer almost exclusively to the work of Kurt Lewin.[4] Lewin's position in relation to Gestalt psychology is not clear-cut, for although he is sometimes classed as a member of the Gestalt school, he is equally often regarded as the developer of a separate but related system. He began working independently but was later closely associated with both Köhler and Wertheimer at the then active center of the Gestalt movement at Berlin. In his productive career as a whole he went well beyond the confines of the orthodox Gestalt group.

Lewin's work is Gestalt-like in orientation, but it centers on needs, personality, and social factors, whereas the Gestaltists emphasized perception and learning. Where the Gestaltists stressed physiological constructs to attempt to explain behavior, Lewin considered psychology more as a social science. It is simplest to consider Lewin's system as an elaboration or outgrowth of the Gestalt movement for two reasons: (a) he was closely associated with the Gestaltists at Berlin for a time, and (b) his position fits the Gestalt system more readily than any other.

THE LIFE OF LEWIN (1890–1947)

Born in Mogilno, Germany, Lewin undertook his university education at Freiburg, Munich, and finally Berlin, where he received his PhD in psychology in 1914. In addition to psychology, he studied mathematics and physics. After a period of military service, he returned to the University of Berlin, where he became such a productive and creative member of the Gestalt group that he was considered a colleague of the three senior Gestaltists. At Berlin he performed much important research on association and motivation, and began developing his field theory.

He was already well known in America when, in 1932, he spent a year as visiting professor at Stanford. He spent two years at Cornell and then decided to leave Germany permanently because of the Nazi menace. In 1935 he went to the University of Iowa, where he conducted a series of studies in the experimental social psychology of the child. As a result of highly successful research efforts in social psychology, Lewin was invited to develop and head a new research center for group dynamics at the Massachusetts Institute of Technology in 1944. Although he died shortly thereafter (in 1947), his program was so effective that the research center remains active and productive in its new location at the University of Michigan.

[4] Tolman's system, discussed in Chapter XI, is also often considered a field theory. We noted his attempted combination of parts of behaviorism and Gestalt psychology.

LEWIN'S FIELD THEORY

Throughout his 30 years of professional activity, Lewin devoted himself consistently to the broadly defined area of human motivation. His research emphasized the study of human behavior in its total physical and social context.

At the outset, Lewin analyzed the basic structure of science, which he believed had evolved through three levels or stages: speculative, descriptive, and constructive. Early Greek science represented the first stage, which was given to large-scale speculative theorizing that attempted to encompass all natural phenomena. At that stage systems were derived from very few basic concepts and were very general in nature.

The descriptive stage involved the accumulation of the greatest possible number of facts, which were described precisely and objectively. Theorizing was minimized, and attempts at classification were made in terms of very broad abstractions.

The third, or constructive, stage was the one within which Lewin developed his system. He envisaged as its goal the discovery of laws that would permit the prediction of individual phenomena. According to this view, events are lawful and orderly even if they occur in only one case. Taking this constructive stage as his model, Lewin argued that laws of behavior need not be based on statistical averages in order to have value. His psychology thus focuses on the individual, not the mean responses of groups of individuals. He contended that the specific individual and the total situation in which he performs must be understood in order to predict behavior.

The theory of fields in physics led Lewin to consider that the psychological activities of a person occur in a kind of psychological field or "life space." The life space comprises all the events that may possibly influence a person, past, present, and future, since from a psychological standpoint each of these three aspects of life can determine behavior in any single situation.

The life space may show varying degrees of differentiation as a function of the amount and kind of experiences the individual has accumulated. Because it lacks experiences, an infant has few, if any, differentiated regions in its life space. A highly educated, sophisticated adult shows complex and well-differentiated life space as a function of his past experiences.

Lewin wanted to use a mathematical model to represent his theoretical concept of psychological processes. Since he was concerned with the single case, statistics were not useful for his purposes. He chose a form of geometry—topology—that he felt was adequate to the task of "mapping the life space" so as to show at any given moment all the possible goals of an individual and all the routes to these goals. Topology deals with transformations in space by representing spatial relationships in nonmetrical fashion. It is a conception of space that deals with the order of relationships, but not with their direction or distance. It can show connections among regions within the life space and their spatial relationships to one another. To represent direction, Lewin developed a new form of qualitative geometry called *hodological space,* in which he used vectors to represent directions of movement toward a goal.

To complete the schematic representation of his system, Lewin introduced the notion of valences to refer to the positive or negative value of objects in the life space. Objects that are attractive to the individual

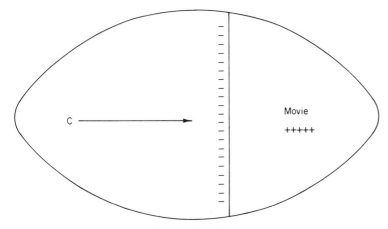

Figure 5. Example of a life space.

or that satisfy his needs have positive valence, while objects that threaten him have negative valence.

Lewin postulated a state of equilibrium between the person and his environment. When this equilibrium is disturbed, a tension (Lewin's concept of motivation or need) arises that leads to locomotion in the attempt to restore the equilibrium. Lewin believed that human behavior involves the continual appearance of tensions, locomotions, and reliefs. This sequence of tension–locomotion–equilibrium is akin to need–activity–relief. Whenever a need is felt, a state of tension exists and the organism acts in order to release the tension by restoring the equilibrium.

Lewin's "blackboard psychology" included complex diagrams representing psychological phenomena. In field theory, all forms of behavior can be represented schematically. A simple example of a bit of behavior as it would be represented in Lewin's system is shown in Figure 5, which illustrates a situation in which a child wants to go to the movies but is forbidden to do so by his mother. The ellipse represents the life space and C represents the child. The arrow is a vector indicating that C is motivated to go to the movie, which, as indicated, has positive valence. The vertical line is the barrier (the mother) to the goal and is shown to have negative valence. (This is but a simple example and is not typical of the highly complex psychological phenomena that Lewin was able to represent through his topological and hodological space.)

Lewin's theoretical system generated a great deal of important and influential research. For example, a series of studies were conducted involving his assumption of a tension-system. Tension, as we have seen, means motivation or need, and Lewin believed that when a goal is reached, the tension is discharged. The first experimental attempt to test this tension-system proposition was performed, under Lewin's supervision, by Bluma Zeigarnik in 1927. Subjects were given a series of tasks and were allowed to complete some of them, but were interrupted prior to their completion of others. The predictions derived from Lewin's system are that: (a) a tension-system develops in a subject when he is given a task to perform, (b) if the task is completed, the tension is dissipated, (c) if, however, the task is not completed, the persistence of the tension results in greater likelihood of recall of the task. Zeigarnik's results confirmed the predictions in that the subjects recalled the uncompleted tasks more easily than the completed ones. Much subsequent research has been performed on this phenomenon; the student is probably familiar with this so-called Zeigarnik effect.

LEWIN AND SOCIAL PSYCHOLOGY

In the early years of his career, Lewin was chiefly concerned with theoretical problems and issues. By the late 1930s, however, he became very interested in social psychology and his pioneering efforts in this field alone are sufficient to justify his prominence in the history of psychology.

Perhaps the outstanding feature of Lewin's social psychology, called group dynamics, is the application of concepts dealing with the individual and group behavior. Just as the individual and his environment form a psychological field, the group and its environment form a social field. Social behaviors are seen as occurring in, and resulting from, total simultaneously existing social entities, such as subgroups, members, barriers, and channels of communication. Thus, group behavior is a function of the total field situation existing at a given time.

Lewin's early social-psychological research was concerned with behavior in various kinds of social climates. A very famous study involving democratic and authoritarian leadership and its effects on the productiveness and general behavior of groups of boys (Lewin, Lippitt, & White, 1939) is a classic experiment in social psychology. Studies such as this opened up important new areas of social research and contributed greatly to the rapid growth of social psychology.

COMMENT

In general, Lewin's experimental programs and research findings are more acceptable to many psychologists than his theoretical views. In spite of this, his theoretical influence in social and child psychology and, to some degree, experimental psychology is considerable. Many of his concepts and experimental techniques are also widely accepted in the areas of personality and motivation.

Lewin's system is still too much in current use to be evaluated. Students of field theory are still actively working in the Lewinian tradition, particularly in the broad area of social psychology.

Criticisms of Gestalt Psychology

The following comments refer only to the original Gestalt formulations, not to latter-day derivatives such as Lewinian field theory. Criticisms of the Gestalt position appeared promptly. They included the major criticism that the Gestaltists were trying to solve problems by simply changing them into postulates. For example, organization of conscious perception is not treated as a problem requiring resolution through one means or another, but as a "given"—a phenomenon that exists in its own right. It can (easily) be said that this is tantamount to solving a problem by denying its existence!

Many tough-minded scientists have asserted that the Gestalt position is too vague. These critics charge that some of its basic concepts and many of its terms (e.g., organization) are not defined with sufficient rigor to be scientifically meaningful. If it is true that the Gestaltists used vague and ambiguous terms, they may not differ greatly from psychologists of other theoretical persuasions in this respect.

The Gestalt psychologists countered these charges by insisting that in a young science, attempts at explanations and definitions must necessarily be incomplete, but that being incomplete is not the same as being vague.

It has also been claimed that the basic tenets of Gestalt psychology are not really new, which is, of course, true since the Gestalt movement, like the others we have discussed, had its historical anticipations. This criticism, however, has no bearing on the relative merits of the Gestalt position.

Some critics allege that Gestalt psychology is too occupied with theory at the expense of adequate experimental research and empirical supporting data. The Gestalt school has been heavily oriented toward theory, but since the time of its founders it has also stressed experimentation and has been both directly and indirectly responsible for a great deal of research.

Related to this criticism is the suggestion that the experimental work of the Gestaltists is inferior to that of S-R theorists in that it lacks adequate control of variables. The same critics argue that the Gestaltists' nonquantified data are not amenable to statistical analysis. The Gestaltists take the position that qualitative results must come first in the investigation of a problem area; therefore, much of their research has deliberately been less quantitative than psychologists of other orientations consider necessary. Much Gestalt research has necessarily been preliminary and exploratory since it often involves investigations of new problem areas (or old areas approached from a completely different point of view). Certain Gestalt psychologists may have conducted inadequately designed and controlled research, but this criticism could be made of some psychologists of any theoretical persuasion. Certainly, no school advocates sloppy experimentation.

A final criticism relates to what some consider the poorly supported and defined physiological assumptions of the system. The Gestaltists readily admit that their theorizing in this area is tentative, but they add that such speculation is recognized as a useful adjunct in any system. In this case, it has generated a great deal of research and the validity of the research results has not been lessened by the speculative framework within which it was conducted.

Contributions of Gestalt Psychology

The Gestalt movement has unquestionably left an indelible imprint on psychology. Like other movements that challenged older traditions, it had a refreshing and stimulating influence on psychology as a whole.

The Gestalt point of view has greatly influenced the area of perception and, to some extent, learning. Its effect on the study of perception is evident in virtually every introductory and experimental psychology textbook. More recent work deriving from the Gestalt school strongly suggests that it is still vital.

Unlike its chief temporal competitor, behaviorism, Gestalt psychology remains a separate entity in that its major tenets have not been fully absorbed into the mainstream of psychological thought. It continues to foster interest in conscious experience as a legitimate problem area for at least part of psychology. (Whether this is a fruitful or inhibiting effect is a moot question among psychologists.) Again, this interest in conscious experience is not of the Wundt–Titchener introspective variety, but centers around a modern version of phenomenology. Contemporary adherents of the Gestalt position are convinced that conscious experience does occur and can (indeed must) be studied. They recognize, however, that it cannot be investigated with the same order of precision and objectivity as overt behavior.

Contemporary proponents of a phenomenological psychology are numerous in Europe and the point of view seems to be gaining support in the United States. While not widely accepted in America, psychologists are becoming more familiar with phenomenology, at least to the point of taking issue with it.

Finally, the pointed and consistent criticisms offered by Gestalt psychology of extant systems have had an important influence by demanding a critical reexamination of the opposing positions.

SUGGESTED FURTHER READINGS

Wertheimer
Asch, S. E. Max Wertheimer's contribution to modern psychology. *Social Research,* 1946, **13**, 81–102.
Köhler, W. Max Wertheimer, 1880–1943. *Psychological Review,* 1944, **51**, 143–146.

Koffka
Köhler, W. Kurt Koffka. *Psychological Review,* 1942, **49**, 97–101.

Köhler
Prentice, W. C. H. The systematic psychology of Wolfgang Köhler. In S. Koch (Ed.), *Psychology: a study of a science.* Vol. 1. New York: McGraw-Hill, 1959. Pp. 427–455.

General
Ellis, W. D. *A source book of Gestalt psychology.* New York: Harcourt, Brace & World, 1938.
Hartmann, G. W. *Gestalt psychology.* New York: Ronald, 1935.
Helson, H. The psychology of Gestalt. *American Journal of Psychology,* 1925, **36**, 342–370; 1926, **37**, 25–62, 189–223.
Henle, M. (Ed.) *Documents of Gestalt psychology.* Berkeley: California University Press, 1961.
Hochberg, J. E. Effects of the Gestalt revolution: The Cornell symposium on perception. *Psychological Review,* 1957, **64**, 73–84.
Katz, D. *Gestalt psychology.* New York: Ronald, 1950.

Phenomenology
Combs, A. W., & Snygg, D. *Individual behavior: a perceptual approach to behavior.* (Rev. ed.) New York: Harper, 1959.
Wann, T. W. (Ed.) *Behaviorism and phenomenology: contrasting bases for modern psychology.* Chicago: University of Chicago Press, 1964.

XIII

PSYCHOANALYSIS:
THE BEGINNINGS

Introduction

THE TERM *psychoanalysis* and the name Sigmund Freud are probably familiar to most literate people. While leaders like Fechner, Wundt, or Titchener are seldom known outside professional psychology, Freud enjoys a phenomenal degree of popularity, although his system may be known to the lay public only superficially or inaccurately. It is often a source of disappointment to teachers of psychology to find that so many beginning students think that Freud *is* psychology, and that psychology deals only with the treatment of the mentally disturbed.

Psychoanalysis cannot be directly related to the evolutionary and revolutionary trends and movements that mark the progress of psychology because psychoanalysis did not originate within psychology. Freud's study of personality and its disturbances was remote from the psychology of the university laboratory. Regardless of their fundamental disagreements, the systems outlined earlier shared an academic heritage; all of these schools formed their basic concepts and approaches in a milieu of laboratories, libraries, and lecture halls. Their traditional areas of concern were perception, sensation, learning, and the like. They were, or strove to be, pure science.

Psychoanalysis, in contrast, was neither a product of academic halls, nor a pure science. Further, it was not (and still is not) a school or systematic theory of psychology directly comparable to the others. Psychoanalysis has not been greatly concerned with the traditional areas primarily because its aim is to provide therapy for the emotionally disturbed. In aim, subject matter, and methods, psychoanalysis diverges from the mainstream of psychological thought: its subject matter is abnormal behavior, which had been relatively neglected by the other schools, and its method is clinical observation rather than controlled laboratory experimentation.

264

Despite the radically different nature of psychoanalysis, it has exerted a great influence on contemporary psychology. In addition, areas outside of psychology—the social sciences, literature, language, religion, philosophy, ethics, and the arts—have felt its impact. We shall see, however, that its acceptance by academic psychology has been, for the most part, less than enthusiastic.

Historical Antecedents

Despite the claims of some of Freud's followers, his insights were not without anticipations. The psychoanalytic movement had very definite intellectual and cultural antecedents. Two main sources of influence led up to the formal founding of psychoanalysis. One was earlier philosophical speculation on the nature of unconscious psychological phenomena, a notion that plays a major role in Freud's thinking. The other was psychopathology, primarily in the French tradition.

EARLY THEORIES OF THE UNCONSCIOUS

We have seen that much of the early history of scientific psychology was concerned with consciousness. The experimental psychology of the late nineteenth century was convinced that the only proper field of study was the content of consciousness. Thus, the main current of work in psychology was directed toward the analysis of conscious experience to the exclusion of consideration of unconscious determinants of behavior. We saw, too, that the background provided for the new psychology by empirical philosophers was also oriented toward conscious experience.

However, not everyone who pioneered the new psychology or its antecedent philosophy agreed with this exclusive focus on conscious mental content; some believed in the importance of nonconscious processes. Although the influence of the unconscious can indeed be traced to Plato, we will begin by considering more recent antecedents.

Early in the eighteenth century, the great German mathematician and philosopher Gottfried Wilhelm Leibnitz (1646–1716) developed his theory of *monadology*. Monads, which Leibnitz considered the individual elements of all reality, were not physical atoms; they were not even material in the usual sense of the word. Each monad was unextended and a psychic entity. Leibnitz went on to insist that although each monad was mental in nature, it had some of the properties of physical matter, and that when enough of them were collected into an aggregate, they created an extension.

Monads were centers of activity and energy. In general terms, they could be likened to perception and are very similar to consciousness. Mental events (the activity of monads) had differing degrees of clᵉ

ness or consciousness, which could range from the completely unconscious to the most clear or definitely conscious. There were, then, according to Leibnitz, lower degrees of consciousness, which he called *petites
perceptions*. The conscious actualization of these he called *apperception*.

For example, the sound of waves breaking on the shore is an apperception. This apperception, however, is made up of all the individual falling
drops of water, none of which is conscious by itself. The individual
drop of water, like the monad, is the *petite perception* and is not consciously perceived by itself. When sufficient numbers of them congregate,
however, they summate to produce an apperception.

A century later, Johann Friedrich Herbart (1776–1841) developed
the Leibnitzian notion of the unconscious into the concept of threshold
or limen of consciousness. Those ideas below the limen are unconscious.
When an idea arises to conscious levels of awareness, Herbart said,
it is apperceived (as Leibnitz had said), but Herbart meant more than
this. In order for an idea to rise into consciousness, it had to be com-
patible and congruent with the ideas extant in consciousness. Incongru-
ous ideas could not exist in consciousness at the same time, and ideas
that were irrelevant were forced out of consciousness to become what
Herbart called inhibited ideas. Inhibited ideas existed below the threshold of consciousness and were akin to Leibnitz's *petites perceptions*.
According to Herbart, there is a conflict among ideas in which they
actively struggle for realization in consciousness. Boring (1950) suggested that Leibnitz foreshadowed the doctrine of the unconscious, but
that Herbart actually began it.

Fechner also contributed to the development of thinking about the
unconscious; he used the notion of limen or threshold, but his suggestion
that the mind is analogous to an iceberg in that a considerable portion
of it is hidden below the surface, where it is influenced by unobservable
forces, was a greater influence on Freud. The latter, therefore, was not
the first to "discover" or even to discuss seriously the unconscious. Although some early thinkers merely mentioned the unconscious, others
attributed importance to it. No one before Freud, however, fully realized
the significance of unconscious motivation or found a way to study it.
Freud believed that in exploring the unconscious he would find explanations for what had previously been considered mysterious. He saw unconscious feelings and thoughts as directly or indirectly influencing
behavior.

THE INFLUENCE FROM PSYCHOPATHOLOGY

We have seen that a new movement needs something to revolt
against—something to push away from in order to gain momentum.

Since psychoanalysis did not develop within academic psychology, the existing order that it opposed was not Wundtian structuralism nor any other psychological school of thought. To discover what Freud opposed, we must note the prevailing thought in the areas of understanding and treating mental disorders.

The history of the treatment of the mentally ill is a fascinating story in its own right. Much of the earlier history presents a striking picture of man's inhumanity to man. In the Middle Ages, the disturbed individual received almost no understanding and, perhaps, even less sympathy. The mind was alleged to be a free agent and hence responsible for its own condition. The "treatment" for the mentally disturbed consisted primarily of blame and punishment, for the causes were considered to be wickedness, magic, and possession by demons.

Nor did conditions improve during the Renaissance; a passage from Boring (1950) recounts events and attitudes characteristic of that period (and presents a message of importance for any time and place).

> The great changes in the social structure at the time of the Renaissance created a general feeling of uncertainty and insecurity . . . . Insecure men, uncertain of the future, frustrated by change, stand ready to exorcise the threat of evil by an uncritical distribution of blame and punishment. Then, as now, they were ready to go witch hunting because they were afraid, and in the fifteenth century the Church did it for them. In 1489 *Jacob Sprenger* and *Heinrich Kraemer*, two Dominican brothers, taking advantage of the recent invention of the printing press, published the *Malleus maleficarum*, a title which perhaps can be best translated as the *Witch Hammer*, since the book was designed to be a tool for hammering at the witches. The *Malleus maleficarum* is a cruel encyclopedia on witchcraft, the detection of witches and the procedures for examining them by torture and for sentencing them. The treatise had the approval of the Pope, of the King of Rome and, after some reluctant resistance, of the Faculty of Theology at the University of Cologne. It identified witchcraft with heresy and for us it identifies witchcraft with the mental disorders, many of whose symptoms it describes with care. For three hundred years in nineteen editions this malevolent compendium remained the authority and guide of the Inquisition as it sought out heresy and demoniacal possession among the people (pp. 694–695).

The Inquisition continued through the eighteenth century, but in the nineteenth century a more humane and rational attitude toward the mentally ill took hold. In Europe and America, the chains were struck (literally) from the insane as the decline in the influence of religious superstition paved the way for scientific investigation of the causes of mental illness.

During the nineteenth century, there were two main schools of thought in psychiatry, the somatic and the psychic. The somatic school held that organic disturbances of the brain account for abnormalities of behavior, while the psychic school sought causes in the mental or psychological sphere. Physical disturbances of the brain had been found in certain kinds of mental illness but not in others. On the whole, however, nineteenth-century psychiatry was dominated by the somatic school.

Psychoanalysis developed as one facet of a revolt against this somatic orientation. As work with the mentally ill continued, the conviction grew that emotional stress was of greater importance than brain lesions in the etiology of abnormal behavior.

Hypnosis played an important role in fostering concern with the psychic causes of abnormal behavior. In the latter part of the eighteenth century, hypnosis was brought to medical attention by Friedrich Anton Mesmer. For a century, *mesmerism* was almost universally rejected by the medical profession, which regarded it as quackery. In England, James Braid (1795–1860) called the phenomena characteristic of the hypnotic state "neurypnology," from which the term hypnosis was later derived; his careful work and disdain for exaggerated claims earned some scientific respectability for hypnosis.

Hypnosis achieved prominence with the work of Jean Martin Charcot (1825–1893), who was a physician and head of a neurological clinic at Salpêtrière, the Parisian hospital for insane women. Charcot treated hysterical patients by means of hypnosis with some degree of success. More important, he described the symptoms of both hysteria and hypnosis in medical terms, making the latter phenomenon more readily acceptable to medicine and the French Academy of Science (which had rejected mesmerism three times). Approval by the Academy was vitally important, for it made it "safe" for neurologists to begin investigating the psychological aspects of mental illness.

Charcot's work, however, remained primarily neurological, so that physical disturbances, paralysis, and the like were emphasized in it. Hysteria, therefore, continued to be ascribed to somatic causes until Charcot's pupil and successor, Pierre Janet (1859–1947), accepted Charcot's invitation in 1889, to become director of the psychological laboratory at Salpêtrière. Janet rejected the opinion that hysteria was a physiological disturbance, and saw it instead as a mental disorder. Accordingly, he emphasized mental phenomena, particularly impairments of memory and fixed ideas, and stressed hypnosis as a method of treatment.

The foregoing précis, of course, barely indicates the important work of Charcot and Janet in the treatment of the mentally disturbed. The relevant point here is the change in the concept of the cause of mental illness from the somatic to the psychic or mental. Janet's work appeared shortly before psychoanalysis and was beginning to exert an impact on psychology and psychiatry when it was superseded by Freud's more dramatic ideas.

OTHER SOURCES OF INFLUENCE

Several other influences on Freud deserve mention. The intellectual climate of the eighteenth and nineteenth centuries included the motivational doctrine of hedonism, which stated, in essence, that man strives to gain pleasure and to avoid pain. Associated primarily with Jeremy Bentham and his notion of utilitarianism, hedonism was also supported by some of the British associationists. One of Freud's doctrines, the pleasure principle, is derived from hedonism.

During Freud's university training, he came in contact with the so-called mechanistic school of thought, as represented by four young physiologists: Carl Ludwig, Emil du Bois-Reymond, Ernst Brücke, and Helmholtz. These students of the great Johannes Müller had united in opposition to the notion of vitalism—the doctrine that life involves forces other than those found in the interaction of inorganic bodies. The "antivitalists" took the position that no forces are to be found in living things that do not exist in inanimate objects. They argued that when an organism is viewed as a mechanical-physical system, there is no unique form of energy to be considered. In other words, there are no forces other than the common physical and chemical ones active within the organism. Freud was a student of Brücke's, and it is possible that the latter's spirit of antivitalism influenced Freud in formulating his notion of the determined nature of human behavior, a concept he called psychic determinism.

Freud's deterministic orientation is also supported by his interest in Darwinian evolution. Like Darwin, Freud tended to take a biological view of man. (Freud acknowledged that Darwin's work, along with an essay on nature by Goethe, influenced his choice of medicine as a profession.)

Thus, there were many diverse sources of influence on Freud's thinking. It has been said that no small part of Freud's genius was the ability to draw on these various sources to develop his system.

Sigmund Freud and the Development of Psychoanalysis

The psychoanalytic movement is a highly personal school centered primarily on Freud and secondarily on his disciples. The system Freud developed is much more intimately related to his own life than is the case with other movements that we have discussed. Consequently, the story of his life is of great importance to an understanding of his system.

THE LIFE OF FREUD (1856–1939)

Freud was born on May 6, 1856, in Freiberg, Moravia (now Pribor, Czechoslovakia). His father was a relatively poor Jewish wool merchant who, when his business failed in Moravia, moved his family first to Leipzig and then (when Sigmund was four years old) to Vienna. Freud remained in Vienna for nearly 80 years.

One of eight children, Freud early demonstrated great intellectual ability, which his family did everything possible to encourage. For instance, his bedroom was the only room in the house to have an oil lamp to provide better light for study; other members of the family had only candles. The other children were not allowed to study music, lest their practice disturb the young scholar. Life for the large Freud family was not easy in Austria, where anti-Semitism was rampant, but at least Jews had been granted citizenship and were able to earn a living, so long as they were "willing to step into the gutter to let a Christian pass" (Miller, 1962, p. 233).

Freud entered the gymnasium a year early and was a brilliant student, graduating with distinction at the age of 17. During this time he was undecided about his choice of career (in Vienna at the time, the only professions open to Jews were medicine and law). His interests included civilization, human culture, human relationships, and even military history. The reading of Darwin's theory of evolution awakened an interest in a scientific approach to an understanding of life and, with some hesitation, Freud decided on medicine. It is reported that he had no real desire to be a practicing physician but selected medicine because he felt that it would enable him to do scientific research.

Freud began his studies at the University of Vienna in 1873. Because of his interest in several fields not directly connected with his medical training, he took eight years to complete his studies. At first he concentrated on biology and dissected over 400 male eels in search of the precise structure of the testes. His results were not very conclusive but it is of interest that his very first attempt at research concerned sex. He then moved on to physiology and work on the spinal cord of the fish. He apparently enjoyed physiology because he worked for six years over a microscope in Brücke's physiological institute. Brücke probably contributed to Freud's concept of man as a dynamic system following the laws of nature. During his medical training, Freud discovered the analgesic properties of cocaine but missed the fame that came to one of his colleagues, who discovered its anesthetic properties. He also took some nonrequired philosophy courses with Franz Brentano.

Freud wanted to remain in scientific work within a university setting but Brücke discouraged this inclination because of Freud's financial circumstances. Freud therefore decided to take his medical examinations and enter private practice as a physician. This necessitated working in clinics and hospitals, for he had neglected the clinical aspects of his medical education in order to pursue his research in physiology.

During his hospital training, he specialized as much as possible in the anatomy and organic diseases of the nervous system, particularly paralysis, aphasia, the effects of brain injuries in children, and speech psychopathology.

Freud received his MD in 1881 and the following year began private practice as a clinical neurologist. It was apparently a difficult step for, although he had become well known for his research in neurology, he was not greatly attracted to private practice in the field. Another reason for his reluctance to begin private practice was his engagement in 1882 to Martha Bernays, who was as poor as he. Their courtship was rather violent at times as Freud evidenced jealousy, depression, and irritability. Their marriage was postponed several times for financial reasons but finally, after a four-year engagement, they were married. It is reported that during the first few months of marriage, Freud had to borrow money and even pawn their watches in order to survive. The situation improved, of course, but the early years of poverty were never completely forgotten.

Freud's extremely long working hours prevented his spending a great deal of time with his wife and children (of which there were eventually six). He also vacationed alone, because his wife could not maintain his fast pace.

A friendship of utmost importance to Freud was developed in these difficult years with Josef Breuer (1842–1925), a physician who had gained some renown for his study of respiration and his discovery of the functioning of the semicircular canals. A highly successful and sophisticated general practitioner, Breuer gave the impoverished and younger Freud advice and friendship, and even loaned him money. The two often discussed some of Breuer's patients, one of whom, Anna O.,[1] is of tremendous importance in the development of psychoanalysis.

A very intelligent and extremely attractive 21-year-old, Anna showed a wide range of severe hysterical symptoms—paralysis, memory losses, mental deterioration, nausea, and disturbances of vision and speech. Breuer began treating her by using hypnosis. He found that while under hypnosis she remembered specific experiences that seemed to have given rise to certain symptoms. Moreover, talking about the experiences while in a hypnotic state seemed to relieve the symptoms. For example, Anna went through a period when she could not drink water despite feelings of thirst. Under hypnosis she related that she had had a similar aversion to water in childhood and then recalled that she had seen a dog she

[1] Watson (1963, p. 553) reports that Anna O's real name was Bertha Pappenheim and that she later became Germany's first social worker; her distinguished career was commemorated by the issuance in 1954 of a West German postal stamp in her honor.

disliked drinking from a glass. After telling this incident to Breuer, she found that she could drink water again with no difficulty, and the symptom never recurred.

Breuer saw Anna every day for over a year. During their meetings, Anna would recount the disturbing incidents of the day, after which she often experienced some relief from her symptoms. She referred to her talks with Breuer as "chimney sweeping" and the "talking cure." The procedure was later called "catharsis."

As the treatment continued, Breuer realized (and mentioned to Freud) that the incidents Anna recalled under hypnosis involved some thought or experience that was repulsive to her. When she was able to relive these experiences under hypnosis, her symptoms either became less severe or disappeared altogether.

Breuer's wife grew jealous of the close emotional relationship that arose between Anna and Breuer. Anna exhibited what was later called a positive transference to Breuer; i.e., she transferred her feelings toward her father to Breuer. Later in the development of psychoanalysis transference was seen to be a necessary part of the therapeutic process; however, Breuer saw the situation as a threat to his career and therefore stopped Anna's treatment. A few hours after he told Anna that he could not continue to see her, she experienced the symptoms of hysterical childbirth. Breuer terminated this experience through hypnosis and did not see her again.

In 1885, a small postgraduate grant enabled Freud to spend four and one-half months studying in France under Charcot. An important incident took place during this stay in Paris: at a reception one evening, Freud heard Charcot assert vehemently that a certain patient's difficulties had a sexual basis. "But, in this kind of case, it is always something genital—always, always, always!" (Boring, 1950, p. 709). To Freud this assessment was an illuminating and exciting insight; thereafter, he was alert to the suggestion of sexual problems in his patients.

In France Freud also had an opportunity to observe Charcot's use of hypnosis in the treatment of hysterics. The French physician had shown that the traditional view of hysteria as an exclusively female malady (the word had derived from the Greek *hystera*, meaning womb) was incorrect by demonstrating the existence of hysterical symptoms in some of his male patients.

On his return from France, Freud presented Charcot's methods and results, including the notion of hysteria in males, to his medical colleagues in Vienna. The poor reception accorded his lecture deeply distressed Freud and intensified his growing animosity toward the medical establishment, which feeling was mutual.

Freud again became associated with Breuer and adopted the methods of hypnosis and catharsis in dealing with his patients. He gradually became less satisfied with hypnosis, however, for although it seemed successful in removing symptoms, it did not seem able to effect a total cure since many patients returned with a different set of symptoms. Furthermore, some neurotic patients could not be easily or deeply hypnotized.

These and other problems induced Freud to abandon the hypnotic portion of the treatment but to retain the so-called talking cure or catharsis. He gradually developed what has been called the most important step in the evolution of the psychoanalytic method: the technique of free association. In this procedure, the patient lies on a couch and is encouraged to talk freely and spontaneously, giving complete expression to every idea, no matter how embarrassing, unimportant, or foolish it might appear. The basic aim of Freud's developing method of psychoanalysis was to bring into conscious awareness memories or thoughts that had been repressed and that were presumably the source of the patient's abnormal behavior. Through the technique of free association, Freud's patients' memories seemed invariably to go further and further back into their childhood experiences. Freud found that many of these repressed memories concerned sexual matters. Already alert to the possible role of sexual factors in the etiology of his patients' illnesses, Freud became more attuned to the occurrence of sexual material in the narratives of his patients.

In 1895, Breuer and Freud published a book, *Studies on Hysteria*, that is often considered the formal starting point of psychoanalysis. It contained a joint paper that had been previously published; five case histories, including that of Anna O.; a theoretical paper by Breuer; and a chapter by Freud on psychotherapy. It was not exactly an overwhelming success. Of the few reviews given the work, most were highly critical, and only 626 copies were sold over the next 13 years. Breuer had been reluctant to publish the book and this seemed to mark the beginning of the break in his personal friendship with Freud. This split was apparently caused by Freud's emphasis on sex in his theories. By around 1898, the break between the two was complete and apparently never healed.

By the mid-1890s, Freud had become convinced that sex played the dominant role in neurosis. He observed that most of his patients reported traumatic sexual experiences in their childhood, often involving members of their own families, and he came to believe that neurosis was not possible in a person with a normal sex life.

In an important paper presented to the Society of Psychiatry and Neurology in Vienna in 1896, Freud reported that his patients had revealed experiences resembling seduction in childhood, with the seducer usually being an older relative, most often the father. These seduction traumas, Freud believed, caused the adult neurotic behavior. He further reported that his patients were extremely reluctant to describe the seduction experience in detail and that the entire situation seemed to contain the feeling of unreality. Patients recounted the events in such a manner as to suggest that they actually did not fully remember them—as though they had never really happened. Jones (1953) reported that the paper was given an "icy reception" and that the chairman of the meeting, the noted Krafft-Ebing, commented, "It sounds like a scientific fairy tale" (I, p. 263).

About a year after the presentation of this paper, Freud experienced the sudden revelation of a "great secret": in most cases, these childhood seduction experiences his patients described had never actually occurred. This realization marked a turning point in the history of psychoanalysis. At first the awareness that his patients were reporting fantasies was a stunning blow to Freud, whose theory of hysteria was based on the reality of these childhood sexual traumas. On reflection, however, he concluded that his patients' fantasies were quite real to them. And since their fantasies centered on sexual matters, sex still had to be the root of their problems. Thus, Freud's basic thesis of sex as a causative factor in neurosis remained intact.

In 1897 Freud began the monumental task of self-analysis. He experienced a number of neurotic difficulties, which were relieved in the course of the analysis, so that he became a more integrated and self-confident person. He undertook self-analysis as a means of understanding his patients better. Our concern here, however, is not his need for self-analysis but the method he used to conduct it—dream analysis.

In the course of his work Freud had discovered that a patient's dreams could be a rich source of significant emotional material. He discovered that dreams often contain valuable clues to the underlying causes of the disturbance. Because of his positivistic belief that everything had a cause, he felt that events in a dream could not be completely without meaning; that they must result from something in the person's mind, probably something of which the person is not consciously aware. (This notion that dream images are symbolic is not unique with Freud, but is actually an ancient theory.)

Realizing that he could not analyze himself by the technique of free association (it is difficult to assume the roles of both patient and therapist at the same time), Freud decided to investigate his dreams. Upon waking each morning, he recorded his dream material of the night before and then free associated to this material.

His self-analysis, which continued for about two years, not only benefitted his personality, but also culminated in the publication of the book,

The Interpretation of Dreams (1900), that was subsequently considered his major work. At the time of its publication, it was either totally ignored or commented on unfavorably. Although it took eight years to sell the first 600 copies, its importance was eventually recognized and it went through eight editions in Freud's lifetime. He incorporated dream analysis into the body of techniques used in psychoanalysis, and for the remainder of his life devoted the last half hour of each day to self-analysis.

In the very productive years after 1900, Freud developed his new ideas. In 1904, he published *The Psychopathology of Everyday Life,* which contained the description of the now famous Freudian slip. He suggested that not only in neurotic symptoms, but also in everyday behavior of the normal person, unconscious ideas are struggling for expression and thus are capable of modifying thought and action. What might appear to be casual slips of the tongue or "forgetting," Freud suggested, are actually reflections of real, though unacknowledged, motives. His next book, *Three Essays on Sexuality,* appeared in 1905. Earlier, in 1902, some students had urged him to begin a weekly discussion group so that they might learn about his psychoanalysis, as he had begun to call his work. These early disciples, including Alfred Adler and Carl Jung among others, later achieved fame through their opposition to Freud (see Chapter XIV), who tolerated no dissent from his emphasis on the key role of sexuality. Anyone who did not accept this tenet was promptly excommunicated, as was the case with several of his major disciples. Later he wrote: "Psychoanalysis is my creation . . . . For ten years I was the only one occupied with it. . . . Nobody knows better than I what psychoanalysis is" (Miller, 1962, p. 238).

During the first decade of this century, Freud's personal and professional positions improved. His practice increased and a growing number of people took his pronouncements seriously. In 1909, he received the first sign of international recognition when he was invited by G. Stanley Hall to speak at the twentieth anniversary celebration of Clark University. He was awarded an honorary doctorate, which moved him deeply, and he met many other prominent psychologists of the day, including James, Cattell, and Titchener. The lack of public attention given his visit disturbed him, however, and he left with a generally unfavorable impression of America.

The official psychoanalytic family was rent by discord, dissent, and defections during the first two decades of this century. The break with Adler came in 1911 and that with Jung, whom Freud considered his spiritual son and heir to psychoanalysis, in 1914. By World War I, three rival groups existed but Freud managed to keep the name "psychoanalysis" for his group. The war years impeded his intellectual advance and reduced the number of his patients and hence his income. With a wife, six children, and a sister-in-law to support, Freud was still greatly concerned over financial matters.

He reached the pinnacle of his fame in the period from 1919 to 1939, the year of his death. He continued to work hard and saw patients for several hours each day, but was able to take three months vacation every summer. During the 1920s psychoanalysis developed as a theoretical system for the understanding of all human motivation and personality, rather than as merely a method of treatment for the disturbed. This conceptual system is discussed later.

In 1923, it was discovered that Freud suffered from cancer of the mouth. (He characteristically smoked 20 cigars a day.) His last 16 years were marked by almost continuous pain. He underwent 33 operations, during which portions of his palate and upper jaw were removed. The prosthetic device that this surgery made necessary hampered his speaking so that he became increasingly difficult to understand. Although he continued to see his patients and disciples, he shunned other personal contact. Meanwhile, his fame spread around the world and he met many prominent people, including H. G. Wells and Thomas Mann.

When Hitler came to power, the official Nazi position on psychoanalysis was made clear when Freud's books were burned in May, 1933, in Berlin. Freud's comment on hearing of this was, "What progress we are making. In the Middle Ages they would have burnt me; nowadays they are content with burning my books" (Jones, 1957, III, p. 182). By 1934, all farsighted Jewish psychoanalysts had left Germany. The vigorous Nazi campaign to eradicate psychoanalysis in Germany was so effective that knowledge of Freud, once so widespread, was almost completely obliterated.

Against the advice of his friends, Freud insisted on remaining in Vienna. In March, 1938, the Nazis invaded Austria and on March 15 his home was overrun by a gang of Nazis. A week later his daughter was arrested and detained for a day. Finally convinced that he should leave, he was not permitted to do so until his unsold books had been brought back from Switzerland to be burned. Partly through the intervention of the American ambassador to France, the Nazis agreed to let Freud go to England. Four of his sisters were later killed in Austria.

A somewhat humorous note attended Freud's departure from Vienna: in order to secure an exit visa, he had to sign a document attesting to his "respectful and considerate" treatment by the Gestapo, and noting that he had no reason to complain. Having signed the form, he asked if he might add, "I can heartily recommend the Gestapo to anyone" (Jones, 1957, III, p. 226).

Though very well received in England, Freud was unable to enjoy the last year of his life because of his illness. His health failed rapidly but he remained mentally alert and worked almost to the very end. He died on September 23, 1939.

Psychoanalysis as a Method of Treatment

Freud found that the "talking-out" method of free association did not always operate so freely, for sooner or later the patient reached a point in his narrative where he was unable, or unwilling, to continue. Freud believed that these *resistances* indicated that the patient had called up a memory or an idea that was too horrible, shameful, or repulsive to be faced. He saw the resistance as a form of protection from emotional pain, and the presence of the pain itself as an indication that the analysis was reaching the source of the difficulty.

Thus, resistance indicated that treatment was proceeding in the right direction and must continue to probe in the same area. Freud placed great stress on helping the patient overcome his resistances. He insisted that the patient face the hidden experience, no matter how disturbing, and see it in the light of reality. In the course of a complete analysis, it was expected that resistance would be encountered and overcome a number of times.

Freud's notion of resistance led to the formulation of a fundamental principle of psychoanalysis: *repression,* which involves the ejecting of painful ideas or memories from conscious awareness. Freud regarded repression as the only adequate explanation for the occurrence of resistance: unpleasant ideas are not only pushed out of consciousness, they are also forcefully kept out. The therapist had to get the patient to bring this repressed material back into conscious awareness so that he could face it squarely and "learn to live with it." (It is sometimes charged that Freud developed the notions of resistance and repression from Schopenhauer. In 1938, Freud noted that he arrived at these ideas without having read Schopenhauer, to whom, however, he did yield precedence.)

Freud recognized that effective work with neurotic patients depended on the development of a personal intimate relationship between patient and therapist. We noted earlier how the *transference* that Anna O. developed toward Breuer disturbed him so that he had to call a halt to the treatment. Freud viewed the transference of a patient's emotional attitudes from parent to therapist as vital and necessary. The therapist had to wean the patient from childish dependence and help him assume a more adult role in life.

Freud's recognition of the importance of dream material has already been noted. He believed that dreams represent a disguised satisfaction of repressed desires and wishes. Therefore, the dream "story" is much more meaningful and complex than it might otherwise seem.

As an aside, we might note that on Wednesday evening, July 24, 1895, at a table in the northeast corner of the terrace of the Bellevue Restaurant in Vienna, Freud realized that the essence of a dream is wish fulfillment. In accord with Boring's notion that genius often flatters itself by dating its own inspirations, Freud quipped that a tablet should be erected at that spot noting that "Here the secret of dreams was revealed to Dr. Sigm. Freud on July 24, 1895" (Jones, 1953, I, p. 354).

Dreams, according to Freud, have both a latent and a manifest content. The manifest content is the actual story told in recalling the events that occurred in the dream. The true significance of the dream, however, lies in the latent content, which is its hidden or symbolic meaning. To interpret this hidden meaning, the therapist must proceed from manifest to latent content, *i.e.*, interpret the symbolic meaning of the events that are related in the manifest content.

This is a complex task, for Freud felt that the forbidden desires in the latent content were expressed in symbolic form in the manifest content. Although many symbols that crop up in dreams are relevant only to experiences of the particular dreamer, Freud believed that others are common to all men and hence always have the same meaning. These universal symbols include gardens, balconies, and doors, signifying the female body; and church spires, candles, and serpents, signifying the male genitals. Dreams of falling represent the giving in to erotic wishes, while dreams of flying represent a desire for sexual achievement. In spite of their universality, Freud warned against interpreting these common symbols without knowledge of a patient's specific conflicts.

Freud believed a long and intensive course of therapy was required to effect a cure. In dealing with his own patients, he found that no less than five sessions a week, for months or even years, were necessary. With such extensive care, an analyst could handle only a few patients in the course of a year.

Freud also had definite ideas about the training of analysts. He felt that each should be analyzed himself, and then work for two years under close supervision before treating patients on his own. He also believed strongly that the practice of psychoanalysis should be a profession independent from medicine.

Freud's Method of Research

Because of the great differences in content and methodology between Freud and the traditional experimental psychology, it is instructive to examine his method of research. It is difficult at times to reconcile some of Freud's theories, particularly the more bizarre, with his thorough training as a scientist, especially his years of physiological research. In spite of his background, Freud eschewed the customary experimental methods of research in his work. Although he was undoubtedly familiar with the experimental psychology movement, he did not collect data from controlled experiments, nor did he analyze his results quantitatively.

Freud derived his theories, then, from his own observations of the narratives and behavior of his patients undergoing analysis. Moreover, since analysis was so lengthy, Freud accumulated great masses of such data, which he then subjected to a critical analysis, using what is called the method of internal consistency.

> Inferences made from one part of the material were checked against evidence appearing in other parts, so that the final conclusions drawn from a case were based upon an interlocking network of facts and inferences. Freud proceeded in his work in much the same way as a detective assembling evidence or a lawyer summing up a case to the jury. Everything had to fit together coherently before Freud was satisfied that he had put his finger upon the correct interpretation (Hall & Lindzey, 1957, p. 56).

Freud saw no inherent obstacles to making relevant and meaningful observations:

> When I set myself the task of bringing to light what human beings keep hidden within them, not by the compelling power of hypnosis, but by observing what they say and what they show, I thought the task was a harder one than it really is. He that has eyes to see and ears to hear may convince himself that no mortal can keep a secret. If the lips are silent, he chatters with his finger tips; betrayal oozes out of him at every pore. And thus the task of making conscious the most hidden recesses of the mind is one which it is quite possible to accomplish (Freud, 1905, pp. 77–78).

Freud's theories were formulated, revised, and extended in terms of the evidence as he alone interpreted it. Thus, his own critical abilities were the predominant, indeed the only, guide in his theory building. He seemed to ignore criticism from others, particularly from those not sympathetic to psychoanalysis, and even the wide-ranging criticism from close friends and colleagues that continued throughout his life had little influence on his thinking. Only rarely did he bother to reply to his critics: psychoanalysis was his system, and his alone.

Psychoanalysis as a System of Personality

Freud's theoretical system did not pretend to cover the topics that were usually included in psychology textbooks of that day. Rather, he attempted to explain areas that other psychologists either neglected completely or, at least, left unsettled. His theoretical formulations dealt almost exclusively with motives, their conflicts, and the effects of these conflicts on the neuroses as well as on everyday behavior.

THE UNCONSCIOUS AND CONSCIOUS ASPECTS OF PERSONALITY

In his earlier work, Freud expressed the belief that man's psychic life consisted of two main parts: the conscious and the unconscious. The conscious part, small and insignificant, presented but a superficial aspect of total personality, whereas the vast and powerful unconscious contained the concealed forces that are the driving power behind all human behavior. Freud also postulated the existence of the preconscious or foreconscious. Unlike the material in the unconscious, that in the preconscious has not been actively repressed; hence it can be easily summoned into conscious awareness.

Freud later revised this simple twofold conscious–unconscious distinction and introduced the famous id, ego, and superego constructs of the mental apparatus. The *id*, corresponding somewhat to Freud's earlier notion of the unconscious, is the most primitive and least accessible part of the personality. The extremely powerful forces of the id include man's instinctive sexual urges and suppressed habit tendencies: "we call it a chaos, a cauldron full of seething excitations." Freud further noted that "The id of course knows no judgements of value: no good and evil, no morality" (Freud, 1933, pp. 73–74). In that the id seeks immediate satisfaction without regard for the circumstances of objective reality, it operates according to what Freud called the pleasure principle, which is concerned with tension reduction.

Man's basic psychic energy or *libido* is contained in the id and is expressed through the notion of tension reduction. Increases in libidinal energy result in increased tension gradients, that the organism attempts to reduce to more tolerable levels. To satisfy his needs and maintain a comfortable tension level, an individual must interact with the real world. For example, the person who is hungry must make appropriate movements in his environment to find food in order to discharge the tension induced by hunger. Thus, an effective and appropriate liaison must be effected between the demands of the id and the circumstances of reality. To facilitate this interaction, the *ego* develops out of the id and serves as a mediating agent between the self and the external world. The ego represents what is ordinarily known as reason and sanity, in contrast to the passions of the id.

The id craves blindly, unaware of reality; the ego, on the other hand, is aware of reality, perceives and manipulates it, and regulates the id with reference to it. The ego thus operates in accord with what Freud called the reality principle, holding in abeyance the pleasure-seeking demands of the id until an appropriate object has been found with which to satisfy the need and reduce or discharge the tension.

The ego does not exist independently of the id; indeed it derives its power from the id. It serves to help, not to hinder, the id, and is constantly striving to bring about id satisfaction.

Freud compared the relation of the ego and the id to a rider on a horse. The horse supplies the energy that the rider directs along the path he wants to travel.

The third part of Freud's structure of personality, the *superego,* develops early in childhood, when rules of conduct taught by parents through a system of rewards and punishments are assimilated. Behaviors that are "wrong" (*i.e.,* bring punishment) become part of the child's conscience, which is one part of the superego. Behaviors that are "good" (*i.e.,* are rewarded) become part of the child's ego-ideal, the other part of the superego. Thus the child's behavior is initially governed by parental control, but once the superego has formed a pattern for conduct, behavior is determined by self-control. That is, the behavior-guiding rewards and punishments are then administered by the individual himself.

Freud said that the superego represents "every moral restriction, the advocate of a striving towards perfection—it is, in short, as much as we have been able to grasp psychologically of what is described as the higher side of human life" (1933, p. 67). It can readily be understood, then, that the superego is in direct conflict with the id. Unlike the ego, the superego does not merely attempt to postpone id satisfaction, but rather to inhibit it completely.

INSTINCTS

Instincts are the propelling or locomotive factors in the dynamics of personality—the biological forces of the individual that release mental energy. They arise from sources of stimulation within the body and their aim is to remove or reduce the stimulation through some activity such as sexual satisfaction.

While Freud did not attempt to delimit the number of instincts, he believed that they could be classified in two distinct categories: the life instincts and the death instincts. The life instincts, including hunger, sex, and thirst, are concerned with self-preservation and racial survival. The libido is the form of energy through which the life instincts are manifested. The life instincts consist of the creative forces which underlie life itself.

In addition to the creative force of the life instincts, there is also the destructive force of the death instinct. This death instinct can be directed either inward, as in suicide or masochism, or outward, as in aggression and hate. Freud believed that man is irresistably drawn toward death, that "The goal of all life is death" (1920, p. 160).

Thus Freud gradually acknowledged that aggression and hostility, as well as sex, are important forces in personality. As he grew older, he became more and more convinced that aggression also powerfully motivates human behavior. He even became more conscious of an aggressive tendency within himself. Some of his closest colleagues described him as a "good hater," and some of his writings, as well as the sharpness and finality of his breaks with dissenters suggest that "his own aggressive drive was not strongly repressed" (Woodworth & Sheehan, 1964, p. 279).

ANXIETY

An important concept in psychoanalysis, particularly when dealing with neurotic and psychotic behavior, is anxiety, of which Freud noted three kinds: objective, neurotic, and moral. Objective anxiety is occasioned by fear of real dangers from the objective world; from it are derived the other two types of anxiety.

Neurotic anxiety arises from the recognition of potential danger inherent in instinctual gratification. It is a fear, not of the instincts per se, but of the punishment likely to follow indiscriminate id-dominated behavior. Thus, neurotic anxiety is a fear of being punished for expressing impulsive desires. Moral anxiety arises out of a fear of the conscience. When a person performs (or even thinks of performing) some act that is contrary to the set of moral values comprising his conscience, he may experience guilt or shame. Moral anxiety, then, is a function of how well developed is the person's conscience. The less virtuous individual is less likely to develop moral anxiety.

Regardless of type, anxiety is a tension-inducing force in human behavior, motivating the person to reduce this state of tension. Freud believed that the ego developed a number of protective defenses against anxiety, the so-called *defense mechanisms*. In the mechanism of *identification*, a person identifies himself with (takes on the manner, dress, style of speech, etc., of) another who seems admirable and less vulnerable to the specific danger giving rise to the anxiety.

Another defense mechanism, *repression*, is the barring from conscious awareness of an anxiety-provoking stimulus. Its importance in Freud's system was noted earlier. *Sublimation* involves substituting a socially acceptable goal for one that cannot be directly satisfied. In *projection*, the source of anxiety is attributed to someone else, *e.g.*, by saying "He hates me" instead of "I hate him."

In another mechanism, *reaction formation*, a person conceals his own disturbing impulse by converting it into its opposite, *e.g.*, replacing hate by love. With the mechanism of *fixation*, a person's development becomes arrested at an early stage because the next stage is too fraught with anxiety. Finally, the mechanism of *regression* involves behavior that indicates a reversion to an earlier developmental stage, one at which there was greater security (*i.e.*, where the current source of anxiety was not operative).

Freud believed that anxiety with which an individual could not adequately cope became traumatic, reducing the person to a state of infantile helplessness.

STAGES OF PERSONALITY DEVELOPMENT

We noted earlier that Freud was convinced that the neurotic disturbances manifested by his patients had originated in childhood experiences. As a consequence, he became one of the first theorists to place great stress on the development of the child. He believed that the adult personality pattern was established very early in life and was almost completely formed by the age of five.

In the psychoanalytic theory of development, the child passes through a series of *psychosexual stages of development* from birth to age five. During these stages, he is considered "autoerotic"; *i.e.*, he derives sensual or erotic pleasure by stimulating the various erogenous zones of his body or being stimulated by his mother in her handling of him. Each stage during this period tends to be localized in specific bodily erogenous zones.

The first, or *oral*, stage lasts from birth into the second year; during it, stimulation of the mouth, such as sucking, biting, and swallowing, is the primary source of erotic satisfaction. Inadequate satisfaction (too much or too little) at this stage may produce an oral type of personality in which the person is preoccupied with excessive mouth habits, such as smoking, kissing, and eating. Freud believed that a wide range of adult behaviors, from excessive optimism to sarcasm and cynicism, were attributable to incidents occurring during this stage of development.

In the *anal* phase, sexual gratification shifts from the mouth to the anus and the child derives pleasure from the anal zone. Watson (1963) imagines this situation as a child might see it:

> There is nothing about the odor, texture, or appearance of the feces that are inherently unpleasant. The infant has no innate repulsion. He has created it, and the mother seems to prize it, since she is pleased when he has a movement and concerned when he does not. According to Freudian thinking, defecation is "perceived" by the infant as the giving of a gift. What happens to his gift? The mother flushes it down the toilet! Often he acts out his puzzlement about this strange behavior by toilet play, throwing toys in the toilet, only to retrieve them again (p. 449).

During this stage (which coincides with the period of toilet training) the child may either expel or withhold, and may in either case thereby defy his parents. Strong conflict during this period can result in an anal expulsive adult, who is dirty, wasteful, and extravagant; or an anal retentive adult, who is excessively neat, clean, and compulsive. (Whether or not they agree with the Freudian interpretation of the struggle between parent and child during toilet training, most parents would agree that it is indeed a contentious period, during which the child is often flushed with victory!)

During the *phallic* stage, which occurs at about the end of the third or fourth year, erotic gratification shifts to the genital region. There is much fondling and exhibiting of the genitals, and sexual fantasizing. In addition, Freud posited the development at this stage of an important phenomenon, the Oedipus complex (named after the Greek legend in which Oedipus unknowingly killed his father and married his mother). At this stage the child becomes sexually attached to the parent of the opposite sex and fearful of the parent of the same sex, whom he now perceives as a rival. Ordinarily, the child overcomes this complex, but the attitudes he develops toward the opposite sex during this time persist and influence his relations with members of the opposite sex in adult life.

If, miraculously, the child is able to get through the many struggles of these three stages, he enters a period of latency lasting from about his fifth to twelfth years. At the start of adolescence (when puberty strikes) the final genital stage begins. During this time, heterosexual behavior is evident and various activities by which the individual prepares for marriage and family are undertaken.

Criticisms of Psychoanalysis

The amount of criticism directed against Freud and his theories, much of which comes from the lay public, is enormous. We shall restrict our discussion to criticisms from professional sources.

Particularly vulnerable are Freud's methods of data collection. We have seen that he drew his insights and conclusions from his patients' responses while they were undergoing psychoanalysis. Consider some of the deficiencies of such an approach in the light of the experimental method of systematically collecting objective data under controlled conditions of observation.

First, the conditions under which Freud collected his data certainly seem to be unsystematic and uncontrolled. He did not make a verbatim transcript of what each patient said, but preferred to work from notes made several hours after seeing a patient. Some of the original data (the patient's own words) must surely have been lost in the interim as a result of the vagaries of recall with its errors of distortion and omission. Data thus consisted of what Freud remembered. Also, it is possible that in the course of recollection Freud reinterpreted the raw data. In drawing his inferences, he may have been guided by his desire to find material supportive of his hypotheses. In other words, he may have recorded only what he wanted to hear. Thus, Freud's reconstruction of the data may not have accurately reflected the actual data as it occurred. Of course, we must consider the possibility that Freud's notes were accurate representations of the raw data but it is impossible to know this with any degree of certainty for the original data did not survive.

There is an even more basic criticism of the raw data itself. Even if a complete record had been kept, it would not have been possible to determine the validity or "truth" of what the patients said. Freud made no attempt to determine the accuracy of what his patients reported and critics argue that he should have tried to verify the patients' reports, e.g., by questioning their relatives and friends about the events described. Thus, the distinct possibility exists that the basic step in Freud's theory building—data collection—may be characterized as incomplete, imperfect, and inaccurate.

As for the next step—drawing inferences and generalizations from the data—no one knows exactly how this was done. That Freud never explained the process fully is, of course, another major point of criticism. As Hall and Lindzey (1957) noted, Freud's writings contain his conclusions but not (a) the data from which the conclusions were derived, (b) the method by which the data were analyzed, nor (c) any systematic account of his empirical findings. Further, since Freud did not attempt to quantify his data, it is impossible to determine the reliability or statistical significance of his findings.

These are serious charges indeed from the standpoint of scientific methodology and theory building. The reader of Freud must, in a sense, accept on faith the validity of his operations and conclusions. Freud's observations cannot be repeated because it is not known for certain exactly what he did in collecting data and in translating observations into generalizations and hypotheses. The language of science is extremely precise and orderly, leaving no room for ambiguities, distortions, and vagaries. It seems that Freud did not speak the same language and it is difficult to translate from one to the other.

Another point of attack concerns the difficulty of deriving empirically-testable propositions from many of Freud's hypotheses. How, for instance, would we empirically test the notion of a death wish? Adherents of operationism argue that Freud's concepts are not operationally defined. (Part of Bridgman's discussion of operationism in Chapter XI included a description of so-called pseudo-problems, or questions that defy answer by any known experimental test.) By this criterion, many of Freud's concepts cannot be experimentally tested, and some critics feel that they are meaningless, indeed useless, for science.

What of the validity of psychoanalytic theory as a whole? It seems that, except in the broadest sense of the word, there is no such thing as a psychoanalytic theory! There are a large number of generalizations and hypotheses but there seems to be no orderly framework of theorems, postulates, or precise relationships so necessary to a scientific theory. "The unfortunate truth is that the *analysts' statements are so general that they can explain whatever behavior occurs.* A genuine scientific explanation cannot do this; it must predict one behavior to the exclusion of all other behaviors. Otherwise the theory is empirically empty . . . (Marx & Hillix, 1963, p. 231).

Since no overall theory exists, no meaningful overall criticism of it can be attempted (save, perhaps, that psychoanalysis as a scientific theory leaves a great deal to be desired). It is noted that specific concepts and generalizations have also come under criticism.

Contributions of Psychoanalysis

Having noted many important and damaging (indeed, damning, to some) criticisms of psychoanalysis, offered primarily by experimentally oriented psychologists, we must ask why psychoanalysis has not only survived, but also prospered.

All theories of behavior can, unfortunately, be criticized as somewhat lacking in scientific validity. However, some are certainly more scientifically respectable than psychoanalysis. As a result, a psychologist in search of a theory must choose on the basis of criteria other than formal scientific rigidity and precision. One who selects psychoanalysis does not do so in the absence of evidence, however; psychoanalysis does offer evidence, although not the variety traditionally accepted by science (*i.e.,* experimental investigations of specific propositions). The psychoanalysts' evidence is based on observation of experience as it occurs.

That psychoanalytic evidence is not the strictly scientific variety does not necessarily mean that the theory is totally incorrect or misleading. Belief in psychoanalysis is based on the intuitive grounds of a perceived appearance of plausibility in Freud's system.

> Any one who accepts or rejects the psychoanalytic theories does so by means of the same kind of reasoning that gives him the thousand and one judgments

he is forced to make in everyday life on the basis of insufficient or inadequate evidence—the kind of judgments, in fact, that he is forced to live by, but which have no standing in science. Such estimates, growing out of a multitude of impressions and interpretations, guesses and insights, often result in unshakable convictions, convictions which may be right or wrong but which, from the standpoint of science, cannot be recognized as either proved or disproved (Heidbreder, 1933, pp. 403–404).

Freud's influence on psychiatry and clinical psychology is profound, and his theories are of considerable significance in the more academic and, in the broad sense of the term, experimental psychology. Certain Freudian concepts have gained rather wide acceptance and been assimilated into American academic psychology. These include the role of unconscious motivation, the importance of childhood experiences in shaping adult behavior, and the operation of the defense mechanisms. Interest in these areas has generated much research. It is a tribute to Freud, moreover, that many of his ardent opponents recognize the value of his contributions.

A more general source of influence is Freud's contribution to the radical change that has taken place in sexual mores. This century has seen a gradual loosening of sexual restraint in behavior as well as in art, literature, and the various media of entertainment. Also, it seems that his emphasis on sex helped to popularize his views. Even when discussed in scientific writings, sex has definite sensational appeal (witness the sales of the Kinsey reports). Also of interest is Freud's exciting and colorful style of writing, rare in scientific work.

Despite criticisms of his lack of scientific rigor and methodology, Freud's psychoanalysis is a vital force in contemporary psychology. It retains a separate identity and, for the most part, has not become part of the mainstream of current psychological thought; indeed, psychoanalysis remains in opposition to the predominantly experimental American psychology.

No matter what one's evaluation of psychoanalysis, and whatever the eventual status of the system, there is no denying that Freud himself possessed the attributes of greatness.

He was a pioneer in a field of thought, in a new technique for the understanding of human nature. He was also an originator, even though he picked his conceptions out of the stream of the culture—an originator who remained true to his fundamental intent for fifty years of hard work, while he altered and brought to maturity the system of ideas that was his contribution to knowledge. . . . It is not likely that the history of psychology can be written in the next three centuries without mention of Freud's name and still claim to be a general history of psychology. And there you have the best criterion of greatness: posthumous fame (Boring, 1950, pp. 706–707).

SUGGESTED FURTHER READINGS

Hypnotism

Shor, R. E., & Orne, M. T. (Eds.) *The nature of hypnosis: selected basic writings.* New York: Holt, Rinehart & Winston, 1965.

Freud

Choisy, M. *Sigmund Freud: a new appraisal.* New York: Philosophical Library, 1963.

Freud, S. *An autobiographical study.* Trans. J. Strachey. New York: Norton, 1963. (First published in 1925.)

Hall, C. S. *A primer of Freudian psychology.* Cleveland: World Publishing Co., 1954.

Jones, E. *The life and works of Sigmund Freud.* New York: Basic Books, 1953–1957. 3 vols.

Nelson, B. (Ed.) *Freud and the 20th century.* New York: Meridian, 1957.

General

Jahoda, M. Some notes on the influence of psychoanalytic ideas on American psychology. *Human Relations,* 1963, **16,** 111–129.

Shakow, D., & Rapaport, D. *The influence of Freud on American psychology.* New York: International Universities Press, 1964.

Skinner, B. F. Critique of psychoanalytic concepts and theories. *Scientific Monthly,* 1954, **79,** 300–305.

XIV

PSYCHOANALYSIS: AFTER THE FOUNDING

AFTER ITS FORMAL founding, psychoanalysis proceeded in two different directions. On the one hand, there was a group of analysts who more or less adhered to the central tenets of Freudian thought, although they modified and elaborated certain concepts after Freud's death. A second group, however, disagreed completely with some of Freud's major points. While refusing to disavow their psychoanalytic orientation, these dissenters devised principles meant to correct what they considered the deficiencies and inadequacies in Freud's thinking. We have seen that Freud did not tolerate dissension, and that those who espoused different positions "left the movement not at all with the tacit agreement to differ but rather in an aura of heavy disapproval and the sort of invective that was once heaped upon the heads of heretics . . ." (Brown, 1963, p. 37).

The Dissenters

Carl Gustav Jung

Once regarded by Freud as heir apparent of the psychoanalytic movement, Jung, when his close friendship with Freud disintegrated in 1914, began what he called analytical psychology.

THE LIFE OF JUNG (1875–1961)

Born in a Swiss village on Lake Constance, of a quite scholarly family, Jung initially considered becoming an archeologist. The story is told that a dream aroused his interest in science and he decided to study medicine. After obtaining his medical degree in 1900 from the University of Basel, he began a long and active career in psychiatry. His first professional appointment was at the psychiatric clinic at the University

289

of Zurich, which was directed by Eugen Bleuler, the well-known psychiatrist noted for his influential work on schizophrenia. In 1905, Jung was appointed a lecturer in psychiatry at the university, but after several years resigned these appointments to devote his efforts to private practice, research, and writing.

Jung became interested in Freud in 1900 after reading *Interpretation of Dreams*, which he described as a "masterpiece." By 1906, the two men had begun to correspond, and a year later Jung went to Vienna to meet Freud. This initial meeting marked the start of their close but short-lived friendship. In 1909 Jung accompanied Freud to America for the Clark University commemorative ceremonies at which they both lectured.

In 1911, largely through Freud's efforts and in spite of strong opposition from its Viennese members, Jung became the first president of the International Psychoanalytic Association. Freud apparently believed that anti-Semitism might impede the movement if a Jew headed the group; the Viennese members, almost all of whom were Jewish, presumably resented Jung, a younger man, because they had seniority in the movement and because of Jung's alleged anti-Semitism.

Shortly after Jung was elected, the friendship between him and Freud showed signs of strain. (Jung had deemphasized the role of sex and expressed a different concept of the libido in his book in 1912 and in a series of lectures at Fordham University.) Friction grew, and in 1912 the two men agreed to terminate their personal correspondence. Relations were completely severed in 1914, when Jung resigned his presidency and withdrew from the association. Although they never saw one another again, Jung retained his admiration for Freud.

In line with an interest in the relevance of myths for the individual, Jung made a number of field expeditions to Africa, Arizona, and New Mexico in the 1920s to study the mental processes of preliterate people. In 1932, he was appointed professor at the Federal Polytechnical University in Zurich, a position he occupied until poor health obliged him to resign in 1942. In 1944 a chair of medical psychology was founded for him at the University of Basel, but again his poor health prevented his keeping the position for more than a year.

He remained actively productive in research and writing for most of his 86 years, publishing an astonishing array of books. His many awards included honorary degrees from Harvard and Oxford. He was read and respected throughout the world, and was known to people in all walks of life.

JUNG'S SYSTEM: ANALYTICAL PSYCHOLOGY

Perhaps the most important point of difference between Jung and Freud concerns the nature of the libido. Whereas Freud defined libido in predominantly sexual terms, Jung regarded it as a generalized life energy, of which sex was only one part. For Jung, this libidinal life energy expressed itself in growth and reproduction as well as other kinds of activity, depending on what was most important for an individual at a given point in time.

Jung's refusal to regard the basic life energy as exclusively sexual left him free to give different interpretations to behavior that Freud could construe only as sexual strivings. For instance, during the first three to five years of life (which Jung called the presexual phase), the Jungian view is that libidinal energy serves the functions of nutrition and growth, with none of the sexual overtones of Freud's conception of these years. Jung rejected the notion of the Oedipus complex (in Freudian terms) and explained the child's attachment to his mother in terms of a dependency need with satisfactions and rivalries associated with the mother's food-providing function. As the child matures and develops in his sexual functioning, Jung maintained, these nutritive functions become overlaid and combined with sexual feelings. To Jung, libidinal energy took a heterosexual form only after puberty.

It is important to note that Jung did not altogether deny the existence of sexual factors. Instead, he reduced the role of sex to only one of a whole range of drives comprising the libido.

THE STRUCTURE OF PERSONALITY

Jung used the term *psyche* to refer to the mind, which he said consisted of three levels: the conscious, the personal unconscious, and the collective unconscious. At the center of consciousness is the ego, which is generally akin to a person's conception of himself. Consciousness comprises perceptions, memories, and the like, and is the avenue of contact with reality that enables a person to adapt to his environment.

Jung believed that too much emphasis had been given to consciousness, which he considered second in importance to the unconscious. The conscious aspect of the psyche is like the visible portion of an island. A larger unknown part exists beneath the (small) part that can be seen above the water, and Jung stressed this mysterious hidden base.

He believed there are two levels or parts of the unconscious. Just beneath consciousness there exists the personal unconscious, which belongs to the individual. It consists of all the impulses and wishes, the faint perceptions, and numerous other experiences that have been either suppressed or forgotten. Incidents from the personal unconscious, however, can be easily recalled to conscious awareness, which indicates that it is not a very deep level of unconsciousness.

Below the personal unconscious is the third psychic level, the collective unconscious. This deepest level of all contains, unknown to the individual, the influence of the cumulative experiences of all past generations, including primitive ancestors. "It is almost entirely detached from anything personal in the life of an individual and it is seemingly universal. All human beings have more or less the same collective unconscious" (Hall & Lindzey, 1957, p. 80). Jung felt that evolutionary theory, by demonstrating a similarity in brain structure in all races of man, could account for the universality of the collective unconscious.

In terms of our island analogy, a number of small islands rising above the surface of the water represent the individual conscious awareness of a number of people. Land areas just beneath the water, which are exposed to view by the action of the tides, represent the individual's personal unconscious. The ocean floor, on which all the islands ultimately rest, is the collective unconscious.

Jung emphasized the powerful forces preserved in the collective unconscious because he felt that it contributed most to psychic development. He called the inherited tendencies in the collective unconscious *archetypes,* and saw them as preexisting determinants of mental experience that dispose an individual to behave in a manner similar to that manifested by his racial ancestors when confronted with an analogous situation.

Jung believed archetypes are experienced as emotions and mental images, and that they are typically associated with such significant human experiences as birth and death, or with particular stages of life (*e.g.,* adolescence) and reactions to extreme dangers. His intensive investigation of the mythical and artistic products of different civilizations resulted in the discovery of certain symbols that were common to all, even cultures so widely separated that there was no possibility of direct influence. In his work with patients, Jung found what he considered definite traces of mythological images in their dreams.

Four of the many archetypes Jung found seemed to recur more often than others; to be laden with emotional significance for man; and to be traceable to ancient historical myths of diverse origins. These four principal archetypes, which Jung considered separate personality systems, are the persona, the anima, the animus, and the shadow.

The *persona,* or outermost aspect of personality, conceals the true self. It is the mask donned by an individual when he comes in contact with others and represents him as he wants to appear to society; thus it may not correspond to his "real" personality. The notion of persona is apparently akin to the sociological concept of role playing, which posits that a person acts the way he thinks others expect him to.

The archetypes *anima* and *animus* reflect the notion that both men and women exhibit both masculine and feminine tendencies. The anima refers to feminine characteristics in man, whereas the animus denotes masculine characteristics in woman. As with the other archetypes, these arise out of the primitive past of the species, in which men and women took on some of the behavioral and emotional tendencies of the opposite sex.

The *shadow* archetype (the darker self) is the inferior, animal-like part of the personality, man's racial heritage from the lower forms of life. As such, it contains all immoral, passionate, and objectionable desires and activities. Jung said that the shadow urges us to do those things that we ordinarily would not allow ourselves to do. Having performed such actions, we usually insist that something "came over us": Jung claimed that the "something" is the primitive part of our nature.

INTROVERSION-EXTRAVERSION

Jung is probably best known for his discussion of introversion and extraversion, which are defined in terms of the direction of libidinal energy. He regarded them as two attitudes or modes of reacting to specific situations.

The *extravert* directs the libido outside the self to external events, people, and situations. A person of this type is strongly influenced by forces in his environment and is very sociable and self-confident in a wide range of situations.

The libido of the *introvert* is directed inward: the individual is more contemplative, introspective, and resistant to external influence. He is less confident in his relations with other people and the external world and tends to be relatively unsociable and shy.

Jung believed that these opposing attitudes exist in every person in varying degrees, but that one is generally more pronounced than the other. He did suggest, however, that no one is a total introvert or extravert, but rather that the dominant attitude at a given moment can be influenced by the situation. For example, a normally introverted person might become quite sociable and unreserved in a situation in which he is vitally interested.

According to Jung, personality differences are also reflected via the *functions*, which are used to orient ourselves to both the external objective world and the internal subjective world. Functions include sensation, thinking, feeling, and intuition. Sensation is the conscious perception of physical objects; thinking is a conceptual process that provides meaning and understanding; feeling is a subjective process of weighing and valuing; and intuition involves perceiving in an unconscious manner.

Jung considered thinking and feeling to be rational modes of responding in that they involve reason and judgment, whereas sensation and intuition he considered irrational because they depend on the concrete and specific stimulus world. Within each pair, only one mode can be dominant at a given time. This dominance of function can be combined with the dominance of either introversion or extraversion to produce a number of possible personality types.

A final part of Jung's system is his notion of *self*, which he considered the most important archetype of all. Comprising all aspects of the unconscious, the self provides unity and stability to the entire structure of personality. As a representation of the "whole man," it attempts to achieve complete personal integration, and can be considered a drive or urge toward self-realization. One symbol that Jung found repeatedly and consistently in various cultures was the *mandala,* or magic circle. He considered it symbolic of the total unity and wholeness toward which all men strive.

WORD ASSOCIATION

Jung developed the now famous word association test as a therapeutic tool. In this test, a list of words is read to a patient, who responds to each with the first word that comes to mind. In addition to measuring the time taken to respond to each word, Jung measured changes in breathing and, using a psychogalvanometer, in the electrical conductivity of the skin. These two physiological measures provided additional evidence of emotional reactions to specific words. If a particular word produced a long response time, irregularity in breathing, and a change in skin conductivity, Jung deduced the existence of an unconscious emotional problem connected with the stimulus word or with the reply.

COMMENT

Jung has influenced not only psychology and psychiatry, but also religion, history, art, and literature. Arnold Toynbee and Philip Wylie, among many others, have acknowledged him as a source of inspiration (Hall & Lindzey, 1957). Scientific psychology has for the most part ignored Jung's analytical psychology. Aside from the fact that not all of his books have been translated into English, his less than lucid writing style impedes understanding. Further, his disdain for traditional scientific methods repels scientifically oriented psychologists, to whom Jung may appeal even less than Freud, for Jung's writings are full of discourse on mysticism and religion.

The same kinds of criticisms noted in relation to Freud's supporting evidence are applicable to Jung, as he too relied on clinical observation and interpretation rather than controlled laboratory investigation. Analytical psychology has received less searching criticism than Freudianism, probably because Freud's overpowering stature in psychoanalysis relegates Jung (and others) to second place in terms of professional attention.

This is not to deny Jung's eminence and importance: his ideas are thought provoking and novel, and he presents an optimistic concept of man that many find a welcome change from Freud. Jung was a scholarly, vital personality who inspired great loyalty in his adherents, and there have been signs of a growing Jungian influence in recent years.

Social-Psychological Theories in Psychoanalysis: the Zeitgeist Strikes Again

The spirit of the times in which Freud developed his system favored a mechanistic and positivistic conception of human behavior. Around the end of the nineteenth century, there appeared new disciplines that suggested the possibility of viewing man in other than a biological and physical frame of reference. Anthropology, sociology, and social psychology were finding evidence to support the proposition that man is the product of the various social forces and institutions that comprise his environment. These ideas suggested that man should be studied as a social animal rather than as a strictly biological one.

As varied cultures were studied by anthropologists, it became clear that the neurotic symptoms and taboos hypothesized by Freud were not found universally, as he had suggested. To give just one example, taboos against incest do not exist in all societies. Further, sociologists and social psychologists found that much human behavior is a result of social conditioning rather than instinctive biological factors.

Thus, the intellectual spirit of the times revised man's concept of himself, but Freud, to the dismay of some of his followers, continued to virtually ignore the possibility of social influences on personality. Some theorists, usually younger and perhaps less constrained by tradition, began to move away from orthodox Freudian psychoanalysis and to reshape psychoanalytic theory along lines congruent with the orientation provided by the social sciences. Three of these socially oriented dissenters, Adler, Horney, and Fromm, are discussed here.

Alfred Adler: Individual Psychology

Adler is usually considered the earliest figure in the social-psychological brand of psychoanalysis because he broke with Freud in 1911. He later developed a theory in which social interest plays a major role.

THE LIFE OF ADLER (1870–1937)

Born of rather wealthy parents in a suburb of Vienna, Adler said that he led an unhappy childhood. The apparent reason was his conviction that he could never live up to the achievements of his eldest brother, who seemed a model child in every way and was his mother's favorite.

(Alfred was his father's favorite.) A sickly youngster who did not walk until the age of four, he was watched over with great care. In spite of his poor health and the feeling of being both ugly and too small, he was a friendly and sociable child.

At five, while recovering from a near-fatal illness, Adler decided to become a physician. This he eventually did, receiving his degree from the University of Vienna in 1895. After first specializing in ophthalmology and then practicing general medicine, Adler went into psychiatry. About 1902, he began meeting with Freud's weekly discussion group, of which he became a highly esteemed leading member.

Over the course of the next several years, Adler developed a theory of personality that differed in important respects from Freud's. By 1911 he had become openly critical of Freud's emphasis on sexual factors. A year earlier, Freud had named Adler president of the Viennese Analytic Society, apparently in an effort to reconcile the growing differences between them. The inevitable split was made complete in 1911, when Adler resigned his presidency and officially broke with the Freudian position.

Adler served as a physician in the Austrian Army during World War I and later organized child guidance clinics in the Vienna school system. During the 1920s, his individual psychology attracted much favorable attention throughout the world and many followers came to study under him in Vienna. He lectured in several countries and in 1926 came to the United States, where he was warmly welcomed. After a number of visits to this country, he made it his home in 1934 and became professor of medical psychology at the Long Island College of Medicine. In 1937, while on a strenuous lecture tour, he died in Aberdeen, Scotland.

Adler wrote numerous books and articles, many of them addressed to the lay public. Adlerian theories continue to be promoted and expounded today in the *American Journal of Individual Psychology* and by the American Society of Individual Psychology.

ADLER'S SYSTEMATIC POSITION

Adler and Freud were quite sharply opposed to one another in their theoretical positions. Whereas Freud's theories emphasized the role of the past in influencing behavior, Adler's orientation was toward the future. The division of personality into separate parts or aspects is an essential part of Freudian theory, whereas the Adlerian approach emphasizes the unity of personality.

Adler developed his system of individual psychology along social lines. This statement represents a basic point of departure from Freud, for Adler saw human behavior as determined not by the biological forces of instinct, but by social forces. He believed that we can understand an individual's personality only through investigation of his social relationships and his attitude toward others. He held that social interest develops very early in infancy:

> The first social situation that confronts a child is its relation to its mother, from the very first day. By her educational skill the child's interest in another person is first awakened. If she understands how to train this interest in the direction of cooperation, all the congenital and acquired capacities of the child will converge in the direction of social sense (Adler, 1930, p. 403).

Social attitude and interest, then, are developed through learning experiences. Adler, like Freud, recognized the importance of the early formative years of childhood, but Adler's focus was on social and not biological forces.

Another point of difference between the theories of Freud and Adler concerns the importance of consciousness. Whereas Freud stressed unconscious determinants of behavior, Adler emphasized the conscious. He considered man first and foremost a conscious being who is aware of his motivations. To Freud, man's behavior is determined by his past experiences. In contrast, Adler believed that man is more strongly influenced by what he thinks the future holds in store. Strivings for future goals can modify and influence what a person does at a given moment. For example, a person living in fear of eternal damnation after death behaves in accordance with this expectation. Thus, anticipations of future events can strongly affect present behavior.

STRIVING FOR SUPERIORITY

Mention was made earlier of Adler's emphasis on the essential unity and consistency of personality. This outlook posits a dynamic driving force that channels the various resources of personality toward one overriding goal. This final goal, toward which all men strive, is superiority, which comprises more complete and perfect development, accomplishment, fulfillment, and realization of the self. In this view, sex is not the dominant drive, but rather one of a number of means to the end of superiority.

Adler saw this striving in every aspect of personality:

> It runs parallel to physical growth. It is an intrinsic necessity of life itself. . . . All our functions follow its direction; rightly or wrongly they strive for conquest, surety, increase. The impetus from minus to plus is never-ending. The urge from "below" to "above" never ceases. Whatever premises all our philosophers and psychologists dream of—self-preservation, pleasure principle, equalization—all these are but vague representations, attempts to express the great upward drive. . . . a fundamental category of thought, the structure of our reason, . . . *the fundamental fact of our life* (Adler, 1930, pp. 398–399).

This striving for superiority is responsible for all progress, not only at the level of the individual, but in all the history of civilization. It carries person and race ever upward from one stage of progress to the next.

INFERIORITY FEELINGS AND COMPENSATION

As we have seen, Adler did not agree with Freud that the primary basis of motivation centers on sexual factors. He believed instead that a general feeling of inferiority is the prime determining force in behavior. At first he related this feeling of inferiority to defective parts of the body. The child with a hereditary organic weakness will develop an inferiority complex and, as a result, will direct his efforts at compensating, and overcompensating, for this defect. He will overemphasize the deficient function, so that just as Demosthenes forcefully overcame his stuttering to become a great speaker, a child with a weak body may, through intensive exercise, excel as an athlete.

Adler later broadened the scope of this concept to include any physical, mental, or social handicap, real or imagined. He believed that the extreme helplessness and smallness of the infant produces a general feeling of inferiority that is experienced by everyone, since all children are totally dependent on their environment. The child, consciously aware of his inferiority, is at the same time driven by his innate striving for superiority. Thus, he is goaded on by the need to overcome his inferiority and insecurity. Adler believed that this "pushing and pulling" process continues throughout life, impelling an individual toward greater accomplishments.

Inferiority feelings, therefore, function to the advantage of both individual and society, since they lead to continuous improvement. However, childhood inferiority feelings that are met with excessive pampering or rejection by the parents can bring about abnormally expressed compensatory behaviors.

STYLE OF LIFE

As noted in the foregoing, man's overriding goal, superiority, is universal, according to Adler. However, he recognized the existence of a wide variety of behaviors that could be used to reach this goal. Thus, different people manifest their striving for superiority in different ways, and each develops his characteristic mode of responding—his own style of life.

> it appears that after the fourth or fifth year of life the style of life has been fashioned as a prototype, with its particular way of seizing upon life, its strategy for conquering it, its degree of ability to cooperate (Adler, 1930, p. 403).

This early formed life-style becomes firmly fixed and difficult to change, and provides the framework within which all later experiences are handled.

Thus, Adler emphasized the importance of the early years of life in forming an individual's personality as much as Freud did. He also greatly stressed the family as a factor in personality development. A child with a handicap, therefore, might consider himself a failure but, through compensation and with the help of understanding parents, might transform his inferiorities to strengths.

On the other hand, a child who is overly indulged by his parents may become self-centered, have no social interest, and expect others always to accede to his wishes; and a neglected child may develop a style of life that involves seeking revenge against society. Both pampering and neglect undermine a person's confidence in his ability to cope with the demands of life.

THE CREATIVE SELF

Considered his crowning achievement as a theorist (Hall & Lindzey, 1957), Adler's concept of the creative self posits an individual's capacity to determine his personality in accord with his unique style of life. The creative self represents an active principle of human existence that may be likened to the older concept of soul. Certain abilities and raw experiences, Adler maintained, are available to man from his heredity and environment, but these are only

> the bricks which he uses in his own "creative" way in building up his attitude toward life. It is his individual way of using these bricks, or in other words his attitude toward life, which determines this relationship to the outside world (1935, p. 5).

The concept of the creative self stresses the idea that man is a consciously active force in shaping his own personality and destiny. Thus, Adler saw man as capable of directly participating in his own fate rather than having it passively determined by past experiences, as Freud had claimed.

ORDER OF BIRTH

In examining the childhood backgrounds of his patients, Adler placed great emphasis on the relation between personality and order of birth. He felt that the oldest, middle, and youngest children had quite different social experiences resulting in the formation of different personalities. Adler noted that the oldest child, for example, received a great deal of attention until he was dethroned by the birth of a second child. As a result, he theorized, the firstborn may feel insecure and hostile toward people. Alder said that criminals, neurotics, and alcoholics are often firstborn children. He found the second child to be intensely ambitious, rebellious, and jealous, constantly trying to surpass the first-born. Nevertheless, Adler considered him better adjusted than either the firstborn or the youngest child. He saw the latter as spoiled and the most likely to be a behavior problem as a child and as an adult.

COMMENT

Adler's theories were warmly received by many people who were dissatisfied, and often repelled, by Freud's picture of man dominated by sexual forces and determined by childhood experiences. It is, after all, more pleasing to consider man as consciously directing his own development and destiny. Adler presented a much more satisfying and optimistic concept of man. His stress on the importance of social factors, to the relative exclusion of biological determinants, is usually considered a positive contribution. This attitude reinforced an already growing interest in the social sciences and the beginnings of a reorientation by the more traditional psychoanalysis in order to render its principles more applicable to the diverse behaviors found in different cultures.

Of course, Adler's system does not lack critics. Many claim his theories are superficial because they rely on a large number of "commonsense" observations from everyday life. Whether this is a criticism, however, is debatable, since many of his observations, regardless of origin, appear to be shrewd and insightful.

It is also argued that Adler was not a very consistent systematic theorist in that his position leaves too many questions unanswered. What, precisely, is this creative force by which an individual directs his behavior? Why do not people become reconciled to their inferiority? What are the relative roles of heredity and environment in this process? Of course, it must be remembered that Adler's is not the only system with questions yet to be answered.

The criticisms that more experimentally oriented psychologists directed at Freud and Jung apply to Adler as well. Finally, it has been said that Adler's influence is much greater than generally recognized:

> The entire neo-psychoanalytic school, including Horney, Fromm, and Sullivan, is no less neo-Adlerian than it is neo-Freudian. Adler's concepts of sociability, self-assertion, security, self, and creativeness permeated the theories of the neo-analysts (Wolman, 1960, p. 298).

Karen Horney

Trained as a Freudian psychoanalyst in Berlin, Horney (1885–1952) considered her work as involving a modification and extension of Freud's rather than as being distinctly non-Freudian.

Horney was born in Hamburg, Germany, but little is known of her childhood years. She entered medical school at the University of Berlin, receiving her MD in 1913. From 1914 to 1918 she undertook psychoanalytic training at the Berlin Psychoanalytic Institute. She began private practice in 1919 and became a faculty member at the institute.

Over the next 15 years, Horney wrote a number of journal articles, most of them concerned with problems of the feminine personality and demonstrating her disagreement with certain of Freud's concepts. In 1932 she came to the United States as associate director of the Chicago Institute for Psychoanalysis. In 1934 she established a private practice and taught at the New York Psychoanalytic Institute, but a growing disaffection for orthodox Freudian theories led her to break with the latter, whereupon she founded the American Institute of Psychoanalysis and remained its head until her death in 1952.

Before discussing Horney's system, let us consider her points of disagreement with Freud. Actually, Horney considered herself a disciple of Freud and accepted several of his basic principles. "Though retaining what I considered the fundamentals of Freud's teaching, I realized . . . that my search for a better understanding had led me in directions that were at variance with Freud" (Horney, 1945, p. 13). Indeed, parts of her system are so strongly at variance with Freud's that it occasionally becomes difficult to recognize her ideas as falling within the Freudian framework.

Horney felt, correctly, that some of Freud's basic assumptions were influenced by the spirit of the times in which he worked, and that times had changed drastically when, in the 1930s and 1940s, she set about formulating her system. Although Freud, as noted earlier, did not change with the times, the intellectual and cultural mores had altered; e.g., attitudes toward sex and the relative roles of the sexes had shifted about, so that many of Freud's theories were no longer in line with the spirit of the times.

Horney did not agree with Freud that personality development depended on unchangeable instinctive forces. She denied the preeminent position of sexual factors, challenged the validity of the Oedipus theory, discarded the libido concept and the Freudian structure of personality. She said that these concepts were a burden on psychoanalysis rather than its cornerstone.

Freud and Horney also differ basically in their conceptions of human nature:

> Freud's pessimism as regards neuroses and their treatment arose from the depths of his disbelief in human goodness and human growth. Man, he postulated, is doomed to suffer or to destroy. . . . My own belief is that man has the capacity as well as the desire to develop his potentialities and become a decent human being . . . I believe that man can change and go on changing as long as he lives (Horney, 1945, p. 19).

There are other differences, but the important point is that Horney rejected much of what Freud had said. She did accept, however, certain of Freud's tenets, including the belief in absolute causality, the notion of unconscious motivation, and the existence of emotional, nonrational motives.

HORNEY'S SYSTEM

The fundamental concept in Horney's theory is basic anxiety, defined as "the feeling a child has of being isolated and helpless in a potentially hostile world" (Horney, 1945, p. 41). This basic anxiety can result from many different expressions of parental attitudes and behavior toward the child, including dominance, lack of protection, lack of warmth, erratic behavior, etc. In short, anything that disturbs the secure relations between the child and his parents is capable of producing anxiety. It must be remembered that this anxiety is not innate but results rather from environmental factors; it is socially created.

In the place of Freud's life and death instincts as major motivating forces, Horney considered the helpless infant to be seeking security in a world that is hostile and threatening. She claimed that the decisive driving power for man is the need for safety, security, and freedom from fear and threat.

Horney shared with Freud the belief that personality develops in early childhood but, whereas Freud detailed psychosexual stages of development, Horney focused on the way the growing child is treated by his parents, denying any such universal instinctual phases as an oral stage or Oedipus complex. She said that a child's possible development of anal or oral or phallic tendencies resulted from parental behaviors. She saw nothing in a child's development as universal, and everything as dependent on culture and social-environmental factors. She attempted to show how all the developmental conflicts that Freud had ascribed to instinctual sources could be attributed to social forces.

Thus, Horney stressed the importance of early childhood experiences and parents' relations with their child, since the latter could either satisfy or frustrate his need for safety and security. The environment provided the child and the way he reacts to it, she said, form the structure of personality.

HORNEY'S THEORY OF NEUROSIS

As noted earlier, Horney's main concept is basic anxiety developing out of a child's relations with his parents. When this socially or environmentally produced anxiety arises in a child, he develops a number of behavioral strategies in an attempt to deal with his feelings of insecurity and helplessness. He thus structures his personality in response to the demands of his specific environment.

When one of these behavioral strategies becomes a fixed part of the personality, Horney believed it then becomes one of the so-called *neurotic needs* (or modes of defense against anxiety) of which she posited ten. Some of these include the need for affection and approval, prestige, personal achievement, perfection, and independence. All these neurotic needs can be reduced to one or another of three directional categories: (*a*) movement toward people, as in the need for love; (*b*) movement away from people, as in the need for independence; and (*c*) movement against people, as in the need for power.

Movement toward people involves acceptance of helplessness and an attempt to win the affection of others and be dependent on them. This is the only way in which the individual can feel secure with others. The movement away from people involves staying apart from others. Movement against people involves an acceptance of hostility, rebellion, and aggression against others.

Horney felt that none of these needs are realistic ways to deal with anxiety and that they themselves can give rise to basic conflicts because of their incompatibility. Once a person firmly establishes his method of coping with anxiety, his behavior ceases to be flexible enough to permit alternative modes of expression. For instance, if his fixed behavior is inappropriate in a particular situation, he is unable to change it to meet that situation's demands. This entrenched behavior intensifies the individual's difficulties because

> the attitudes do not remain restricted to the area of human relationships but gradually pervade the entire personality, as a malignant tumor pervades the whole organic tissue. They end by encompassing not only the person's relation to others but also his relation to himself and to life in general (Horney, 1945, p. 46).

Horney also invoked the concept of the neurotic's *idealized self-image*, which provides him with a false picture of his personality. This self-image is an imperfect and totally misleading mask that prevents the neurotic from understanding and accepting his "true" self. In donning it, the neurotic denies the existence of his inner conflicts. The image, which to the neurotic is genuine, enables him to believe that he is far superior to the man he actually is.

Horney believed the neurotic's basic conflicts are neither innate nor inevitable, but arise out of undesirable social situations in childhood and can be prevented if the child's homelife is characterized by understanding, security, love, and warmth.

COMMENT

Horney's optimism about the possibility of avoiding neurotic conflicts was welcomed by many as a relief from the pessimism of Freudian theory. Wolman (1960) suggested that Horney's contribution to psychological theory is considerable in that she has introduced a model of personality that stresses social factors, attributing little, if anything, to innate factors.

Horney's theory of personality may be weaker than Freud's in clarity, internal consistency, and level of formal development. Many feel that it is easier to simply accept or reject Freud's theory than to attempt to reshape it as Horney did. So radical is her departure from basic Freudian concepts that her system is frowned on by more orthodox psychoanalysts. Her evidence, like that of Jung, Adler, and Freud, is taken from clinical observations and is thus subject to the same questions regarding its scientific legitimacy noted earlier.

Erich Fromm

Unlike Jung, Adler, and Horney, Fromm (1900–   ) studied sociology and psychology before training in psychoanalysis and becoming a therapist. Because of these early interests, Fromm's theories may be described as social philosophy rather than as strictly psychological theories (Cofer & Appley, 1964).

Born in Frankfurt, Germany, in 1900, Fromm studied psychology and sociology at Heidelberg, Frankfurt, and Munich, receiving his PhD from Heidelberg in 1922. He took his psychoanalytic training in Munich and at the Berlin Psychoanalytic Institute, and came to the United States in 1933. He lectured at the Chicago Psychoanalytic Institute before moving to New York, where he engaged in private practice. He has taught at a number of universities and institutes in the United States and Mexico.

One of Fromm's basic interests is the effect of large aspects of society on the individual. He believes, for instance, that political organizations no longer provide the firm guidance and secure framework they once did. He suggests that contemporary man has succeeded in freeing himself from dependence on nature, only to find himself isolated from his fellow man. Consider the sense of belonging, dependence, and security a child has in his relations with his parents. When he reaches adulthood, he achieves independence but at the expense of his earlier security. Similarly, in the evolution of society toward greater mobility, complexity, and impersonality, man has lost his once secure relationship with smaller, more primary groups, such as the tribe or village, as well as with nature itself.

Fromm suggests that man is motivated to escape his ever-growing freedom and return to a more secure existence. He believes that the prime motivating force in human existence is not the satisfaction of instinctual drives, but the desire to revert to a condition of dependence.

In his book *Escape from Freedom* which was written during the Nazi regime, Fromm suggested that Nazism attracted people because it offered an escape from intolerable freedom back to secure dependency. In short, Fromm views man's nature as culturally or socially, and not biologically, determined.

The two most common systems through which man can regain security, according to Fromm, are humanism and authoritarianism. Authoritarianism involves the external imposition on a society of a highly rigid set of guiding principles, producing a state of bondage or slavery. Fromm rejects this system as an effective solution to man's problem of isolation because he believes that a society that prevents the individual from realizing his full potential thereby generates hostility against itself.

A far more effective solution. Fromm claims, is humanism, in which man unites with his fellow man in the spirit of love and shared work, or mutual cooperation. Fromm envisages a society, called Humanistic Communitarian Socialism, in which each person is a brother to every man and hence does not feel alone.

According to Fromm, man has five specific needs that arise from the conditions of his lonely existence: the need for a sense of individual identity; to feel that he belongs to society (rootedness); to transcend his base animal nature as a creative human being; to relate satisfactorily to his fellows; and for a stable and consistent orientation or frame of reference.

Fromm notes that society, unfortunately, does not provide adequate means for satisfying these needs. Further, social and political institutions often produce conflicts by satisfying certain needs at the expense of others; *e.g.*, a strong identification with an industrial or national symbol frustrates the need for personal identity.

Fromm's system offers four ways to escape the isolation and insecurity he believes predominates in modern society. In his *Man for Himself* (1947), he identifies them as dynamic orientations of character: receptive, exploitative, hoarding, and marketing. Although no one exhibits only one such orientation, Fromm believes that one may be dominant in a given person.

> In the receptive orientation a person feels "the source of all good" to be outside, and he believes that the only way to get what he wants—be it something material, be it affection, love, knowledge, pleasure—is to receive it from that outside source. In this orientation the problem of love is almost exclusively that of "being loved" and not that of loving (Fromm, 1947, p. 62).

The person becomes submissive and dependent on others, needing someone (or some system) to take care of him. Such individuals will go to great lengths to maintain strong identification with others. (In Horney's terms, this orientation involves a movement toward people.)

The exploitative orientation is manifested as very aggressive behavior and corresponds to Horney's movement against people. People thus oriented do not expect to receive from others, but rather take from or exploit others, by force or cunning, according to the philosophy "might makes right."

The hoarding orientation involves the perception of the outside world as threatening, which leads to distrust of and rigidity toward people. The hoarding person tends to save and possess, becoming frugal, miserly, and letting as little as possible (material things or emotions) out; he evaluates his security in terms of tangible possessions and wealth.

The final orientation—marketing—reflects the advent of capitalism, according to which personal success is adjudged by one's acceptability to those who use his services or employ him. The person therefore plays a variety of socially approved roles and concentrates on selling himself rather than on fulfilling his potential. Since a person's value depends more on his success in the market-place and less on his personal qualities, the situation does not lead to a feeling of security. In this kind of orientation, a man says to others, in essence, "I am as you want me to be."

COMMENT

The overall theme in Fromm's writings is man's relations to society. He remains optimistic about man's ability to shape a society that would allow him to develop into a fully human creature. This point of view is highly acceptable to many in that it offers the hope that man can introduce constructive forces into his society to render the human condition more distinctly human. It has been suggested, however, that Fromm's philosophy of life does not really justify such a high degree of optimism. He sees man in a never-ending conflict with nature; since man knows "too much, he is unable to accept his fate naïvely. . . . there is never peace of mind, never harmony between man and universe, but only a continuous struggle and search for new solutions, none of them ever a final one. This is, to quote Fromm, man's tragic fate: 'to be part of nature, and yet to transcend it'" (Wolman, 1960, p. 368).

Fromm's descriptive analyses are not defined to the degree of precision required of scientific evidence.

Critique of the Social-Psychological Theories

The theorists discussed in this section share an obvious point of similarity in that their work may be labeled "social-psychological." They all place considerable emphasis on the role of social variables in the development of the individual personality. Although they do concede some intellectual debt to the work of Freud, each constitutes a vigorous protest against the Freudian notion of the primacy of instinct in personality formation.

Thus, they see man's behavior as determined not exclusively by instinctual, biological forces, but rather by the types of interpersonal relationships to which the individual is exposed, particularly in childhood. Sexual forces in personality development are minimized by these theorists, who believe that sexual experiences do not determine personality, but rather that the socially developed personality determines the nature of sexual responses.

Just as the role of instinct is minimized, so too is the role of the libido and its manifestations, such as the Oedipus complex and psychosexual stages of development. Anxiety and expressions of abnormal behavior do not originate in instinct, libido, and sex, but instead develop from early social relationships experienced. To these theorists, man is not irrevocably doomed to anxiety, as in Freud's deterministic theory, since anxiety can be avoided by the proper kinds of childhood social experiences.

According to Freud, man's behavior is universally static; the social-psychological theorists, on the other hand, consider man's behavior quite flexible and capable of being consciously changed by the individual. Man's social organizations, too, are flexible and liable to alteration by man. While recognizing that social mores can be modified only gradually and with difficulty, these theorists optimistically agreed that man is able to develop the kind of social system most appropriate to his requirements.

Hall and Lindzey (1957) discussed two points of criticism that have been directed against the social-psychological theorists. First, it is argued that their conception of man as a rational, conscious, and socialized being is unconvincing in the light of his frequently disappointing and irrational behavior. One rejoinder to this charge is to blame man's past and present displays of violence, injustice, etc., on the social system. As noted earlier, however, these theorists imply that man shapes society to best suit his needs. We are left with the paradox of man, an eminently rational, perfectible, socialized being, who has nevertheless developed an abundance of social systems inadequate to his needs.

The second criticism accuses these theorists of neglecting the social processes through which a person is shaped, i.e., of leaving unanswered the question of how a person learns to be a properly functioning member of society. The social-psychological theories draw on the general concept of learning to explain personality formation, but neglect the specific mechanisms of the learning process. This neglect, moreover, is the more serious since learning has been a topic of paramount importance in American psychology for many years.

The Mainstream after Freud

We have noted that Freud alone fashioned and shaped the development of psychoanalysis. When he died, his loyal followers were left the difficult problem of what to do with Freud's system now that he could no longer determine its direction. The course they chose involved: (a) amplifying certain less well-developed aspects of his system, (b) making more explicit some of his postulates, (c) attempting more precise definitions of certain basic concepts, (d) extending the range of behavior covered by psychoanalytic interpretations, and (e) employing research methods other than the psychoanalytic interview (Hall & Lindzey, 1957, p. 64).

These neo-Freudians used Freud's system as a base; his pronouncements are not radically changed so much as they are extended and amplified. A very strong allegiance and intellectual debt to Freud is obvious in their writings, where Freud's works are continually used as the most important authority to support newer positions. Nevertheless, a number of important trends have appeared in psychoanalysis since Freud's death.

Hall and Lindzey (1957) discuss several recent modifications in psychoanalysis, the first of which concerns the emergence of the ego as a more independent part of personality. Although Freud attributed important functions to the ego, he considered it subservient to the id, which was the center of attention in his system. The neo-Freudians have accorded greater status and autonomy to the ego, which they consider independent of the id in both function and origin. This newer concept proposes that the ego and id are formed early in life and have distinct origins in inherited predispositions and separate courses of development. Thus, the ego is looked on as a rational guiding system responsible for intellectual and social development, independent of the id, with its own sources of energy as well as its own motives and goals.

A second modification is a diminished emphasis on instinctual determinants of personality. Though perhaps not departing so radically from Freud's system as the social-psychological theorists, these more recent psychoanalysts have recognized the influence on personality of psychological and social variables. In more contemporary psychoanalytic literature, there is less use of the term "instinct" and more of the term "drive." Personality development is more often explained in terms of the individual's life history instead of innate forces. Biological factors tend to be de-emphasized in favor of an approach wherein personality formation is accounted for through primarily psychological structures arising from early experiences.

The third important modification in Freud's system of psychoanalysis arises from the change in emphasis just discussed. Increased interest in early experiences of the individual has brought about more studies of infants and children. Freud, as we have seen, was also interested in early experiences, but he worked with inferences drawn from the remembered childhood experiences of his patients. The new approach, in contrast, observes developmental processes directly, as they take place in childhood. In recent years, psychoanalytically oriented investigators have conducted much research on development, using this method of direct observation. Much of this work has been reported in the annual volumes of *The Psychoanalytic Study of the Child,* of which Anna Freud has been co-editor since its beginning in 1945.

A fourth change in the direction of psychoanalysis has to do with increased interest in the experimental testing of psychoanalytic propositions. There has been more frequent use of nonanalytical methods, such as the observational studies of children just mentioned. Patients' reports are no longer the sole means of verifying psychoanalytic hypotheses. A growing body of experimental literature, reporting research with both human and animal subjects, has drawn heavily on psychoanalytic concepts, for which it has in turn provided some measure of experimental support.

Finally, there is evidence of a steadily though slowly growing rapprochement between psychoanalysis and academic experimental psychology. Prominent representatives from both camps have, through their research and writing activities, helped to bring about some degree of reconciliation. Both psychoanalysis and experimental psychology have tended to investigate problems of common interest, such as factors in motivation. The rapid growth of clinical psychology in the years since World War II has led many psychologists to recognize the possible value of psychoanalysis as a therapeutic device. There is also the undeniable fact that psychoanalysis has strongly influenced the entire Western culture; this has not gone unrecognized by psychologists. Hall and Lindzey (1957) note that, "As Freud's reputation grows in the world at large, it is difficult for psychologists not to claim him as their own" (p. 68).

Nevertheless, profound differences between psychology and psychoanalysis remain. A great deal of mutual disaffection, indeed, hostility, still separates the two approaches, and many psychologists still openly reject the validity and utility of psychoanalytic theory, regardless of the extent of its modifications.

SUGGESTED FURTHER READINGS

Jung

Evans, R. I. *Conversations with Carl Jung.* Princeton: Van Nostrand, 1964.

Fordham, F. *An introduction to Jung's psychology.* Baltimore: Penguin, 1959.

Jacobi, J. *The psychology of C. G. Jung.* (Rev. ed.) New Haven: Yale University Press, 1951.

Adler

Ansbacher, H. L., & Ansbacher, R. R. (Eds.) *The individual psychology of Alfred Adler.* New York: Basic Books, 1956.

Orgler, H. *Alfred Adler: The man and his work.* New York: Putnam, 1965.

Horney

Horney, K. *The collected works of Karen Horney.* New York: Norton, 1963. 2 vols.

General

Brown, J. A. C. *Freud and the post-Freudians.* London: Cassell & Co. Ltd., 1963.

Hartmann, H. *Essays on ego psychology: selected problems in psychoanalytic theory.* New York: International Universities Press, 1964.

Rapaport, D. Structure of psychoanalytic theory. In S. Koch (Ed.), *Psychology: a study of a science.* Vol. 3. New York: McGraw-Hill, 1959. Pp. 55–183.

XV

EPILOGUE

WE HAVE SEEN how the various systems of psychological thought came into being, prospered for a time, and then, with the exception of psychoanalysis, were absorbed by the mainstream of contemporary psychology. We also saw that the movements grew strong through opposition to another system. When there was no longer any need for strong and vociferous protest, the schools, as such, died a gradual death. Yet each of these protests died a successful death because they made substantial contributions to psychological thought. Thus, each was a fruitful protest—each accomplished its mission.

There may be one exception—the structuralists left little, if any, direct mark on the contemporary scene. Yet we cannot deny the substantial influence of the structuralist position on the subsequent course of psychology's development. It served as a formidable and well-defined starting point—a substantial base to inspire opposition. Even this rather thoroughly destroyed system, then, served a valuable purpose.

For a time, primarily in the 1920s and 1930s, the psychology of the day made a rather sorry showing. Heidbreder noted in 1933 that:

> System after system announces its principles, each imposes its order on the facts that arrest its attention, and each puts its case with a degree of plausibility. The difficulty is that they all do so and that they are all more or less at odds with each other . . . this is the situation after more than half a century of effort: systems in plenty, but no one interpretation of the facts of psychology to which all psychologists, or even a majority, agree (p. 413).

Thus, the leaders of each school attempted to establish psychology in their own image. There was disagreement over the problems of definition, subject matter, and methodology. The intensity of the debates among the various schools reached a peak in the 1920s. Psychologists as well as outside observers witnessing these controversies viewed the future of psychology pessimistically. Many felt that psychology could never realize its ambition of becoming a science on a par with the

311

natural sciences. The division of psychology into separate camps was spoken of as "one of the scandals of contemporary science" at the Ninth International Congress of Psychology in 1929.

In retrospect, however, a more optimistic picture of the role of the schools emerges. It now can be seen that the period of the schools represents a phase of normal development and serves as an important milestone in the development of psychological thought. It is recognized that each school made contributions, some presenting new empirical data, some offering new insights and generalizations, and others correcting or destroying the propositions of a rival school.

The Dissolution of the Schools

With the exception of psychoanalysis, the distinctiveness of the various schools began to fade around 1930, and controversy began to subside. One of the many factors that helped to bring about this change in the psychological scene, was the death, or at least withdrawal from active and open debate, of the leaders of the schools. This was particularly evident in the case of Titchener, who died in 1927. No one of his stature and ability remained to carry the banner of structuralism and do battle with its opponents. The effect of Titchener's death was noted by Boring (1927):

> The death of no other psychologist could so alter the psychological picture in America. . . . The clear-cut opposition between behaviorism and its allies, on the one hand, and something else, on the other, remains clear only when the opposition is between behaviorism and Titchener, mental tests and Titchener, or applied psychology and Titchener. His death thus, in a sense, creates a classificatory chaos in American systematic psychology (p. 489).

Another factor involved the differences of opinion that arose within the schools themselves and weakened their solidarity. Within the behaviorist camp, for instance, we discussed the emergence of theorists who adhered to the basic behavioristic emphasis on increased objectivity, yet differed from strict Watsonian behaviorism. The same kind of divisive emphasis within psychoanalysis was also noted.

Finally, it became apparent to many psychologists that the various approaches were not as irreconcilable as had been thought. A mutual recognition and acceptance of contributions, both conceptual and methodological, by the rival systems developed. The various lines of theory and research began to converge. Even Titchener remarked, as early as 1921, that the terms and concepts of "functional" and "structural" as descriptive qualifications in psychology were becoming obsolete. Woodworth noted in 1930 that the schools actually had more in common than had first appeared.

Individual psychologists became more and more suspicious of the schools' claims that all psychological data could be ordered within the framework of one system. By the 1930s, many psychologists declined to align themselves with a particular school (and even to theorize at all) because of the division and controversy. The schools came to be viewed as too restrictive and dogmatic, and many felt that the development of final systems and global theories that attempted to encompass all behavior was premature at a time when many facts were still undetermined and many relationships not yet investigated.

And so the schools passed into history, although their heritage lingers on. We have discussed some of the more current efforts in psychology that grew out of the schools, and will now consider the mainstream of contemporary American psychology. Psychologists today no longer exclusively rally around a Gestalt, behaviorist, or functionalist flag. There is a greater tendency toward eclecticism with regard to theories, methods, and concepts.

Woodworth and Sheehan (1964) note, however, that in spite of the dissolution of the schools, if you ask a psychologist, "What do you think of psychoanalysis?" or "Are you a behaviorist?" his reply will not be one of total indifference. Major points of difference still exist between contemporary objective (neo-behavioristic) psychology and psychoanalysis, which still stands as an orientation not integrated into the mainstream of psychology. This situation will no doubt persist until psychoanalysis achieves scientific status—and many question whether this will ever occur.

Contemporary American Psychology

Before we discuss the nature of contemporary psychology in America, consider again its phenomenal growth. Only a few psychologists constituted the charter membership of the American Psychological Association in 1892. By the time of the demise of the schools in 1930, membership had risen to 1100. By 1968, the membership had grown to over 26,000 members and is increasing rapidly. Two out of every three psychologists today live in the United States (Watson, 1965).

Psychology is growing not only in numbers, but also in degree of specialization. The size of the APA has necessitated the formation of separate divisions: those representing scientific interests include experimental psychology, evaluation and measurement, developmental psychology, and physiological and comparative psychology, among others; professional divisions include industrial, school, clinical, military, and consumer psychology. The annual national meeting and various regional meetings are well supported, often to the extent that several hotels are needed to accommodate those attending.

This "population explosion" is paralleled by an "information explosion" of journal articles, books, and other publications, making it increasingly difficult for a psychologist to keep up with all the developments outside of his own specialty areas. An idea of the rate of increase in reported research can be had by comparing the number of articles reported in the *Psychological Abstracts* in 1961 (over 7000), with those appearing only six years later: by 1967, the number had jumped to 17,000. To be aware of all the literature in all areas of psychology would require the reading of at least two books and some 50 journal articles every day!

The nature of American psychology today is that of a functional-istic behaviorism; other terms, such as deterministic, environmentalistic, and naturalistic, also describe the American psychological scene. Chaplin and Krawiec (1960) suggest that contemporary American psychology deals with objective behavioral events, but that these events are meaningful only when considered as expressions of functional processes in the individual. Hence, psychology has become more behavioristic in definition and functionalistic in spirit.

A renewal of interest in theoretical issues occurred in the late 1940s and 1950s but today's theorizing differs considerably from that of the 1920s and 1930s. During the era of the schools, theories or systems existed on a grand scale and attempted to encompass all of psychology within a single framework. John B. Watson, for example, attempted to explain all aspects of behavior—thinking, emotion, learning, etc.—within one behavioristic system. The newer attempts at theorizing are more circumscribed and restricted.

> The modern psychologist is both more modest and more timid than his predecessor. Not for him is the grand canvas of the whole of human nature captured by one artist. Broad systematic issues are no longer seen as being as important as they were at one time. Specific research facts are now sought with less attention to an examination of views of the fundamental nature of psychology. In fact, psychology, today, is less adventurous, less inclined to stake its all on some issue, and more sober in its outlook (R. I. Watson, 1963, p. 486).

Thus, topics in current theorizing are specific, so much so that the term "miniature theory" has come to describe, aptly, today's theories. Some of these theories deal with a single area, such as learning, motivation, or personality. Most, however, are concerned with even more restricted functions or processes; *i.e.*, they attempt to explain a very small portion of behavior, such as performance in a very specific and restricted learning situation.

The foregoing comments do not mean to imply that all contemporary psychologists are conducting research in the light of a particular miniature theory. A substantial portion of current research is conducted in the absence of *any* formally stated theoretical structure. Very often, the results of a particular study suggest further research on that topic. For example, it is common for a study to be replicated, but with a change (*e.g.*, from children to adults) in the subject population. Research to determine the effect of a laboratory stress situation on performance on a particular kind of test is likely to be followed by research using tests that measure other functions.

Thus, we have a distinct trend toward specificity in theory construction, and research problems concerned with quite limited areas of behavior. It has been said that such specialization "consists in knowing more and more about less and less" (R. I. Watson, 1963, p. 487).

METHODS

It was noted earlier that contemporary American psychology is primarily behavioristic in nature and definition. From this statement it follows that the methods of psychology today are characterized by operationism and objectivity. The experimental method remains fundamental; indeed, its use as well as its rigor has increased.

Progress in electronics and engineering has led to the development of very sophisticated and elaborate laboratory apparatus and measuring devices. These advances have greatly increased both the objectivity and precision of data collection in psychology. Thus, psychology today is much more quantitative than during the era of the schools.

Not only the techniques of data collection, but also the methods of analyzing data have improved. A development of major importance is the widespread use of computers, which are able to analyze vast amounts of data in very short periods of time. Their use has intensified the trend toward greater quantification in psychology.

Thus, we can see that the methods of modern psychology closely emulate those of the natural sciences—a direction in which psychology has been moving since the days of Wundt. Developments in computers and in sophisticated electromechanical apparatus and measuring techniques have perhaps complicated the training requirements of modern psychologists. An experimental psychologist today must be part engineer, electrician, and mathematician if he is to adequately use the tools at his disposal. This trend is evidenced by the publication in recent years of books dealing with the design of electrical circuits and aspects of instrumentation written for behavioral scientists (*e.g.*, Cornsweet, 1963; Sidowski, 1966).

In addition to methodological changes in experimental psychology, there have been changes in the scope or range of application of those methods. The term "experimental psychology" no longer refers exclusively to basic research, nor is it restricted to the once traditional areas of sensation, perception, and learning. Today, social, child, industrial, and educational psychologists as well as "pure" research psychologists use the experimental method. Further, in keeping with America's functional orientation, experimental psychology is no longer exclusively academic, as laboratory research is being conducted in industrial and military situations.

MAJOR RESEARCH AREAS

Although research of today covers a wide field, four areas—learning, perception, motivation, and personality—comprise the major fields of research by academic psychologists. The following comments on these areas are not all-inclusive, but provide the highlights of the current scene.

Learning

Research on learning attracts the greatest attention in the United States and perhaps reflects the environmentalistic cast of American psychology. In our discussions of the schools, we noted the great interest in learning on the part of Pavlov, Watson, Thorndike, and others that has presaged the work of a great many modern-day psychologists. We have already mentioned the more recent developments in learning of Hull, Skinner, Guthrie, and Tolman, and the continuing work of their followers.

Learning behavior has been studied over the entire range of the phylogenetic scale, from the flatworm to the college sophomore (who may or may not be the highest form of animal studied). For the most part, contemporary American learning research and theory is based on animal research and is behavioristically oriented. In learning theory, as in all psychology, the day of the large-scale global theory is past, and modern miniature theories, and more specific and restricted types of learning, are being tested and studied.

The current focus is on such areas as human verbal learning, instrumental learning, animal learning (also, in specific species), and human motor learning. Many workers in these areas see them as fundamental to the understanding of all other aspects of human functioning. While not denying the importance of perception, emotion, personality, and the like, many believe that these areas are studied more fruitfully when considered as problems in learning.

Although the most striking development in the history of learning theory is the domination of behavioristic conditioning oriented systems based on animal studies, contemporary learning theory and research also emphasize the study of intervening variables. Though retaining a strong behavioristic cast, theorists are evidencing great interest in the covert aspects of learning, such as the role of reinforcement, retroactive interference, and so on. Indeed, the most important variable investigated in the last 25 years or so is the nature of reinforcement and its function in learning. This trend strongly suggests that the strict S-R brand of behaviorism has proven less than adequate in understanding the nature of the learning process.

Published studies on learning theory and research constitute a substantial part of the extensive literature in psychology as a whole. Many comprehensive textbooks and professional monographs have appeared, and much learning research is published in journals whose scope extends beyond learning per se, such as the *Journal of Experimental Psychology* and the *Journal of Personality and Social Psychology*. In addition, specialized journals concentrating on specific problems in learning have appeared, such as the *Journal of Verbal Learning and Verbal Behavior* (begun in 1962).

Research findings in learning have been applied in the field of education in the form of programmed instruction and teaching machines. Thus, learning is an area that receives much attention in contemporary American psychology.

Perception

Perception, a traditional research area in psychology, continues to attract substantial attention, but is not as frequent a subject of study as learning. The approach to the study of perception has altered drastically in recent years. Under the aegis of the so-called "new look" in perception, there has been a pronounced tendency to emphasize certain inner determinants of perception, such as needs, values, attitudes, and personality factors.

The process of perception is no longer regarded as the mere combination of sensory impressions deriving their meaning from stimulus organization or past experience. Motivational, emotional, and social factors are now recognized as influential in determining not only what an individual perceives but also the manner in which he perceives it. This does not mean that the role of stimulus factors has been neglected or ignored in contemporary research, but interest in inner determinants of perception reflects one of the major emphases of the contemporary scene.

Current theoretical work in the area of perception has developed within Gestalt, behaviorist, and functionalist frameworks. As noted in the discussion of the Gestalt point of view, that school's most significant contribution has been in the area of perception. The Gestaltists' emphasis on the innate factors of organization and their tendency to minimize experience and stimulus–observer interactions have received considerable support from the research work of Lewin, Gordon Allport, Postman, and others.

Working within a behaviorist framework, the Canadian psychologist Donald Hebb developed a neurological theory of perceptual functioning that stresses the importance of learning in perception. Hebb postulates a cell assembly conceived of as a group of cortical neurons that, through learning, become associated with each other. This associationistic theory, with its neurological foundation, has revitalized the role of learning in perception, a role that had declined because of the strong influence of Gestalt psychology.

Regardless of systematic position, contemporary psychologists seem to be taking a functionalistic approach to perception. Perception is increasingly being treated as a fundamentally important process in man's interactions with his experiential world. As a result of this trend, applied psychologists as well as academic researchers have been compelled to recognize and study perceptual processes.

Motivation

Motivation, perhaps the most central of all aspects of human functioning, remains one of the least developed areas of contemporary psychology. In the early years of psychology's development, it received little direct attention. (Perhaps the "determining tendencies" of the Würzburg group were a prelude to later study.) More direct interest was provided by the evolutionary emphasis on adaptation and biological drives, and by Freud's concern with unconscious motivation.

In spite of these few early efforts and the practical importance of the area, theories of motivation remain much less well formulated than those of learning and perception. There has been much research of value in recent times, but a general theory of motivation is lacking.

Progress in the area has been deterred by the many opposing points of view, differing experimental approaches, and disagreements over proper terminology and problems of definition. A fundamental dichotomy exists between the behavioristic-comparative theorists working with animal subjects, who are concerned with the physiological basis of motivation, and the often nonexperimental theorists of an analytic persuasion, concerned with the more psychological basis of motivation.

As in other areas of psychology, miniature theories devoted to a single motive or a small group of motives have been developed. Working with an isolated and specific problem area, such theories, while often providing well-supported accounts of one aspect of behavior, cannot account for human motivation in general.

Although progress in motivational theory has been the slowest of all contemporary psychological theory in this country, there are signs of increasing recognition of, and concern over this unsatisfactory state of affairs. There is, further, a growing awareness that the area of motivation is a central problem for psychology. A final source of encouragement is that many learning theorists have become interested in motivation as an integral aspect of learning, and those working in perception and personality are also recognizing the role of motivational determinants in their areas of study.

Personality

As noted earlier, concern with personality theory was not evidenced in the early schools of psychology and was but little developed in the American schools. Psychoanalysis, more than any other orientation, has generated an interest in the study of personality. As a consequence of the development and spread of psychoanalysis, theories of personality have proliferated both in Europe and America. In addition to the psycho-analytic–nurtured personality theories, other systems of personality have developed since the 1930s. Consequently, there now exist in American psychology several theoretical and methodological orientations. This diversity is partly the result of the extremely broad nature of the subject matter of personality which has attracted psychologists with sharply different theoretical orientations. It is hard to imagine a conceptual or methodological orientation that could not include the study of personality.

Some current theoretical efforts stress a biological approach to personality study, whereas others use a social or cultural approach. Some emphasize conscious aspects of personality, others the unconscious; some are highly objective and rely heavily on empirical research, whereas others are very subjective and rely on uncontrolled observation, primarily of patients' behavior. American psychologists on the whole seem to prefer experimental-learning approaches, in keeping with the general objective, behavioristic, environmentalistic flavor of contemporary American psychology. (The nonexperimental approaches to personality study have, by definition, little in the way of empirical support.)

Other Developments

An outstanding feature of contemporary psychology is the intensive research interest in the area of physiological psychology. Prompted by quite recent advances in physiology and endocrinology, physiological psychologists have studied the physiological functioning of the organism and biochemical factors in behavior. Recent years have seen rapid advances in the development of more precise physiological measuring apparatus, largely of the electronic variety.

Particularly impressive is the research in brain physiology. With the development of new techniques for implanting electrodes in the brain has come exciting research involving self-stimulation of the organism and mapping of functional areas of the cortex. The combination of physiological methods of investigation with operant conditioning techniques has opened up several new research areas emphasizing both overt behavior and neurophysiology, as well as their interaction. Recent research on the reticular activating system of the brain and its relation to the amount and kind of stimulation to which the organism is exposed has led to other new research areas (such as sensory deprivation) and theoretical considerations. Some psychologists see the mushrooming activities in physiological psychology as the most potentially productive in the understanding of behavior.

The area of social psychology has flourished since its modest beginnings in the early years of this century. Its research methods have become increasingly sophisticated and the range of behavior it encompasses is enormous. It has made substantial contributions to the traditional areas of learning, perception, motivation, and personality by drawing attention to the influence of social and cultural forces on these basic processes. Concerned with group behavior and the effects of group membership on individual behavior, social psychology is working effectively in such areas as group problem-solving ability, mass behavior, leadership, communication, attitude formation and change, and prejudice. Social psychology has been applied to so-called "real world" problems in industry and politics in the areas of propaganda and public opinion, and the national concern over racial prejudice. Findings from social psychological research were cited in the 1954 Supreme Court decision against racial segregation in the public schools. This rapidly growing area enjoys enormous research productivity.

The initial impetus provided by Galton, Cattell, and Binet has carried the field of psychological testing to a prominent position in contemporary American psychology. Literally millions of psychological tests are given each year to school children, college students, military personnel, and people in government, business, and industry. It is almost impossible to reach maturity in the United States today without having taken at least one psychological test. No matter what an individual's plans, there seems to be a psychological test to be taken first.

Many psychologists in academic settings have conducted a great deal of research on the development and use of psychological tests. Others in business, government, or the military, have been administering, scoring, and interpreting these tests, thereby influencing the lives and careers of a great many people. The widespread use of these tests has evoked some concern in recent years. The United States Congress has held hearings to determine whether and to what degree psychological testing constitutes an invasion of privacy, with the result that at least one well-known personality test has been barred from use by government agencies. Despite the reaction against testing, the advantages gained from the use of well-constructed tests by competent and conscientious testers seems to outweigh any possible disadvantages—at least thus far.

The area of clinical psychology has also expanded rapidly since its beginnings in the work of Freud and others. In America, thousands of clinical psychologists are involved in the diagnosis and treatment of the emotionally disturbed. Some nonclinical psychologists express concern and dismay at the relative lack of well-controlled research in this area and the fact that psychotherapy remains more art than science. The number of psychologists working in clinical settings in mental institutions or in private practice is increasing, but a shortage of trained personnel still exists.

Another area of more professional than scientific orientation includes the complex of activities subsumed under the label "industrial psychology," which has grown considerably since its beginnings around the time of World War I. Industrial psychologists work in industrial, governmental, and military settings, and are primarily concerned with selecting the right man for the right job, training workers to do their jobs more efficiently, and solving problems of supervision and other factors (such as fatigue and morale) that affect job performance. A number of clinical psychologists also work on the industrial scene and claim success in reducing accidents, absenteeism, sickness, etc., by their concern with various social and emotional factors relevant to the work environment.

A recently developed branch of industrial psychology is concerned with the design of highly technical and sophisticated military equipment such as is found in aircraft, missile and space systems, submarines, and the like. Called engineering psychology (or human engineering), it strives to design equipment to fit the man, i.e., to make the best possible use of man's capabilities in operating the equipment quickly and efficiently.

Finally, some industrial psychologists are concerned with areas of marketing and motivation research, such as advertising, packaging, and creating consumer demand.

While many industrial psychologists apply their knowledge of psychology to practical problems, others conduct relevant research in academic settings. Some research is carried out by those working in industry, but it is less in quantity (and perhaps also in quality) compared to the academic research.

PROFESSIONALIZATION

We have noted that several of the important pioneers in psychology strongly opposed any application or professionalization of psychology. Our discussion of contemporary psychology makes it plain that no such climate of thought exists today. Indeed, fewer than half of today's psychologists are in academic situations and psychology has been applied to almost every aspect of American life.

Miller (1962) noted that:

> Psychological dogma influences the way we discipline our children, manage our businesses, and run our marriages. Studies of abnormal behavior modify our conception and treatment of mental illness, incompetence, perversion, criminality, and delinquency. The priest and the rabbi agree in their use of psychological techniques to guide their flocks to salvation. Novels, plays, and movies now feature psychological themes as one of their standard formulas. Psychological drugs have already changed the situation in our mental hospitals, and more are yet to come (p. 7).

The differences between the purely scientific and the applied aspects of psychology have come into sharp focus since World War II, when the major growth in applied psychology occurred. Relations between science and practice, between "pure" and applied, have shown evidence of considerable strain. Some consider that those who apply psychology have sacrificed their scientific integrity and have not contributed sufficiently or effectively to the advancement of knowledge in the field. The practitioners of psychology counter by accusing the academic psychologists of leading an "ivory tower" existence and showing no concern about problems in the real world to which they might be able to offer solutions.

A major source of contention between the two groups is that not all attempts at application of psychology have been supported by adequate scientific evidence. This situation comes about for several reasons: very often there is simply no time to conduct full-scale well-controlled research into real problems that require quick action. Then, too, many industrial organizations balk at the cost of such adequate research programs.

Also, the practitioner may be pressed for a quick answer, possibly to permit the meeting of a contract deadline. He is forced to make a decision within a period that does not allow him to wait for research findings. He therefore presents an "educated guess" based on available evidence no matter how fragmentary or inconclusive. Moreover, many feel such a guess is better than no answer at all.

Since the answers the applied psychologist is called on to provide rest in large measure on the availability of the findings of the academic research psychologist, perhaps a closer working relationship between the two groups is in order. In this way the practitioner would be able to suggest, for the attention of the academician, urgent problem areas in which a paucity of research data exists.

Contemporary Psychology in Other Countries

To forestall the impression that psychology is the exclusive property of the United States, we offer some comments on the status of psychology in other countries.

GERMANY

Psychology in Germany suffered a serious setback during the Nazi era and World War II. Since the war, however, the task of rebuilding psychology has been actively pursued until a number of branches of the discipline, particularly social, industrial, and educational psychology, as well as the study of personality and guidance are now flourishing.

Laboratory experimentation is not widely practiced, nor has the use of quantitative methods been generally accepted. Thus, German psychology remains much more subjective than American psychology. German research and experimental methods, as compared to their American counterparts, are somewhat lacking in rigor. A great many theories exist, but most of them remain untested. The German public seems less disposed to accept psychology as a profession than the American, and therefore it has not had a comparable impact on society.

ENGLAND

Psychology developed rather slowly in English universities but the field has grown rapidly since World War II. It bears some resemblance to psychology in this country, though there is less of an objective emphasis and learning is not a primary topic. In recent years, psychology in England has gained considerable prestige and public and governmental support.

British psychology evidences a strong bent toward practical application, as reflected in the very rapid growth of clinical psychology in recent years. While experimental psychology has progressed slowly, albeit substantially, England's most important contributions have been in the areas of statistics, psychometrics, and educational psychology.

SOVIET UNION

Direct extensive political influence has rendered the development of psychology in the Soviet Union entirely different from that in other countries. After 1936, all Western psychological influences, such as testing and industrial psychology, were eliminated. A turning point in the history of Soviet psychology occurred in 1950, when Pavlovian theory was given the sanction of official state doctrine. Since this change, Soviet psychology has become much more active and productive.

Recent years have seen a marked increase of interest in the areas of personality study, social psychology, and information theory. Psychophysiological research, conducted primarily by physiologists, has included studies of conditioning and physiological psychology, and has produced important research on brain processes. Research and practice in the areas of testing and industrial psychology, however, are not favored by the state, clinical psychology is underdeveloped, and Freud is banned. Psychology as a profession is practically nonexistent.

A greater exchange of ideas is occurring between Russian psychologists and those of the Western world. Soviet works have been translated into other languages and Russian translations have been made of a number of American books. A significant event was the 1966 meeting, in Moscow, of the Eighteenth International Congress of Psychology.

OTHER COUNTRIES

Among the Asian countries, psychology has developed most fully in Japan, where research attitudes are quite similar to those of the United States. The rest of Asia lags in both scope and rate of growth of psychology. For the most part, Japanese experimental psychology shows an American influence and focuses on research in learning and visual perception. The areas of clinical and social psychology are advancing rapidly, but little research has been conducted in industrial psychology or personality. The vigorous Japanese psychology now boasts three journals and active scientific meetings.

Psychology in Canada is difficult to distinguish from that in the United States. The same positivistic, behavioristic climate seems to exist and the two countries freely exchange both personnel and published literature.

In the South American countries, the growth of psychology has so far been negligible although signs of development, notably the establishment of psychology departments in universities, are becoming evident.

Psychology in the Scandinavian countries closely resembles American psychology in research attitudes toward industrial as well as academic psychology.

It seems that the United States leads in the vigorous promotion of both research and application of psychology and in its acceptance and use by society at large. (Wundt's comment, *ganz Amerikanisch*, comes to mind.) We cannot, however, minimize the growth and increasing vigor of psychology throughout the world.

The Future: Continuation or Cleavage?

What will be psychology's future? Many believe it will continue within the same behavioristic framework, with the experimental method remaining the *sine qua non* of psychological research. Indeed, the experimental method may become even more precise and objective as more sophisticated equipment and apparatus become available (as they surely will), and as more advanced electronic computers for data analysis are developed. As a result, psychology may become all the more empirical, and the future may see even greater specialization as the storehouse of data grows in both depth and detail.

It must be noted, however, that all is not calm within contemporary American psychology. Since the 1950s, voices of dissent have been heard, largely from without the behavioristic camp, although of late some behaviorists themselves have joined in the call for a new movement, a *humanistic psychology*. This approach is still too new and tenuous to be considered an integral part of the history of psychology, but we cannot ignore its growing strength.

The members of this new force feel that behaviorism is a narrow artificial, and relatively sterile approach to the understanding of man. The emphasis on studying only overt behavior tends, they suggest, to rehumanize man and reduce him, "to a larger white rat or a slower computer" (Bugental, 1967, p. vii). They argue that the image of man provided by the S-R orientation presents, at best, an incomplete picture of human nature and, at worst, one that may be totally inaccurate. Behaviorism, in other words, does not "come to grips" with what is unique about man: those highly subjective qualities and capacities that set him apart from the laboratory animal. A psychology based on separate and discrete conditioned responses makes of man a mechanized computer-like organism responding deterministically to the stimuli presented to him. The humanists argue that man is much more than an Orwellian robot, and cannot be objectified, quantified, and reduced to S-R units. Man is not such an "empty organism."

The humanistic psychologists argue that the vast amounts of research on overt behavior have added little to our understanding of man: "we are offered beautifully executed, precise, elegant experiments which, in at least half the cases, have nothing to do with enduring human problems . . ." (Maslow, 1965, p. 21).

These strong words of protest leave no doubt about the humanists' perception of behaviorism. What do they offer as an alternative? Humanistic psychology is, or at least hopes to be, a new orientation—a new attitude toward psychology, rather than a new psychology per se. It is not a new school of thought or a specific content area, but rather an attempt to reshape and supplement (not supplant) the existing form of psychology. James F. T. Bugental, the first president of the American Association for Humanistic Psychology (1962–1963), describes the movement:

> Humanistic psychology has as its ultimate goal the preparation of a complete description of what it means to be alive as a human being. . . . Such a complete description would necessarily include an inventory of man's native endowment; his potentialities of feeling, thought, and action; his growth, evolution, and decline; his interaction with various environing conditions . . . the range and variety of experience possible to him; and his meaningful place in the universe (1967, p. 7).

All aspects of uniquely human experience thus come under the purview of the humanistic psychologist: love, hate, fear, hope, happiness, humor, affection, responsibility, the meaning of life, etc. Most of these aspects of human existence are not found in any form in current textbooks of psychology, for they are not amenable to operational definition, precise quantification, and laboratory manipulation.

Bugental (1967) noted six fundamental points of emphasis that distinguish humanistic psychology from behaviorism.

1. Adequate understanding of human nature cannot be based exclusively (or even in large part) on research findings from animal studies. Again, man is not "a larger white rat," and a psychology based on animal data obviously excludes distinctly human processes and experiences.

2. The research topics chosen for investigation must be meaningful in terms of human existence and not selected solely on the basis of their suitability for laboratory investigation and quantification. Currently, topics not amenable to experimental treatment tend to be ignored.

3. Primary attention should be focused on man's subjective internal experiences, not on elements of overt behavior. This is not to suggest that overt behavior be discarded as a subject of study, but rather that it should not be the only subject of investigation.

4. The continuing mutual influence of the so-called pure psychology and applied psychology should be recognized. The attempt to sharply divorce them is detrimental to both.

5. Psychology should be concerned with the unique individual case instead of the average performance of groups. The current group emphasis ignores the atypical, the exception, the person who deviates from the average.

6. Psychology should seek "that which may expand or enrich man's experience . . ." (Bugental, 1967, p. 9).

This overview of humanistic psychology is deliberately brief, for its purpose is to acquaint the student with the existence of the movement and not to outline it in detail. It is, of course, too early to attempt any evaluative commentary on humanistic psychology. The extent of its impact, if any, remains to be seen, but it certainly warrants watchful and critical attention.

We must note, however, that humanistic psychology seems to be reflecting a similar kind of unrest and disaffection currently being voiced against Western culture. Humanistic psychology implies that behaviorism is, if not antihuman, then ahuman. This appears evident from the very title of the movement itself, which suggests that the quality of "human–ness" is lacking in behaviorism. Representatives of the movement resist the conception of man as an animal functioning mechanically and deterministically in response to his environment.

Many current social critics suggest that Western, and particularly American, culture has also dehumanized, depersonalized, and de-individualized man to the extent that he is regarded as an infinitesimal part of an immense societal machine. It has been suggested that people are no longer viewed as humans, but as personnel, statistics, and averages. As individuals, we have a reduced sense of personal identity and a lessened ability to actively shape our own lives. Society, through the giant bureaucracies, molds our destiny for us to a greater extent. "In an acceleratingly rationalized, pervasively systematized society, we are numbered—quite literally. Count the numbers through which your existence is proved—by machines" (Hentoff, 1966, p. 277). Even our names have less importance; if we lose our numbers, how soon may we only with difficulty prove that we exist!

The critics tell us we grow increasingly estranged from society and from ourselves: regimented, controlled, computerized, manipulated, numbered, and helpless, all of which seems ideal for a behavioristic view of man as a nicely functioning well-ordered machine. Indeed, it has been suggested that modern psychology has reinforced this dehumanizing influence of contemporary society. Koch (1964) commented:

> That modern psychology has projected an image of man which is as demeaning as it is simplistic, few intelligent and sensitive non-psychologists would deny. . . . Of all fields in the community of scholarship, it should be psychology which combats this trend. Instead, we have played no small role in augmenting and supporting it (pp. 37–38).

But, like the humanistic movement in psychology, there are voices of dissent speaking out against the dehumanizing forces of modern society. They are few in number (so far) and often have trouble being heard as they speak against the prevailing wind, but they are speaking, warning us against the dangers of an overly objective and numbered society. This *Zeitgeist* of social criticism, then, may be reflected in the humanistic psychologists' plea for the study of man as a distinctly human being.

SUGGESTED FURTHER READINGS

Contemporary American Psychology

Hebb, D. O. The American revolution. *American Psychologist,* 1960, **15,** 735–745.

Helson, H., & Bevan, W. *Contemporary approaches to psychology.* Princeton: Van Nostrand, 1967.

Koch, S. *Psychology: a study of a science.* New York: McGraw-Hill, 1958–1963. 6 vols. (Vol. 7 in preparation.)

Langfeld, H. S. The development of American psychology. *Scientia,* 1951, **86,** 264–269.

Professionalization

Bingham, W. V. Psychology as a science, as a technology, and as a profession. *American Psychologist,* 1953, **8,** 115–118.

Tryon, R. C. Psychology in flux: the academic-professional bipolarity. *American Psychologist,* 1963, **18,** 134–143.

Other Countries

Brozek, J. Soviet psychology. In M. Marx & W. Hillix, *Systems and theories in psychology.* New York: McGraw-Hill, 1963. Pp. 438–455.

Drever, J. European psychology. In M. Marx & W. Hillix, *Systems and theories in psychology.* New York: McGraw-Hill, 1963. Pp. 425–437.

Iwahara, S. Oriental psychology. In M. Marx & W. Hillix, *Systems and theories in psychology.* New York: McGraw-Hill, 1963. Pp. 456–472.

Misiak, H., & Sexton, V. S. *History of psychology: an overview.* New York: Grune & Stratton, 1966. Chapter 14, Psychology in Great Britain, France, and Italy; Chapter 15, Psychology in the Soviet Union; Chapter 16, Psychology in Asia.

Woodworth, R. S., & Sheehan, M. R. *Contemporary schools of psychology.* (3rd ed.) New York: Ronald Press, 1964. Chapter 4, Soviet psychology as a "school."

The Future

Murphy, G. The psychology of 1975: an extrapolation. *American Psychologist,* 1963, **18,** 689–695.

Murray, H. A. Prospect for psychology. *Science,* 1962, **136,** 483–488.

Humanistic Psychology

Bugental, J. F. T. *Challenges of humanistic psychology.* New York: McGraw-Hill, 1967.

Severin, F. T. (Ed.) *Humanistic viewpoints in psychology.* New York: McGraw-Hill, 1965.

Bibliography

History and Systems

Boring, E. G. *Sensation and perception in the history of experimental psychology.* New York: Appleton-Century-Crofts, 1942.

Boring, E. G. *A history of experimental psychology.* (2nd ed.) New York: Appleton-Century-Crofts, 1950.

Chaplin, J. P., & Krawiec, T. S. *Systems and theories of psychology.* New York: Holt, Rinehart, & Winston, 1960.

Esper, E. A. *A history of psychology.* Philadelphia: Saunders, 1964.

Flugel, J. C., & West, D. J. *A hundred years of psychology: 1833–1933.* New York: Basic Books, 1964.

Heidbreder, E. *Seven psychologies.* New York: Appleton-Century-Crofts, 1933.

Marx, M. H. *Theories in contemporary psychology.* New York: Macmillan, 1963.

Marx, M. H., & Hillix, W. A. *Systems and theories in psychology.* New York: McGraw-Hill, 1963.

Miller, G. A. *Psychology.* New York: Harper & Row, 1962.

Misiak, H. *The philosophical roots of scientific psychology.* New York: Fordham University Press, 1961.

Misiak, H., & Sexton, V. S. *History of psychology: an overview.* New York: Grune & Stratton, 1966.

Murphy, G. *Historical introduction to modern psychology.* (Rev. ed.) New York: Harcourt, Brace & World, 1949.

Peters, R. S. (Ed.) *Brett's history of psychology.* New York: Macmillan, 1953.

Postman, L. (Ed.) *Psychology in the making.* New York: Knopf, 1962.

Roback, A. A. *History of American psychology.* New York: Library Publishers, 1952.

Watson, R. I. *The great psychologists.* Philadelphia: Lippincott, 1963.

Wolman, B. B. *Contemporary theories and systems in psychology.* New York: Harper & Row, 1960.

Woodworth, R. S., & Sheehan, M. R. *Contemporary schools of psychology.* (3rd ed.) New York: Ronald Press, 1964.

Readings

Dennis, W. *Readings in the history of psychology.* New York: Appleton-Century-Crofts, 1948.

Drever, J. (Ed.) *Sourcebook in psychology.* New York: Philosophical Library, 1960.

Herrnstein, R. J., & Boring, E. G. *A source book in the history of psychology.* Cambridge: Harvard University Press, 1965.

Rand, B. *The classical psychologists.* New York: Houghton Mifflin, 1912.

Sahakian, W. S. (Ed.) *History of psychology: a source book in systematic psychology.* Itasca, Ill.: F. E. Peacock, 1968.

Shipley, T. (Ed.) *Classics in psychology.* New York: Philosophical Library, 1961.

329

In addition, the *Journal of the History of the Behavioral Sciences,* begun in 1965, contains scholarly articles on a wide variety of topics. Also of interest are the autobiographical sketches of the major figures in the history of psychology in the following.

Murchison, C. (Ed.) *A history of psychology in autobiography.* 3 vols. Worcester, Mass.: Clark University Press, 1930–1936.

Boring, E. G., *et al.* (Eds.) *A history of psychology in autobiography.* Vol. 4. Worcester, Mass.: Clark University Press, 1952.

Boring, E. G., & Lindzey, G. *A history of psychology in autobiography.* Vol. 5. New York: Appleton-Century-Crofts, 1967.

References

Adler, A. Individual psychology. In C. Murchison (Ed.), *Psychologies of 1930.* Worcester, Mass.: Clark University Press, 1930. Pp. 395–405.

Adler, A. The fundamental views of Individual Psychology. *International Journal of Individual Psychology,* 1935, **1,** 5–8.

American Psychological Association, Committee on Distinguished Scientific Contribution Awards. The American Psychological Association Distinguished Scientific Contribution Award for 1958. *American Psychologist,* 1958, **13,** 729–738.

American Psychological Association, Committee on the Role of Psychology in Small and Large Institutions, Subcommittee of Curriculum Differences. Undergraduate training for psychologists. *American Psychologist,* 1958, **13,** 585–588.

American Psychological Foundation. Presentation of the First Gold Medal Award. *American Psychologist,* 1956, **11,** 587–589.

Angell, J. R. The province of functional psychology. *Psychological Review,* 1907, **14,** 61–91.

Bakan, D. Behaviorism and American urbanization. *Journal of the History of the Behavioral Sciences,* 1966, **2,** 5–28.

Bekhterev, V. M. *Objective psychology.* Leipzig: B. G. Teubner, 1907. (First published in German.)

Bergmann, G. The contribution of John B. Watson. *Psychological Review,* 1956, **63,** 265–276.

Berkeley, G. *An essay towards a new theory of vision.* 1709.

Berkeley, G. *A treatise concerning the principles of human knowledge.* 1710.

Boring, E. G. Edward Bradford Titchener 1867–1927. *American Journal of Psychology,* 1927, **38,** 489–506.

Boring, E. G. *A history of experimental psychology.* New York: Century, 1929.

Boring, E. G. *Sensation and perception in the history of experimental psychology.* New York: Appleton-Century-Crofts, 1942.

Boring, E. G. *A history of experimental psychology.* (2nd ed.) New York: Appleton-Century-Crofts, 1950.

Boring, E. G. *History, psychology, and science: selected papers.* New York: Wiley, 1963.

Boring, E. G. Introduction. In G. Fechner, *Elements of psychophysics,* Vol. 1. Trans. H. Adler. New York: Holt, Rinehart & Winston, 1966. (First published in 1860.)

Brentano, F. *Psychology from an empirical standpoint.* Leipzig: Duncker & Humblot, 1874. (First published in German.)

Brett, G. S. Associationism and "act" psychology: a historical retrospect. In C. Murchison (Ed.), *Psychologies of 1930.* Worcester, Mass.: Clark University Press, 1930. Pp. 39–55.

Breuer, J., & Freud, S. *Studies on hysteria.* Leipzig: Franz Deuticke, 1895. Trans. A. A. Brill. New York: Nervous & Mental Disease Publishing Co., 1936.

Bridgman, P. W. *The logic of modern physics.* New York: Macmillan, 1927.

Brown, J. A. C. *Freud and the post-Freudians.* London: Cassell & Co. Ltd., 1963.

Bugental, J. F. T. *Challenges of humanistic psychology.* New York: McGraw-Hill, 1967.

Carr, H. *Psychology.* New York: Longmans, Green, 1925.

Carr, H. Functionalism. In C. Murchison (Ed.), *Psychologies of 1930.* Worcester, Mass.: Clark University Press, 1930. Pp. 59–78.

Chaplin, J. P., & Krawiec, T. S. *Systems and theories of psychology.* New York: Holt, Rinehart & Winston, 1960.

Cofer, C. N., & Apply, M. H. *Motivation: theory and research.* New York: Wiley, 1964.

Cornsweet, T. N. *The design of electric circuits in the behavioral sciences.* New York: Wiley, 1963.

Darwin, C. *On the origin of species by means of natural selection.* London: Murray, 1859.

Darwin, C. *The descent of man.* New York: Appleton, 1871.

Darwin, C. *The expression of the emotions in man and animals.* London: Murray, 1872.

Darwin, C. *Biographical sketch of an infant.* 1877.

Dewey, J. *Psychology.* New York: Harper, 1886.

Dewey, J. The reflex arc concept in psychology. *Psychological Review,* 1896, **3**, 357–370.

Ebbinghaus, H. *On memory.* Leipzig: Duncker & Humblot, 1885. (First published in German.) Trans. H. Ruger & C. Bussenius. New York: Teachers College, Columbia University, 1913.

Ebbinghaus, H. *The principles of psychology.* 1902.

Ebbinghaus, H. *A summary of psychology.* 1908.

Esper, E. A. *A history of psychology.* Philadelphia: Saunders, 1964.

Fechner, G. *Elements of psychophysics.* Leipzig: Brietkopf and Härtel, 1860. Trans. H. Adler. New York: Holt, Rinehart & Winston, 1966.

Flugel, J. C., & West, D. J. *A hundred years of psychology: 1833–1933.* New York: Basic Books, 1964.

Freud, S. *The interpretation of dreams.* 1900. New York: Macmillan, 1913.

Freud, S. *The psychopathology of everyday life.* 1904. New York: Macmillan, 1915.

Freud, S. *Three essays on sexuality.* 1905. Trans. A. A. Brill. New York: Nervous & Mental Disease Monograph Service, 1910.

Freud, S. Fragment of an analysis of a case of hysteria. In *Collected Papers,* Vol. III. London: Hogarth Press, 1933. (First published in 1905.)

Freud, S. Beyond the pleasure principle. In J. Rickman (Ed.), *A general selection from the works of Sigmund Freud.* New York: Liveright, 1957. (First published in 1920.)

Freud, S. *New introductory lectures on psychoanalysis.* Edited by J. Strachey. New York: Norton, 1965. (First published in 1933.)

Fromm, E. *Escape from freedom.* New York: Holt, Rinehart & Winston, 1941.

Fromm, E. *Man for himself.* New York: Holt, Rinehart & Winston, 1947.

Galton, F. *Hereditary genius.* London: Macmillan, 1869.

Galton, F. *English men of science*. 1874.

Galton, F. *Natural inheritance*. London: Macmillan, 1889.

Guthrie, E. R. *The psychology of learning*. New York: Harper, 1935. (Rev. ed., 1952.)

Hall, C. S., & Lindzey, G. *Theories of personality*. New York: Wiley, 1957.

Hall, G. S. *Adolescence*. New York: Appleton, 1904.

Hall, G. S. *Jesus, the Christ, in the light of psychology*. Garden City, New York: Doubleday, 1917.

Hall, G. S. *Recreations of a psychologist*. 1920.

Hall, G. S. *Senescence*. New York: Appleton, 1922.

Hall, G. S. *The life and confessions of a psychologist*. New York: Appleton, 1923.

Harrison, R. Functionalism and its historical significance. *Genetic Psychology Monographs*, 1963, **68**, 387–423.

Hartley, D. *Observations on man*. 1749.

Heidbreder, E. *Seven psychologies*. New York: Appleton-Century-Crofts, 1933.

Helmholtz, H. v. *Physiological optics*. Leipzig: Voss, 1856–1866. (First published in German.)

Helmholtz, H. v. *On the sensations of tone*. Braunschweig: Vieweg & Sohn, 1913. (First published in 1863.)

Hentoff, N. The cold society. *Playboy,* September, 1966, 133 ff.

Herrnstein, R. J., & Boring, E. G. *A source book in the history of psychology*. Cambridge: Harvard University Press, 1965.

Hilgard, E. R. *Theories of learning*. (2nd ed.) New York: Appleton-Century-Crofts, 1956.

Holt, E. B. *The Freudian wish and its place in ethics*. New York: Holt, Rinehart & Winston, 1915.

Horney, K. *Our inner conflicts*. New York: Norton, 1945.

Hull, C. L. *Hypnosis and suggestibility*. New York: Appleton-Century-Crofts, 1933.

Hull, C. L., et al. *Mathematico-deductive theory of rote learning: a study in scientific methodology*. New Haven: Yale University Press, 1940.

Hull, C. L. *Principles of behavior*. New York: Appleton-Century-Crofts, 1943.

Hull, C. L. *Essentials of behavior*. New Haven: Yale University Press, 1951.

Hull, C. L. *A behavior system*. New Haven: Yale University Press, 1952.

Hume, D. *A treatise on human nature*. Oxford: Clarendon Press, 1949. (First published in 1739.)

James, W. *The principles of psychology*. New York: Holt, 1890.

James, W. *Talks to teachers*. New York: Holt, 1899.

Jones, E. *The life and work of Sigmund Freud 1856–1900*. 3 vols. New York: Basic Books, 1953–1957.

Koch, S. Psychology and emerging conceptions of knowledge as unitary. In T. W. Wann (Ed.), *Behaviorism and phenomenology*. Chicago: University of Chicago Press, 1964. Pp. 1–41.

Koffka, K. *The growth of the mind*. New York: Harcourt, Brace & World, 1921.

Koffka, K. Perception: an introduction to Gestalt-theorie. *Psychological Bulletin,* 1922, **19**, 531–585.

Koffka, K. *Principles of Gestalt psychology*. New York: Harcourt, Brace & World, 1935.

Köhler, W. *The mentality of apes*. 1917. Trans. E. Winter. New York: Humanities Press, 1927.

Köhler, W. *Static and stationary physical Gestalts*. Braunschweig: Vieweg, 1920. (First published in German.)

Köhler, W. *Gestalt psychology.* New York: Liveright, 1929.

Köhler, W. *The place of value in a world of facts.* New York: Liveright, 1938.

Köhler, W. *Dynamics in psychology.* New York: Liveright, 1940.

Köhler, W. *Gestalt psychology.* New York: Liveright, 1947.

Köhler, W., & Wallach, H. Figural after-effects. *Proceedings of the American Philosophical Society,* 1944, **88,** 269–357.

Kuhn, T. S. *The structure of scientific revolutions.* Chicago: University of Chicago Press, 1962.

Külpe, O. *Outline of psychology.* Leipzig: Engelmann, 1893. (First published in German.)

Lachman, S. J. *History and methods of physiological psychology.* Detroit: Hamilton, 1963.

Lashley, K. *Brain mechanisms and intelligence.* Chicago: University of Chicago Press, 1929.

Lewin, K., Lippitt, R., & White, R. Patterns of aggressive behavior in experimentally created social climates. *Journal of Social Psychology,* 1939, **10,** 271–299.

Locke, J. *An essay concerning human understanding.* Oxford: Clarendon Press, 1924. (First published in 1690.)

Mach, Ernst. *The analysis of sensations.* 1885.

McDougall, W. *Introduction to social psychology.* London: Methuen, 1908.

MacLeod, R. B. Review of *Cumulative record* by B. F. Skinner. *Science,* 1959, **130,** 34–35.

Marx, M. H., & Hillix, W. A. *Systems and theories in psychology.* New York: McGraw-Hill, 1963.

Maslow, A. H. A philosophy of psychology: the need for a mature science of human nature. In F. T. Severin (Ed.), *Humanistic viewpoints in psychology.* New York: McGraw-Hill, 1965. Pp. 17–33.

Mill, James. *Analysis of the phenomena of the human mind.* 1829.

Miller, G. A. *Psychology.* New York: Harper & Row, 1962.

Misiak, H., & Sexton, V. S. *History of psychology.* New York: Grune & Stratton, 1966.

Mueller, C. G., Jr., & Schoenfeld, W. N. Edwin R. Guthrie. In W. K. Estes *et al., Modern learning theory.* New York: Appleton-Century-Crofts, 1954. Pp. 345–379.

Müller, J. *Handbook of physiology.* 1833–1840.

Müller-Freienfels, R. *The evolution of modern psychology.* New Haven: Yale University Press, 1935.

Murphy, G. *Historical introduction to modern psychology.* (Rev. ed.) New York: Harcourt, Brace & World, 1949.

Nance, R. Current practices in teaching history of psychology. *American Psychologist,* 1962, **17,** 250–252.

Perry, R. B. *The thought and character of William James.* Boston: Little, Brown, 1935.

Peters, R. S. (Ed.) *Brett's history of psychology.* New York: Macmillan, 1953.

Postman, L. (Ed.) *Psychology in the making.* New York: Knopf, 1962.

Roback, A. A. *William James: his marginalia, personality and contribution.* New York: Science & Art, 1942.

Roback, A. A. *History of American psychology.* New York: Library Publishers, 1952.

Romanes, G. J. *Animal intelligence.* London: Kegan Paul, 1883.

Ruckmich, C. A. The use of the term *function* in English textbooks of psychology. *American Journal of Psychology,* 1913, **24,** 99–123.

Sidowski, J. B. (Ed.) *Experimental methods and instrumentation in psychology.* New York: McGraw-Hill, 1966.

Skinner, B. F. *Walden two.* New York: Macmillan, 1948.

Skinner, B. F. *Science and human behavior.* New York: Macmillan, 1953.

Skinner, B. F. *Verbal behavior.* New York: Appleton-Century-Crofts, 1957.

Skinner, B. F. John Broadus Watson, behaviorist. *Science,* 1959, **129,** 197–198.

Skinner, B. F. Behaviorism at fifty. *Science,* 1963, **140,** 951–958.

Spencer, H. *The principles of psychology.* London: Williams and Norgate, 1870–1872. (First published in 1855.)

Stumpf, C. *Psychology of tone.* Leipzig: Hirzel, 1883. (First published in German.)

Thorndike, E. L. Animal intelligence. *Psychological Review Monograph Supplement,* 1898, **2.**

Thorndike, E. L. *The elements of psychology.* New York: Seiler, 1905.

Thorndike, E. L. *Human learning.* New York: Appleton-Century-Crofts, 1931.

Thorndike, E. L. *Selected writings from a connectionist's psychology.* New York: Appleton-Century-Crofts, 1949.

Titchener, E. B. *An outline of psychology.* New York: Macmillan, 1896.

Titchener, E. B. The postulates of a structural psychology. *Philosophical Review,* 1898, **7,** 449–465.

Titchener, E. B. *A primer of psychology.* New York: Macmillan, 1898.

Titchener, E. B. *Experimental psychology.* New York: Macmillan, 1901–1905.

Titchener, E. B. *A text-book of psychology.* New York: Macmillan, 1909–1910.

Titchener, E. B. The schema of introspection. *American Journal of Psychology,* 1912, **23,** 485–508.

Tolman, E. C. *Purposive behavior in animals and men.* New York: Century, 1932.

Tolman, E. C. A stimulus-expectancy need-cathexis psychology. *Science,* 1945, **101,** 160–166.

Tolman, E. C. Autobiography. In E. G. Boring et al. (Eds.), *A history of psychology in autobiography.* Vol. 4. Worcester, Mass.: Clark University Press, 1952. Pp. 323–339.

Watson, J. B. Psychology as the behaviorist views it. *Psychological Review,* 1913, **20,** 158–177.

Watson, J. B. *Behavior: an introduction to comparative psychology.* New York: Holt, Rinehart & Winston, 1914.

Watson, J. B. *Psychology from the standpoint of a behaviorist.* Philadelphia: Lippincott, 1919.

Watson, J. B. *Behaviorism.* New York: Norton, 1925. (Rev. ed., 1930.)

Watson, J. B. *Psychological care of the infant and child.* New York: Norton, 1928.

Watson, J. B. Autobiography. In C. Murchison (Ed.), *A history of psychology in autobiography.* Vol. 3. Worcester, Mass.: Clark University Press, 1936. Pp. 271–281.

Watson, J. B., & McDougall, W. *The battle of behaviorism.* New York: Norton, 1929.

Watson, R. I. *The great psychologists.* Philadelphia: Lippincott, 1963.

Watson, R. I. The historical background for national trends in psychology: United States. *Journal of the History of the Behavioral Sciences,* 1965, **1,** 130–138.

Watson, R. I. The role and use of history in the psychology curriculum. *Journal of the History of the Behavioral Sciences,* 1966, **2,** 64–69.

Weiss, A. P. *A theoretical basis of human behavior.* 1925.

Wertheimer, Max. Experimental studies of the perception of movement. *Z. Psychol.,* 1912, **61,** 161–265. (First published in German.)

Wertheimer, Max. *Productive thinking.* New York: Harper & Row, 1945.

Wertheimer, Michael. Rationales for and approaches to the teaching of psychology's history. Paper presented to the American Psychological Association, New York, New York, 1966.

White, A. D. *A history of the warfare of science with theology in Christendom.* New York: Free Press, 1965.

Wolman, B. B. *Contemporary theories and systems in psychology.* New York: Harper & Row, 1960.

Woodworth, R. S. *Dynamic psychology.* New York: Columbia University Press, 1918.

Woodworth, R. S. *Psychology.* New York: Holt, 1921.

Woodworth, R. S. Dynamic psychology. In C. Murchison (Ed.), *Psychologies of 1930.* Worcester, Mass.: Clark University Press, 1930. Pp. 327–336.

Woodworth, R. S. *Experimental psychology.* New York: Holt, 1938. (Rev. ed., 1954, with H. Schlosberg.)

Woodworth, R. S. *Contemporary schools of psychology.* (2nd ed.) New York: Ronald Press, 1948.

Woodworth, R. S. *Dynamics of behavior.* New York: Holt, Rinehart & Winston, 1958.

Woodworth, R. S., & Sheehan, M. R. *Contemporary schools of psychology.* (3rd ed.) New York: Ronald Press, 1964.

Wundt, W. *Contributions to the theory of sensory perception.* 1858–1862. (First published in German.)

Wundt, W. *Vorlesungen über die Menschen- und Thierseele.* Leipzig: Voss, 1863.

Wundt, W. *Principles of physiological psychology.* Leipzig: Engelmann, 1873–1874. (First published in German.)

Wundt, W. *Grundriss der Psychologie.* Leipzig: Engelmann, 1896.

Wundt, W. *Folk psychology.* Leipzig: Engelmann, 1900–1920. (First published in German.)

AUTHOR INDEX

Numbers in italics show the pages on which complete references are listed.

A

Adler, A., 6, 275, 295–300, 304, 310, *330*
Allen, G. W., 122
Allport, G., 122, 123, 318
Angell, J. R., 6, 58, 101, 124, 126–145, 146, 151, 183, 185, *330*
Ansbacher, H. L., 310
Ansbacher, R. R., 310
Appley, M. H., 228, 304, *331*
Aristotle, 14, 16, 80, 152, 153, 154
Asch, S. E., 263

B

Babkin, B. P., 181
Bakan, D., 83, 185, *330*
Baldwin, J. M., 119
Balz, A. G. A., 28
Beach, F. A., 237
Bekhterev, V. M., 6, 163–164, *330*
Bentham, J., 269
Bentley, M., 83
Bergmann, G., 211, 212, 237, *330*
Berkeley, G., 6, 23–24, 25, 139, *330*
Bevan, W., 328
Binet, A., 121, 320
Bingham, W. V., 328
Bixenstine, V. E., 237
Blanshard, B., 238
Bleuler, E., 290
Boring, E. G., 2, 4, 8, 11, 12, 14, 17, 26, 31, 34, 38, 41, 42, 44, 47, 52, 55, 57, 61, 62, 65, 69, 83, 88, 101,

Boring, 102, 106, 112, 113, 117, 122, 123, 147, 150, 155, 157, 158, 179, 181, 213, 238, 246, 248, 266, 267, 272, 278, 287, 312, *329, 330, 332, 334*
Braid, J., 268
Brazier, M. A. B., 42
Brentano, F., 6, 55–57, 62, 73, 74, 78, 79, 80, 242, 270, *330*
Brett, G. S., 152, *331*
Breuer, J., 271, 272, 273, 277, *331*
Bridgman, P. W., 217–218, 237, 286, *331*
Broca, P., 30
Brown, J. A. C., 289, 310, *331*
Brozek, J., 328
Brücke, E., 269, 270
Bugelski, B. R., 181, 238
Bugental, J. F. T., 325, 326, 328, *331*
Bühler, K., 60–61
Burnham, W. H., 123

C

Carmichael, L., 237
Carr, H., 6, 145–146, 149, 151, *331*
Cattell, J. M., 2, 6, 52, 62, 114, 117–122, 123, 146, 147, 165, 183, 215, 275, 320
Chaplin, J. P., 2, 203, 235, 314, 329, *331*
Charcot, J. M., 6, 268, 272
Choisy, M., 288
Cofer, C. N., 228, 304, *331*
Combs, A. W., 263
Comte, A., 6, 20, 183

337

SUBJECT INDEX